FOURTH EDITION

A GUIDE TO CUSTOMER SERVICE SKILLS FOR THE SERVICE DESK PROFESSIONAL

Badal – 2, 3, 6, 3
Rocha – 8, 9, 4, 1

DONNA KNAPP

CENGAGE
Learning·

Australia • Brazil • Japan • Korea • Mexico • Singapore • Spain • United Kingdom • United States

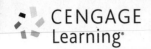
CENGAGE
Learning®

**A Guide to Customer Service Skills
for the Service Desk Professional,
Fourth Edition**
Donna Knapp

Senior Product Manager: Jim Gish

Senior Content Developer: Alyssa Pratt

Developmental Editor: Robin M. Romer

Product Assistant: Gillian Daniels

Content Project Manager:
  Jennifer Feltri-George

Art Director: Cheryl Pearl, GEX

Manufacturing Planner: Julio Esperas

Copyeditor: Mark Goodin

Proofreader: Jeri Freedman

Indexer: Sharon Hilgenberg

Compositor: Integra Software Services

For product information and technology assistance, contact us at
Cengage Learning Customer & Sales Support, www.cengage.com/support
For permission to use material from this text or product,
submit all requests online at **www.cengage.com/permission**
Further permissions question can be e-mailed to
permissionrequest@cengage.com

Library of Congress Control Number: 2014934994

ISBN-13: 978-1-285-06358-4

Cengage Learning
20 Channel Center Street
Boston, MA 02210
USA

Some of the product names and company names used in this book have been used for identification purposes only and may be trademarks or registered trademarks of their respective manufacturers and sellers.

Any fictional data related to persons or companies or URLs used throughout this book is intended for instructional purposes only. At the time this book was printed, any such data was fictional and not belonging to any real persons or companies.

Cengage Learning reserves the right to revise this publication and make changes from time to time in its content without notice.

The programs in this book are for instructional purposes only. They have been tested with care, but are not guaranteed for any particular intent beyond educational purposes. The author and the publisher do not offer any warranties or representations, nor do they accept any liabilities with respect to the programs.

Cengage Learning is a leading provider of customized learning solutions with office locations around the globe, including Singapore, the United Kingdom, Australia, Mexico, Brazil, and Japan. Locate your local office at: **www.cengage.com/global**

Cengage Learning products are represented in Canada by Nelson Education, Ltd.

Purchase any of our products at your local college store or at our preferred online store: **www.CengageBrain.com**

Printed in the United States of America
1 2 3 4 5 6 7 20 19 18 17 16 15 14

Brief Contents

Contents

CONTENTS

ix

Preface

It has been close to 15 years since the first edition of this text was published as *A Guide to Customer Service Skills for Help Desk Professionals*. In some respects, little has changed since that first edition. The function we now call the service desk is still first and foremost a customer service organization. What has changed, and what continues to change, are the customers themselves. Today's technology users are increasingly technically savvy and self-sufficient. They expect technology to work, and they expect easy access to a wide range of support services when it does not. They expect options! Businesses expect the service desk to offer these options and also to help people use technology to be more productive in the workplace, not just reactively fix technology when it does not work. They expect the service desk to proactively anticipate customer needs, and they expect the people working in the service desk to meet those needs in the most innovative, cost-effective ways possible.

The technologies used by service desks have also changed considerably since this book was first published. Service desk web sites and self-help services are now commonplace. Technologies such as incident management systems, knowledge management systems, and remote control systems have found their way into even the smallest service desks. Technologies such as instant messaging, chat, and social media have become viable tools in the battle to deliver services more efficiently and effectively. All of these changes have prompted service desks to rethink how they deliver support, the skills of their analysts, and, most importantly, how they interact with their customers.

What has not changed is the fact that customer service is fundamentally about people, not technology. It is about customers and their expectations, and it is about front-line service providers and their desire and ability to meet and exceed those expectations. Great service providers understand this and are working hard to continuously improve their skills and the quality of their service. They are also working hard to ensure that the technologies that are now readily available facilitate great service, rather than getting in the way of it. This book is dedicated to helping you do both.

For more than 30 years I have worked in the Information Technology industry. More than 20 of those years have been devoted to providing service desk–related consulting and training services. I understand how difficult it can be for an individual and for an organization to deliver high-quality technical customer support. I understand that customers can be demanding and company policies sometimes make it difficult to satisfy customers. I understand that technologies that are meant to help can quickly become a hindrance. I also understand that service providers are often asked to support complex technologies with inadequate training, tools, and information. This book is designed to provide the skills and insight you need to enjoy and excel in the challenging and dynamic environment that a service desk offers. In addition, the business, soft, and self-management skills described in this book are excellent life skills that will serve you well regardless of your chosen profession.

Intended Audience

This book is intended primarily for three kinds of readers.

- Readers who are taking a course in service desks and technical customer support or a related degree program. They can use this book to obtain additional knowledge and depth about the ins and outs of providing quality customer support, as well as clear definitions and explanations of key concepts. They can use this book to learn about ITIL®and its guidance and best practices relative to the service desk role. (ITIL® is a registered trade mark of AXELOS Limited.) They can also use this book to learn business concepts and techniques that are increasingly relevant to technical professionals. These readers will especially benefit from the end-of-chapter activities that provide practical experience with the concepts and skills they will use on the job.

- Readers who are considering career opportunities at a service desk, and who want to understand how to provide high-quality technical customer support in any situation. They can use this book to develop the skills needed to interact effectively and appropriately with customers, coworkers, and managers, whether face-to-face, on the telephone, via web-based technologies, or in written documents.

- Readers who are working in a service desk and want a better understanding of how to communicate effectively, handle difficult customer situations, solve and prevent incidents and problems, be a team player, and minimize stress. They can use this book to learn proven techniques for meeting and exceeding customer expectations, using data and information to improve individual and service desk team performance, and maintaining a positive attitude and sense of well-being while providing support.

Service Desk Curriculum

This book is designed for a customer service course in any Service Desk Curriculum. It is intended for use in community and technical college courses, such as Customer Service Skills, Customer Service and the Service Desk, and Problem Solving for the Service Desk. These courses are part of rapidly emerging programs in schools that aim to prepare students for the following degrees or certificates: IT Support Professional; Computer Service Desk Specialist; Computer Technical Support; Service Desk Support Specialist; Computer User Support; and Computer Support Technician. As the need for service desks grows, companies are turning to community and technical colleges to prepare their graduates to fill existing positions in the technical support industry.

No longer are technical skills the only requirement for the field of technical support. Companies now want to attract individuals who have the appropriate balance of business, technical, soft, and self-management skills that contribute to making their service desks successful. Increasingly, organizations that are committed to providing high-quality technical customer support view their service desks as a strategic asset. Whether the service desk provides support to the customers who use their companies' products or the service desk provides technical support to the companies' employees, the need for qualified service desk professionals is on the rise.

Approach

This text is designed to provide an in-depth look at the business skills, soft skills, and self-management skills people need to provide effective customer service and support in a technical environment. The first chapter is devoted to a discussion about the evolving role of the service desk, trends influencing the service desk, and the dynamic nature of customer expectations. Chapters 2 through 6 explore in detail the soft skills needed for a successful career in customer support. The goal was to provide readers with proven techniques they could implement immediately. These techniques are introduced in chapters dedicated to subjects such as listening and communicating, handling telephone calls, technical writing, handling difficult customer situations, and solving and preventing incidents and problems. Chapter 7 explores the basic business skills commonly needed for analysts as well as the more advanced skills used by senior technical professionals, team leaders, supervisors, and managers. Chapters 8 and 9 are devoted to self-management skills, including being part of a team, minimizing stress, avoiding burnout, and effectively managing time.

Although this book is very how-to oriented, it describes the bigger picture benefits of acquiring and demonstrating business skills, soft skills, and self-management skills. For example, this book will help readers understand that business skills enable them to understand the goals of the company where they work (or where they want to work) and how they can contribute to those goals. This book will also help readers understand that soft and self-management skills will enable them not only to find a good job and achieve success in the technical customer support industry, but also to feel considerable job satisfaction while avoiding the frustration and burnout that is inherent in that industry.

To derive maximum benefit from this book, readers must be an active participant in the learning process. The end-of-chapter activities are specifically designed to develop their knowledge and help them assimilate the chapter concepts. They encourage readers to expand their knowledge through self-study as well as help prepare them for the team-oriented technical support environment by having them work with classmates in project groups or teams. Many of the end-of-chapter activities encourage readers to use information resources and solve problems—skills that are essential in the dynamic service desk industry.

Assumed Knowledge

This book assumes that readers have experience in the following areas, either through course work, work experience, or life experience:

- Basic service desk and customer service concepts

- Basic computer concepts or computer literacy

- Internet and World Wide Web concepts

Overview

The outline of this book takes a detailed look at the characteristics of excellent technical customer support and at the business skills, soft skills, and self-management skills needed to deliver it. Each chapter explores in detail a particular skill required to provide effective customer support and includes proven techniques for implementing the concepts.

Chapter 1, Achieving High Customer Satisfaction, explores what is involved in delivering excellent customer support, the role of the service desk and all of the technical support providers within a support organization, and trends influencing the service desk role. It also discusses the mix of business, technical, soft, and self-management skills required in today's dynamic technical support setting.

Chapter 2, Developing Strong Listening and Communication Skills, focuses on how support providers can become better listeners and communicate effectively with customers and coworkers. These skills are considered the two most basic and important skills that support providers must possess.

Chapter 3, Winning Telephone Skills, discusses the skills that support providers need to interact with customers over the telephone as well as how to avoid the most common call handling mistakes. This chapter helps support providers develop excellent telephone skills that will send a positive, professional message to customers.

Chapter 4, Technical Writing Skills for Support Professionals, discusses the impact that technologies such as the Internet, email, instant messaging, chat, knowledge management systems, and social media have had on the service desk in terms of how it collects information and delivers support. It also discusses how these changes have prompted the need for support professionals to add technical writing to their list of required skills. This chapter describes the characteristics of good technical writing and provides tips and techniques to help support providers improve their writing skills.

Chapter 5, Handling Difficult Customer Situations, focuses on the leading cause of stress in customer support—difficult situations such as calming irate customers, handling extremely demanding customers, and saying no to customers while maintaining their goodwill. This chapter includes specific techniques for handling difficult situations and minimizing the frustration and stress support providers may feel afterward.

Chapter 6, Solving and Preventing Incidents and Problems, presents a methodical approach that support providers can use to navigate the incident management process, along with proven problem-solving techniques to diagnose and resolve incidents. It discusses the concept of incident ownership and describes when and how to communicate the status of incident resolution activities to customers and management. It also discusses how to use the problem management process to prevent incidents by identifying and eliminating the root cause of problems.

Chapter 7, Business Skills for Technical Professionals, introduces some of the business topics and disciplines technical professionals may encounter when they join the workforce. This chapter also describes advanced business skills that managers are increasingly requiring more senior technical professionals to acquire and use, such as project management, cost-benefit analysis, and return on investment analysis.

Chapter 8, Teams and Team Players in a Service Desk Setting, discusses the fact that customer support is an ideal environment for working in teams due to the complexity of the work and the diversity of skills required. This chapter helps support providers understand their role in the service desk and the support organization, and how to respect and value their team members' contributions.

Chapter 9, Minimizing Stress and Avoiding Burnout, deals with the fact that customer support is one of the most stressful professions. It helps support providers determine the factors that may be causing them stress and provides specific techniques they can use to manage their stress, time, and workload as well as avoid the physical and emotional exhaustion—burnout—caused by long-term stress.

New to This Edition

Concepts and features new to this edition include:

- **Up-to-Date Concepts.** Up-to-date research and resources are referenced throughout the text. Chapter 1 provides an in-depth overview of current support industry trends and how those trends are influencing the skills needed by service desk professionals.

- **Up-to-Date Interviews.** Comprehensive interviews with industry professionals performing a variety of roles in the service desk industry appear throughout the text.

- **Strategic, Proactive Service Desk.** Chapter 1 describes the transition from reactive help desk to strategic, proactive service desk. Service desk best practices are reflected throughout the remaining chapters.

- **Social Support.** Chapter 1 introduces the rise of social media as a support channel and specific techniques for leveraging social media technologies are described throughout the text.

- **Technical Writing.** Chapter 4 has been expanded to include topics such as Knowledge-Centered Support (KCS), blogs, and developing scripts for successful videos.

- **Emerging Concepts.** Chapter 7 introduces the emerging business productivity team and enterprise genius bar concepts.

- **DevOps.** Chapter 8 introduces the DevOps movement and describes the role of the service desk in DevOps.

- **ITIL 2011.** References to ITIL best practices throughout the text have been updated to reflect ITIL 2011.

Features

To aid you in fully understanding service desk concepts, the following features in this book are designed to improve its pedagogical value:

Chapter Objectives. Each chapter in this book begins with a list of the important concepts to be mastered within the chapter. This list provides you with a quick reference to the contents of the chapter as well as a useful study aid.

Illustrations, Photographs, and Tables. lllustrations and photographs help you visualize common components and relationships. Tables list conceptual items and examples in a visual and readable format.

Notes. Notes expand on the section topic and include resource references, additional examples, and ancillary information.

Tips. Tips provide practical advice and proven strategies related to the concept being discussed.

Want More Info? Want More Info? pointers direct you to other chapters in the text or the Internet for more information about a topic, an example related to the chapter content, and other points of interest.

Bulleted Figures. Selected figures contain bullets that summarize important points to give you an overview of upcoming discussion points and to later help you review material.

Interviews. Interviews detail real-life examples of the chapter topic. Using a case study approach, interviews describe actual experiences and confirm the importance of the topic. Also, interviews with industry experts expand upon and give additional insight into real-world applications of the topic.

Case Studies. Case Studies introduce and explore a concept related to the chapter content. They provide helpful information that give a broader perspective of the service desk industry.

Chapter Summaries. Each chapter's text is followed by a summary of chapter concepts. These concise summaries provide a helpful way to recap and revisit the ideas covered in each chapter.

Key Terms. Each chapter contains a listing of the boldfaced terms introduced in the chapter and a short definition of each. This listing provides a convenient way to review the vocabulary you have learned.

Review Questions. End-of-chapter assessment activities begin with a set of at least 30 review questions that reinforce the main ideas introduced in each chapter. These questions ensure that you have mastered the concepts and have understood the information you have learned.

Hands-On Projects. Although it is important to understand the concepts behind service desk topics, no amount of theory can improve on real-world experience. To this end, along with conceptual explanations, each chapter provides eight to ten Hands-On Projects aimed at providing practical experience in service desk topics. Some of these include applying service desk concepts to your personal life and researching information from printed resources, the Internet, and people who work in or have experience with the support industry. Because the Hands-On Projects ask you to go beyond the boundaries of the text itself, they provide you with practice implementing service desk concepts in real-world situations.

Case Projects. The Case Projects at the end of each chapter are designed to help you apply what you have learned to business situations much like those you can expect to encounter in a service desk position. They give you the opportunity to independently synthesize and evaluate information, examine potential solutions, and make recommendations, much as you would in an actual business situation.

Capstone Project. The Capstone Project is designed to be an active learning experience that brings together in a real-world setting all of the concepts and techniques described in this book.

Instructor Resources

The following teaching tools are available to the instructor for download through our Instructor Companion Site at sso.cengage.com.

Electronic Instructor's Manual. The Instructor's Manual that accompanies this textbook includes additional instructional material to assist in class preparation, including teaching tips, quick quizzes, class discussion topics, and additional projects.

Test Bank. Cengage Learning Testing Powered by Cognero is a flexible, online system that allows you to:

- Author, edit, and manage test bank content from multiple Cengage Learning solutions.

- Create multiple test versions in an instant.

- Deliver tests from your LMS, your classroom, or anywhere you want.

PowerPoint Presentations. This book comes with Microsoft PowerPoint slides for each chapter. These slides are included as a teaching aid for classroom presentation; teachers can make them available on the network for chapter review, or print them for classroom distribution. Instructors can add their own slides for additional topics they introduce to the class.

Solution Files. Solutions to all Review Questions are provided.

Acknowledgments

I wish to thank the staff at Cengage Learning who contributed their talents to the creation of this book, including Jim Gish, Senior Product Manager, and Alyssa Pratt, Senior Content Developer, along with all of the individuals who have worked "behind the scenes" to bring this book to life.

Special thanks to Robin Romer who served as developmental editor on this book, a role she also played on earlier editions. Robin's guidance, attention to detail, and calm and caring nature make my job considerably easier. As always, thank you, Robin!

I want to express my great appreciation to Cay Robertson, TECO Energy, and Joyce Parker, Independent IT Service Management Instructor, who reviewed the draft manuscript and made suggestions that significantly enhanced the quality and completeness of the book and its usefulness as a learning tool. My good friend Joyce Parker also contributes to the project by writing exam questions, and for that I am grateful.

I am also very grateful to the following people for their valuable contributions to the "Interview with…" sections that offer a real-world view of the subject matter presented in each chapter: Jeffrey Brooks, Gartner, Inc.; Bill Clement, TECO Energy; Benjamin Compton, TECO Energy; Ann Cook, American Accent Training; Nancy Flynn, The ePolicy Institute; Joe Leggiero, Information Technology Consultant; Lori Smiley, Metro Government of Nashville.

Love and thanks to my family and friends who suffer the neglect that comes with any book project. Good news! It's done! I greatly appreciate your support and encouragement.

Finally, I tip my hat to the thousands of service desk professionals who are out there doing a great job day in and day out. Your efforts have enabled this industry to become what it is—an exciting and growing professional career choice. You have a tough job and you rarely receive the support and respect that you deserve for doing it. I hope through this book you see that you certainly have mine.

Donna Knapp
Tampa, Florida

Achieving High Customer Satisfaction

In this chapter you will learn:

◎ The role the service desk plays in delivering high-quality technical customer support

◎ The four components of a successful service desk

◎ Trends influencing the service desk

◎ What customers need and expect

◎ How to meet and exceed customer expectations

◎ The mix of skills needed for a career in technical customer support

Technology pervades our lives. People of all ages, backgrounds, and skill levels use information and communications technology at work, at school, and at home. Mobile devices such as smartphones and tablets enable people to use technology anywhere. This widespread use of technology results in an enormous need for technical support. Many companies meet this need by setting up service desks. A **service desk** is a single point of contact within a company for managing customer incidents and service requests. Companies worldwide know that they must provide high-quality customer service and support if they want to survive in today's fiercely competitive business environment. Companies also know that today's savvy and self-sufficient technology users expect easy access to a wide range of support services. They expect options. The service desk plays an extremely important role in delivering that service and support.

An integral component of the service desk is people. Having the right people on a service desk facilitates high customer satisfaction. Finding and keeping people who enjoy working with technology and helping customers is a great challenge facing companies. Historically, the service desk was considered a stepping stone to other professions within the information technology (IT) industry. Today, the service desk has been elevated to a profession in and of itself and provides a tremendous opportunity for people who want to pursue an exciting career in the IT field. Because the service desk is such a critical part of any customer-oriented business, people who possess the skills needed to deliver high-quality customer service and technical support are extremely valuable and highly employable. To work in a service desk, you must possess a mix of skills, including business skills, technical skills, soft skills, and self-management skills. You must understand the characteristics of high-quality customer service and technical support. Finally, you must understand that how you interact with each and every customer influences that customer's perception of your company and its products and services.

Delivering High-Quality Technical Customer Support

We are living in a connected age, and the technology we employ to obtain and use information and to stay connected has found its way into every aspect of our lives. For the average person, it can be a challenge to keep that technology up and running and get it to do what he or she wants and needs it to do. A person may turn to any number of service desks for support. For example, to obtain assistance with a personal mobile device, a person may call, chat online with, or walk into a retail store of a product manufacturer or service provider. When at home, that person may contact the particular company that manufactured his or her computer or the company that publishes a software package he or she uses. When at work, that person may contact his or her company's service desk for aid in using programs that are unique to that company. A person working as a service desk analyst may even contact other service desks, such as a vendor's service desk, for assistance in diagnosing a hardware, software, or network incident. How a service desk treats people influences their level of satisfaction and perception of the entire company and its products. People's level of satisfaction with and perception of a company can determine whether that company succeeds or fails.

Customer Support and the Service Desk Role

The role of the service desk has evolved considerably since the late 1970s when organizations first began directing technology users to a single point of contact for support. Known initially as the "help desk," this function was originally established simply to screen calls, determine the nature of the call, and then **dispatch**, or send, a vendor or other technical support specialist to the customer's site. A **help desk** is a single point of contact within a company for technology-related questions and incidents. Today, the service desk offers a broader range of services and is a key part of any technical support organization.

Technical support refers to the wide range of services that enable people and companies to effectively use the information technology they acquired or developed. Technical support services include selecting and installing the hardware, software, network, and application components that enable technology users to do their work; keeping the systems and devices in good repair; upgrading hardware, software, and application components when needed; and providing customer support. **Customer support** includes services that help a customer understand and benefit from a product's capabilities by answering questions, solving problems, and providing training. The service industry makes the distinction that a **customer** buys products or services and a **user** consumes products or services. This distinction is made to clarify that customers are individuals with budgeting responsibilities and so are responsible for making purchasing decisions and for negotiating agreements or contracts. For example, the managers (customers) within an organization typically make purchasing decisions based on both their employees' (users) requirements and the organization's financial constraints. However, it is important to note that in practice, many organizations—and this text— informally use the term *customer* instead of *user* in recognition of the service desk's role as a customer service organization. Many companies consider the service desk a strategic corporate resource because of its constant interaction with the company's external customers, internal employees, vendors, and partners.

Customer service and support organizations come in all shapes and sizes and deliver a wide range of services. These organizations can be either a company or a department within a company devoted to customer service and support. One type of customer service and support organization is a **call center**, which is a place where telephone calls are made or received in high volume. The term **contact center** refers to a call center that uses technologies such as email and the web in addition to the telephone to communicate with its customers. These various routes of communication to and from the service desk are typically called **channels**.

Major businesses use call or contact centers because they need to handle a high volume of customer contacts. A cost-efficient solution is to handle these contacts from one or more centralized locations. The actual services delivered by each call or contact center vary, and the services provided may or may not be technology oriented.

Examples of call centers and contact centers include airline reservation centers, catalog ordering centers, and home shopping centers. Large software publishers and hardware manufacturers such as Apple, Dell, Hewlett-Packard, and Microsoft use call or contact centers to provide technical and customer support. Large corporations may use call or contact centers to provide technical and customer support to internal employees. Or, large corporations may **outsource** their support services—that is, have services provided by an outside supplier instead of providing them in-house. These suppliers typically run call centers that serve the employees or customers of many corporations.

The help desk and the service desk are also customer service and support organizations. This book focuses on the service desk, a successor to the help desk. Simply put, a service desk is a help desk with a broader scope of responsibilities.

The transition from help desk to service desk was prompted mainly by wide-scale adoption in the mid 1990s of the **Information Technology Infrastructure Library© (ITIL©)**, which is a set of best practices for IT service management. A **best practice** is a proven way of completing a task to produce a near optimum result. Best practices are proven over time through experience and research to work for a large number and variety of people and organizations. **IT service management (ITSM)** is a discipline for managing IT services that focuses on the quality of those services and the relationship that the IT organization has with its customers. An **IT service** is a service that is based on the use of information technology and supports business processes.

 ITIL was developed in the 1980s by the United Kingdom government's Central Computer and Telecommunications Agency (CCTA) and consists of a series of books that gives best practice guidance on IT service management-related topics.

A fundamental premise of ITIL is that IT organizations must adopt a service-oriented approach to managing IT services, instead of the traditional product- or technology-centric approaches. In other words, IT organizations must recognize their role as service providers and strive to satisfy their customers' requirements. This philosophy applies whether IT serves internal customers, such as other departments or divisions within the same company, or external customers. ITIL provides guidance that IT organizations can use to meet customer needs by managing IT services as efficiently and effectively as possible.

ITIL considers technical and customer support vitally important, and it introduced organizations to the concept of the service desk. In addition to managing customer incidents, ITIL considers the service desk responsible for handling service requests and communications with customers.

ITIL defines an **incident** as an unplanned interruption to an IT service or a reduction in the quality of an IT service. Common incidents include a broken device, an error message, and a system outage. Historically, such unplanned events were referred to as problems (and still are in some organizations). ITIL, however, defines a **problem** as the cause of one or more incidents. Common problems include hardware defects, corrupt files, software errors or bugs, and human error. ITIL defines a **service request** as a formal request from a user for something to be provided. Common service requests may include requests for information, advice, or a standard change. Common standard changes may include installing preapproved software, setting up a new employee within an organization, or providing access to an IT service.

 Some organizations handle password reset requests as incidents, while others view them as service requests.

Although this book focuses on the service desk, many of the concepts covered in this book apply to any organization devoted to customer service and support. Skills such as listening and communicating (Chapter 2), creating a positive telephone image (Chapter 3), effective writing skills (Chapter 4), and handling difficult situations (Chapter 5) are important in any profession, but are particularly important when dealing with customers.

The service desk makes a significant contribution to business goals by providing a single point of contact for all technical and customer support services, delivering value to customers, and capturing and distributing information. Because people working in a service desk have daily contact with customers, they enjoy a unique opportunity to capture an enormous amount of information about customers' wants and needs. Successful service desks share this information with managers and other groups within the organization that are involved in supporting customers.

The service desk and these other support groups are often structured in a series of levels, an approach commonly known as a multi-level support model. In a **multi-level support model**, shown in Figure 1-1, the service desk refers incidents it cannot resolve to the appropriate internal group, external vendor, or subject matter expert. Level one is the service desk because it is the first point of contact for customers. If the level one service desk cannot resolve an incident, it hands off the incident to the next highest level, level two. Level two might consist of a support group for a particular software application or a network support group. Level two might be a specialist group within the service desk team that has greater technical skills or authority than the front-line service desk analysts who initially handle incidents. If level two cannot resolve the incident, then it hands off the incident to level three, which is usually a software vendor, a hardware vendor, or a subject matter expert. A **subject matter expert (SME)** is a person who has a high level of experience or knowledge about a particular subject.

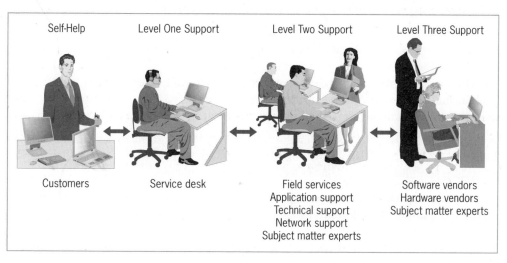

Figure 1-1 Multi-level support model

In the context of a multi-level support model, customers solving incidents on their own is known as **level zero** or tier zero and may also be referred to as **self-help**. Self-help services such as a service desk web site that contains answers to frequently asked questions (FAQs) and a knowledge base of solutions empower customers to support themselves.

The goal of this multi-level support model is to have the service desk resolve as many incidents as possible at level one. This approach ensures the most efficient use of level two and three resources.

In an effort to satisfy their customers, the industry average is for IT service desks to resolve just under 66 percent of reported incidents at level one according to HDI, an international membership association that focuses on the needs of internal and external support organizations (2013 Support Center Practices and Salary Report, HDI). They also take ownership of all incidents, whether or not they can resolve them. Taking **ownership** of an incident means tracking the incident to ensure that the customer is kept informed about the status of the incident, that the incident is resolved within the expected time frame, and that the customer is satisfied with the final resolution.

Not all service desks require three levels of support. Technology and a broader scope of responsibilities are making it possible for many level one service desks to function at a much higher level than in the past, eliminating the need for a third level. Also, it is not uncommon for smaller service desks to have only two levels of support. This is particularly true in organizations that support primarily off-the-shelf computer software products or cloud-based applications. In those organizations, a level one analyst who cannot resolve an incident contacts the appropriate vendor.

Historically, the level one service desk delivered customer support services, and the level two groups handled technical support services such as repairing systems and upgrading hardware and software when needed. As the support industry has evolved, that division of responsibilities has changed. Many companies have consolidated some or all of their support services into the service desk in an effort to deliver faster, more cost-effective services.

This consolidation of support services has many benefits. The service desk handles incidents and service requests with greater efficiency because it hands off fewer incidents and service requests to other groups. This increases the value of its services to customers and the company. Level two and level three support groups can focus on their primary responsibilities, which include tasks such as projects, operational activities, and maintenance activities. The company achieves a maximum return on its investment in the service desk.

Technology also makes it possible for the service desk to absorb many activities that relate directly to the customer from other support groups, such as network support, field support, and system administration. Available technologies may include:

- **Knowledge management systems (KMSs)**—Tools and databases that are used to store, manage, and present information sources such as customer information, documents, policies and procedures, incident resolutions, and known errors. The databases that underpin a knowledge management system may be referred to as knowledge bases or known error databases. A **knowledge base** is a logical database that contains data used by a knowledge management system. A **known error** is a problem that has a documented root cause and a workaround. A **known error database (KEDB)** is a database that contains known error records.

- **Configuration management systems (CMSs)**—Tools and databases for managing IT asset information and linking that information to related incidents, problems, known errors, changes, and releases.

- **Network monitoring systems**—Tools used to observe network performance.

- **Remote control and diagnostic systems**—Systems that allow the service desk to take remote control of the keyboard, screen, or mouse of connected devices and then troubleshoot problems, transfer files, and even provide informal training by viewing or operating the customer's screen.

By expanding its responsibilities to include activities such as network monitoring and network and system administration, the service desk can be more proactive and timely because it does not have to engage other groups to perform these tasks. **Network monitoring** involves activities that use tools to observe network performance in an effort to minimize the impact of incidents. **Network and system administration** activities include day-to-day tasks such as setting up and maintaining user accounts, ensuring that the data the company collects is secure, and performing email and database management.

The web has also had a profound impact on the support industry. According to HDI, 63 percent of service desks maintain web sites that provide customers with self-help or self-service options such as the ability to report incidents, submit service requests, obtain answers to FAQs, and search online help systems or knowledge bases (2013 Support Center Practices and Salary Report, HDI). Empowering customers to help themselves increases customer satisfaction because customers can get the help they need when they need it. Self-services also benefit support organizations because they are a cost-effective way for the service desk to assist large numbers of customers while freeing human resources to work on more complex incidents and service requests.

The technical support services that a company delivers as well as how and by whom those services are delivered vary according to company size, company goals, and customer expectations. The service desk contributes significantly to its company or department by serving as the first point of contact for all technical support services and by taking ownership and ensuring that customer incidents and service requests are resolved as quickly and cost effectively as possible.

Components of a Successful Service Desk

A successful service desk plays an important role in providing high-quality technical customer support. A successful service desk also is made up of several tightly integrated components. Each component relates to the others in some way and, together, these components enable the service desk to satisfy customers. Four critical components—people, processes, technology, and information—determine a service desk's success.

People

The **people** component consists of the staff and structure put in place within a company or department to support its customers by performing processes. The principal roles played by people who work in a service desk include the **front-line service providers**, who interact directly with customers. Although titles and job descriptions vary from one service desk to the next, front-line service provider positions include dispatcher or call screener, level one analyst, and level one specialist. Depending on the size of the organization, service desk management positions include service desk supervisor or team leader, service desk manager, and senior service desk manager.

Several supporting roles such as knowledge management system administrator, technical support, and training are also important and commonplace in the service desk. A **knowledge engineer**, also called a **knowledge base administrator (KBA)**, develops and oversees the knowledge management process and ensures the information contained in the knowledge management system is accurate, complete, and current. Technical support staff maintains the hardware, software, and applications used by the service desk. Training staff ensures the service desk team receives training that addresses the business, technical, soft, and self-management skills it needs.

Processes

A **process** is a collection of interrelated work activities that take a set of specific *inputs* and produce a set of specific *outputs* that are of value to a customer. **Value** is the perceived worth, usefulness, or importance of a product or service to a customer. The consistent use of processes leads to customer confidence and employee satisfaction because customers and service desk employees know what and how something needs to be done and the time frame within which it needs to be done. Some common processes found in a service desk include incident management, problem management, request fulfillment, knowledge management, access management, and service level management.

Technology

In a service desk setting, people use a wide array of tools and technologies—collectively referred to as technology—to do their work. A **tool** is a product or device that automates or facilitates a person's work. A **technology** is an invention, process, or method that enables the creation and enhancement of tools. Service desk employees and managers use technology to perform processes. They also use technology to capture, use, and share information about their customers and their work. Service desks use technology to automate routine tasks such as password resets and to automatically distribute software. Service desks also use technology to enable self-help and self-service and to facility communication and collaboration with their customers and other support groups. Some tools found in a typical service desk include incident management systems, knowledge management systems, telephone systems, web-based systems, and Web 2.0 technologies.

Web 2.0 is a concept that emphasizes enabling web users to interact, collaborate, and generate content via blogs, wikis, and social networking sites, for example, rather than passively view content created by others.

Incident management systems offer enhanced trouble ticketing and management reporting capability. Incident management systems are the technology used to log and track customer incidents and service requests. Incidents and service requests are often collectively called contacts. **Contact** is a generic term used to describe different types of customer transactions such as questions, incidents, and service request. By logging all customer contacts, the service desk prevents a common customer complaint, which is that incidents and service requests are lost or forgotten. Furthermore, when analysts log all contacts in an incident management system, they can use the many features this tool provides to track contacts from start to finish. For example, many incident management systems generate alerts that remind analysts to periodically contact customers with status updates when incidents cannot be resolved immediately. Many systems also allow analysts to access a knowledge management system.

Information

Information is data that is organized in a meaningful way. People need information to do their work. For example, service desk analysts need information about customers and the details of their incidents and service requests to provide support. Management needs information to evaluate team and individual performance and identify improvement opportunities. For example, service desk managers need information that tells them how quickly, completely, and accurately services are delivered. Other groups within the organization need information about the company's customers. For example, a company's Research and Development department needs information about how customers are using the company's products and services, and how customers would like those products and services to be improved. Without data, service desks have trouble creating the information required to understand customer needs and expectations and measure customer satisfaction. Consequently, successful companies consider information a resource in the same way that well-trained employees, well-defined processes, and well-implemented technology are resources. Types of data captured by service desks include customer data, incident data, status data, and resolution data.

People working in a service desk must understand that customers, managers, and coworkers use the data they collect on a daily basis to create information. The knowledge gained by analyzing this data and information can be used to increase customer satisfaction, enhance productivity, improve the quality of products and services, increase the efficiency and effectiveness with which services are delivered, and create new products and services.

Of the four components, people are by far the most important and expensive component of a service desk. Finding qualified people to deliver high-quality customer support is a great challenge being faced throughout the support industry. People are the most important component because customers are people who have feelings and expectations that only other people can understand. In fact, customers do not buy products or services so much as they buy expectations. Customer **expectations**, results that customers consider reasonable or due to them, are a moving target, and it is this movement that makes it so difficult for companies to get and stay ahead.

Customer expectations are a moving target for a number of reasons. As customers become more dependent on technology, they become more demanding of the support they require.

Also, as companies improve the quality of the services they deliver, the standard that represents great service gets redefined. When companies consistently deliver a high level of service, that high level becomes the standard, making it extremely difficult, and sometimes quite costly, for companies to go beyond what customers have come to expect. Companies must manage and, when possible, exceed customers' expectations to compete in today's business world. The best companies listen rigorously to their customers' suggestions and complaints in an effort to fully understand their customers' wants and needs. Those companies communicate what they *can* do for customers and work hard to ensure they deliver the products and services customers really want and need—not products and services they *think* their customers want and need.

Customers have expectations not only about what a product can do, but also about what the company can do to enable them to fully use that product. This is particularly true in the world of technology where customers often use customer service and technical support to differentiate between companies and their products. Vendors are constantly striving to duplicate the features offered by their competitors. Companies that gain a competitive edge through product innovation can quickly lose that edge when a competitor publishes its next release. In other words, the products themselves can be very similar at any point in time. Companies that deliver excellent service—that is, they meet and exceed their customers' expectations—can use that excellent service, as well as a great product, to maintain their competitive edge. Also, the more complex and pervasive technology becomes, the more people crave personalized service and support. Companies that deliver excellent customer service work hard to treat every customer as an individual. They pay attention and attend to the details of each customer's need.

Delivering high-quality services can be very costly, so most companies also strive to deliver cost-effective self-services that meet and exceed their customers' expectations. Self-services offered through the web, such as knowledge bases, FAQs, and online forms that can be used to submit incidents and service requests, are excellent examples of ways companies use technology to support customers 24 hours a day, 7 days a week.

To meet and exceed customers' expectations, technology must make customers feel they are getting personalized service. For example, many web sites enable users to create a profile to specify personal preferences, and some use cookies to identify users and track their preferences. A **profile**, or user profile, is a collection of personal data associated with a specific user. A **cookie** is a very small text file created by a web server that is stored on a user's computer either temporarily for that session only or permanently on the hard disk. Cookies are assigned to a user's profile and can only be read by the web server that stored the cookie on the user's computer. When a profile or cookie is present, the web server remembers the user and displays information the user requested or that is relevant.

Benefits of Quality Customer Support

Companies that deliver excellent customer support receive substantial benefits, as do their employees. Some of those benefits are very tangible, such as return business and the positive word of mouth that leads to new business. These, in turn, lead to higher sales and profits. Industry recognition is another benefit, and many companies are striving to be recognized as "world class." A **world class** company has achieved and sustains high levels of customer satisfaction. World class companies often reap the benefit of customer loyalty. Loyal customers are willing to pay slightly more for products and suffer minor inconveniences, such as temporarily living without a feature provided by a competitor's product, in exchange for excellent service.

A less tangible benefit of high-quality customer support is customer feedback. Companies that deliver great service often receive customer feedback about how they can improve their service even more: "This is great, but you know what would be even better…" Companies that deliver poor service do not receive that kind of feedback because few dissatisfied customers complain. Most dissatisfied customers just walk away and do not come back.

Service providers need to understand that customer complaints are a good thing, and they need to be responsive to, and even encourage, complaints. Companies that make it easy for customers to complain by, for example, conducting customer satisfaction surveys, receive a greater number of complaints. Technology is also making it easier for customers to complain when, for example, a company provides a link on its web site or an email address that can be used to provide feedback. The challenge is for companies to collect and analyze that feedback and take action to improve their services. Companies that are receptive to customer feedback often are given an opportunity to further improve or a second chance when they fall down. Companies that deliver poor service or fail to listen to their customers do not typically receive that second chance—customers just take their business elsewhere.

Another benefit of high-quality customer support is the very real phenomenon that happy customers result in happy employees, who in turn create more happy customers. Some companies believe that if they treat their employees well, their employees in turn will treat their customers well. Regardless of who came first, the happy customer or the happy employee, companies that are committed to delivering high-quality service and support derive many benefits, and those benefits are often passed on to their employees.

The most obvious benefits that companies pass on to their employees are reward and opportunity. Many companies offer their employees "pay for performance" plans that are tied to customer satisfaction. Some companies offer profit-sharing plans that enable employees to directly benefit when the company is doing well. Other companies offer bonuses to employees who consistently go the extra mile for their customers. Job security is another benefit, and although few companies guarantee life-long jobs, people with the right mix of skills are highly employable and can more easily find work.

One of the most important principles of success is developing the habit of going the extra mile.

NAPOLEON HILL

Employees also derive intrinsic benefits from supporting customers, such as the pride and satisfaction that come from helping other people. People who enjoy the technical customer support field also tend to demonstrate a strong sense of purpose. They know the role they play is important to their customers and their company, and they take it very seriously.

Establishing and maintaining a service desk can be costly, and the cost is even greater when a company strives to achieve world class status. Not all companies are able or willing to invest in the service desk. People working in a service desk must promote the benefits of high-quality customer support and show they understand and are committed to satisfying their customers' needs and expectations.

Trends Influencing the Service Desk

An irreversible dependence on technology has prompted customers to demand ever cheaper, better, and faster support services. This demand has prompted companies to considerably expand and reinvent the role of the service desk. Although companies originally considered service desk jobs to be entry-level positions, today's service desk has a more strategic position because the service desk can and does contribute to the company's bottom line. This is because the service desk helps companies to make the most of their technology investments and also helps to minimize the impact when that technology fails.

This huge demand for support, coupled with a shortage of IT professionals, has created a tremendous career opportunity in the field of customer service and technical support. According to the United States Department of Labor, computer support is projected to increase by 18 percent from 2010 to 2020 (*Occupational Outlook Handbook*, 2012–13 Edition, U.S. Department of Labor Bureau of Labor Statistics). The service desk offers—and for the foreseeable future will continue to offer—considerable opportunities to people who want to be a part of this dynamic and growing industry. For example, pursuing a career in the service desk provides the opportunity to:

- Learn about and support a wide range of information technologies, such as hardware, software, databases, applications, and networks.

- Work with people and technology.

- Use relevant skills acquired in other industries, such as customer service skills or multilingual skills, to gain entry into the IT industry.

- Gain entry into a company at which you want to work.

- Learn about all the various departments within a company and gain a full appreciation of the opportunities available within that company.

- Advance your career along either a technical career path or a managerial career path.

- Work a flexible schedule, work from home, or potentially travel for work, including traveling abroad.

- Achieve the personal satisfaction that comes from helping others.

As service desks evolve, they face many challenging business trends. These trends, listed in Figure 1-2, influence the direction in which the service desk industry is heading and the opportunities available to people pursuing a service desk career. Each of these trends affects how service desks are run and the opportunities they present to service desk analysts.

- Multi-generational support
- Multichannel support
- Anytime, anywhere, any device support
- Collapsing support levels
- 24/7 support
- Fee-based support
- Global support
- Use of best practice frameworks and standards
- Outsourcing
- Service desk as a profession

Figure 1-2   Service desk industry trends

Multi-Generational Support

The workforce is more diverse today than ever before in history. The demographics span four different generations of workers, including the mature, World War II generation; the Baby Boomers; Generation X; and the Millennials (also known as Generation Y). These different generations of technology users tend to have varying needs and expectations with regard to the service desk and support.

By 2020, Millennials will make up nearly half (47 percent) of the workforce (*The 2020 Workplace*. J. Meister. K. Willyerd. HarperCollins Publishers, 2010).

Most customers in Generation X and the Millennials have grown up interacting heavily with technologies such as social networking sites, wikis, blogs, and podcasts, and tend to be quite comfortable using these technologies for self-help. Service desks must respond by providing these self-help resources and ensuring these resources provide customers the answers they need in an efficient and effective way.

Younger customers also tend to bypass formalized support channels such as the telephone or email and turn first to crowdsourcing as a means of problem solving. **Crowdsourcing** involves outsourcing a task traditionally performed by a single individual to a large group of people or community (in other words, a crowd). In the context of technical support, crowdsourcing may involve posing a question or problem to a large group of people via Facebook, Twitter, or an online forum in an effort to quickly get an answer. Although this approach could be viewed as desirable because it reduces the number of contacts at the service desk, crowdsourcing can be ineffective. For example, the "crowd" may not have a solution, and so the customer wastes time waiting for one. Also, the solutions provided might not be the best solutions, or they might violate existing policies, such as security policies. Service desks must respond by offering social media channels and forums that are monitored to ensure customers get the right answers at the right time or are directed to more formalized channels.

Generally speaking, older workers do not fit any one profile. Their level of comfort using technology varies. Some older workers feel quite comfortable using self-help and crowdsourcing as their first option, whereas others require help adapting to these technologies. Still other older workers have "grown up" contacting a help desk or service desk and may be more comfortable obtaining human assistance and receiving step-by-step instructions. Service desks must respond by ensuring that self-help is not viewed as a one-size-fits-all solution that becomes a barrier to customer service.

 Older generations are increasingly expected to work longer, many beyond the usual age of retirement, and some retired workers will return to the workforce for reasons such as a desire to be a productive member of society, personal satisfaction, or perhaps in response to financial pressures.

Regardless of age, customers demand better and faster service and are increasingly willing to use any and all options provided. These demanding customers want the freedom to choose when, where, and how they obtain support, and they want whatever option they choose to be easy to use and effective.

Multichannel Support

Customer experience is a critical component of customer satisfaction. If companies fail to make customer experience a priority, it has become easier for customers to both vocalize their dissatisfaction and to change services and service providers. If companies get it right, customers can just as easily broadcast their praises. Multichannel support is one way that service desks can positively influence customer experience.

The telephone will continue to be a heavily used contact channel for some time. One reason is that self-help is not always an option, whether because of poor connectivity or because the customer is experiencing a unique or complex issue that is beyond the scope of self-help. Another reason is that some workers are unwilling to take the time required to use self-help options and view calling the service desk as the fastest way to obtain support. Examples include highly compensated workers, such as lawyers and doctors, and workers who handle financial transactions such as stock brokers or workers taking orders in a call center. Furthermore, some people simply prefer to speak with a human being, particularly when they need help. Given the increase in user mobility, some service desks are seeing and providing for an increase in the number of people walking in to the service desk for much the same reason—the desire to speak one-on-one with a human being.

Customers are also willing to use alternative support channels such as email and web-based services such as self-help, online chat, and video demonstrations. A "trend within a trend" is that many interactions involve multiple technologies. For example, customers may begin interacting with the service desk via the telephone, a chat session, or social media and then be directed to download a fix from a web site. Customers may begin interacting with the service desk via a web site and be directed by an avatar to download a video demonstration. In the context of computing, an **avatar** is a computer user's representation of himself or herself. Avatars may be three-dimensional, such as those found in video games, or two-dimensional, such as those used in many Internet-based instant messaging forums such as Skype. Or, customers may begin interacting with an avatar embedded in an application or service, and the avatar directs the customer to the service desk only if automated diagnostic techniques fail to produce a solution.

Service desks should provide input to service design activities that result in support being a natural extension of people's work. In other words, meet customers where they are, and where they need support, rather than requiring that customers conform to the processes that are convenient or cost-effective for the service desk.

Historically, companies have tended to handle these alternative support channels informally—for example, incidents might not be logged—and few, if any, performance measures, or **metrics**, were captured. However, to meet the needs of today's technically savvy and demanding customers, service desks must look at multichannel support differently.

Smart service desks know that customers will embrace self-help and web-based services only if the content is current, well organized, and easy to use. As with telephone calls, chat services must enable customers to interact with a knowledgeable professional who can quickly deliver a resolution. These same service desks also know that, as discussed previously, some customers are still going to use channels such as the telephone and email to obtain support.

And herein lies the trend. Multichannel support changes the skills that service desk analysts must have and the types of incidents and service requests they resolve. Because customers can handle their simpler incidents through the web, they contact the service desk with more complex incidents or with incidents that require an immediate resolution, such as connectivity-related incidents. As a result, good problem-solving skills are important for analysts. Writing skills are important because analysts must interact with customers through email and chat and because they are expected to contribute to the content that customers access on the web. Internet skills, such as the ability to use browsers, find content online, and use Internet-based diagnostic tools such as remote control systems, also are imperative.

Multichannel support also creates a need for people to develop, maintain, and support the service desk's systems. Roles such as technical support and knowledge engineer have greater importance, as service desks rely more heavily on their support systems and use these systems to collect and maintain content for their web sites.

Service desks also face the challenge of ensuring they are capturing the data needed to efficiently and effectively manage the various support channels they offer to customers. This means they must determine how best to integrate the various tools needed to capture this data, such as automatic call distributors (ACDs), email response management systems, integrated service management tools, web-based systems, and social media, to name just a few. An **automatic call distributor (ACD)** is a telephone technology that answers a call and routes, or distributes, it to the next available analyst. If all analysts are busy, the ACD places the call in a queue and plays a recorded message, such as "We're sorry, all of our service representatives are currently assisting other customers. Your call will be answered in the order it has been received." An **email response management system** is a system that enables service desks to manage high-volume chat, email, and web form messages.

Service desks must also begin to produce meaningful metrics, such as response time and cost per contact, relative to each channel they offer. They must track usage trends, understand their customers' preferences, and invest in options that reflect those preferences. They must understand that, when sites are well designed, web-based contacts cost less than contacts that involve analysts—but still they are not free. Companies must bear the cost of maintaining their web sites, and they must work hard to keep them useful and current, or customers will turn to another channel. Companies must also understand that the cost of telephone contacts may begin to rise, because they represent complex and unique incidents that typically cannot be resolved using self-services.

Social media has made it easier for service desks to understand their customers' perceptions and preferences. Smart service desks monitor Facebook and Twitter postings and respond quickly to customer inquiries, complaints, and suggestions.

Anytime, Anywhere, Any Device Support

A number of IT industry trends are prompting changes to how the service desk is structured, along with its policies and processes. These IT industry trends include bring your own device, desktop virtualization, and cloud computing, to name just a few. **Bring your own device (BYOD)** involves using personally-owned mobile devices to access business applications. **Desktop virtualization** separates a PC desktop environment from a physical machine using the client/server model of computing. **Cloud computing** involves delivering hosted services over the Internet. Each of these trends is affecting the service desk as they result in a more complex computing environment. Collectively, these trends are enabling the even faster adoption of what was already a strong trend—worker mobility. The variety of mobile and wireless devices and applications, combined with the speed at which individuals are adopting these devices, make supporting mobile workers particularly challenging for service desks.

Mobile devices such as tablets and smartphones are also being used by level two and level three support groups and service desk managers, prompting many service desks to revise their escalation and notification procedures.

This constant barrage of new technologies and in some cases an absence of standards with regard to these technologies, are causing service desks to realize they must look strategically at how to serve their customers going forward. The complexities of supporting a multivendor environment, compounded by the emergence of technologies such as cloud computing, reinforce this need to take a strategic view. Such a strategic assessment includes assessing the skills of their staff, redesigning their processes, evaluating their tools, and rethinking their data and information needs. In other words, service desks must holistically address all aspects of their services to meet the requirements of their customers whenever they need assistance (anytime), wherever they are (anywhere), regardless of the device they are using (any device).

 The challenges facing today's service desks can be overcome by effectively using people, processes, technology, and information.

In response to these trends, service desks are getting engaged earlier in the service lifecycle and working with other parts of the IT organization to define standards in terms of what devices and applications best serve the needs of technology users and ensure the security of corporate data assets. Service desks are also participating in efforts to modify Service Level Agreements to include policies and procedures relating to process areas such as information security management, change management, service asset and configuration management, request fulfillment, and access management. A **Service Level Agreement (SLA)** is a written document that spells out the services the service desk will provide the customer, the customer's responsibilities, and how service performance is measured.

In light of these trends, service desks recognize that today's workers are increasingly technically savvy and self-sufficient. When they do need support, however, their need is often immediate, and so the service desk must be prepared. Practices such as improved knowledge management, self-help, and the introduction of social or communal forms of support can help but are still relatively reactive in nature.

 Service desks are being challenged to adopt proactive practices that focus on user productivity and that support strategic business goals.

To make the transition to a more strategic, proactive service desk, a more formalized approach to problem management is needed—one that not only feeds knowledge management (e.g., workarounds and known errors), but also seeks to eliminate recurring incidents, thus freeing service desk resources to work on new and more complex incidents. A more innovative approach to knowledge management is also needed—one that integrates the creation and maintenance of knowledge into the problem solving process, such as the approach presented in the Knowledge-Centered Support methodology. **Knowledge-Centered Support (KCS)** is a knowledge management strategy for service and support organizations developed by the Consortium for Service Innovation (*www.serviceinnovation.org*). KCS is a set of practices and processes that focuses on knowledge as a key asset of the support organization.

An important point here is that self-help can be used effectively to handle known issues (such as answers to how-to questions), and it can also be used to automate recurring requests (such as password resets). However, the technological changes facing the IT industry are resulting in new incidents, many of which are complex in nature because people want to be able to access data, information, and knowledge across a wide array of platforms and technologies. Furthermore, as organizations adopt practices such as virtualization and cloud computing, connectivity becomes critical, and incidents that stand in the way of that connectivity are now viewed as major. These incidents are viewed as major because they affect business productivity.

This transition to a more strategic, proactive service desk and the focus on continual process improvement is supported by the expanded role service desks are taking as organizations adopt ITIL best practices. This expanded role has broadened the service desk's scope of responsibility and has created jobs that require more advanced skills, pay better, and offer a greater diversity of advancement opportunities for service desk analysts.

The constant barrage of new technologies creates job opportunities as well and requires people in support positions to continuously update their skills. Many companies offer a considerable amount of training in an effort to attract and retain analysts who have, and want to maintain, state-of-the-art skills and who are comfortable using and supporting state-of-the-art technologies.

Collapsing Support Levels

Historically, service desks have used a multi-level support model. Although three levels was the standard, many organizations have collapsed that model to only two levels of support. Level one triages contacts, resolves those that can be resolved at the service desk, and escalates those that cannot to other support groups. Incidents that are escalated are handled by specialists, such as the network group or an applications support group. A "trend within a trend" is for **major incidents** that cause significant business impact to be handled by virtual teams of experts that come together to resolve incidents and then disband. This practice is also known as swarming. Gartner defines **swarming** as a work style characterized by a flurry of collective activity by anyone and everyone conceivably available and able to add value (*www.gartner.com/it/page.jsp? id=1416513*). Although such an approach would prove too costly for all incidents or for noncritical incidents, it represents a more efficient way to handle complex or critical incidents than the historical approach of escalating incidents from one level of support to the next.

This trend to collapse support levels is prompted by the need to resolve incidents quickly and minimize the impact of those incidents on business operations. It also reflects the fact that many customers are unwilling to be placed on hold, transferred from one group to the next, or told they will receive a call back. Instead, they want an immediate resolution.

Because of this trend, companies are striving to ensure that their service desks are able to assist customers at the first point of contact whenever possible. To do so, techniques companies are using include hiring and promoting more highly skilled and certified analysts as well as using technologies, such as knowledge management systems and remote control systems, to expand analysts' capabilities. Companies also are using ACD features, such as skills-based routing, voice response units (VRUs), and web-based features such as chat because these technologies make it possible to route contacts directly to the analyst who has the skill needed to handle the incident or service request. All of these techniques enable organizations to reduce handoffs. As a result, the level one service desk is able to handle contacts previously handled by both level one and level two. These techniques also make it possible for companies to reduce the number of escalated incidents (and therefore more effectively use IT resources), reduce wait times, and provide the immediate response today's demanding customers require.

24/7 Support

Customers are challenging companies to provide **24/7 support**, which means that support services are provided 24 hours a day, 7 days a week. The need to support an increasingly self-sufficient customer base, a global customer community, a mobile workforce, or a business that operates around the clock leads to this demand for continuous support.

24/7 support does not mean that service desk analysts must be on site at all times. Many service desks use their phone system to direct customers to their web site after hours where they can use self-help services, submit an incident or service request, or obtain the status of an outstanding incident or service request. Some service desks forward calls to a data center or supplier after hours where the calls are then logged and handled. Some service desks use their phone system to transfer callers to analysts who are working at home or to instruct callers about how to obtain emergency support if needed—typically by contacting an on-call analyst. Some service desks enable customers to chat via the service desk's web site with analysts who may be working at home.

Emergency support is often provided by on-call analysts who carry smart mobile devices. The compensation that on-call analysts receive varies by company. For example, some companies pay an hourly overtime rate, which is typically 1.5 times the analyst's base rate. Some companies offer analysts compensatory time ("comp time"), which means employees earn time off when they work extra hours. Some companies convert on-call availability time to comp time. For example, two to four hours of on-call time equals one hour of comp time. Other companies are more generous. A night of on-call time equals a day off. Conversely, some companies simply expect analysts to be on call as a regular part of their job. They may, however, pay a flat rate per incident, which means analysts are compensated only when they actually handle customer contacts. Or, they may pay a bonus when an analyst spends a lot of time working on a particularly severe or complex incident.

This 24/7 support trend creates many opportunities for service desk professionals. It creates positions for service desk analysts as well as positions for team leaders and supervisors. Companies that provide 24/7 support often have three work shifts: a day shift, a midday (or "mid") shift, and a night shift. The hours that these shifts work vary from company to company. Companies often pay a shift premium, or shift differential, to employees who work an undesirable shift such as the night shift. The shift periods that qualify for a premium and the amount paid vary from one company to the next. Most shift premiums range from 5 to 8 percent of an employee's salary.

Companies that provide 24/7 support often offer very flexible schedules for their employees. For example, people may work 10 hours per day for 4 days and then have 3 days off. Or they may work part-time, such as 20 hours per week. These scheduling alternatives help accommodate the needs of people such as students and retirees who want to continue their education, have family demands, and so on.

 Flexibility is an important characteristic for both individuals and companies. To meet dynamic business challenges, companies will increasingly adopt on-demand staffing models that give the flexibility to scale staffing levels up or down based on current needs.

This trend also creates opportunities for people who assume supporting roles in the service desk. For example, the service desk's technical support staff maintains the service desk's web site, which allows customers to gain access to web-based self-services after hours. Knowledge engineers also make it possible for customers to get answers to FAQs and search knowledge bases for solutions after hours.

For some companies, demand for support may be light after hours. As a result, support may be provided by a supplier, by an on-call employee, or via the web. Customers may not receive the same depth of service after hours that they receive during normal business hours. Most customers are satisfied, however, if they are at least able to find answers to FAQs and known errors on their own, submit a request to obtain service during normal service desk business hours, or obtain support in the event of an emergency.

Fee-Based Support

With **fee-based support**, customers pay for support services on a per-use basis. In other words, each time a customer contacts the service desk or accesses a designated area of the company's web site for billable services, a fee is charged. Service desks that charge for support then have funds available to acquire resources and continuously improve their services. This creates job opportunities. Also, charging for support is an effective way to manage customer expectations. For example, the service desk can charge a higher rate for premium or value-added services. As a result, higher-level, more challenging, and higher-paying job positions are created.

The trend is that some web-based support services will most likely continue to be free, such as FAQs, online knowledge bases, downloadable software fixes, and so on. However, more service desks will likely charge for at least some of their services, such as premium services. As the BYOD policies put in place by some companies are requiring that a service contract is in place for the device itself, it is also likely that there will be an increase in the number of companies providing fee-based consumer support services.

People entering the service desk industry need to be aware of this trend and determine whether and how their employer, or prospective employer, charges for support. A company's policy on this practice greatly influences how analysts account for their time and effort as well as how they interact with customers. For example, analysts who work at service desks that charge for their services are typically required to log all incidents and to verify that a customer is entitled to support before they begin working on an incident. Service desk managers value people who understand that the service desk is a "business within a business" that must justify its existence and that can be run profitably.

Global Support

Some companies are being challenged to provide **global support**, which means they support customers anywhere in the world. This demand for global support may be caused by the need to support a large company that has foreign divisions and subsidiaries or by the need to support customers who are doing business with the company through the web. Companies providing global support must address the culture, language, time zone, and legal issues that come with working in an international market. They also must consider matters affecting the regions of the world in which they do business such as economic conditions, natural disasters, crime, and terrorism. They can do that several ways, including regional, in-country service desk; follow the sun support; and one centralized, global service desk.

Regional, In-Country Service Desks

Traditionally, large companies establish multiple, in-country service desks that each provide localized support. These in-country service desks are able to provide highly personalized service because they understand issues such as language, culture, and local expectations. Some companies prefer this highly personalized form of support even though it can be expensive. To mitigate their costs, these companies may require that all service desks use the same processes and technologies, such as cloud-based technologies. Each service desk may also produce a standard set of metrics that are forwarded to the corporate headquarters for review. Conversely, some companies allow each service desk to establish its own processes and technologies and focus only on its own needs and the needs of its customers.

Follow the Sun Support

Follow the sun support means that companies establish two or more service desks, each on a different continent, and as one service desk closes, another opens. For example, if a company has service desks in Australia, the United Kingdom, and the United States, when Australia completes its business day, support transfers to the service desk in the United Kingdom. When its business day is complete, the United Kingdom service desk transfers support to the service desk in the United States, which transfers support back to Australia when its day is done. These service desks use common tools and common processes and are able to share common data and information sources such as knowledge and configuration management systems. The advantage of this approach is that the company is able to leverage technology and maximize its return on investment, while analysts within each service desk are able to deliver personalized service to their customers—that is, service that addresses issues such as language and culture. This approach also eliminates the costs associated with shift work, as each service desk works only a single shift. Large, multinational companies often take a follow the sun approach.

One Centralized, Global Service Desk

One centralized, global service desk means that one physical service desk provides 24/7 support. This approach tends to be less costly than follow the sun support because companies are not required to set up and staff multiple facilities, nor are they required to replicate their processes and technologies across multiple sites. These companies must, however, address issues such as language and culture, and they must also determine how to deliver localized support when necessary. For example, a service desk may need to determine how to ship a replacement laptop to a mobile worker in another country. Companies that need to provide global support but lack a large support staff, such as a small web-based company, often opt to have a single global service desk.

Regardless of how companies provide global support, this trend presents a number of opportunities for people pursuing a service desk career. First, companies that provide global support often operate 24 hours a day, 7 days a week, which means more job opportunities. Second, people with the right skills may be given the opportunity to travel and gain experience working abroad. Third, global support often requires people who speak multiple languages and understand the cultural issues that are unique to a particular part of the world. For example, in Germany, people consider it rude to address someone by their first name prior to being given permission. In the United States, however, people often use first names. Also, while some companies provide information and deliver support through the web in English only, others offer a choice of languages. These companies often depend on their analysts to translate solutions and publish them in a variety of languages. Companies that provide global support value and are willing to reward people who understand cultural differences and can read and write as well as speak multiple languages. Rewards may include higher salaries and perks such as the opportunity to telecommute or travel abroad.

Use of Best Practice Frameworks and Standards

The trends discussed above require service desks to determine how best to use each of the components discussed throughout this book—people, processes, technology, and information. Many companies are taking the first step toward meeting this challenge by using best practice frameworks such as ITIL to redesign their processes. These frameworks view the service desk as a critical role within IT, and so adopting them often results in increased responsibility and opportunity for service desk professionals.

Some companies are using the ITIL framework along with ISO/IEC 20000 specifications to redesign their processes. **ISO/IEC 20000** is an international standard for IT service management. ISO/IEC 20000 requires evidence in the form of records and documents that the specifications are being met. This evidence is often created by the service desk or uses data and information collected by the service desk.

By redesigning their processes, service desks are able to determine how best to use their existing people and technology, before hiring new people or acquiring new technology. Service desks can use information to determine which processes need to be designed (or redesigned), and they can also use information to measure the efficiency and effectiveness of their new processes.

Most process-related initiatives are handled as projects to ensure all stakeholders are engaged and to ensure the new processes and associated tools achieve the desired outcome. These initiatives present tremendous opportunities for individuals who understand these frameworks and standards and who also have some project management skills, whether as a project manager or as an effective project team member. These initiatives also demand many of the soft and self-management skills discussed in this book, such as being a good listener, being an effective communicator, and being able to manage stress. Individuals with these skills who understand the benefits of a best practice approach are in the best position to survive and even thrive in today's rapidly changing workplace.

The more you can contribute to improvement initiatives and bottom-line benefits, the more valuable you become to an organization. At a minimum, you gain marketable experience that enhances your resume.

Outsourcing

Many of the service desk industry trends discussed above, combined with the need to reduce costs, prompt companies to outsource some or all service desk services. While the outsourcing of services is cyclical, sometimes up and sometimes down, outsourcing will always be a part of the service desk industry for a number of reasons. Companies that outsource may want to take advantage of an outsourcer's experience or flexibility, such as an outsourcer's ability to accommodate peak periods, seasonal call volumes, or after-hours call volumes. Companies that outsource may also want to leverage an outsourcer's investment in and use of new technologies. Frequently, companies are partnering with these external service agencies to deliver high-quality support services at a reduced cost. Some companies outsource all of their support services. Others outsource a portion of their services, such as after-hours support, hardware support and repair, or off-the-shelf PC software support. Some companies outsource support for these industry-standard hardware and software products so they can dedicate their resources to supporting systems developed in house. This desire to outsource all or some support services has spawned a tremendous increase in the number of companies that offer service desk outsourcing services and, consequently, an increase in the number of job opportunities.

Outsourcing requires that the two companies involved—the supplier and the company that hires them—work closely together to define the services to be delivered and the expected level of performance.

This outsourcing trend represents a great opportunity for people who want to pursue a service desk career because it has created many jobs that offer a lot of flexibility. Each outsourcer needs the right number of people with the right skills to support its clients. Outsourcers are constantly looking for people who have great customer service skills along with the necessary mix of business and technical skills to satisfy their customers' needs, which naturally vary considerably from one customer to the next. As a result, people have the opportunity to work with a diversity of customers while being employed by one company. Outsourcers often base raises and bonuses on people's performance and ability to satisfy customers. The best and the brightest people are regularly rewarded and promoted. Service agencies also tend to offer flexible work hours and even the opportunity to work on a contract basis. This means that people who want to work for a time and then take time off (for example, to go to school or to care for a child or family member) have the opportunity to do so as long as they give the supplier adequate notice.

People working in service desks tend to be frightened by the prospect of outsourcing because it can result in the loss of jobs. However, successful outsourcing creates job opportunities for the external supplier, which they may then offer to service desk employees. It is not uncommon for companies to allow a supplier to hire qualified members of their service desk staff when it takes over support because knowledge about the customer community is very important. This is particularly true when the supplier employees who deliver support services are physically located at the company's facilities. Companies may enter into this type of arrangement for security reasons or because they want to leverage an existing investment in technology. Regardless of where the analysts are physically located, people with the right skills are valued.

Service Desk as a Profession

Historically, the service desk was considered a stepping stone to other professions. Today, a number of trends indicate that the service desk has been elevated to a profession in and of itself. For example:

- In many organizations, service desks report directly to a chief information officer (CIO) or senior executive. This shows the importance of service desks within companies.

- Many companies have rewritten their service desk job descriptions to create higher-level job positions. This reflects the expanded responsibility of the service desk. Because the expanded responsibility includes the service desk being asked to solve more incidents at level one, many companies are increasing the amount of training and authority given to analysts. In addition, some companies have been raising the starting salaries for service desk positions.

- Organizations often offer bonuses based on a person's performance and ability to satisfy customers.

- Some companies are creating new team leader and supervisor positions within the service desk in recognition of the need to provide feedback, coaching, and counseling to front-line staff. As a result, more management positions are available.

- Some companies rotate personnel through different positions in the department or company in an effort to reduce burnout and increase the experience and skill of service desk analysts. This practice enables front-line staff to acquire a broad base of experience and to better understand the needs of the business. This practice also enables service desks to reduce turnover and retain the knowledge and experience of seasoned analysts.

- Individual and site certification programs are being used by service desk managers and service desk analysts to demonstrate their business, technical, soft, and self-management skills.

Certifications are necessary for organizations that provide service desk outsourcing services. Potential clients often consider both site and individual certifications held by both service desk management and staff when evaluating potential suppliers. For individuals, certification coupled with experience is what is most valued in today's competitive job market, along with a willingness to learn new skills and stay current. Figure 1-3 lists the top certification programs relevant to a service desk career. The need for these certifications varies from one industry to the next, from one organization to the next, and from one stage in an analyst's career to the next.

- HDI certification
- TSIA certification
- ITIL certification
- Project management certification
- CompTIA certification
- Vendor certification

Figure 1-3   Service desk-related certification programs

The service desk is no longer an entry-level position that people enter and leave as if through a revolving door. The number of opportunities the service desk offers continues to expand, as shown in Figure 1-4.

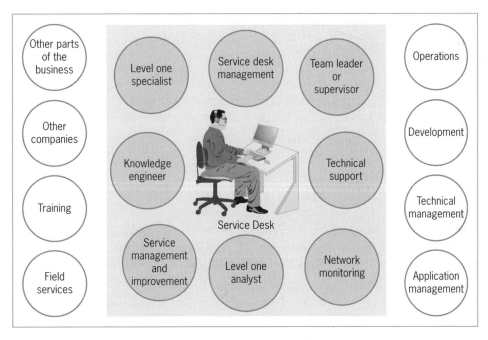

Figure 1-4   Career opportunities within and beyond the service desk

The Service Desk Analyst's Role in the Customer Service Value Chain

There are two principal types of service desks: internal service desks and external service desks. An **internal service desk** responds to questions, distributes information, and handles incidents and service requests for its company's employees. Each employee is considered an

internal customer, a person who works at a company and at times relies on other employees at that company to perform his or her job. A company can have any number of internal service desks that employees contact for support. For example, employees may contact the Human Resources department when they have questions about their medical insurance or other employee benefits. They may contact the Facilities department to have office fixtures installed or repaired. And they may contact the company's IT department when they need help with the hardware and software they use to accomplish their work.

An **external service desk** supports customers who buy its company's products or services. An **external customer** is a person or company that buys another company's products or services. For example, most companies that manufacture hardware, publish software packages, or offer cloud-based services have external service desks to support their customers. Many computer stores offer service desk services to customers who purchase products or equipment at the store. And, as discussed earlier, some suppliers offer fee-based service desk services to external customers.

The relationship between internal and external customers is tightly linked. Every interaction the internal service desk has with an internal customer affects that person's ability to provide excellent service to his or her customers, who may be the external customers of the company. Conversely, the support an external service desk receives from other people or groups within the company (such as the internal service desk or the Sales, Marketing, Field Services, and Research & Development departments) greatly affects its ability to support the company's external customers. To be effective, each and every person involved in this linked set, or chain, of activities must add value. This linked set of activities during which value is added when serving customers, shown in Figure 1-5, is known as a **customer service value chain**.

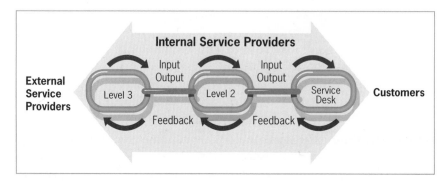

Figure 1-5   Customer service value chain

The customer service value chain shows the relationship that exists between customers, internal service providers, and external service providers. Feedback is used to communicate customer expectations through the value chain. Using the feedback as a guide, internal service providers receive input from other service providers and deliver output to other service providers until a service of value to the customer is delivered. Sometimes external service providers are engaged by internal service providers in an effort to meet the customer's expectations. A service desk analyst, a level two service provider, or a level three service provider may contact a vendor for help resolving a particularly difficult incident. The internal service provider at that point becomes the vendor's customer. The vendor will have its own customer service value chain that must now work together to meet *its* customer's expectations.

The customer service value chain illustrates that all of the departments within a company—all of its internal service providers—are interdependent and must work together to deliver services to external customers. Even departments that do not interface directly with customers perform work that results in the delivery of services to external customers. Because of this, each and every role in a company's customer service value chain must be respected and supported.

Day in and day out, everyone can be considered at times a customer and at other times a service provider. A coworker may ask you to provide information needed to complete a project. In this case, you are the service provider and your coworker is the customer. Later in the day, you may ask this same coworker to help you resolve an incident. Now you are the customer, and your coworker is the service provider. Whether a customer or a service provider, you must respect that each person with whom you interact has a role to play—a job to do—and you must strive to understand the other's needs and expectations. Ultimately, the job each of you does leads—through the customer service value chain—to the delivery of service to the company's external customers. As a result, you must also strive to understand your external customers' expectations. In other words, you must understand what they value. Typically, how your efforts contribute to meeting those expectations will be communicated in the form of your job description and feedback relative to your job performance.

Customer-oriented companies understand and nurture each of the customer–service provider relationships that make up their customer service value chain. Such companies understand that every link is important and that the chain is only as good as its weakest link. These companies also realize that productivity and profit gains are possible only when the service desk, whether it is an internal service desk or an external service desk, is seen as a strategic corporate resource. How customers perceive the entire company—that is, the entire service value chain—is influenced every single time they interact with the service desk— meaning each and every time they interact with you!

Influencing Customer Perception

Customer satisfaction reflects the difference between how a customer expects to be treated and how the customer perceives he or she was treated. This reality is one of the things that makes supporting customers a challenge. It is common knowledge that two people who experience the same event will *perceive* the event differently. For this reason, service desks must work hard to manage their customers' expectations by clearly defining their mission, spelling out their services and policies, and continuously assessing their mission, services, and policies in light of their customers' needs. To do this, some companies have established Service Level Agreements with their customers. Service Level Agreements are an excellent way to manage customer expectations because they spell out exactly what services can and cannot be delivered. These agreements can also be used as the basis for continual service improvement.

According to HDI, more than 73 percent of its members have SLAs with some or all of their customers (2013 Practices and Salary Survey, HDI). The reason most service desks have SLAs is that they realize they cannot keep pace with customers' rising expectations. SLA negotiations ensure that the service desk understands its responsibilities and that customers understand their responsibilities. Customer responsibilities may include complying with policies and providing needed funding. While negotiating SLAs, the service desk and the customer discuss the company's cost to meet the customer's expectations to ensure the company does not spend more than is necessary. Consequently, service desks use SLAs as a tool for managing customer expectations and, when possible and appropriate, enhancing customer self-sufficiency.

As illustrated in Figure 1-6, SLAs must take into consideration every group in the company's customer service value chain, or customer expectations will not be met. For example, if the company guarantees a customer that certain types of incidents will be resolved in 2 hours, and one of the groups in the service value chain cannot respond within 2 hours, the customer's expectations will not be met.

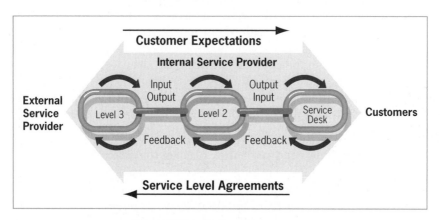

Figure 1-6 Impact of SLAs on the customer service delivery chain

SLAs are an excellent way to influence customer perception because they show how well the service desk is meeting customer expectations. Furthermore, the service desk does not have to guess at what customers expect—the service desk knows what customers want and need because it is all clearly defined in the SLAs.

SLAs can be quite complex, or they can be simple one-page documents such as the sample shown in Figure 1-7. For example, an SLA between a company and a supplier that provides service desk outsourcing tends to be quite complex because it is a legally binding contract. It will provide measurable performance metrics for all parties involved and may provide for incentives or penalties based on performance. An SLA between a company and an internal IT service provider may reflect all or some of the IT services provided by an IT organization, not just its service desk services. Other IT services may include communication services such as email, network services, and personal computing services. Services may also include those that support the unique needs of the organization, such as an online banking service for a financial institution, or a point-of-sale (POS) service for a retail organization. Such SLAs typically include the services provided by the service desk. On the other hand, some organizations have simple SLAs between the service desk and the various departments within the company. These agreements are used primarily to clarify expectations and responsibilities.

ABC SERVICE DESK
SERVICE LEVEL AGREEMENT

This document is an agreement between the ABC service desk and its customers. This service level agreement (SLA) has been designed to promote a common understanding about the services the service desk provides, and customer responsibilities relative to those services. This document also describes how service level performance is measured.

Parties: The *service desk* provides a single point of contact for the ABC IT Department. *Customers* are ABC employees who seek technical support services from the ABC IT Department.

Responsibilities: The service desk provides first level support to customers using the processes and technology implemented by the ABC IT Department. The service desk also facilitates second and third level support by engaging resources as needed to resolve incidents beyond the scope and authority of the service desk. *Customers* obtain service using the processes and technology implemented by the ABC IT Department and described in this document. Specifically, ABC employees must contact the service desk when support services are needed.

Hours of operation: The service desk is available to ABC employees 24 hours a day, 7 days a week.
- During *normal business hours*—Monday through Friday 7 a.m. to 8 p.m.—customers can contact the service desk and speak directly with an analyst.
- *After-hours*—8 p.m. to 7 a.m. weekdays, weekends, and holidays—customers can access the service desk's web site. For priority 1 incidents only, customers can contact the service desk and obtain support from on-call analysts.

Contact methods: Customers can use the following methods to obtain support:
- Telephone—Customers can contact the service desk by calling **(555) 451-4357**. The target response time for calls is thirty (30) seconds. Following a brief introduction, customers may hear a system outage message. This message is broadcast only when a priority 1 incident exists.

- Voice mail—Voice mail is offered to customers who call the service desk during normal business hours after a two (2) minute delay. Customers can use this option in lieu of waiting in the queue. Voice mail messages will be answered within thirty (30) minutes during normal business hours. Customers calling with a priority 1 incident are encouraged to wait in the queue. Voice mail messages left after-hours will be answered the next business day.

- Email—Email messages sent to **servicedesk@example.com** will be answered within one (1) hour during normal business hours. Emails sent after-hours will be answered the next business day.

- Internet—The service desk's web site at **example.com** provides forms that can be used to submit incidents and service requests. Submitted incidents and service requests are automatically logged in the service desk's incident management system and are handled according to their priority. The web site also provides self-services such as FAQs, a solution knowledge base, a password reset utility, and access to remote diagnostic and control utilities.

Incident priorities: Incident *priority* reflects the impact of an incident on the ABC business and when the incident must be solved. Service desk analysts and customers will work together to determine the priority, using the following guidelines:

Priority	Business Impact	Target Resolution Time
1	Service, system, or device down, business halted	2 hours
2	Service, system, or device down or level of service degraded, business impacted	8 hours
3	Not critical, customer can wait without business impact	48 hours

This agreement is effective through December 31st of the current year and will be evaluated and republished yearly or as needed.

Figure 1-7 Sample service desk SLA

Nearly 29 percent of service desks have **Operational Level Agreements (OLAs)** in place, which are agreements between internal support groups. OLAs underpin SLAs by ensuring that all parties involved in meeting SLA targets understand their respective responsibilities. SLAs may also be underpinned by contracts with external suppliers. Figure 1-8 shows the relationship between SLAs, OLAs, and contracts.

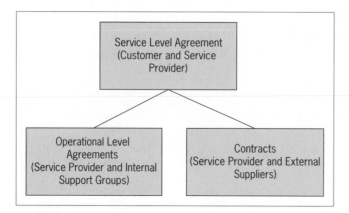

Figure 1-8   The relationship between SLAs, OLAs, and contracts

Understanding Customer Needs and Managing Expectations

Managing expectations in today's rapidly and radically changing business world is indeed a challenge. It is not hard to understand why. Expectations are influenced by many factors and vary from person to person, situation to situation, and even day to day. Although the varying nature of customer expectations may make it seem that satisfying customers is an impossible task, Figure 1-9 lists three things you can be certain customers will want. Each of these characteristics of excellent customer support addresses a particular customer need, and ignoring any one of these characteristics can cause customer dissatisfaction.

- Responsiveness

- A caring attitude

- Skills

Figure 1-9   Customer needs

Responsiveness

Responsiveness refers to the service desk's ability to be available when customers need help and to make it easy for customers to obtain help. Responsiveness involves answering the telephone and chat requests promptly or responding to voice mail and email inquiries within the time frame promised. A company might guarantee that during normal business hours all voice mails will be returned within 30 minutes and all email inquiries will be answered within 1 to 4 hours. Given these options, customers can decide whether to wait to speak on the telephone or chat with an analyst, or send an email for a less immediate response.

Responsiveness also involves anticipating customers' support needs and, when possible and practical, providing self-services through the web. Unfortunately, some service desks do not seem very responsive. They are not available when they say they will be, or their hours of operation do not match the needs of their customers. They provide an email address on their web site, but the email box is frequently full. They implement complex telephone systems that have long menus with numerous confusing options and no easy way to reach a live person, or they offer a telephone number that more often than not connects customers to a voice mailbox where they can leave a message. The message then goes unanswered or, from the customer's perspective, takes a long time to answer.

Optimally, responsive service desks have hours of operation that are comparable to the business hours during which their customers are most likely to need support. They also set up technology in a way that is easy for customers to navigate and that actually adds value to the interaction. For example, some telephone systems capture information about the customer and use that information to transfer the customer to the service desk analyst best suited to handle the customer's incident or service request. Others prompt customers for an account number or product ID and then use that information to greet the customer by name. Some web sites provide customers the ability to automatically check for software updates and download software patches. Simply put, responsiveness refers to the service desk's ability to *be there* for customers.

A Caring Attitude

A caring, positive, and helpful attitude goes a long way toward keeping customers satisfied. A **caring attitude** is a service desk's ability to communicate that it wants to satisfy its customers' needs. One of the biggest reasons that customers choose to stop doing business with a company is that they feel an attitude of indifference. In other words, no one made the customers feel that the company wanted to satisfy their needs. Although the service desk may not always be able to give customers exactly what they want, when they want it, there is always something the service desk *can* do. It can log the customer's incident or service request in its incident management system so the contact is not lost or forgotten. It can take ownership of the customer's incident or service request and ensure it is forwarded to the person or group that can satisfy it. If nothing else, it can let the customer know where to obtain help. Customers occasionally contact the service desk with questions about a product or system that the service desk does not support. What the service desk can do in those situations is give the customer the name and telephone number or web site of the person or group that does support the product. In other words, the service desk must *be willing* to assist customers in any way it can.

Your customers don't care how much you know until they know how much you care.

GERHARD GSCHWANDTNER

Skill

Skill refers to the service desk's ability to quickly and correctly resolve customer incidents and service requests. Given today's complex technology and sophisticated, demanding customers, it is not enough for service desk analysts to be polite, perky, and caring. Service desk analysts must also be efficient and knowledgeable. They must have the ability and authority to solve incidents or know exactly how to get incidents solved. If customers perceive the service desk cannot help, they will simply go around it. They may turn to crowdsourcing or **peer-to-peer support**, a practice in which users bypass the formal support structure and seek assistance from their coworkers or someone in another department.

Peer-to-peer support is effective when a coworker can help a person in the same department understand how to use a product or system for department-specific work. Peer-to-peer support has its drawbacks, however. For example, when a person asks a coworker for help solving a complex incident that neither one has the skill to resolve, they not only waste time trying to solve the incident, but they could also make the incident worse. Or, they may "fix" the incident incorrectly so that it is likely to recur. Also, because incidents solved via peer-to-peer support are typically not logged, the service desk does not know about the incidents and so it cannot assess their impact nor minimize that impact by helping others who experience similar incidents.

When the service desk lacks the required skill, customers may also simply give up and take their business elsewhere. The service desk must convince customers that contacting the service desk is the fastest, cheapest, and best way to obtain a solution. It must *be able* to handle any request that comes its way.

Although these characteristics may seem very nice and "fluffy," they are actually very measurable. Most companies use metrics to evaluate the performance of their service desk in all or some of these areas. Figure 1-10 shows some of the metrics that service desks use to ensure they understand their customers' expectations and are meeting their customers' needs.

Metrics are used to measure the service desk's responsiveness and its ability to demonstrate a caring attitude and skill. Metrics enable each and every member of the service desk team to know how well they are meeting their customers' needs and managing their expectations. In addition, metrics provide service desk analysts the information needed to determine what else they can do to satisfy their customers.

Service desks use data captured by tools and technology to produce these metrics. They also use techniques such as customer satisfaction surveys and monitoring. A **customer satisfaction survey** is a series of questions that ask customers to provide their perception of the support services being offered. **Monitoring** is when a supervisor or team leader observes an analyst's interactions with customers in order to measure the quality of that analyst's

Be There

✓ Answer the telephone within 20 seconds.
✓ Respond to voice mail messages within 30 minutes.
✓ Respond to email messages within 1 hour.
✓ Maintain a monthly average abandon rate of less than 5 percent.

Be Willing

✓ Answer the telephone with a smile on your face.
✓ Gather the facts and approach each incident in a methodical fashion.
✓ Speak clearly and use terms your customer can understand.
✓ Accurately assess the priority of the incidents you must escalate.
✓ Take ownership and track 100 percent of incidents to closure.
✓ Maintain a high customer satisfaction rating.

Be Able

✓ Use all available resources in an effort to resolve incidents and service requests.
✓ Resolve 70 percent of reported incidents and service requests.
✓ Resolve or escalate 100 percent of incidents and service requests within the time required for the stated priority.
✓ Assign 100 percent of escalated incidents and service requests to the correct level two group.

Figure 1-10   Sample service desk customer satisfaction metrics

performance. Monitoring may include a supervisor or team leader listening to a live or recorded call, watching an analyst's data entry and key strokes during an email or chat session, or sitting beside an analyst to measure the quality of the analyst's performance during a customer contact.

Demonstrating a Positive Can Do Attitude

Delivering high-quality customer support is incredibly challenging for a number of reasons. One, customers are people whose feelings and expectations can change from minute to minute. Two, customers today are more sophisticated and demand cheaper, faster, and better service. Three, technology is increasingly complex and changes so rapidly that it can be difficult for service desk analysts to keep up. Although these factors may tempt you to consider the possibility of satisfying customers a hopeless scenario, remember, there is always something you can do.

A **can do attitude** means telling a customer what you *can* do that rather than what you cannot do. A subtle distinction, for sure, but it goes a long way toward satisfying customers. That is, customers *perceive* that they have been helped.

There is little difference in people, but that little difference makes a big difference. The little difference is attitude. The big difference is whether it is positive or negative.

W. CLEMENT STONE

To be successful, service desk analysts must learn to strike all negative phrases from their vocabulary. Rather than telling a customer, "We do not support that product," say "What I can do is give you the web site of the company that supports that product." If you were the customer, wouldn't being pointed in the right direction satisfy you more than simply hearing "We can't help"?

Saying "no" is one of the most difficult things for service desk analysts to do. This is because many of us grew up hearing phrases such as "The customer is king" and "The customer is number 1."

Although the spirit of these phrases lives on, the execution is often much more difficult and costly than companies expect. In today's competitive marketplace, few companies have the resources to give customers everything they want, when they want it. Rather, companies are trying to maximize their resources and provide a high level of service, even if it means limiting the scope of their services. For example, many companies are establishing standards in terms of the products they support, rather than supporting all of the possible products their customers may want to use. In doing so, the service desk can acquire the training, tools, and talent needed to support that limited set of products. If the service desk tried to be all things to all people, its resources would quickly be stretched too thin and its entire level of service would decline.

A common phrase is "The customer is always right." Unfortunately, companies have found that customers are not always right. A customer may install a product that conflicts with the company's product and then ask, "What are you going to do about it?" Or, a customer may download a document from the web that contains a virus and corrupts his or her system. Again, the customer turns to the service desk for support. Should the service desk support customers in these situations? Absolutely. Although the customer may not always be right, he or she is always the customer. Your company's SLAs or policies will spell out what you *can do* in these situations.

When facing these challenging situations, a *can do* attitude will always serve you well. Sometimes it is necessary to say "no" to customers. Sometimes it is impossible to respond as quickly as customers would like when they need help. A *can do* attitude enables you to give customers this information without offending or alienating them. Throughout this book, you will learn how to maintain a *can do* attitude day in and day out, and how that attitude will positively influence not only your interactions with customers, but each and every person with whom you come into contact each day.

Going the Extra Mile

Are satisfied customers loyal? Not necessarily. Satisfying a customer simply means that the company has fulfilled the customer's need. The customer contacted the service desk with an incident and that incident was resolved. If the service desk resolves incidents consistently, will customers contact the service desk when they have a need in the future? Yes. Will they, however, rave about the service they received, thus attracting new customers? Not necessarily.

Feeling an attitude of indifference is one of the most common reasons that customers choose to do business with another company. The scary part is that customers do not always tell *you* how you are doing, but they will tell *others* when they are dissatisfied. A large percentage of unhappy customers never speak up. Many just take away their business. Others describe their dissatisfaction to many other people. When that dissatisfaction is communicated via the Internet, a company's reputation and profits can be severely impacted. Although it is sometimes hard to listen to complaints day in and day out, it is important to thank customers who provide feedback because it enables your organization to improve.

How, then, do companies generate customer loyalty? How do companies go beyond customer satisfaction to customer delight? Companies must go the extra mile—and give a little something extra. Most service desks define boundaries of what analysts can do to delight their customers. Some service desks authorize analysts to make exceptions to company policies in certain situations. Other service desks authorize analysts to waive product shipping charges or offer a free product upgrade in certain situations. Those situations are typically clearly spelled out. These boundaries are important. Without boundaries, the cost of going the extra mile might quickly deplete the company's profits.

Most customers understand that products can fail and human beings can make mistakes. How a company handles those situations ultimately determines whether customers remain loyal or take their business elsewhere. Companies that train employees to quickly take responsibility, empathize with what the customer is experiencing, and offer a viable solution can retain even the most dissatisfied customer.

In technical support, just as in customer service, it is often the little things that delight customers—the unexpected. Two key ways to delight customers are to: (1) save them time, and (2) enhance their self-sufficiency. You can save customers time by teaching them a faster or easier way to use their computer, such as clicking the right mouse button or setting up shortcuts on their desktop. You can enhance customer self-sufficiency by teaching them how to maintain their system and prevent problems by performing maintenance tasks, such as backing up their data and using system tools such as tools designed to clean out temporary Internet files, cookies, and other unused or unwanted files that affect performance. Taking a few minutes to teach customers a simple trick or a way that they can diagnose and perhaps fix incidents on their own comes back to you tenfold in customer good will.

Good will is the one and only asset the competition cannot undersell or destroy.

MARSHALL FIELD

Developing the Right Mix of Skills

The support industry is evolving, and companies are continuously changing the ways they do business in an effort to gain customer loyalty. This dynamic business climate represents a tremendous opportunity for people who possess the mix of skills needed to meet the service desk's expanding responsibilities. Figure 1-11 shows the principal skills needed to work successfully at a service desk.

- Business skills
- Technical skills
- Soft skills
- Self-management skills

Figure 1-11　Principal service desk skills

Each service desk role—dispatcher, level one analyst, level one specialist, and service desk manager—requires a specific set of skills. The level of skill and experience required will vary from company to company, but most companies will explore a job candidate's qualifications in each of the following categories:

- **Business skills**—The skills people need to work successfully in the business world. In a service desk setting, business skills include the ability to understand and speak the language of business; the skills that are unique to the industry or profession the service desk supports, such as accounting skills or banking skills (industry knowledge); and the skills that are specific to the customer service and support industry, such as understanding the importance of meeting customers' needs and knowing how to manage their expectations (service industry knowledge).

- **Technical skills**—The skills people need to use and support the specific products and technologies the service desk supports. Technical skills also include basic computer and software literacy.

- **Soft skills**—The qualities that people need to deliver great service, such as active listening skills, verbal communication skills, customer service skills, problem-solving skills, temperament, teamwork skills, and writing skills.

- **Self-management skills**—The skills, such as stress and time management, that people need to complete their work effectively, feel job satisfaction, and avoid frustration or burnout. Self-management skills also include the ability to get and stay organized and to continuously and quickly learn new skills.

Filling front-line positions with people who have the right mix of skills is one of the most difficult challenges facing service desk managers today. People who have very strong interpersonal skills—that is, soft skills—may lack the technical skills required to support today's increasingly complex technology, or the self-management skills needed to thrive in a highly active and dynamic service desk setting. People with strong technical skills may lack the skills such as patience and empathy that are needed to support customers with varying skill levels. Some people prefer a more hands-on approach to technical support and may be more comfortable working in a field service role away from the front line. The employee and the company benefit when those with the right skills are matched with the right position.

When hiring people for front-line positions, companies look for people with positive, *can do* attitudes who genuinely enjoy helping other people and enjoy solving problems. Companies also look for individuals who are team oriented and enjoy working with other people. This is because technical skills are generally considered to be more easily developed than interpersonal skills. Companies are willing to provide technical training to individuals with good interpersonal skills and a customer service orientation. Also, technology is constantly changing, and technical skills must be continuously updated.

This does not mean that technical skills are unimportant. At times, companies may hire people with very strong technical skills and then provide extensive customer service training. Or, companies may need people who have a very specific business skill or technical skill that would take an extensive amount of training to develop, so they hire people who already possess that skill. Smart companies let their customers' needs and expectations drive their hiring decisions. For this reason, people who understand that all these skill sets—business, technical, soft, and self-management—are important create the greatest opportunity for themselves.

Companies worldwide know they must deliver high-quality customer service and support or lose business to their competition. These companies are seeking people who have the mix of skills and the desire needed to satisfy as well as delight customers day in and day out. The rapidly growing support industry represents a tremendous opportunity for people who want to use all of their skills—business, technical, soft, and self-management. To seize this opportunity, you must understand the characteristics of excellent technical customer support and remember at all times that you are supporting people using technology and not just technology. Those people will have needs and expectations that will take all of your skills to meet and exceed.

This book focuses on the soft skills and self-management skills, and touches briefly on the business skills needed to pursue a successful career in technical customer support. Although the business skills and the technical skills you may choose to develop are wide ranging and diverse, soft skills and self-management skills are somewhat universal. It is possible to build a solid foundation of these latter skills from which you will always be able to draw.

Chapter Summary

- The pervasive nature of increasingly complex computing technology has created a tremendous demand for technical support. The service desk is the first point of contact for this support. How people are treated by the service desk influences their level of satisfaction and how they perceive the entire company and its products. To be successful, a service desk must effectively use all of its assets: people, processes, technology, and information. People are by far the most important component because customers are people who have needs and expectations that only other people can understand.

- An irreversible dependence on technology has prompted customers to demand ever-cheaper, better, and faster support services. This huge demand for support, coupled with a shortage of information technology (IT) professionals, has created a tremendous career opportunity in the field of customer service and technical support. Trends such as multigenerational support, multichannel support, anytime, anywhere, any device support, collapsing support levels, 24/7 support, fee-based support, global support, use of best practice frameworks and standards, outsourcing, and the elevation of the service desk to a profession are influencing the direction in which the service desk industry is heading. Each of these trends affects how service desks are run and the opportunities they present to service desk analysts.

- Managing customer expectations is a challenge, but you can be certain that customers want the service desk to be there, be willing, and be able. Even when it seems that customer expectations cannot be met, you can avoid offending or alienating customers by demonstrating a *can do* attitude and by going the extra mile. A *can do* attitude means that rather than telling customers what you cannot do, you tell them what you *can* do.

- The support industry is evolving, and the dynamic nature of this industry represents a tremendous opportunity for people who possess the right mix of skills. Skills needed include business, technical, soft, and self-management. This book focuses on the soft and self-management skills, and touches briefly on the business skills needed to pursue a successful career in technical customer support. These skills are somewhat universal and will serve you well throughout your life and career.

Key Terms

24/7 support—Service desk services that are provided 24 hours a day, 7 days a week.

automatic call distributor (ACD)—A telephone technology that answers a call and routes, or distributes, it to the next available analyst. If all analysts are busy, the ACD places the call in a queue and plays a recorded message.

avatar—A computer user's representation of himself or herself.

best practice—A proven way of completing a task to produce a near optimum result.

bring your own device (BYOD)—The practice of using personally owned mobile devices to access business applications.

business skills—The skills people need to work successfully in the business world.

call center—A place where telephone calls are made or received in high volume.

can do attitude—Telling a customer what you *can do* rather than what you cannot do.

caring attitude—A service desk's ability to communicate that it wants to satisfy its customers' needs.

channel—A route of communication to and from the service desk, such as the telephone, voice mail, email, and the web.

cloud computing—Delivering hosted services over the Internet.

configuration management system (CMS)—A set of tools and databases for managing IT asset information and linking that information to related incidents, problems, known errors, changes, and releases.

contact—A generic term used to describe different types of customer transactions such as questions, incidents, and service request.

contact center—A call center that uses technologies such as email and the web in addition to the telephone.

cookie—A very small text file created by a web server that is stored on a user's computer either temporarily for that session only or permanently on the hard disk.

crowdsourcing—Outsourcing a task traditionally performed by a single individual to a large group of people or community (in other words, a crowd).

customer—A person who buys products or services.

customer satisfaction—The difference between how a customer expects to be treated and how the customer perceives he or she was treated.

customer satisfaction survey—A series of questions that ask customers to provide their perception of the support services being offered.

customer service value chain—A linked set of activities during which value is added when serving customers.

customer support—Services that help a customer understand and benefit from a product's capabilities by answering questions, solving problems, and providing training.

desktop virtualization—The separation of a PC desktop environment from a physical machine using the client/server model of computing.

dispatch—To send.

email response management system—A system that enables service desks to manage high-volume chat, email, and web form messages.

expectation—A result that a customer considers reasonable or due to them.

external customer—A person or company that buys another company's products or services.

external service desk—A service desk that supports customers who buy its company's products or services.

fee-based support—Support services that customers pay for on a per-use basis.

front-line service provider—A service desk staff member who interacts directly with customers.

global support—Support for customers anywhere in the world.

help desk—A single point of contact within a company for technology-related questions and incidents.

incident—An unplanned interruption to an IT service or a reduction in the quality of an IT service (ITIL definition).

incident management system—Technology that offers enhanced trouble ticketing and management reporting capability.

information—Data that is organized in a meaningful way.

Information Technology Infrastructure Library (ITIL)—A set of best practices for IT service management.

internal customer—A person who works at a company and at times relies on other employees at that company to perform his or her job.

internal service desk—A service desk that responds to questions, distributes information, and handles incidents and service requests for its company's employees.

ISO/IEC 20000—An international standard for IT service management.

IT service—A service that is based on the use of information technology and supports business processes.

IT service management (ITSM)—A discipline for managing IT services that focuses on the quality of those services and the relationship that the IT organization has with its customers.

knowledge base—A logical database that contains data used by a knowledge management system.

knowledge base administrator (KBA)—Another name for a *knowledge engineer*.

Knowledge-Centered Support (KCS)—A knowledge management strategy for service and support organizations developed by the Consortium for Service Innovation (*www. serviceinnovation.org*).

knowledge engineer—A person who develops and oversees the knowledge management process and ensures that the information contained in the service desk's knowledge management system is accurate, complete, and current; also called a *knowledge base administrator (KBA)*.

knowledge management system (KMS)—A set of tools and databases that are used to store, manage, and present information sources such as customer information, documents, policies and procedures, incident resolutions, and known errors.

known error—A problem that has a documented root cause and a work-around.

known error database (KEDB)—A database that contains known error records.

level zero—Customers resolving incidents on their own; also referred to as *tier zero* or *self-help*.

major incident—An incident that is causing significant business impact.

metrics—Performance measures.

monitoring—When a supervisor or team leader observes an analyst's interactions with customers in order to measure the quality of that analyst's performance.

multi-level support model—A common structure of service desks, where the service desk refers incidents it cannot resolve to the appropriate internal group, external vendor, or subject matter expert.

network and system administration—Activities that include day-to-day tasks such as setting up and maintaining user accounts, ensuring the data that the company collects is secure, and performing email and database management.

network monitoring—Activities that use tools to observe network performance in an effort to minimize the impact of incidents.

network monitoring system—A tool used to observe network performance.

Operational Level Agreement (OLA)—An agreement between internal support groups that underpins a Service Level Agreement by ensuring that all parties involved in meeting SLA targets understand their respective responsibilities.

outsource—To provide services through an outside supplier instead of providing them in-house.

ownership—The tracking of an incident to ensure that the customer is kept informed about the status of the incident, that the incident is resolved within the expected time frame, and that the customer is satisfied with the final resolution.

peer-to-peer support—A practice in which users bypass the formal support structure and seek assistance from coworkers or someone in another department.

people—The service desk component that consists of the staff and structure put in place within a company or department to support its customers by performing processes.

problem—The cause of one or more incidents (ITIL definition).

process—A collection of interrelated work activities that take a set of specific inputs and produce a set of specific outputs that are of value to a customer.

profile—A collection of personal data associated with a specific user; also called a *user profile*.

remote control and diagnostic systems—Systems that allow the service desk to take remote control of the keyboard, screen, or mouse of connected devices and then troubleshoot problems, transfer files, and even provide informal training by viewing or operating the customer's screen.

responsiveness—The service desk's ability to be available when customers need help and to make it easy for customers to obtain help.

self-help—Customers resolving incidents on their own; also referred to as *level zero* or *tier zero*.

self-management skills—The skills, such as stress and time management, that people need to complete their work effectively, feel job satisfaction, and avoid frustration or burnout; also includes the ability to get and stay organized and to continuously and quickly learn new skills.

service desk—A single point of contact within a company for managing customer incidents and service requests.

Service Level Agreement (SLA)—A written document that spells out the services the service desk will provide the customer, the customer's responsibilities, and how service performance is measured.

service request—A formal request from a user for something to be provided (ITIL definition).

skill—The service desk's ability to quickly and correctly resolve customer incidents and service requests.

soft skills—The qualities that people need to deliver great service, such as active listening skills, verbal communication skills, customer service skills, problem-solving skills, temperament, teamwork skills, and writing skills.

subject matter expert (SME)—A person who has a high level of experience or knowledge about a particular subject.

swarming—A work style characterized by a flurry of collective activity by anyone and everyone conceivably available and able to add value (Gartner, Inc. definition).

technical skills—The skills people need to use and support the specific products and technologies the service desk supports; also includes basic computer and software literacy.

technical support—A wide range of services that enable people and companies to effectively use the information technology they acquired or developed.

technology—An invention, process, or method that enables the creation and enhancement of tools.

tool—A product or device that automates or facilitates a person's work.

user—A person who consumes products or services.

value—The perceived worth, usefulness, or importance of a product or service to a customer.

pg 6 **Web 2.0**—A concept that emphasizes enabling web users to interact, collaborate, and generate content via, for example, blogs, wikis, and social networking sites, rather than passively view content created by others.

pg 11 **world class**—Refers to a company that has achieved and sustains high levels of customer satisfaction.

Review Questions

1. Why is there a tremendous need for technical support?

2. What is a service desk?

3. What influences customers' level of satisfaction and how they perceive a company and its products?

4. Technical support services are the same as customer support services. True or False? Explain your answer.

5. How are service desks and help desks the same? How are they different?

6. What is the relationship between ITIL and IT service management?

7. What is an incident?

8. Provide examples of an incident, a problem, and a service request.

9. What are the goals of a multi-level support model?

10. List and describe the components of a successful service desk.

11. What are customer expectations?

12. Why do companies have a hard time meeting and exceeding customer expectations?

13. List three benefits that companies derive when they deliver excellent customer support.

14. List two reasons that customer support is projected to increase as an occupation through the year 2020.

15. How are technically savvy customers changing the way that service desks interact with customers?

16. What are three skills service desk analysts must have when delivering multichannel support?

17. What are three ways that service desks can ensure that mobile devices and applications meet the needs of users and ensure the security of corporate data assets?

18. Describe three ways that the need to deliver 24/7 support creates opportunities.

19. What are three ways that companies provide global support?

20. How do frameworks and standards benefit the service desk?

21. In light of the outsourcing trend, list four ways professionals can reduce the risk of losing their jobs and create opportunities for themselves.

22. Certifications are what is most valued in today's competitive job market. True or False? Explain your answer.

23. What are the two principal types of service desks?

24. What is a customer service value chain?

25. What is customer satisfaction?

26. What is a Service Level Agreement?

27. What three characteristics of excellent customer support can the service desk count on customers wanting?

28. Name three ways that companies produce the metrics needed to measure their performance.

29. What should you do rather than telling a customer what you cannot do?

30. Is a customer always right? Explain your answer.

31. What turns a satisfied customer into a loyal customer?

32. What are two things that service desk analysts can do to delight customers?

33. What are the four principal skills needed to work successfully at a service desk?

34. Which of the four principal skills are universal or life skills?

Discussion Questions

1. Some would say that highly personalized service, such as interacting live with an analyst via the telephone or chat, is better than self-service. Do you agree or disagree? Explain why.

2. What impact do you think Web 2.0 will have on the support industry?

3. A common perception is that soft and self-management skills, such as listening, communication, and stress management, are innate. In other words, you are either born with them or you are not. Do you agree or disagree? Explain why.

Hands-On Projects

1. **Evaluate technical support needs.** The average person may contact any number of service desks for support. Talk to at least three friends or classmates who use computers or mobile devices about their experiences with technical support. Ask each person the following questions, and then write a one-page report that summarizes each experience and presents your conclusions:

   a. Have you ever contacted a service desk for support?

   b. How did you contact the service desk?

c. Did you interact live with an analyst via the telephone or chat?

d. Did you use any self-services?

e. What were your expectations when you contacted the service desk?

f. Did the service desk set your expectations or were you left to set them on your own (for example, did the service desk indicate how quickly calls, chats, emails, and so forth would be answered)?

g. Were your expectations met?

2. **Analyze the pros and cons of walk-in support.** Assemble a team of at least three classmates or use your school's online message or discussion board. Search the web as needed to learn about the genius bar concept. Discuss the genius bar concept in the context of a corporate or university service desk. Consider both customers' expectations relative to walk-in support and the capabilities the service desk must have to deliver such support successfully. Write a brief summary of your findings, and discuss them with the class.

3. **Learn about service desk certification.** Search the web to locate an organization that certifies service desk professionals or select one of the organizations discussed in this chapter. Visit the organization's web site and then determine the following:

a. What levels of certification are available?

b. What skills are certified?

c. What must you do to get certified?

d. What are the benefits of being certified?

Write a report that summarizes what you have learned about certification from visiting this web site.

4. **Learn about service desk outsourcing.** Search the web to locate three organizations that provide service desk outsourcing services. For each company, visit its web site, and then write a paragraph that answers the following questions:

a. What services do they deliver?

b. What do they consider standard services, and what do they offer as optional services?

c. How do they distinguish themselves from their competition?

d. What do they say about their staff?

e. What do they say about their hiring practices?

f. What do they say about satisfying their customers?

5. **Understand the customer service value chain.** Day in and day out we are all at times a customer and other times a service provider. Think about your experiences as a customer and as a service provider during the past week or so.

Write a paragraph describing your experiences as a customer (for example, contacting a company for technical support or going to a store to purchase needed equipment or to obtain support) that addresses the following questions:

a. Were your expectations for service and support met?

b. What did the service provider do well?

c. How could the service provider have done better?

Write a second paragraph describing your experiences as a service provider (for example, assisting customers at the company where you work or helping a friend or family member with a project) that addresses the following questions:

a. Do you feel you met your customer's expectations?

b. What did you do well?

c. How could you have provided better service?

6. **Compare perceptions and expectations.** Describe in a paragraph or two a situation where your perception of an event was different than what you expected. Include, if possible, a description of how a person who experienced the event with you had a different perception and different expectations. For example, you go to Mardi Gras in New Orleans expecting it to be fun and exciting, but find that you are actually overwhelmed by what you perceive is the unruly nature of the crowd. On the other hand, your friend has a great time and cannot wait to go back next year.

7. **Discuss customer needs and expectations.** Assemble a team of at least three classmates or use your school's online message or discussion board. Assume the perspective of an office-based worker, and discuss each of the three things you can count on customers wanting: responsiveness, a caring attitude, and skill. Discuss the ramifications if any one of these customer needs is not consistently met. Assume the perspective of a mobile worker, and repeat the discussion. Are the ramifications different if any one of these customer needs is not consistently met? Write a brief summary of your findings, and discuss them with the class.

8. **Demonstrate a can do attitude.** Sometimes we forget that there is always something you can do. For the next 24 hours, write down any negative phrases you catch yourself using, such as "I can't," "It's not my job," and "There's nothing I can do." For each situation, restate the negative phrase in a positive way. Place your list of negative and restated phrases somewhere easy to locate. You'll revisit these phrases in Chapter 9.

9. **Assess your interpersonal skills.** When hiring people for front-line positions, companies look for people with good interpersonal skills and a customer service

orientation. Write down your answers to the following questions. You will consider your answers in Chapter 9.

a. Do I have a positive attitude?

b. Do I enjoy helping other people?

c. Do I enjoy solving problems?

d. Do I consider myself a team oriented person?

e. Do I enjoy working with other people?

Case Projects

1. **Way Cool, Inc.** Way Cool, Inc. has hired you to determine how it can minimize costs in terms of customer service and support. Its focus is on its product, a state-of-the-art virtual reality game that is extremely popular and attracting new users each day. The company wants to invest as much as possible in developing its game and as little as possible in terms of providing support. In fact, the company believes the game is so easy to use that support is unneeded and is thinking of eliminating customer support services all together. Prepare a brief report that outlines the pros and cons of minimizing the company's investment in support. Suggest ways the company can minimize its costs without eliminating support services altogether. Also suggest ways the company can ensure its minimized services are meeting customers' needs.

2. **Bill's Cyber Cycle Shop.** Bill, the owner of Bill's Cyber Cycle Shop, has hired you to help survey his customers and determine whether his business is meeting its customers' needs. Bill wants his customers to perceive that his staff is there, willing, and able to support customers when they need help ordering bicycles and associated accessories from his web site. Draft a customer satisfaction survey that Bill can use to measure his customers' satisfaction. Remember, Bill wants to know if customers perceive his staff members as responsive, if staff members demonstrate a caring attitude, and if staff members have the skill needed to answer customer inquiries.

3. **Bayside Unlimited.** You work for a service desk that supports the internal employees of Bayside Unlimited. Due to budget constraints and the need to maximize resources, the service desk is reducing the number of products it supports. Historically, the service desk supported any laptop, telephone, or mobile device employees used. Going forward, a list of standard products and services will be published, and the service desk will support only those products and services. Your boss has asked you to identify ways that you can manage customer expectations and increase customer satisfaction, despite the decrease in services. Search the web for articles about topics such as "managing customer expectations" and "managing user expectations." Prepare a report of your findings, and include why it is important to manage customer expectations, along with specific techniques.

CHAPTER 2

Developing Strong Listening and Communication Skills

In this chapter you will learn:

- ◎ The characteristics and benefits of active listening
- ◎ How to avoid the distractions that prevent good listening
- ◎ What to listen for
- ◎ How to build rapport and trust with customers
- ◎ How to identify and understand customer communication styles

Listening and communication skills are two of the most basic and important skills that service desk analysts must possess. Analysts take in information by listening. They use both verbal and nonverbal skills to communicate. These skills are important because analysts must communicate and listen actively when customers provide information about their incidents or service requests. In return, analysts must respond in ways that give customers a sense of confidence they are being heard and understood. Analysts must also deliver information in a way that is meaningful to their customers. Good listening and communication skills benefit both of the parties involved in a conversation and can be improved through practice.

Learning to communicate with customers around the world is particularly important to the growing number of service desks that provide global support. Communicating with people of different cultures can be challenging. Languages and rules about proper behavior when communicating may vary from one country to the next. A willingness to learn about cultural differences and make a conscious effort to overcome those differences is key to communicating with international customers.

When working as a service desk analyst, you must develop strong listening and communication skills so you can communicate effectively with customers, coworkers, managers, and other service providers such as internal support groups and vendors. This chapter focuses on how to be an active listener and avoid the distractions that prevent good listening. You will also learn how to be an effective communicator and how to identify and respond to the varying communication styles you may encounter.

The Power of Active Listening

Listening means making an effort to hear something—paying attention. Listening is a skill that is important to many professions. Skilled negotiators listen carefully and understand the other party's needs before they make a compromising offer. Top salespeople concentrate on listening to avoid talking customers out of a sale. Effective leaders and managers must be able to listen to people at all levels of the organization and to speak directly with employees in an authentic way.

 Great leaders are great listeners!

If your actions inspire others to dream more, learn more, do more and become more, you are a leader.

JOHN QUINCY ADAMS

What does this have to do with customer support? Well, at times in customer support, analysts must be skilled negotiators—remember that *can do* attitude. At times, analysts must be salespeople. You cannot always give customers what they want, but if you listen actively you can at least acknowledge and try to address what customers need. At times, analysts must also be leaders who take ownership of incidents and service requests and who serve as a customer advocate.

Listening is consistently cited as the most important skill for a support person. Why? Because customers are living, breathing human beings, and a basic human need is to be heard and understood.

You can convey no greater honor than actually hearing what someone has to say.

PHILIP CROSBY

The Importance of Listening

Listening, like speaking and writing, is hard work. It requires thought and can be improved through practice. You have to *want* to listen. Listening is even more challenging when you are facing a difficult situation such as an upset or angry customer. In difficult situations, you need to stay calm and focused and avoid becoming defensive or offensive.

Chapter 5 explores techniques for handling difficult customer situations.

Self-listening is an important form of listening, particularly in difficult situations. If you could hear what you say and how you say it from other people's perspectives, you might, at times, be appalled. You need to listen to yourself to ensure you are presenting yourself in a positive manner. When others do not respond in the way you expect, you need to honestly assess your words and tone of voice in an effort to become a better communicator.

Whether you are interacting with customers, coworkers, friends, or family members, listening enables you to understand the other person's needs. Only then can you concentrate on fulfilling those needs. Furthermore, it is not enough to just listen; you must listen *actively* so the other person knows that you are listening.

Being an Active Listener

Analysts with good listening skills can focus on what the speaker is saying to obtain the information needed to handle incidents and service requests quickly and correctly. They can convey a caring attitude and build rapport with the speaker by using active listening. **Active listening** involves participating in a conversation and giving the speaker a sense of confidence that he or she is being heard. **Passive listening** involves simply taking in information and shows little regard for the speaker. Table 2-1 compares the characteristics of active and passive listening. The following sections explore each active listening characteristic and discuss ways you can demonstrate that you are actively listening.

Active Listeners	Passive Listeners
Ask questions and respond to the speaker	Take in information without questions
Verify understanding	Accept information at face value
Pay attention to *what* is being said and *how* it is being said	Show little regard for the feeling with which the information is being communicated

Table 2-1 Active listening versus passive listening

Ask Questions and Respond to the Speaker

Customers do not typically contact the service desk because everything is going well. They are calling to report an incident or to request service. Sometimes customers articulate their needs succinctly. Other times customers are not exactly sure why they are experiencing an incident or what they need. They just know they cannot get their job done. By asking appropriate and relevant questions and by assimilating and acknowledging the information the customer is providing, you can resolve the incident or at least determine the next steps to take.

Successful analysts often develop checklists they can use to diagnose incidents and methodically identify solutions. In some companies, level two service providers also develop checklists in an effort to enhance the abilities of level one analysts. These checklists help to ensure that analysts have correctly identified the failing hardware, software, network, or application component. A methodical approach also enables analysts to avoid making assumptions when diagnosing incidents. Remember, just because a customer was using Microsoft Word when an incident occurred does not mean that the software package is the failing component. By asking questions and validating the facts given, you can better ensure that you fully understand what the customer needs.

 Chapter 6 discusses how to develop problem-solving checklists.

Knowing what questions to ask is an important skill for analysts. It is also important to know when to question the answers received. This is because customers occasionally provide information that can be misleading. Customers do not intentionally provide misleading information. They may simply lack the skills to provide an accurate diagnosis. Good listening and tactful questions help you assess your customers' skill level, which in turn helps you determine how to respond or proceed. Tactful questions obtain information without offending customers. Asking a customer "Can you describe the steps you took before this incident occurred?" is much better than asking "What did you do?" The latter question has a condemning tone and most likely will make the customer defensive.

Keep in mind, too, that not all customers feel comfortable using technology. Some customers may be just getting started and have not yet mastered the basics. Asking a customer questions such as "Do you have Internet access?" or "Do you know how to clear your cache?" is much better than assuming that the customer has Internet access or simply stating that the customer should clear his or her browser's cache and cookies. On the other hand, some customers may be quite sophisticated and, in fact, may have a better understanding of a product or system than some analysts do. Active listening enables you to avoid asking questions that are unnecessary or too simple. If a customer says, "I looked on your web site and could not find any information about this incident," you know that the customer has Internet access and do not need to ask. Asking questions that are too simple will offend a sophisticated customer just as quickly as asking questions that are too complicated will alienate a customer who is just getting started. Asking overly simple questions may also undermine the analyst's authority and effectiveness in the customer's mind. In other words, the customer may perceive that the analyst is new to the job or unskilled.

You can get a good idea of customers' skill levels by listening to how they use jargon to describe an incident or service request. **Jargon** is the specialized or technical language used by a trade or profession, in this case, the computer industry. A customer who reports in a panicked voice that he has "lost" the report for his boss that he worked on all afternoon will need to hear some assurance that you can help before you begin asking questions in a nontechnical manner. On the other hand, a customer who reports that she is having a chronic, repeatable incident when running a spreadsheet macro, but only in a certain spreadsheet, will need you to acknowledge the detailed information she has given and then proceed accordingly.

How or if a customer uses acronyms can be another indicator of skill. An **acronym** is an abbreviation formed from the first letters of a series of words, such as *TSC* for *Technology Support Center*. For example, a customer who reports that he is new in the Accounting department and is having trouble logging on to the system will need tactful probing in an effort to determine what system he is trying to use. On the other hand, a customer who calls and indicates that she got a "Cannot Open" message when trying to access a file in the AAS (Advanced Accounting System) is demonstrating a higher level of skill.

However, resist the temptation to make assumptions about customers' skill levels based on their use of jargon, acronyms, and terminology. Customers may be very familiar with the technologies they use on a daily basis, but may be unfamiliar with others. Conversely, many long-term users have a fairly broad base of technical knowledge, but may not have any experience at all with specific systems. It is also important to remember that customers may know and use jargon, acronyms, and terminology that are unfamiliar to analysts. For this reason, it is best to avoid or explain language that may be confusing or uncommon to customers.

Good listening also enables you to learn the business language that customers are using to describe their work. When you understand how customers are using the technology you support to do their work, you can better comprehend the business impact or potential business impact when that technology is failing. Conversely, awareness of how customers are using technology makes it possible for you to provide useful tips that will help them. You may also identify ways your company's product can be enhanced to better fit your customers' business needs. If nothing else, you can help bridge the gap that can exist between the business needs of your company and the technology used to fill those needs. Remember that many customers simply want to use technology to do their work. When they have an incident using technology or want to use the technology more efficiently or effectively, they turn to the service desk for support. Good listening enables you to understand and adjust to your customers' needs—no matter what their skill level.

Knowing when *not* to ask questions while still being responsive to customers is one of the nuances of customer service. Sometimes asking additional questions is not going to help and may, in fact, cause frustration or dissatisfaction. Such cases include when an analyst lacks the ability or authority to handle an incident or service request, when a customer lacks the level of skill or information needed to adequately handle the contact, when time is of the essence because the impact is high, or when the product in question is not supported by the service desk. Many service desks have policies and procedures that help determine when it is time to stop asking questions and take an action such as escalating the incident to the next line of support or directing the customer to another organization for support.

Another situation where asking questions may not be appropriate is when the customer is angry or in a highly agitated state. In these instances, it is best to let the customer vent before asking questions. Customers who are upset have a story to tell. If you interrupt their story with questions, they may become more upset.

In most cases, it is best to curb any tendency you may have to interrupt a speaker. Interrupting is generally considered rude and sends a signal to the speaker that you are unwilling to listen. If you catch yourself interrupting, quickly halt your interruption and say, "Excuse me. Please continue."

One situation where it may be appropriate to interrupt a customer is if the customer is being abusive, such as if the customer is criticizing you personally or using particularly foul language. Your company's policies will typically provide guidance for how to handle such situations.

Generally speaking, however, when customers are angry or upset, it is best to simply listen and, in the least intrusive way possible, respond to what the customer is saying. When interacting with a customer face to face, you can maintain eye contact and nod your head to let the customer know you are listening. When interacting with an upset or angry customer over the telephone, let the customer know you are listening by using acknowledging and encouraging phrases such as "Uh-huh," "I see," "Go on," and "I understand" at appropriate points in the conversation. The phrases "Uh-huh" and "Go on" encourage the customer to continue. Phrases such as "I see" and "I understand" let the customer know you can appreciate his or her point of view or that you comprehend what the customer is telling you. Although you may be tempted to just be quiet and listen, that may cause the customer to become more upset. If a customer asks, "Are you listening?" you are not being responsive enough.

Verify Understanding

One of the most important aspects of active listening is to verify understanding. As a service desk analyst, this means verifying that you understand what a customer said and verifying that the customer understands your reply. If you are unsure of the customer's meaning or think he or she may be unsure of yours, you can ask a follow-up or clarifying question. For example, when interacting with a customer face to face, the customer may furrow his brow or stare vacantly at you, his computer, or something on his desk. In other words, he may *look* confused. When interacting with a customer over the telephone, you may hear silence on the other end of the line. In either situation, the customer may question the course of action you are suggesting by inquiring, "Are you sure?" The following questions enable you to determine the customer's level of understanding in any of these situations and confirm that the customer understands the course of action that you are proposing:

- Would you like me to repeat that?
- Would you like to go through that again?
- How does that sound?

 When in doubt, keep asking questions until you feel comfortable that you have the information you need to resolve the incident or escalate it to the next line of support.

Another good technique for verifying that you understand what a customer is telling you is to **paraphrase**, or restate the information given by the customer using slightly different words. Paraphrasing repeats something using new words and enables you to verify the meaning of, or clear away any confusion about, the information you have received, as shown in the following example.

Customer: I printed the page and the words were okay, but the clip art and boxes didn't print right.

Analyst (paraphrasing): Let me make sure I understand. You printed a document and the text printed correctly, but the pictures and graphics did not?

When you verify understanding, you not only satisfy the customer by ensuring the customer's needs are being met, but you also promote a good working relationship with other service providers. Level two service providers commonly complain that they receive incidents from the service desk that they perceive the service desk should have been able to resolve or that should have been assigned to a different level two group. Very often this occurs because service desk analysts failed to ask a sufficient number of questions or assumed they knew the answer to an unasked question. If a customer reports that her printer is not working, you may be tempted to send a field engineer to her office to investigate. However, that customer may have trouble printing for a number of reasons, many of which can be diagnosed over the telephone. Asking questions is the only way to determine the actual source of the incident. Again, it never hurts to ask additional questions in an effort to make sure you fully understand your customer's needs. Be sensitive, though, and be aware that customers can become impatient or frustrated if you ask too many questions or if you ask the same question over and over. Choose your questions carefully, and actively listen to the responses so you can quickly determine what your customers need.

Pay Attention to What *Is Being Said* and How *It Is Being Said*

Ultimately, your goal as an analyst is to resolve an incident a customer is experiencing or to provide the customer with needed information or instructions. This is the *what* component of a conversation for which you need to listen. How the customer is delivering that information is also important. Customers are often experiencing emotion as a result of having an incident or not having what they need to use the products or services you support. They may be confused by the instructions for configuring a software package or application. Or, they may be frustrated that the device they purchased is not functioning properly and they have just spent a considerable amount of time trying to determine why. Or, they may be angry because they have experienced this same incident before and they perceive that a solution offered by another member of the service desk did not work. By listening actively, you hear both the incident and the emotion, and acknowledge both. You hear *what* is being said and *how* it is being said.

As mentioned previously, a basic human need is to be heard and understood. When you acknowledge customers' emotions, you address those needs. Often, what customers want most is for analysts to say that they understand. When you acknowledge customers' emotions in a sincere way, customers perceive that you care about their well-being and are more willing to work with you to resolve the incident. When you do not acknowledge customers' emotions, or when you are insincere, customers may become more upset or angry. Have you ever contacted a company and expressed dissatisfaction with a product or service only to hear, "There's nothing we can do." Or, have you ever had an analyst reply in a way that was clearly scripted and insincere? Such a response probably made you feel more frustrated or angry than you were to begin with. A much better response would be, "I'm sorry you're frustrated," or "Those instructions can be confusing. Let's walk through them together."

Some service desk analysts have a hard time dealing with emotions, and they lack the people skills needed to interact effectively with customers. They are very logical thinkers and just want to resolve the incident. Most customers, however, are unable to actively participate in problem solving until the analyst acknowledges their emotions.

Being a good listener requires concentration. Communicating the fact that you are listening requires thought and caring. If a customer does not *perceive* that you are listening, you must take responsibility and determine why that is. Are you ignoring what the customer is saying? Are you failing to acknowledge how he or she feels? Determining how you can be more responsive requires that you listen to what the customer is saying. When a customer says, "That doesn't answer my question" or "Let me say this again," you are being given strong cues that the customer *perceives* you are not listening. Good listeners acknowledge what the customer has said when responding and they respond to both *what* is being said and *how* it is being said.

It is important to control your own emotions when interacting with customers. In other words, it is important to pay attention to what you say as well as how you say it. When a customer is angry or upset, it is neither helpful nor appropriate for you to become angry or upset as well.

Chapter 5 provides specific techniques you can use when facing difficult customer situations, such as calming an irate or extremely demanding customer or saying "no" to customers while maintaining their goodwill.

It is also important to pay attention, or "listen," when communicating with customers through channels such as email, chat, and social media. Customers may ask multiple questions in a single email or chat message and will quickly become frustrated if each question is not answered—particularly if they have had to wait for a response. Customers may use a social media technology such as a forum, wiki, or social network to pose their questions or voice their frustrations. **Social listening**, also known as social media listening, is the process of identifying and evaluating what is being said about a company, individual, product, or brand on the Internet. Service desks must actively listen to what their customers are saying via social media, even if they do not currently offer a social media channel for contacts.

Regardless of the channel being used to communicate, customers may provide cues to their emotions by using words, punctuation, and capital letters. For example, customers may include words such as *frustrated* or *disappointed* to describe their feelings about a situation. Or, they may use an exclamation point or capital letters for emphasis.

Do not assume, however, that you can fully understand the customers' point of view when it is provided in writing. Although an email written entirely in capital letters could have been written in anger, it may just be that the customer mistakenly hit the Caps Lock key. When in doubt, ask questions as needed to verify understanding.

Chapter 4 explores how to effectively use technologies such as email and chat to communicate with customers.

Nothing is ever gained by winning an argument and losing a customer.

C. F. NORTON

The Benefits of Active Listening

The benefits of active listening far exceed the benefits of speaking. Active listening helps you establish rapport with a customer. The most common way to build rapport is to listen for the customer's name and use it respectfully during the remainder of your conversation.

Listen carefully to how customers provide their name. If a customer uses a title, such as Professor Brown, Dr. Jones, or Ms. Smith, address the customer using that title until the customer gives you permission to use a first name or nickname. When supporting international customers, avoid using first names unless you have been given permission to do so.

Active listening also enables you to determine the customer's emotional state. If a customer is upset or angry, you must acknowledge and address that emotion before you can begin to address the technical incident. Active listening can help you build trust by enabling you to respond in a way that acknowledges your customer's sense of urgency. Helping a customer route a presentation she is scheduled to make in an hour to another nearby printer when her personal printer jams will go a long way in terms of building trust. Quick thinking and a viable workaround may not resolve the actual incident, but it can satisfy the customer's immediate need. If you do not at least try to satisfy the customer's immediate need—that is, if you do not respond in a way that acknowledges the customer's sense of urgency—the customer may become demanding and challenge you to do more than is possible. When customers understand that you will go the extra mile when they have a critical need, they may not feel the inclination to be as demanding in the future.

In addition to enabling you to establish rapport, address emotions, and build trust, active listening helps you keep the conversation on track so you can quickly determine the nature and likely source of the customer's incident or service request. If you are not listening carefully, you may miss an important detail or have to ask the customer to repeat what he or she said. Either scenario may instill a lack of confidence if the customer perceives you were not listening. Active listening will also enable you to determine situations that require management involvement. If a customer is unhappy with the service he or she received from another department in your company, you need to pass on that information to your manager. It is then your manager's responsibility to relay that information to the manager of the other department.

Most importantly, active listening enables you to show customers that they are important and that you want to do all you can to satisfy their needs. This leads to customer confidence, and the customer is left with a positive image of you and your company.

Avoiding Distractions That Prevent Good Listening

At least half of our time is spent listening, and, yet, we are not good listeners (*The Business of Listening: Become a More Effective Listener*, Crisp Publications, 2009). In fact, studies indicate that we usually listen using about 25 percent of our listening capacity and that we ignore, forget, distort, or misunderstand 75 percent of what we hear. Given that we spend much of our time listening, why are we not better listeners? In today's society, a lot of things get in the way, including those listed in Figure 2-1.

- Distractions and interruptions
- "Third ear" syndrome
- Jumping ahead
- Emotional filters
- Mental side trips
- Talking

Figure 2-1   Factors that prevent good listening

Distractions and Interruptions

Whether you work for a large or small service desk, you work in a high-energy environment. In a typical service desk on a typical day, telephones are ringing, electronic reader boards are flashing information and may be sounding alarms, customers and service providers are wandering about talking and perhaps entering your workspace, and all are demanding your attention. Figure 2-2 shows these typical distractions at a service desk. It is easy to lose focus

Keith Brofsky/Photodisc/Getty Images

Figure 2-2   Distractions and interruptions at a service desk

in this dynamic working environment. Good listeners find ways to minimize these distractions by, for example, turning into their workspace when talking on the telephone or working on incidents and signaling to visitors when they are already engaged.

"Third Ear" Syndrome

Many analysts believe they can listen to their customers and keep a "third ear" tuned in to what is happening around them. This concept of being aware of what is happening is valid, but must be used appropriately. Few people can truly listen and still do other things at the same time. If you are speaking with a customer and hear a coworker discussing a similar incident, you may want to ask the customer if you can put him or her on hold while you determine if there is a systemwide incident. On the other hand, if you are speaking with a customer and hear several coworkers talking about their lunch plans, you must focus on your customer's needs and avoid the distraction your chatting coworkers represent.

Jumping Ahead

The concept of jumping ahead is best explained by the adage, "Listening is not waiting for your turn to talk." Unfortunately, analysts sometimes decide they know the solution to an incident, or they have rehearsed a standard response to an inquiry and they are simply waiting for the customer to stop talking so they can begin. Analysts who jump ahead run the risk of missing key information from the customer that changes the nature of the incident. They may waste time diagnosing the wrong incident because they were not listening and missed important information. They may also appear insensitive because they have failed to hear out the customer. As a result, the customer may become defensive or uncooperative. The customer may reject an analyst's solution because the customer does not feel that he or she has been heard or understood. Good listeners wait until the speaker has provided all available information before reaching a conclusion.

Emotional Filters

We all have prejudices that influence our thinking and, as a result, our ability to listen. You may not like a speaker's appearance, voice, race, religion, or nationality. You may not like a speaker's temperament. Some people have a hard time dealing with negative people or people who whine. You may simply disagree with what the customer is saying. It is important to remember, however, that as a service desk analyst it is your job to uphold the policies of your company and assist all customers to the best of your ability.

Mental Side Trips

As a member of the human race, it is inevitable that your life will at times intervene when you are working. It may occur to you that you need to buy your friend a birthday gift or that you have to take your child to baseball practice after school. As these thoughts race through your mind, they make it hard to listen. This ability to manage several conversations in your mind at once is because most people can listen to 125 to 250 words per minute, but can think more than 1,000 to 3,000 words per minute ("Sssh! Listen Up!," HighGain Inc., June 2000). Good listeners focus on what the speaker is saying and resist thoughts that sidetrack their attention.

Keep paper and a pen or a digital note-taking tool handy to maintain your personal "To Do" list. Write down items that you don't want to forget to give your mind a sense of satisfaction so you can focus on the task at hand.

Talking

Talking is a necessary part of communication, but it is possible to talk too much. A common mistake in customer service is delivering too much information. For example, a customer asks you for the status of an outstanding incident and you answer by saying that Joe Brown in the Programming department is working on it. The customer promptly calls Joe Brown and asks him for the status, thus taking him away from solving the incident. Also, the customer now has Joe Brown's name and telephone number and may call him directly in the future, rather than calling the service desk. A more appropriate response is to let the customer know the incident is being worked on and that you will give the customer a call when the incident has been resolved. Or, if the incident is critical, promise the customer you will provide periodic updates. Then, make sure you do!

In Western cultures, silence is perceived as negative and so people often feel compelled to fill quiet moments by talking. People tend to speak first, listen second, and observe third. If you are working in or visiting Eastern cultures, a better approach is to observe first, listen second, and then speak. Seek to understand the varying approaches to communication that you encounter, and make an effort to avoid misunderstandings and appearing rude.

Knowing when not to talk too much is also an important part of communication. This is because it is sometimes necessary to listen for cues that the customer is following your instructions. If you asked a customer to restart his or her computer, you can listen for the Microsoft jingle to know the restart is under way. There is sometimes the tendency to engage in idle chatter during a lull in the problem-solving process, but remember, you cannot listen if you are talking too much. It is better to stay focused on working with the customer to resolve an incident. Rather than simply chatting while a customer is restarting his or her computer, you may want to describe for the customer what steps you will be taking once the computer has restarted. Use the active listening techniques described earlier in this chapter to verify that the customer is following the plan of action.

Knowing What to Listen For

Listening requires concentration, and it helps to know what you are listening for and how to record the information you receive. Begin by taking note of the key points the customer is making. If your company has an incident management system, record the information directly into that system so you do not have to handle the information again when you finish your conversation with the customer. If your company does not have a system, the system does not facilitate real-time logging of information, or you are simply not in a position to log information (such as when you are at a customer site), take notes as neatly and precisely as possible. Be as specific as possible so you can restate, using the customer's words when appropriate, the information the customer provides. A good guideline is to note who, what, when, where, and how. That is, who is experiencing an incident or has a service request? What product or service is involved? When is the incident occurring: chronically, intermittently, and so forth? Where is the incident occurring: for example, where is the failing device located or on what server is the failing software installed? How severe or widespread is the incident or how is the incident affecting the customer? *Why* the incident is occurring is determined once a solution is identified.

When listening to customers, your ultimate goal is to determine their needs. It is important to remember that customer needs can go beyond obtaining details about a technical incident or service request. It is also important to remember that you and your company can learn a lot by listening closely to customers. Challenge yourself to comprehend and retain as much as possible when communicating with customers. Skillful listening will enable you to:

- Detect any emotion the customer is experiencing that you need to acknowledge and address.

- Obtain the details of the customer's incident or service request.

- Graciously receive any complaints or compliments the customer has about your company, its products, or its services.

- Detect any misconceptions the customer has about your company and its products, which you or others in your company such as the Sales or Marketing department need to clarify.

- Learn ways that your products and services can be enhanced and improved.

- Gain insight about your customers that will enable you to improve the quality of your services.

Remember, too, that listening involves keeping your eyes open as well as your ears. When interacting with customers face to face, watch their face and body language. Speakers often deliver information through nonverbal cues, such as folded arms, a furrowed brow, or poor eye contact. These cues may indicate the customer is having a hard time understanding or believing what you are saying. If a customer rubs her eyes or scratches his head, it may be because he or she is confused and needs you to slow down or restate your instructions.

 In the Americas and most of Europe, steady eye contact is considered a sign of trust and respect. In Asia, eye contact is considered a personal affront and is kept to a minimum.

When interacting with customers over the telephone, remember that silence can be very telling. If a customer is unresponsive or fails to comment on the information you are delivering, the customer may be confused or may disagree with what you are saying. Although there is nothing wrong with a brief interlude of silence (the customer may be processing what you have said), you want to avoid the temptation to view that silence as acceptance. A tactful clarifying question, such as "Would you like for me to repeat that?" or "Is that acceptable to you?" will enable you to avoid incorrect assumptions.

Good listening requires discipline and begins with a willingness to fully comprehend and retain everything that customers are saying, in terms of both *what* they are saying and *how* they are saying it. Also, good listening does not begin and end with the conversations you have with customers. Listening is a skill that you can use and apply on a daily basis in all areas of your life.

Communicating with Customers

Communication is the exchange of thoughts, messages, and information. It requires skills such as listening, speaking, and writing. It also requires the desire to convey information in a meaningful and respectful way. Technology is helping us to communicate faster and with a larger audience, but it cannot help us formulate the information we transmit. Knowing what to say and how to say it when communicating with customers takes practice and patience.

Chapter 4 explores ways that you can improve your writing skills and use those skills to communicate technical information accurately, completely, and comprehensively. Communicating via technologies such as email and chat is discussed along with common service desk documents.

Building Rapport and Trust with Customers

What you say is a matter of knowing and selecting the right words to use for a given situation. The words you choose should also communicate to customers that you appreciate their business and want to assist them in any way you can. *How* you say it is much more complex and requires an understanding of how people communicate. Figure 2-3 illustrates the factors that influence customer perception when people are communicating face to face and over the telephone. It is easy to see from this chart that communicating with customers over the telephone requires a very different approach than communicating face to face. When communicating over the telephone, *how* people say it makes all the difference.

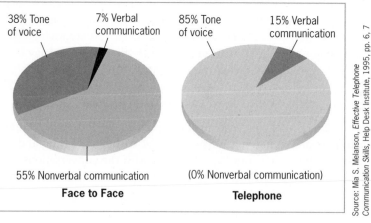

38% Tone of voice   7% Verbal communication   85% Tone of voice   15% Verbal communication

55% Nonverbal communication   (0% Nonverbal communication)

Face to Face   **Telephone**

Source: Mia S. Melanson, *Effective Telephone Communication Skills*, Help Desk Institute, 1995, pp. 6, 7

Figure 2-3   How people communicate

Be aware that customers will sometimes say things over the telephone or via a text message that they would never say in person. Customers may also tend to come on strong if they think their request is going to meet with resistance. This can cause analysts to become defensive because the analysts perceive they have not even been given the opportunity to try to help. A better approach is for analysts to remain calm and avoid overreacting. Controlled breathing is an excellent way for analysts to release tension and reduce any symptoms of anxiety or panic.

Chapter 9 describes techniques such as controlled breathing that analysts can use to relax and stay in control.

Verbal Communication

Verbal communication is the exchange of information using words. The words you choose to use can greatly influence the response you receive from customers. If you speak in a straightforward manner using everyday language that customers can understand, your message will be well received. If you speak in riddles or use technical language that customers cannot understand, you can alienate customers. If you acknowledge customers' emotions and let them know that you will do all you can to help, most customers will be willing to open up and describe their incident. If you use phrases such as those listed in Figure 2-4, you can quickly turn even a reasonable, calm customer into a charging bull. These phrases tend to provoke customers and should be considered forbidden.

Figure 2-4 Forbidden phrases

There may be times when you are faced with the need to deliver the messages these forbidden phrases represent. However, even when you have to deliver bad news to customers, you can present it in a positive, respectful way. Look at how these "forbidden phrases" can be replaced with more positive statements.

IT'S AGAINST OUR POLICY. This is a tough one because what your customer is asking for may very well be against your company's policy. Rather than state the negative, try stating your response as a positive: "Our policy states...." Or, if the policy enables you to offer the customer options, let the customer know what those options are: "According to our policy, what I *can do* is...."

THAT'S NOT MY JOB. It may not be your job, but it *is* your job to determine who *can* assist the customer. Here is where you put your *can do* attitude to work. Phrases such as "What I can do is transfer you to the person who handles that area" or "What I can do is give you the web site of the company that supports this product" let you keep the customer's goodwill even when you are unable to assist the customer directly.

THAT'S NOT THE WAY WE DO THINGS. This phrase rejects the customer's request without offering an alternative or positive option. Rather than stating the negative, turn this phrase into a positive statement that addresses the customer's need. "I am sending you a link for a web form you can complete and return with your manager's signature. I can then assign those rights to your account."

THERE'S NOTHING ELSE I CAN DO. This phrase, and its counterpart, "I don't know what else I can tell you," rejects the customer's request and implies you are unwilling to explore other ways to meet the customer's needs. It also undermines your credibility. Remember, there is always something you *can* do. When in doubt, offer to let the customer speak with your manager. Although you do not want to engage your manager in every conversation you have, there are times when management involvement is needed to satisfy the customer.

YOU NEED TO LOOK THIS UP ON OUR WEB SITE. This phrase begs the response, "I don't need to do anything!" A better way to approach this situation is to replace "You" with "Let me" or "Let's." For example, "Let me show you how to locate that information on our web site." Although customers may prefer that you simply give them the answer, this technique enhances their self-sufficiency while acknowledging their need to get information quickly.

YOU SET IT UP WRONG. There is nothing to be gained by pointing out the fact that a customer has made a mistake. Here is another example of where the "Let's" technique can be used. "Let's look at the system parameters and make sure they are set up correctly." If the customer figures out that he or she made a mistake, offer empathy. Giving the customer an encouraging "It happens to the best of us" response will go a long way in restoring the customer's confidence.

WE DON'T SUPPORT THAT. YOU NEED TO CALL... Stating the negative disempowers you and may alienate the customer. Remember that there is always something you can do. A more appropriate response would be, "What I *can* do is give you the web site of the group that supports this product." Using a positively stated phrase leaves the customer with the impression that you have helped. And you have! You have directed the customer to the best possible source of assistance.

WE'RE SWAMPED. I CAN'T GET TO THAT UNTIL LATER. Everyone is busy. The fact that you are busy is not the customer's fault nor does the customer really want to hear about it. Although it is appropriate to let the customer know that there are other customers who also are waiting for service, the best thing to do when you cannot respond to a customer's incident or service request immediately is give an *honest* estimate of how long it will take. When an SLA is in place, you may want to communicate the terms of that agreement. "Per our SLA with your department, this service request will be completed within 48 hours."

WHAT'S YOUR POINT? A more appropriate way to ask this question would be "Let me make sure I understand." or "Would you explain that again? I'm not sure I understand." Remember that you are the one not getting the point or you would not be asking that question. If you do not understand, ask the customer in a respectful way to clarify what he or she means.

WHOA! SLOW DOWN! You may be tempted to use this phrase when a customer is speaking very quickly. Although it is appropriate to let the customer know you are having trouble following the conversation, a more appropriate approach would be to get the customer's attention (you can call the customer's name if it has been given), and then respectfully ask the customer to slow down. "Mr. Lee, could I ask you to slow down just a bit so I can be sure I am getting all of your information correctly?"

YOU'VE GOT TO BE KIDDING! This is where the golden rule—treat others the way you would want to be treated—comes into play. How would you feel if a service provider said this to you? There will be times when you are amazed by what a customer says or requests, but you must always be respectful. Consider the customer's request, and positively and respectfully let the customer know what you *can* do. For example, "What I can do is take control of your system and work on this incident remotely. That will save the time it would take a technician to travel to your home office."

Choose your words carefully when communicating with customers. The wrong words not only can alienate your customer, they also can disempower you and undermine the credibility of your entire company. Practice using phrases that are positive and respectful.

INTERVIEW WITH...

Courtesy of Ann Cook

ANN COOK
AMERICAN ACCENT TRAINING
AUTHOR/DIRECTOR
STUDIO CITY, CALIFORNIA
www.americanaccent.com
One of the things that analysts may find difficult in a customer support setting is understanding people who have accents. Conversely, customers sometimes have difficulty understanding analysts who have accents. When you add technical jargon to the equation, communication can quickly break down. Ann Cook, author of *American Accent Training*, answers a few questions about accents, particularly as they relate to American English. Ann Cook is the director of American Accent Training, an international program that teaches people who speak English as a second language how to speak standard American English. She has developed a diagnostic speech analysis that identifies each aspect of a person's accent and pronunciation.

Question: What is an accent?

Answer: An accent is how we deliver a particular language. An accent has three main parts: the speech music or intonation, word connections, and the actual pronunciation of each sound. If you don't have speech music, your speech will sound flat and monotone: "He. Is. In. A. Dark. Room." With intonation, you'll be able to say, "He is in a DARK room" (developing photographs) or "He is in a dark room" (the room is dark). With intonation, you can also indicate how you feel about something. Think of the difference between "I should CALL him" and "I SHOULD call him." In the first case, it is likely that you will pick up the telephone; in the second case, you are indicating some degree of reluctance.

How you run words together, or make word connections, is also very important. A sentence that looks like "He is in a meeting room" actually sounds like "heezina meeding room."

Finally, pronunciation is the difference between phrases such as "I like tennis" and "I like Dennis."

Question: How do people get an accent?

Answer: People learn their original accents in infancy. Babies hear the speech rhythms of the people around them and mimic those rhythms, long before they acquire grammar and vocabulary. When they learn a second language in adulthood, they bring those patterns and pronunciations with them, and that results in a "foreign" accent. For instance, in languages other than American English, the R sounds like a D, the T always sounds like a T, and there are only five vowel sounds. In American English, the R is a kind of growly semivowel (*arrr*), the T is frequently pronounced as a D (*meeting* sounds like *meeding*), and American English has 14 vowel sounds. The result is that when a person who was not born in America says, "Eet eess hoeddeebel," they are trying to say, "It is horrible." In American English, it would come out "Idiz horrabul."

Question: What perceptions do people have about people who have accents?

Answer: To a large extent, it depends on the accent. If a person's accent is very light, people frequently respond positively. If an accent makes communication difficult, however, the response can be extremely negative, to the point of considering the speaker less capable or less intelligent. Americans and Europeans generally understand each other's accents, as they all speak Western languages. Asians, on the other hand, tend to have difficulty both speaking and understanding Western languages.

Question: Are there any stereotypes associated with people who have accents?

Answer: Quite sadly, people think that someone with nonstandard speech is speaking with an accent on purpose or isn't quite bright enough to talk "right." Many age-old notions about people from other countries arise, in large part, from the fact that foreign-born people don't use intonation the way a native American English speaker does. For example, to a native speaker, the sentence "Ben has a red pen" can be inflected many different ways:

- BEN has a red pen (not Sue)

- Ben HAS a red pen (he already has it, so don't offer him one)

- Ben has a RED pen (not a blue one)

- Ben has a red PEN (but no pencils)

A nonnative American English speaker will frequently say "BEN HAS A RED PEN," so the listener has to try to imagine which interpretation to make. Also, most other languages don't use the words A and *The* so words that are important in American English may be left out. Think about the difference between:

- A teacher bought a book (an unspecified teacher bought an unspecified book)

- The teacher bought a book (a specific teacher bought an unspecified book)

- A teacher bought the book (an unspecified teacher bought a specific book)
- The teacher bought the book (a specific teacher bought a specific book)

Given all of those possible interpretations, it is easy to see that if a person were to say, "Teacher bought book," the American listener would have to struggle to interpret what the speaker meant.

Question: What techniques can people use to better understand people who have a strong accent?

Answer: To better understand people who have a strong accent:

1. Speak slowly and clearly, but not loudly.

2. Acknowledge and accept that their speech isn't "perfect."

3. Don't sweat the details: try to grasp their main idea, as opposed to trying to understand each and every word they are saying.

4. Don't try to correct them, even if inadvertently. (Oh! THE teacher bought THE book.)

5. Listen for a key word, no matter how it's pronounced.

6. Don't interrupt. Make notes and go back to the problem when the person finishes speaking. The calmer you are, the calmer the other person will be.

7. Avoid colloquial, or conversational, speech. Foreign-born speakers are usually more familiar with longer words rather than the short words Americans prefer. For instance, *postpone* would be more familiar to someone who does not speak American English than *put off*, and *arrange* would be more familiar than *set up*. When you think about English verbs and prepositions, it's mind-boggling. With the word *get* alone, you have *get up*, *get over*, *get away*, *get away with*, *get off*, *get on*, *get through to*, and many, many more. These are very difficult for foreign-born speakers.

Question: Is there one most important thing that people can do to better understand people who have an accent?

Answer: It's like learning a new dance—try to catch the rhythm without being judgmental of how it "should" be.

Question: How is interacting over the telephone with a person who has an accent different than interacting face to face with that person?

Answer: There is so much more information available face to face. You can point to things, hand things back and forth, and use facial expressions and body language to communicate. Over the phone, you are limited to the sound of the other person's voice.

Question: What techniques can people use to reduce their accent?

Answer: To reduce an accent:

1. Focus on the rhythm of an entire phrase instead of word by word.

2. Learn to "hear." Listen to the radio, and write down exactly what the person says based on pronunciation, not spelling. For example, the word *water* would be *wahdr*, not *wa-ter*.

3. Don't worry about sounding fake—Americans don't tend to notice if a foreign-born person speaks with a heavy American accent. They'll just think that your English has improved.

4. Don't sound too perfect—native American English speakers don't talk that way. Let all your words run together. "I'll get it" should sound like "I'll geddit." This is not slang; it's perfectly standard colloquial American speech.

5. Take a course that is specifically oriented to "accent training" or "accent reduction," rather than grammar or vocabulary based.

Question: Is there one most important thing that people can do to reduce their accent?

Answer: Imitate and learn the American intonation. One way to do that is to listen to and repeat ballads and children's books on tape.

Question: Is there anything else that you think is important for students to know about accents?

Answer: For a person to have an accent means that they communicate perfectly in an entirely different language—not that they are deficient in their second language, which is English. Also, English is the hardest language in the whole world. It has more synonyms than any other language. Think of the difference between to tap, to rap, to pat, to pet, to stroke, to caress—these are all very similar words for using your hand to touch something, but look how different and specific each one is.

Nonverbal Communication

Nonverbal communication is the exchange of information in a form other than words. Nonverbal communication can say as much as words and includes qualities such as facial expressions, body language, and even clothing. When communicating with customers over the telephone, by email, or by chat, these nonverbal qualities have no impact whatsoever. When communicating face to face, however, they make up over half of our conversation. This is because people read meaning into nonverbal cues. If you wink while telling a story to a friend, he knows that you are kidding or teasing. If you avoid eye contact and tightly fold your arms across your chest when speaking with a customer, she may perceive that you are not listening or that you are rejecting what she is saying. If you dress sloppily or do not practice good grooming, people may perceive your thinking is sloppy as well and may resist your ideas.

To communicate effectively, learn to use your nonverbal vocabulary in the same positive way you use words. Be respectful, be attentive, and "listen" to what the speaker is telling you with his or her nonverbal cues. If a customer steps back when you approach him or her to discuss an incident, you may be standing too close. Allow the customer to establish a distance that feels comfortable. You can also observe and consider emulating the nonverbal techniques used by someone that you believe is an excellent communicator. Also, be aware of the culture at the company where you work. Although some companies allow a more casual dress code, there is such a thing as too casual. A neat appearance and good grooming always serve you well.

People in the United States are much more casual in terms of how they speak and dress than are people in other countries. When interacting with a customer, an effective technique is to mirror that customer's behavior. If the customer's manner is formal, respond in a formal manner. If the customer's manner is more casual, you can relax a bit. However, it is your responsibility to remain professional at all times. When traveling for business, ask people who have been to the country you are visiting, or ask your coworkers who live in that country, for guidance on how to make a good impression.

Tone of Voice

Figure 2-3 illustrated the dramatic difference tone of voice makes when you are interacting with customers face to face and even more so over the telephone. A number of factors, including those listed in Figure 2-5, make up your tone of voice. We all have different voices, and we can change our voices by controlling the energy, rate of speech, volume, and pitch we use when we speak.

- Energy
- Rate of speech
- Volume and pitch

Figure 2-5   Factors that influence tone of voice

ENERGY Enthusiasm is contagious, and the energy in your voice often reflects your personality and your attitude. Answering the telephone with a bored "Yeah" will not impress and instill confidence in customers. Facial expression mirrors mood, and mood mirrors facial expression. One technique that works well is to approach all interactions with customers as if they were standing in front of you. In other words, even if you are speaking to a customer over the telephone, put a smile on your face, focus your attention on what the customer is saying, and be as responsive as possible. Do not overdo it, however. False enthusiasm can be just as offensive and distracting as no enthusiasm. Be yourself! And remember, some days it can be tough getting excited by the prospect of handling one incident after another. Stay focused on the fact that you chose the field of customer support because you enjoy helping people. Hang inspiring quotes in your office, or place a funny picture on your desk that will help you put a smile back in your voice on even the toughest days.

Everyone smiles in the same language.

AUTHOR UNKNOWN

To monitor your facial expressions and posture, place a mirror on your desk at eye level. Placing the mirror at eye level ensures that you are sitting straight and practicing good posture. By taking a quick look in the mirror before you answer the telephone, you can ensure you have a relaxed and pleasant facial expression. You can put a smile on your face, give the customer (who you pretend to see in the mirror) your full attention, take a deep breath if needed to get focused, and then answer the telephone. Give it a try!

RATE OF SPEECH A normal rate of speech is 125 words per minute (*Telephone Courtesy & Customer Service*, Fourth Edition, Crisp Publications, 2009). Speaking too quickly or too slowly can be distracting to customers and affect their ability to listen. A good technique is to determine your normal rate of speech. You can do this by placing an audio recording device such as an MP3 player, smartphone, computer, or tape recorder next to you to record yourself while you are conversing or reading aloud casually from a book. The trick is to forget about the recording device so you get a more accurate reading of your rate of speech. You can then replay the recording, marking time with a stopwatch, to determine the number of words you speak per minute. After you have determined your normal rate of speech, strive to adapt your pace to the needs of your customer. Factors to consider include your customer's rate of speech and the information you are delivering. If you tend to speak quickly and a customer is speaking slowly, you may want to slow your speech slightly as well. Or, if you are walking the customer through an important set of instructions, you may want to slow your speech slightly. You may also want to slow down a bit if you are speaking to a customer in his or her second language. On the other hand, if you are asking a routine set of questions or simply validating information, you can pick up the pace *a little*.

Speaking too quickly at any point in a conversation can cause confusion or alienate the customer. This is particularly true when you are wrapping up a call. There is often a temptation to rush through the closing and move on to the next call. Unfortunately, you can undo any goodwill you have created by hanging up before the customer is satisfied. Take your time and listen to your customers. Their needs will help you adapt and adjust your pace.

Chapter 3 describes steps for closing a call effectively.

VOLUME AND PITCH The volume of your voice should always be loud enough that your customer and any of the other people involved in your conversation can hear you. The volume of your voice should not, however, be so loud that it disturbs the people around you. Service desks can get loud. All analysts must do their best to be courteous and respectful in terms of keeping the volume of their voice at an appropriate level and using speakerphones appropriately. If things get too loud on any given day, do not be afraid to politely signal coworkers that they need to keep it down. Graciously accept and respond to any such signals you receive from coworkers.

Make sure you are speaking closely, but not too closely, into your headset or telephone receiver. Speaking too far away from the receiver can make it hard for the customer to hear properly and allow outside noise to interfere with your speech. Speaking too closely to the receiver may cause your voice to sound muffled or so loud that the customer may perceive that you are shouting.

Pitch refers to the highness or lowness of vocal tone. Generally speaking, high-pitched voices are viewed as weak. We also tend to associate a high-pitched voice with someone who is excited, possibly even in a state of panic or being out of control. Low-pitched voices are typically viewed as strong, and we tend to associate a low-pitched voice with someone who is confident and in control.

Voice pitch is influenced by the way you hold your head and by the way you breathe. If you tend to have a high-pitched voice, practice lowering your head slightly when you speak. If you tend to have an exceptionally low-pitched voice, practice raising your head slightly when you speak. Your posture could also be influencing the quality of your voice. Good posture enables you to project your voice and makes it easier for customers to understand what you are saying. You can improve your posture by making sure you have a good chair that enables you to sit up straight and by making sure your workspace is ergonomically aligned.

Chapter 9 discusses how to set up an ergonomically aligned workspace.

You can also influence the pitch of your voice by learning to take long, slow, deep breaths, especially when you are under pressure. Most people become shallow breathers when they are under pressure. When this happens, your vocal cords tend to tighten, making your voice go up and sound strained. By slowing down your breathing, you lower the pitch of your voice and create a calmer tone.

Coupled with the right words, the tone of voice you use can dramatically change the message you communicate to a customer. Consider the differences between the following two phrases.

Stated using a frustrated tone of voice: What do you expect me to do about it?

Stated using a calm tone of voice after taking a deep breath: How would you like to see this situation resolved?

Both questions ask how the customer wants to see the situation resolved. The first example not only fails to engage the customer, it also fails to have the speaker take responsibility for the customer's satisfaction. The second example encourages a dialogue with the customer and at the same time avoids false promises. Selecting positive words and using a calm tone of voice communicates a completely different message—one that is much more empowering to both you and your customer.

Customers recognize and respond to your "words," whether they are spoken or communicated through nonverbal cues or your tone of voice. Practice using each of these techniques to establish rapport with your customers and gain their trust. Understanding the communication style of your customer is another tool you can use to enhance communications.

Identifying and Understanding Customer Communication Styles

Becoming an effective communicator requires that you acknowledge that customers are people, and people are different. They have different personalities, different ways of handling change and stress, and different communication styles. To communicate effectively, you must first identify the communication style of your customer. You can then respond, rather than react, to your customer in a way that is meaningful. Figure 2-6 lists some of the most common communication styles you will encounter.

- Aggressive people
- Chatterers
- Complainers
- Know-it-alls
- Passive people

Figure 2-6 Common communication styles

You determine every customer's communication style by listening to the information he or she provides and to the responses given when you ask questions. Use the following techniques to determine which communication style each customer exhibits and how to respond to that person.

Aggressive People

Aggressive people like to be in control. They are usually unwilling to engage in social conversation and want to get to the point immediately. Aggressive people may be quick to inform you that they "don't have time for this." They can become hostile and often try to bully and intimidate people, or they make a scene in order to get their way. An aggressive person may challenge you to "Get someone out here right away" or "Put your supervisor on the phone." When interacting with aggressive people, give them time to tell their story and then jump into the conversation when they pause or ask you a question. You can also try to get their attention and then take control of the conversation. Respectfully call out their name, and then state specifically what you *can* do. Always restate the information that aggressive people give you and their opinions of the incident. "John, I understand this situation with your power cord is frustrating. Let's verify the problem is with the power cord, and then I can order a new one for you." This technique lets aggressive people feel that they have been heard.

Chatterers

Chatty customers can be fun, but they can also be a challenge when you are busy. The first way to deal with chatty customers is to avoid encouraging them. Resist the temptation to ask a chatty customer how his or her vacation was. You are asking for a prolonged answer. When a chatty customer asks you a question that lends itself to a prolonged answer, reply with a minimum response. If a customer asks if you are busy, you can politely respond, "Yes, very. How can I help you?" Another great technique is to take control of the conversation by asking closed-ended questions. A **closed-ended question** prompts short answers such as "yes" and "no." After you have taken control, you can ask open-ended questions as needed to obtain more information. An **open-ended question** cannot be answered with a "yes" or "no" response.

Closed-ended questions:
Have you ever been able to access this application? [Yes/No]
Is there another printer close by that you can use? [Yes/No]
Open-ended questions:
What other applications did you have open when this incident occurred?
When was the last time you were able to use this device?

Complainers

Complainers whine and object but cannot always identify reasons why a solution will not work. They cannot or will not take responsibility for problem solving and often deflate the creativity or optimism of others. When interacting with complainers, empathize but do not necessarily sympathize with the customer's complaint. It is okay to acknowledge that computers can be frustrating, but agreeing that they should all be banished from the face of the earth is probably not a good idea. Also, when interacting with complainers, paraphrase their main points and make sure you understand the specific nature of their complaint. Try not to waste time talking about generalities. You can also ask complainers how they would like things to turn out. By empowering complainers to participate in developing a solution, you enhance their self-sufficiency and increase the likelihood that they will be satisfied with the final outcome.

Know-It-Alls

Know-it-alls believe they know everything and tend to resist advice or information they receive from others. They may go to great lengths to convince you that they are right. They can be condescending and pompous and in extreme cases take pleasure in making other people feel stupid. When interacting with know-it-alls, suggest alternatives without attacking their opinions. Avoid phrases such as "That won't work," which tend to be perceived negatively. Instead, use positive phrases such as "In my experience, this will work." Also, be respectful when asking questions and acknowledge the customer's knowledge.

When appropriate, use phrases such as "What if…" and "Let's try this." These phrases engage customers in the problem-solving process without rejecting their perspective.

Passive People

Passive people avoid controversy at all costs, and they often cannot or will not talk when you need information. They rarely volunteer opinions or comments and tend to go along with suggestions from other people whether or not they feel those suggestions are correct. When interacting with passive people, ask open-ended questions to encourage a prolonged reply rather than a "yes" or "no" response. Also, do not feel you have to fill the silence when waiting for a passive person to respond. If you have posed a question, wait for him or her to answer. Resist the temptation to jump in and put words in the person's mouth. Listen responsively when passive people are talking. If they perceive you are not listening, they may resume their silence.

Although these are the most common communication styles, they represent only a handful of the different kinds of people that you will encounter during your career in the support industry. It is also important to remember that people can use different communication styles depending on the situation they are facing or the response they are receiving. A customer who is getting pressure from his or her boss may be much more aggressive than usual when experiencing an incident. Or, a customer who perceives that you have been rude may suddenly become very passive and unresponsive. The more carefully you listen and strive to understand the different ways that people communicate, the more effective a communicator you will become.

Speaking the Customer's Language

It may not have occurred to you before, but you and your customers are bilingual. You may not speak French or Spanish in addition to English, but you *do* speak Business and Technology. Customers tend to speak Business. Analysts tend to speak Technology. Table 2-2 lists some examples of how customers and analysts speak different languages.

Customers Say	Analysts Hear
I can't log on.	The application is down.
I can't print.	The printer is down.
Analysts Say	**Customers Ask**
FPS1 (File and Print Server #1) is down.	Why can't I print?
The ERP system will be unavailable this weekend.	Does this affect payroll?

Table 2-2 Sample translations between Business and Technology languages

To keep communications on track and to avoid alienating your customers, avoid jargon and acronyms that your customers may not understand, or worse, may think they understand but actually do not. When customers use jargon or an acronym, ask clarifying questions to avoid making an invalid assumption they fully understand what they are saying. We all know it is possible for two people to have a conversation and walk away thinking they agree, only to find out later that they did not communicate. The excessive use of jargon and acronyms increases the likelihood that this will occur.

Remember that most people consider technology a tool. They typically are using it to *do* something, not just for the sake of it. The best way to serve your customers is to understand their business and learn to speak its language. Understand the business goals customers are using technology to achieve. Understand the impact when that technology fails. Really listen to what the customer is saying and respond with an appropriate sense of urgency.

Enabling user productivity is a critical success factor for service desks. Some days a tablet is just a tablet. Some days it is a sales tool that is being used to close a million dollar deal. Listening enables a support person to understand the difference.

Chapter Summary

- Listening is the most important skill for a support person. Active listening involves participating in a conversation by asking questions, responding to the speaker, and verifying understanding. Good listening requires discipline and begins with a willingness to fully comprehend and retain everything that customers are saying in terms of both *what* they are saying and *how* they are saying it. Listening brings many benefits and is a skill you can use and apply daily in all areas of your life.

- At least half of our time is spent listening, and, yet, we are not good listeners. Factors that prevent good listening include distractions and interruptions, "third ear" syndrome, jumping ahead, emotional filters, mental side trips, and talking. A service desk is a high-energy environment, and it is easy to lose focus. Good listeners use proven techniques to minimize these distractions and remain focused on customer needs.

- Listening requires concentration, and it helps to know what you are listening for and how to record the information you receive. A good guideline is to capture details such as who, what, when, where, and how. *Why* the incident is occurring is determined once a solution is identified. Be as specific as possible so you can restate the information the customer provides and record that information accurately in your company's incident management system.

- Communication is the exchange of information. It requires skills such as listening, speaking, and writing. It also requires the desire to convey information in a meaningful and respectful way. What you say—the words you choose to use—greatly influences the response you receive from customers. If you avoid forbidden phrases and speak in a straightforward manner using everyday language that customers can understand, your message will be well received. How you say it—the nonverbal ways you communicate and your tone of voice—can say as much as your words because people can read meaning into your nonverbal cues. Customers recognize and respond to your "words," whether they are spoken or communicated through nonverbal cues or your tone of voice. Effective communicators use proven techniques to establish rapport with customers and gain their trust. One of the most effective ways to build rapport is to listen for the customer's name and use it respectfully throughout your conversation.

- Customers have different personalities, different ways of handling change and stress, and different communication styles. To determine a customer's communication style, listen to the information he or she provides and to the responses given when you ask questions. You can then respond, rather than react, to your customer in a way that is meaningful.

- You can determine and influence your customers' response by learning to speak their language. Most people consider technology a tool. They typically are using it to *do* something, not just for the sake of it. The best way to serve your customers is to understand their business and learn to speak its language. You can then translate that language into your language, the language of technology.

Key Terms

acronym—An abbreviation formed from the first letters of a series of words.

active listening—Listening that involves participating in a conversation and giving the speaker a sense of confidence that he or she is being heard.

closed-ended question—A question that prompts short answers, such as "yes" and "no."

communication—The exchange of thoughts, messages, and information.

jargon—The specialized or technical language used by a trade or profession.

listening—To make an effort to hear something; to pay attention.

nonverbal communication—The exchange of information in a form other than words, including facial expressions, body language, and clothing.

open-ended question—A question that cannot be answered with a "yes" or "no" response.

paraphrase—To restate the information given by a customer using slightly different words in an effort to verify that you understand.

passive listening—Listening that involves simply taking in information and shows little regard for the speaker.

pitch—The highness or lowness of vocal tone.

social listening—The process of identifying and evaluating what is being said about a company, individual, product, or brand on the Internet; also known as *social media listening*.

verbal communication—The exchange of information using words.

Review Questions

1. What is the most important skill a support person must possess?
2. What is a basic human need?
3. Explain the difference between active and passive listening.
4. How can analysts use checklists?
5. What are tactful questions?
6. What can you learn about a customer by listening to how the customer uses jargon?
7. When a customer is angry or upset should you ask questions? Explain your answer.
8. What are two ways to let a customer know you are listening when you are interacting face to face?
9. When a customer is speaking, the best thing to do is remain quiet and listen. True or False? Explain your answer.
10. How can you obtain the information you need to resolve an incident?
11. What are three cues that a customer may give when he or she is confused or unsure?
12. What is paraphrasing?
13. What two things should you listen for when interacting with customers?
14. Why is it important to acknowledge a customer's emotion?
15. What must you do if a customer indicates he or she does not perceive you are listening?
16. List six benefits of active listening.
17. List the six distractions that prevent good listening.
18. What should you do if you are speaking to a customer and hear one of your coworkers discussing a similar incident?
19. What are three risks you run when you jump ahead?

20. What information should you capture about a customer's incident or service request?

21. What can silence tell you when you are interacting with a customer over the telephone?

22. What factors influence customer perception when communicating face to face?

23. What factors influence customer perception when communicating over the telephone?

24. What is a good substitute for "forbidden phrases"?

25. What are three nonverbal ways that people communicate?

26. Name the three factors that influence tone of voice.

27. Speaking slowly is the best way to ensure a customer can understand you. True or False? Explain your answer.

28. What are three techniques you can use to change the pitch of your voice?

29. How can you determine the communication style of your customer?

30. List three ways you can get an aggressive person's attention and take control of the conversation.

31. What is an open-ended question?

32. An effective way to interact with a complaining customer is to sympathize with his or her situation. True or False? Explain your answer.

33. What is the benefit of using phrases such as "What if…" and "Let's try this" when interacting with know-it-alls?

34. Which language do you need to speak—Business, Technology, or both Business and Technology? Explain your answer.

Discussion Questions

1. People often pride themselves on their ability to multitask. A person might work on the computer while talking on the telephone, or check instant messages while in a meeting. Can people really do two things at one time and still be active listeners?

2. Many technical support providers believe that customers need to become more technical, so they use jargon and acronyms in an effort to teach customers. Conversely, many customers believe that technical support providers could avoid jargon and acronyms, but they just do not want to. Who is right?

3. Have you ever forgotten someone's name within minutes of meeting them? Why does that happen?

Hands-On Projects

1. **Assess your listening skills.** Table 2-1 compares the characteristics of active and passive listening. Review these characteristics, and identify the active listening characteristics that you possess. Discuss these characteristics with at least three friends or family members. Ask them to provide feedback in terms of what kind of listener you are. Review your list, consider the feedback you received, and then prepare a list of ways you can become a more active listener.

2. **Develop a social listening strategy.** Assemble a team of at least three classmates or use your school's online message or discussion board. Search the web for information about social listening or social media listening. Prepare a brief presentation that describes the following:

   a. What is social listening?

   b. What are the benefits of social listening?

   c. How are companies using the data captured via social listening tools?

   d. What three to five key steps must companies take to implement an effective social listening strategy?

   As a team, present your findings to the class. As a class, discuss how social listening can be used in a service desk setting.

3. **Practice becoming a better listener.** Two common traits of poor listeners are (1) assuming you know what a person is about to say or that you understand the point he or she is trying to make, and (2) interrupting. For the next 21 days—at which point these techniques will become habit—pick at least one good listening technique and apply it at least once a day. Techniques you may want to practice include using acknowledging phrases ("Uh-huh," "I see," "Go on," "I understand"), paraphrasing, and halting your tendency to interrupt. Prepare a one-page report describing your efforts and observations.

4. **Pay attention when you are the customer.** Over one or more days, pay close attention during customer service experiences such as visiting a restaurant, grocery store, or department store. Other customer service experiences may include contacting a company over the telephone or via the web. The goal is to have multiple customer service experiences. Keep a list of any situations where you experienced an emotion, such as confusion, frustration, or anger, as a result of a customer service encounter. For each situation, answer the following questions:

   a. How did the service provider treat you?

   b. Did the service provider acknowledge your emotion?

   c. How did that make you feel?

   Then, write a paragraph describing the conclusions you can draw from your experiences.

5. **Avoid distractions.** Review the list of distractions that prevent good listening. Select two distractions that you can honestly say have influenced you in the past or continue to affect you in your current job, hobby, or home life. Prepare a list of three things you can do to minimize the impact of each distraction.

6. **Collect and rewrite forbidden phrases.** During the next week, pay close attention to the service you receive (see Project 4) and keep a list of any "forbidden phrases" that you hear. Refer to Figure 2-4 for a sample list of forbidden phrases. For each phrase, state a more positive, respectful way of delivering the message. Share your list via the class message board and have your classmates critique your restatements.

7. **Determine your rate of speech.** Record your voice while you converse or read aloud casually from a book. If you do not have a recording device, simply read aloud casually from a book. Determine the number of words you speak per minute. Is your rate of speech faster or slower than the average rate of 125 words per minute? Prepare a list of situations in which you may want to adjust your rate of speech.

8. **Assess the effectiveness of nonverbal communication.** Over the course of a day, take note of the various nonverbal ways that people communicate. Write a paragraph describing two or three nonverbal cues that you found to be particularly effective. Also, write a paragraph describing two or three nonverbal cues you found to be particularly ineffective or annoying. Write a final paragraph describing any conclusions you can draw from your observations.

9. **Determine your voice pitch.** Record your voice and replay the recording, listening for the pitch of your voice. If you do not have a recording device, leave a voice mail message somewhere that you can play it back. Do you have an exceptionally low- or high-pitched voice? Prepare a list of ways that you can adjust the pitch of your voice to project confidence and strength. Practice changing the pitch of your voice. Record your voice again, and replay the recording. Have you improved the pitch of your voice? Consider asking a classmate to listen to your recording and provide feedback.

Case Projects

1. **Diagnose Printer Incidents.** Your boss wants you to develop a problem-solving checklist that can be used to diagnose printer incidents. She has asked you to "keep it simple" and list only a half a dozen questions. Prepare a list of three open-ended questions and three closed-ended questions that can be used to determine why a customer may be having trouble printing a report.

2. **Coach an Analyst to Keep It Positive.** You are the team leader for a large internal service desk. Your boss recently overheard an analyst ask a customer, using an incredulous tone of voice, "You want it by when?" He asks you to provide the analyst with some coaching. Speak with the analyst (choose a classmate) and help the analyst determine a more positive, respectful way to respond to a customer's seemingly unreasonable request.

3. **The Business of Listening.** This exercise illustrates how to be an effective communicator and a good listener.

   a. Select volunteers to read out loud to the class.

   b. Students who are not reading close their books and prepare to listen.

   c. Volunteers read from an article in one-minute sequences.

   d. As a class, discuss how effectively each volunteer communicated, and how well the students listened. Consider such questions as:

      - Was the volunteer's tone of voice energetic?

      - How was the volunteer's rate of speech? Fast? Slow?

      - Did the volunteer read as fast or slow as the class perceived?

      - How was the volunteer's volume?

      - How was the volunteer's pitch?

      - Did any factors influence the students' ability to be good listeners? If so, what factors?

      - What were the students listening for?

   e. As a class, discuss the main points of the article that was read aloud.

4. **One-Way Communication.** This exercise illustrates how analysts and customers benefit when they can ask questions and receive responses. In other words, they engage in two-way conversation as opposed to one-way communication, which does not allow the exchange of questions and answers.

   a. Select one volunteer to describe a diagram to the class.

   b. Other students place a clean sheet of paper in front of them and prepare to listen. Students are *not* allowed to ask questions or communicate in any way with the volunteer. Students must remain silent throughout this entire exercise.

   c. The volunteer describes the diagram to the class. The volunteer must use only words to describe the diagram. The volunteer cannot use any nonverbal techniques to communicate, such as facial expressions, hand motions, or body movements. The volunteer cannot ask the students if they understand the information that is being communicated.

   d. Students draw the diagram the volunteer is describing on their clean sheet of paper. Remember, students cannot ask clarifying or follow-up questions.

   e. After the volunteer has finished describing the diagram to the class, reveal the diagram. Compare the students' drawings to the original diagram.

f. As a class, discuss how effectively the volunteer communicated, and how well the students listened. Consider such questions as:

- How explicitly did the volunteer describe the diagram?

- Did the volunteer use any jargon that the class did not understand?

- Did the volunteer go too fast or too slow?

- Did any students become confused or frustrated and just quit listening? Why?

- Why was the one-way communication difficult to follow?

- If the students had been allowed to speak, what questions would they have asked the volunteer?

g. As a class, discuss the benefits of being able to engage in two-way conversation. Also, discuss ways to become better listeners and communicators.

CHAPTER 3

Winning Telephone Skills

In this chapter you will learn:

- ◎ The power of the telephone
- ◎ How to handle calls professionally
- ◎ How to avoid the most common telephone mistakes
- ◎ How to place callers on hold and transfer calls in a positive, professional way
- ◎ How to continuously improve your telephone skills
- ◎ How to consistently convey a positive, caring attitude

For many service desks, the telephone is the primary way that customers obtain assistance. According to HDI's 2013 Support Center Practices and Salary Report, nearly 97 percent of its members receive customer incidents through the telephone. Although many service desks offer customers the ability to use channels such as email, chat, and Internet-based support services, the telephone will always play a role in customer service. Professional telephone skills help to ensure the service desk handles customer contacts in a prompt, courteous, and consistent manner. Consistency is particularly important because it builds trust between the analyst and customers, and it teaches customers what they can expect during the call so they know how to prepare.

To communicate effectively with customers over the telephone, you must understand how to handle calls professionally and how to avoid the most common call-handling mistakes. You must also let your caring attitude and personality shine through and use your telephone skills to send a positive, proficient message to your customers. How you answer the telephone and handle telephone calls greatly influences how customers feel about your entire company.

Creating a Positive Telephone Image

Two characteristics of excellent customer support discussed earlier—responsiveness and a caring attitude—are fundamental to a positive telephone image. How long it takes analysts to answer the telephone and the energy and enthusiasm they convey greatly influence a customer's perception of the analysts and the entire company. Although conducting business over the telephone can be frustrating and impersonal for both analysts and customers, when handled properly, the telephone can be an efficient, effective way to deliver support.

Understanding the Power of the Telephone

The telephone continues to be one of the most common ways that businesses and customers communicate. At a service desk, analysts may handle incoming calls (calls received), such as calls from customers, or they may handle outgoing calls (calls they make), such as follow-up calls to customers or calls to vendors. Telephone technology automates and facilitates many of these activities. The most common telephone technologies are listed in Figure 3-1.

- Voice over Internet Protocol (VoIP)
- Voice mail
- Fax
- Automatic call distributor (ACD)
- Voice response unit (VRU)

Figure 3-1 Common telephone technologies

Service desks use telephone technologies that range from simple voice mailboxes to highly complex, automated systems. Which telephone technologies a service desk selects are determined by a number of factors, such as the service desk's size, the company's goals, the nature of the company's business, and customer expectations. Smaller service desks may opt to use a simple set of telephone technologies, such as voice mail and fax. Larger service desks and those in high-technology industries tend to use more sophisticated technology, such as automatic call distributors and voice response units. The technology a service desk uses affects how customer contacts are directed to analysts and how analysts' performance is measured.

Most analysts use telephone headsets to prevent neck pain and leave their hands free to use the keyboard or a touch-screen device such as a smartphone or a tablet.

Chapter 9 describes how to adjust your telephone and headset, chair, monitor, keyboard and mouse, and lighting to create a workspace that fits your needs.

Many organizations integrate recording systems with their telephone technologies to monitor calls and evaluate analysts' performance. Organizations may also record calls for security and compliance purposes. **Recording systems** record and play back telephone calls. Companies that use this technology often inform customers about the recording system by playing a message such as, "Please be advised that this call may be monitored or recorded for quality purposes."

Voice over Internet Protocol (VoIP)

Voice over Internet Protocol (VoIP) systems translate voice communications into data and then transmit that data across an Internet connection or network. At the other end, the data is converted back into its original voice form and emerges like a regular phone call. In other words, VoIP transmits voice communications in the same way that email and instant messaging systems send messages across the Internet.

Popular VoIP providers include ITP, Phone Power, Skype, Via Talk, and Vonage.

A benefit of VoIP in a service desk setting is that an organization can reduce its costs by using its existing data network to route phone calls. Cost reductions include the ability to reduce telephone company fees, long-distance charges, and costs associated with supporting and maintaining both a voice and a data network. Other benefits include integration with existing data systems and analyst mobility. For example, VoIP systems enable many of the computer telephony integration features offered by traditional telephone systems such as screen pops. VoIP also makes it easy for companies to link local service desks and analysts working at home. Analysts use VoIP telephones to handle calls just as they would a regular telephone or ACD console.

 VoIP can also be used to transmit text messages across the Internet. Analysts may use VoIP to text with a level two specialist or subject matter expert while at the same time handling a customer via the telephone.

One obstacle to VoIP is that companies using traditional telephone systems need to invest in significant upgrades to their data network to support VoIP traffic and guarantee both call quality and network reliability. Without such upgrades, a network-related incident could result in poor call quality and a network-related outage could result in all channels used to contact the service desk being unavailable. Despite these concerns, most companies are moving to VoIP rather than upgrading or replacing their existing telephone systems when those become obsolete. Newer call centers and service desks are likely to be VoIP only.

Voice Mail

Voice mail is an automated form of taking messages from callers. Companies often combine voice mail with automatic call distributors and voice response units, enabling customers to choose between waiting in a queue and leaving a message. More than 51 percent of companies use voice mail to take after-hours calls, according to HDI (2013 Support Center Practices and Salary Report, HDI).

Customers can perceive voice mail negatively if they are not given an idea of when the call will be returned or if a previous voice mail message was not returned. For customers to view voice mail positively, they must be given a target response time, and then customers must receive that return call within the promised time frame. For example, some companies state that calls received prior to a designated time will be returned by the end of that same day, while calls received after the designated time will be returned the next business day.

To ensure expectations are set in a consistent way, a best practice is for analysts to always provide customers the service desk's telephone number, not their personal telephone number or extension. This ensures that voice mail greetings reflect the company's policies and that voice mail messages are returned in accordance with those policies. Some companies provide analysts with a script for their direct business extension or telephone number voice mail greeting that directs the customer to the service desk's main number for assistance.

You have reached the voice mail box of Andy Smith. I am unavailable to take your call at this time. If you are calling about a technical matter, please contact the service desk at extension 4387 and a member of our team will be happy to assist you. Otherwise, I will return your call within 24 hours or on the next business day. Thank you for calling. Have a great day.

People often mistrust a voice mail greeting such as "I will get back to you as soon as possible." Be specific. Provide a realistic target response time.

The best companies diligently manage voice mail messages and promptly return all customer calls, even if only to let the customer know that (1) the call was received, (2) the call has been logged in the company's incident management system, and (3) the call is being handled. In other words, acknowledging the voice mail is not the same as resolving the customer's incident or service request. Rather, acknowledging the call simply lets the customer know that the voice mail message has been received and logged. In some companies, voice mail messages are logged and automatically acknowledged via email. Analysts may also contact customers who have left a voice mail message to verify the accuracy of the customers' information or to gather additional information.

To minimize the number of exchanges required to handle voice mail messages, the voice mail recording customers hear should list the specific information they should provide when leaving a message. Such information may include their name, a telephone number where they can be reached, their account number or product number when applicable, the product they are calling about, and a brief description of their incident or service request.

You have reached the IT Service Desk. Our office is currently closed. Our business hours are 7 a.m. to 7 p.m., Monday through Friday. You can obtain basic services and answers to common questions 24 hours a day, 7 days a week, by accessing our web site at www.example.com. If this is an emergency, press 1 now to obtain after-hours support. Otherwise, please wait for the tone and leave your name, telephone number, and a detailed description of your inquiry including any device- or service-related information we may need to assist you. We will return your call the next business day. Thank you for contacting the IT Service Desk.

Voice mail requests are typically logged in the service desk's incident management system in the same way as a telephone call. Most incident management systems automatically assign a ticket number or unique identifier to logged customer incidents or service requests.

The term *ticket* is a throwback to the days when customer contacts were recorded on paper forms. Today contacts are logged electronically, but the term *ticket* is still widely used. In this context, a **ticket** is a record stored in a database that contains the details of a customer contact. Tickets may also be called cases, incidents, logs, records, and service requests.

A best practice is to provide customers with their ticket number as assurance that their incident or service request will not be lost or forgotten. Also, inform customers they can reference the ticket number when calling to obtain a status update for an incident or service request. If the service desk's web site provides the capability, inform customers they can use the ticket number to obtain a status update online.

Fax

A **fax**, short for *facsimile*, is an image of a document that is electronically transmitted to a telephone number connected to a printer or other output device. Faxes can be sent and received via fax machines, multifunction printers, or computers. Faxes can also be sent and received via email. Although the use of fax is declining in popularity, some companies allow their customers to fill out forms requesting service and then fax the form to the service desk. According to HDI, just under 9 percent of companies use fax, down from more than 20 percent in 2009 (2013 Support Center Practices and Salary Report, HDI). Occasionally, a service desk analyst may ask a customer to fax information, such as a report that has an error message, to the service desk so the analyst can see the error and better diagnose the incident. Faxed incidents and service requests are typically logged in the service desk's incident management system in the same way as a telephone call.

Automatic Call Distributor (ACD)

An ACD answers a call and routes, or distributes, it to the next available analyst. If all analysts are busy, the ACD places the call in a queue and plays a recorded message, such as "We're sorry, all of our service representatives are currently assisting other customers. Your call will be answered in the order it has been received." Some companies provide an estimate of the time customers can expect to wait for the next available analyst and may let customers choose between waiting in the queue and leaving a voice mail message. According to HDI's 2013 Support Center Practices and Salary Report, 64 percent of its members use ACDs and another 4 percent plan to add ACDs within 12 months.

A **queue** is simply a line. The term *queue* can be used to refer to a list of calls, tickets, email messages, or chat requests waiting to be processed.

ACD software determines what calls an analyst receives and how quickly the analyst receives those calls. Analysts use an ACD console to perform ACD functions. Figure 3-2 shows a sample ACD console.

Figure 3-2   Sample ACD console
Courtesy of American Telebrokers, Inc.

With an ACD console, like the one shown in Figure 3-2, analysts at their desks can:

- Log on at the start of a scheduled shift each day, and place the telephone in an available state. An **available state** means the analyst is ready to take calls.

- Log off anytime they leave their desk for an extended period of time, and log on when they return.

- Log off at the end of a scheduled shift each day.

- Answer each call routed to them within a certain number of rings, as specified by service desk policy. When analysts do not answer calls within the designated number of rings, the ACD transfers the call to the next available analyst. Because service to the customer is delayed, this practice is discouraged.

- Correctly use **wrap-up mode**, a feature that prevents the ACD from routing a new inbound call to an analyst's extension. Service desk analysts use this wrap-up time to finish documenting the customer's incident or service request after they have hung up, to escalate a call, and to prepare for the next call. Many companies establish guidelines for how long analysts can stay in wrap-up mode before making themselves available to take the next call.

 The terminology used to describe these ACD functions and states varies slightly from one ACD system to the next.

ACDs provide a wealth of statistical information the service desk can use to measure individual and team performance. Also, some ACD systems enable companies to use this tool to queue and manage email, voice mail, fax, and Internet inquiries such as chat requests, along with traditional telephone calls. This feature is very attractive to companies because they can then use a single tool to produce statistics about their workload.

ACDs can integrate with and use other technologies to deliver information to analysts and customers. For example, when integrated with an announcement system, an ACD can inform customers about the status of a system that is down. An **announcement system** is a technology that greets callers when all service desk analysts are busy and can provide valuable information as customers wait on hold such as answers to frequently asked questions, information about current system outages, or information customers can use to access self-services such as the web address for the service desk's web site. Or, the ACD can use caller ID data to provide the service desk analyst with the name of the caller. ACDs also can use the caller's telephone number or information collected from the caller, such as an account number or a product number, to route the call. This information can be captured in a number of different ways, such as an automated attendant, a voice response unit, or automatic number identification. Automated attendants and skills-based routing are common ACD features.

Some organizations, particularly larger organizations and those that provide external customer support, post a Privacy Agreement or Privacy Policy on their web site that describes how customer information is used and protected. Customers concerned about how their information is being used can typically "opt out" of information-sharing activities.

An **automated attendant** is an ACD feature that routes calls based on input provided by the caller through a touch-tone telephone. Systems that have speech-recognition capability allow customers to speak their input, rather than key it in through their telephone keypad. A basic automated attendant prompts the caller to select from a list of options or enter information, such as the extension of the party the caller wants to reach, and then routes the call based on the caller's input. Automated attendants can be much more sophisticated. They can also be integrated with other technologies to enhance functionality. For example, automated attendants can use caller ID or automatic number identification data to identify the customer and then route the caller to an appropriate analyst or group of analysts.

Skills-based routing (SBR) is an ACD feature that matches the requirements of an incoming call to the skill sets of available analysts or analyst groups. The ACD then distributes the call to the next available, appropriately qualified analyst. Skills-based routing determines the call requirements from the customer's telephone number or information collected from the customer or from a database. This information is obtained from services such as caller ID and automatic number identification, or from a voice response unit. Companies that use SBR require analysts to create and maintain a skills inventory that correlates the products, systems, and services supported by the service desk to each analyst's level of skill. Then, calls can be routed to an analyst who has the skill needed to handle the customer's incident or service request. For example, with SBR, a call concerning a spreadsheet application can be routed to an analyst who has a depth of experience supporting spreadsheets.

Voice Response Unit (VRU)

A **voice response unit (VRU)** , which may also be called an interactive voice response unit (IVRU), integrates with another technology, such as a database or a network management system, to obtain information or to perform a function. A VRU obtains information by having callers use the keys on their touch-tone telephone, or, when speech recognition is available, speak their input into the telephone. For example, a VRU can collect a unique identifier, such as a customer's employee ID or product number, and then use it to verify the customer is entitled to service. A VRU can prompt customers to specify the nature of their inquiry or the type of product they are using and then route the call to an analyst skilled in that product. Some companies also use a VRU to automate routine tasks, such as changing a password or checking the status of an order. Other companies use a VRU to provide access to a reduced set of service desk services during nonbusiness hours. For example, after business hours a VRU can enable a customer to hear system status information, leave a voice mail message, or contact an on-call analyst if the customer is experiencing a critical incident.

Customers often become frustrated when prompted to select an option from a long list of choices. To increase customer acceptance, the optimum number of choices for a VRU menu is four options that lead to no more than four additional options. Optimally, one of the options enables customers to speak with an analyst. To avoid confusion and frustration, VRUs should also be programmed to provide callers with the ability to repeat the menu options, return to the main menu, and cancel input, such as by pressing the asterisk key. A well-designed VRU enables callers to feel that they are in control of calls and that they have options, rather than feeling that the company is simply trying to avoid human interaction.

When poorly implemented or when used improperly, telephone technology can lead to customer frustration and be perceived negatively. When customers mistrust or dislike technology, it affects how they interact with service desk analysts and how analysts receive their work. Consider the following examples:

- Some companies fail to respond to voice mail and fax messages in a timely fashion. As a result, customers may mistrust that technology and choose to wait in the queue instead. This means that service desk analysts are required to be on the telephone for extended periods of time.

- Some companies are not staffed properly, causing customers to spend an extended time waiting in the queue. When customers finally reach an analyst, they may be more upset about having to wait than they were about the incident they were originally calling to report.

- Some companies offer long VRU menus with a number of confusing options. Because there may not be any way to reach a human being who can help, customers select the option they *think* most closely matches their need. As a result, service desk analysts occasionally receive calls from disgruntled customers or calls they are not qualified to handle because a customer inadvertently selected the wrong option or was unsure of which option to select.

- Some companies fail to provide customers with the ability to leave a message or reach a human being. As a result, customers are forced to wait in a queue, hang up and call back later, or seek an alternate form of support.

These negative effects are a result of telephone technology that has been poorly implemented. By listening to customers and service desk analysts and implementing the technology in a way that both perceive as useful and beneficial, companies can minimize these negative effects.

Telephone technology is not a substitute for service desk analysts. Implemented correctly, it is a powerful communication tool that can enhance the services a service desk offers and benefit service desk analysts. Tools such as voice mail and fax offer flexibility to customers and time away from the telephone to analysts. Automatic call distributors can broadcast messages at the beginning of the call that inform customers about, for example, a virus that is affecting the network, reducing the number of calls that analysts must handle. Automatic call distributors and voice response units can also use caller ID data or automatic number identification data to provide the analyst with the name of a caller. **Caller identification (caller ID)** is a service provided by a *local* telephone company that discloses the telephone number of the person calling and, where available, the name associated with the calling telephone number. **Automatic number identification (ANI)** is a service provided by a *long-distance* service provider that discloses the telephone number of the person calling. ACDs and VRUs can also use the caller's telephone number or information collected from the caller through automated prompts to route the call to the analyst best suited to handle the customer's incident or service request. As a result, analysts receive only the calls they can handle, which reduces their stress.

Many companies use computer telephony integration to further enhance the services offered via the telephone. **Computer telephony integration (CTI)** links computing technology with telephone technology to exchange information and increase productivity. Companies use CTI at the service desk to perform functions such as screen pops and simultaneous screen transfers. CTI can also facilitate fax server transmissions and outgoing calls, which means that people can send faxes or dial an outgoing call right from their computer.

A **screen pop** is when information about the caller appears, or pops up, on an analyst's monitor based on caller information captured by the telephone system and passed to a computer system. Figure 3-3 illustrates how the telephone system can use caller ID to determine the caller's telephone number and how the computer system can look up the number in the company's customer database to find additional information, such as the caller's name and address. The computer can add this information to the telephone number and create a new ticket that pops up on the screen of the analyst taking the call.

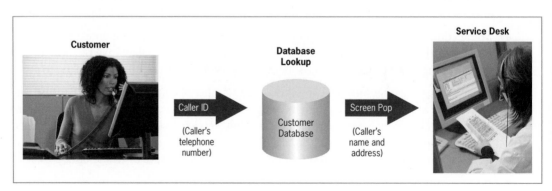

Figure 3-3 Computer telephony integration
© JGI/Blend Images/Getty Images, © Ternovoy Dmitry/Shutterstock.com

The analyst can quickly verify the customer's information and then ask questions and add details about the customer's incident to the ticket. A history of the caller's previous incidents and service requests can also pop up on the screen. The analyst can then use that history to diagnose the customer's incident or provide a status update. A screen pop reduces the amount of data that an analyst must gather to create a ticket, and enables the analyst to quickly verify the customer's information and begin determining the customer's need. A screen pop also ensures that the data collected is accurate and complete because much of the information is entered automatically, rather than by an analyst.

When working in a service desk, you must understand the telephone technology that is available and strive to use it properly. Regardless of the technology available, there are proven techniques that can facilitate faster and smoother telephone transactions. These techniques enable you to present a positive image to customers and leave them feeling confident that their call has been handled professionally.

Handling Calls Professionally from Start to Finish

To be excellent, customer service providers must view each and every customer encounter as critical to the success of the company. This is particularly true when interacting with customers over the telephone. Over the telephone, customers cannot see an analyst's body language to know that the analyst is ready to assist them or is listening. They cannot see that the analyst is using a tool to determine an answer to their question. All they have to go on is *what* the analyst says and *how* the analyst says it. Figure 3-4 lists some of the most critical interactions that occur in the course of a call to a service desk. Each of these interactions— along with how calls are placed on hold and transferred—contributes considerably to how customers perceive an analyst and the entire company.

 Most organizations establish targets and measure how quickly these activities are performed in an effort to minimize business impact. Chapters 7 and 8 describe common metrics used to measure individual and team performance in a service desk setting.

- Answering the telephone
- Handling calls about unsupported products or services
- Taking a message
- Closing a call

Figure 3-4 Critical interactions during telephone calls

The use of a **script**, or a standard set of text and behaviors, is a common service desk practice that is particularly useful when providing technical support. Using scripts and turning them into a habit enables analysts to focus their energy on resolving incidents and service requests and handling unique situations. Analysts may use scripts when they need to find a positive way to say something they do not feel comfortable saying, such as "No," to a customer. Scripts also enable customers to perceive that service desks deliver services consistently. By learning and applying the following proven techniques, you can feel confident you are providing the best service possible, regardless of the situation.

Customer service should flow smoothly, almost effortlessly. Everything about the business is touched and nourished by it. It's not a department, it's an attitude.

AUTHOR UNKNOWN

Answering the Telephone

How you answer the telephone sets the tone for the entire conversation. Grunting your last name into the telephone, or even stating only "Hello," is not good telephone etiquette. When answering the telephone, pick up the telephone promptly, but with composure. Customers like timely service, but they also like working with someone who is composed and in control. Put a smile on your face, and if you have one, glance in a mirror to ensure you appear willing and ready to assist the customer. Remember that your smile, energy, and enthusiasm are communicated to the customer through your tone of voice. Take a deep breath so the customer perceives you are relaxed and in control.

 Most companies strive to answer the telephone in less than 30 seconds. Factors that influence an organization's target answer speed include customer expectations, staffing levels, budgetary considerations, and competitive considerations.

Answer the telephone using your company's standard script. This ensures customers are greeted in the same, consistent way. Many companies use the following approach:

1. **Announce the name of your company or department.** This lets customers know they have reached the right place. Some companies place a greeting such as "Hello," "Thank you for calling," or "Good morning" in front of the department name. This is because customers very often do not hear the first word or two that is stated, so the first thing they do hear is the department or company name. Be careful when using greetings such as "Good morning" and "Good afternoon." If you state the time of day incorrectly or if the customer is in a different time zone, the customer may perceive that you are inattentive or insensitive. The best practice is to keep it simple.

2. **Give the caller your name.** Say your name slowly, so it can be understood. Providing your name is a simple courtesy, and it lets customers know that you are taking ownership of their incident or service request. Your company's policy will dictate whether you provide your first name or your title and surname. When only first names are provided, your company's policy will dictate what to say when a customer is asking for your last name.

3. **Ask the first question.** By asking the first question, you take control of the call and begin gathering needed information. Your company's policy and the technology you use will determine the question you ask. Some service desks must determine if customers are entitled to service before they begin handling a call. In

this case, you may ask customers for a customer ID or a product serial number. You can then use their response to look up information in the company's incident management system. Other service desks simply ask customers how they can help. Resist the temptation to ask personal questions or questions that can veer the call off track. This is a common mistake that analysts make when they know customers personally or have established a high degree of rapport. Greeting a customer with a hearty, "Hey, Jan, how was your vacation?" elongates the call and may offend a customer who is being severely impacted by an incident and needs immediate help. The best practice is to take care of business first and keep personal conversation to a minimum.

The following are a few examples of standard service desk greetings.

Service Desk, this is Carmen. How may I help you?

Service Desk, this is Sue. May I have your name please?

Hello, Options Unlimited, this is Leon. May I have your customer ID?

After greeting the customer, listen *actively* to the customer's incident or service request. When asking the customer for the information you need to log the contact, ask every customer for the same information *in the same order every time*. For example, if you must determine a customer's name, location, and employee ID to log the contact, ask for that information in the same order every time. Over time, customers learn what information they need to provide when they call. Customers can then be prepared and often begin to volunteer the information before being asked. As a result, you will be able to quickly and easily log the customer's contact.

If you speak with a customer regularly and know, for example, his address or telephone number, a good practice is to verify the information rather than skipping that step and assuming that what you have is correct. For example, ask, "Julian, do you still live at 123 Main Street?" You want to verify the information because the customer may have moved or some information may have changed. This also ensures that the customer knows the call is being logged and manages the customer's expectation of how calls are handled no matter who answers the call.

Remember that you are usually not the only person in the service desk. Although it may seem that you are making it easier for the customer by skipping steps and failing to ask questions, you are actually doing the customer and your coworkers a disservice. A customer who has gotten used to speaking with you may be dissatisfied when your coworker follows the standard procedure. As a result, the customer may ask to speak with only you in the future. Although this seems like a compliment, it actually is not in the customer's best interest because you may not always be available when that customer needs help. The service desk is a team setting. By being consistent, you communicate your company's policies and you convey to customers that anyone in the service desk can assist them.

Quality is never an accident; it is always the result of high intention, intelligent direction, and skillful execution. It represents the wise choice of many alternatives.

WILL A. FOSTER

Handling Calls about Unsupported Products or Services

Few companies are in a position to be all things to all people. This means that few companies can support every product or service their customers may conceivably use. The costs would simply be too high. As a result, many companies define a list of supported products and services. This list is typically published on the service desk's web site.

Many companies offer self-services via their web sites that customers can use to obtain support without having to wait to speak with a service desk analyst. Chapter 4 discusses self-service in greater detail.

In an internal service desk setting, the service desk supports those products that are most commonly used by the company's employees and those products that most directly contribute to the company's goals. In an external service desk setting, the supported products and services are limited to those developed or sold by the company, or those the service desk has been contracted to support. Most external service desks do not support products and services that are developed or sold by another company unless they are being compensated to do so.

The service desk receives training, documentation, and procedures related to the products and services it does support. It also typically has a copy of supported software and may have access to a lab environment that contains supported hardware that it can use to replicate and diagnose incidents. Thus, the service desk is able to deliver high-quality support.

Service desk analysts often have a hard time referring customers to another group or company when customers need help with unsupported products or are requesting unsupported services. In other words, they have a difficult time saying "No" to customers. This is particularly difficult for service desk analysts who may be familiar with the product the customer is calling about because they supported that product in the past or they use the product on a daily basis. Analysts want to help. It is important to remember, however, that the number of analysts assigned to the service desk is determined by the service desk's projected workload, which is based on the list of supported products and services. When service desk analysts assist customers with incidents related to unsupported products, they are undermining the ability of the entire team to handle work that is within its scope of responsibility. This is why it is the policy of most service desks to simply refer the customer to the correct group or company, rather than contacting that group or company for the customer. Then, service desk resources can be devoted to assisting customers who call about supported products and services. Analysts may also try to help customers only to realize that they lack the ability or authority to handle the incident. This is a disservice to customers because time and effort have been wasted working on the incident, finding a solution has been delayed, and the customer may need to start over with another group or company. Assisting a customer with an unsupported product also leads the customer to expect that he or she can contact the service desk about this product in the future. The customer will become dissatisfied if another analyst refers him or her to the correct group or company.

Referring a customer who needs help with an unsupported product or service to another group or company is different than escalating an incident to a level two support group. Typically, the service desk does not retain ownership of incidents relating to unsupported products. This means that the service desk does not follow up to ensure the incident is resolved to the customer's satisfaction. It lets the other group or company assume that responsibility.

Remember that while your service desk may not support some products and systems, there is always something you *can do* for the customer. Many service desks develop scripts that analysts can use to advise customers of their options, such as the following examples.

> What I can do is provide you with the web site of the company that supports that product. They will be able to help you.
>
> What I can do is transfer you to the group that supports that product. They will be able to help you.

Sometimes you may not know who supports a product. In that case, let the customer know you will look into the matter and get back to him or her with an answer, as in the following example.

> What I can do is research this matter and call you back with the name and contact information of someone who can help.

Although uncommon, some companies allow an exception to this scenario by establishing a "best effort" policy. **Best effort** means you do your best to assist the customer within a predefined set of boundaries, such as a time limit. For example, you may try to assist the customer, but if you cannot resolve the incident within 15 minutes, you refer the customer to the correct group or company. This practice is sometimes found in companies that support PC-based off-the-shelf products. **Off-the-shelf** products are personal computer software products that are developed and distributed commercially. Because these products, particularly products that operate in Microsoft Windows, function similarly, service desk analysts can sometimes assist customers even though they have not received specialized training on a given product. By setting a time limit, the service desk can assist customers while minimizing wasted effort. A good practice is to let customers know in advance that you are working under a time constraint or that there is a possibility you will have to refer them to another group or to a vendor. The following example shows how this might sound.

> This product is supported by Superior Software Solutions, Inc., but what I can do is work with you for 15 minutes to see if we can resolve the incident. If we can't, I can give you Superior Software's telephone number and they will be able to assist you. Would you like to continue working on the incident, or would you like to contact Superior Software?

If your company does not have a policy of giving "best effort" support, or if you feel you do not have the ability or authority to resolve a customer's incident or service request, the best practice is to quickly refer the customer to the correct group or company. Even though it may seem like you are not supporting customers when you refer them to another group or company, you are actually helping them obtain assistance from the people who are best suited to support the products or services in question. You are also contributing to the goals of your team by resisting the temptation to devote time and effort to support services that are outside the scope of your mission.

Taking a Message

Sometimes a customer calls the service desk and asks to speak with a specific analyst. If that analyst is unavailable, let the customer know and ask who is calling. Then, in an effort to ensure the customer receives service as quickly as possible, ask the customer if you can do anything to help.

Inform the customer of the analyst's availability *before* asking for the customer's name. If you ask for the customer's name first, the customer may perceive that the analyst is available but avoiding his or her call.

When communicating to a customer the fact that an analyst is not available, explain the analyst's absence in a positive way. Also, resist the temptation to give out too much information. For example, rather than informing the customer that the analyst is meeting with a supervisor, simply say that he or she stepped away for a couple of minutes or that the analyst is currently not available. Avoid saying things the customer may perceive negatively, such as "I don't know where he went" or "She hasn't shown up yet today."

In the best service desks, any analyst can assist a customer even if that analyst did not initially handle the customer's incident or service request. If the customer is inquiring about the status of an outstanding incident, you can look up the ticket in the incident management system and give the customer a current status. If the customer is calling to provide information, you can log that information in the ticket. If the call is personal, or concerns a matter that requires a particular analyst, such as a special project, or if there is nothing you can do to assist the customer, offer to transfer the customer to the analyst's voice mailbox or take a message.

When transferring a caller to a voice mailbox, be careful to dial correctly so the call is not disconnected during the transfer. When appropriate, provide the customer with the telephone number of the person to whom you are transferring the call so the customer can reach that person directly in the future. Make sure that providing a direct telephone number is, however, an acceptable policy at your company. Also, learn what you can do in the event a call is inadvertently disconnected. If you have the caller's telephone number, you can call the customer back and ensure a successful transfer. Or, you can contact the person the caller was trying to reach and leave a message with the name, and, when available, telephone number of the caller.

When taking a message, write down all of the important information. Obtain the caller's name, preferred contact method such as a telephone number or email address, the required time frame for a response, and any message the caller chooses to leave. Be sure to read the information back to the caller and verify that you have gotten everything correct. The following is an example of this interaction.

> Joyce has stepped away from her desk. May I ask who is calling? (Get the caller's name.)
>
> Mr. Brown, Joyce should be back in 10 minutes. In the meantime, is there anything that I can help you with? (If not...)
>
> I can take a message for you, or I can transfer you to Joyce's voice mailbox. Which would you prefer? (If a message is preferred, record all important information. Read it back to the customer.)
>
> Okay, Mr. Brown, I have written that you would like Joyce to call you at (503) 555-1234 before the end of the day about your printer. Is there anything else that I can help you with today? (If not...)
>
> Thank you for calling, Mr. Brown. Feel free to call anytime.

Use the quickest method possible to relay the message to the analyst. If the technology is available—and particularly if the message is urgent—you may want to text the analyst, send the analyst an email message, or contact the analyst by cell phone. When using a message pad or Post-it note, place the message where the analyst will see it immediately upon his or her return. If the message is urgent, you may also want to relay the message to the analyst electronically on behalf of the customer rather than simply leaving the message on the analyst's desk.

Closing a Call

There is always something to do in technical support, and a service desk can be a particularly busy place. Because of this, a temptation exists to rush the closing of a call in an effort to take the next call or move on to the next contact. Trust and customer confidence come, however, from taking a little extra time and making sure that the customer is comfortable with the steps you have taken before you hang up the telephone. Ending the call on a positive note leaves the customer with a lasting, good impression.

Be quick, but do not hurry.

JOHN WOODEN

Figure 3-5 lists some points to consider when ending the call. Each item is important and helps close the call effectively and professionally.

Step 1: Recap the call.

Step 2: Repeat any actions that you are going to take.

Step 3: Be specific about when the customer can expect a resolution or a status update.

Step 4: Share any information that enables the customer to be more self-sufficient.

Step 5: Ask the customer if there is anything else you can do.

Step 6: Thank the customer for calling.

Step 7: Let the customer hang up first.

Figure 3-5   Steps for closing a call effectively

STEP 1: RECAP THE CALL. Take a moment to ensure that you have collected all the information needed to log the customer's incident or service request and any information that may be required by level two service providers. Verify that all the information you have collected is accurate and complete. Provide the customer a ticket number, and let the customer know how he or she can use that number to obtain a status update in the future. For example, some service desks encourage customers to call or email the service desk for status updates. Others provide customers the ability to enter the ticket number into a form on the service desk's web site to obtain a status at any time.

STEP 2: REPEAT ANY ACTION STEPS THAT YOU ARE GOING TO TAKE. Provide the customer an overview of what you are going to do. For example, "I need to try to duplicate this incident in our lab" or "I need to check with our Accounting department to verify the correct policy." If the incident must be escalated to level two, let the customer know that. Remember to resist the temptation to impart too much information. The customer usually does not need to know the name of the person who will be working on the incident. You may not even know that yourself. Keep it simple, as shown in the following example.

Dr. Rogers, I'm assigning this ticket to the network administration group. They will be able to make this change to your account.

STEP 3: BE SPECIFIC ABOUT WHEN THE CUSTOMER CAN EXPECT A RESOLUTION OR A STATUS UPDATE. This is one of the greatest challenges in technical support. On the one hand, customers do not want vague time frames, such as "We'll get to it as soon as possible." On the other hand, level two support groups are sometimes hesitant to commit to deadlines they may not be able to meet. This is not a problem you can solve. It is up to your management team to establish SLAs that clearly define the time frame within which incidents and service requests must be handled. Then you can state these guaranteed times to your customers.

As shown in Table 3-1, most companies establish guidelines for target resolution times that consider the incident priority and the combined efforts of service providers in level one, level two, and level three that may be called upon to resolve an incident. A **target resolution time** is the time frame within which the support organization is expected to resolve an incident. ITIL defines **priority** as a category used to define the relative importance of an incident, problem, or change and is based on impact and urgency. In other words, priority determines the order in which incidents, problems, or changes are handled. ITIL defines **impact** as the effect an incident, problem, or change is having on business processes. For example, an incident that affects many customers is typically considered to have a higher impact than an incident that affects one customer. Other factors that influence impact include risk to life or limb, potential financial loss or regulatory breach, and the role of the customer. Incidents affecting very important people (VIPs) such as executives or high-ranking politicians are often assigned a higher impact.

Criteria for determining impact, urgency, priority, and target resolution time are typically defined in SLAs or, in the absence of SLAs, an organization's policies and procedures.

As defined by ITIL, **urgency** is a measure of how long it will be until an incident, problem, or change has a significant impact on the business. Impact and urgency combine to determine priority. Typically, the service desk analyst and the customer determine the priority of an incident together.

Priority	Definition	Example
1	System or device down, critical business impact such as loss of revenue, no workaround available, begin resolution activities immediately, bypass/recover within 1 hour, resolve within 4 hours.	A network device is not working and many customers are affected. The only printer that can print checks or special forms is malfunctioning. A real-time critical application, such as payroll or the company's web site, is down.
2	System or component down or level of service degraded, potential business impact, alternative or workaround available, resolve within 8 hours.	A slow response time on the network is severely affecting a large number of customers. The network is down, but customers can temporarily work offline. A product is usable, but its use is restricted due to memory constraints.
3	Not critical, customer can wait, a workaround is possible, resolve within 24 hours.	A printer is down, but customers can route their output to a similar printer down the hall. One of many registers in a retail store is down at a slow time of the month.
4	Not critical, customer can wait, a workaround is possible with no operational impact, resolve within 48 hours or negotiate time with customer.	Intermittent errors that the customer can work around. One of two speakers attached to a PC is not working.

Table 3-1   Sample priority definitions

The priority assigned to an incident often considers the availability of a workaround. A **workaround** is a temporary way to circumvent or minimize the impact of an incident. For example, helping a customer route his report to a printer down the hall when the printer in his office is jammed is an excellent workaround. The jammed printer must still be repaired, but because a workaround is available, the incident has a lower impact, and the target resolution time is therefore greater.

Make sure you understand the priority definitions for any company where you work. More importantly, make sure you understand the target resolution time associated with each priority so you can be specific when telling a customer when to expect a resolution or a status update. Promising a swift resolution may make a customer happy in the short term; however, the customer will become dissatisfied and distrusting if the support organization cannot deliver a resolution in the time promised.

In the absence of SLAs, you can work closely with level two support groups to gain an understanding of their workload. Then, even if you cannot provide an estimated resolution time, you can let the customer know where his or her incident or service request stands in the backlog. That is, you can tell the customer how many incidents or service requests the support group must handle before they get to this customer's ticket. If nothing else, you can explain how the customer can easily obtain a status update or offer to call the customer at an agreed upon time with a status update, particularly if the customer is being impacted by a high-priority incident. Another approach is to provide the customer a time frame within which level two will contact him or her to schedule a time to work on the incident or service request, as shown in the following example.

> Someone from the field services group will contact you within the next 2 hours to schedule a time when they can come out and configure your device.

Many organizations provide a time range within which service will be provided, such as between 9 a.m. and noon tomorrow, and then provide a more specific time when that information is available.

STEP 4: SHARE ANY INFORMATION THAT ENABLES THE CUSTOMER TO BE MORE SELF-SUFFICIENT. Although the service desk's role is to support customers, service desk analysts best serve their customers when they enable them to help themselves. When appropriate, let customers know they can use resources such as online help or the Internet to find answers to FAQs or solutions to common incidents. You can also let customers know alternate ways to request support. For example, customers may not know that they can use email or chat to contact the service desk or that they can download and electronically submit forms from a web site. If a customer does not have the time to discuss these options, let the customer know that you will email information that describes alternative ways to obtain support and self-service options.

STEP 5: ASK THE CUSTOMER IF THERE IS ANYTHING ELSE YOU CAN DO. Analysts are sometimes hesitant to ask if they can do more for a customer because they are afraid the customer will say "yes." This is particularly true in a busy service desk where contacts are stacking up in the queue. The only alternative is to have the customer hang up and call back. This is neither practical nor good customer service. Although difficult, do not worry about the next call until you have fully satisfied the current customer. If the customer does have another incident or service request to report, politely ask the customer to wait for a moment while you complete the first ticket. Then handle the next incident or service request as a new ticket. If the customer has an incident or service request that is beyond the service desk's mission (for example, the customer may ask you to have someone come out and repair the soda machine in the break room near his or her office), use the techniques discussed in the "Handling Calls About Unsupported Products or Services" section of this chapter to direct the customer to the group or company that can handle the request.

STEP 6: THANK THE CUSTOMER FOR CALLING. Remember that whether you are supporting internal customers or external customers, they are indeed customers, and you have a job because they need your help. Always thank your customers for calling, and let them know they should not hesitate to call if they need help in the future.

STEP 7: LET THE CUSTOMER HANG UP FIRST. We have all experienced the frustration of getting cut off midsentence. This frustration is even greater when we must work our way through a series of menu options or wait in a queue to get back to the service provider. By letting the customer hang up first, you avoid rushing the customer or cutting the customer off. If the customer seems to be waiting for you to hang up, tactfully ask, "Is there anything else?" If not, then go ahead and hang up the telephone. As a courtesy to the customer, make sure the line disconnects before you begin talking to yourself, a coworker, or another customer.

The following examples demonstrate how to close a call that the analyst has not been able to resolve as well as how to close a call that the analyst has resolved.

After searching unsuccessfully for an answer: Liz, I have logged your incident and your ticket number is 40304. I am going to assign this ticket to the database administration group. You can expect this incident to be resolved within 2 hours. Is there anything else that I can help you with today? (If not...)

Thank you for calling the service desk. If you need further help or would like a status update, please feel free to give us a call.

After finding the answer and giving it to the caller: Kevin, did you know that you can find similar information on our web site? (If the customer did not...)

The address of our web site is *www.example.com*. Other information you'll find includes answers to FAQs and information about our other products. Is there anything else that I can help you with today? (If yes...)

Okay, please give me a moment while I save your first request. (Update and save the ticket.)

Now, what else can I help you with?

When possible, log all important information in the ticket before you hang up the telephone or, if necessary, immediately after you hang up the telephone. Use the first couple of moments after you hang up the telephone to complete the ticket and, if necessary, escalate the call properly. Again, this can be difficult when there are other calls in the queue or other customers waiting, but this is time well spent and it ensures that the customer receives the best possible service. It also ensures that anyone else who works on the ticket has the most up-to-date information.

A common misperception is that service desk analysts and people whose job consists primarily of handling telephone calls are the only ones who must develop professional telephone skills. Managers and level two service providers, particularly highly specialized technicians, often believe they do not need telephone skills because it is the service desk's job to handle calls. Not true. On any given day, anyone may receive telephone calls and may need to place a caller on hold or transfer a caller to another person or group. In a business environment where telephones are a common communication tool, excellent telephone skills are indispensable regardless of your position.

Avoiding the Most Common Telephone Mistakes

Two things that most frustrate customers are being placed on hold for an extended period and being transferred repeatedly. Pay attention when you are the customer. How do you feel when someone asks, "Can you hold please?" and then puts you on hold without waiting for a response? How do you feel when you have given a service provider a detailed explanation and they transfer you to someone else who asks, "May I help you?" and you have to begin again? When working in a service desk, it is sometimes appropriate to place a customer on hold or transfer the customer to another service provider. The proven techniques that follow enable you to conduct these transactions in a way that engages your customer and minimizes frustration.

Avoid embarrassment and customer frustration by understanding how to use your company's telephone system to put customers on hold and transfer customer calls. Follow available policies and procedures, or request training to be confident that you will not inadvertently disconnect your customers.

Putting a Customer on Hold

At times it will be necessary to put a customer on hold while you look up information or consult with another service provider. You may need to put a customer on hold if someone is in front of you demanding your attention and is urgently insisting on speaking with you. If you have one customer on hold for an extended period of time and another customer who is receiving only half of your attention, it is likely that neither customer will be satisfied. The best practice is to focus your energies on one customer at a time. Remember that it takes only a little extra time to put customers on hold in a professional manner that instills confidence. It is also important to let customers decide if they would prefer to have you call back rather than being placed on hold. Figure 3-6 lists some points to remember when placing a caller on hold.

1. Ask the customer if you can put him or her on hold.

2. Tell the customer why he or she is being put on hold.

3. Tell the customer approximately how long to expect to be on hold.

4. Wait for the customer to respond.

5. Use the Hold button on your telephone to place a customer on hold.

6. When you return, thank the customer for holding.

Figure 3-6   Steps for putting customers on hold

1. **Ask the customer if you can put him or her on hold.** Put yourself in the customer's shoes. Do you find it frustrating when someone puts you on hold without giving you a choice?

2. **Tell the customer why he or she is being put on hold.** If you need to investigate the error message or consult an expert, briefly explain that to the customer. It will instill confidence in the customer and create trust.

3. **Tell the customer approximately how long to expect to be on hold.** Be realistic when estimating the time it will take to complete that task. If you tell the customer it will take just a second, the customer will immediately mistrust the estimate. Many companies have policies such as never asking a customer to hold if you are going to be longer than 3 minutes. Others encourage analysts to check back with customers every 60 seconds to let the customers know that they have not been forgotten.

4. **Wait for the customer to respond.** If the customer does not want to be placed on hold, ask what he or she would prefer. If the customer would prefer to call back, save the information collected thus far and provide the customer a ticket number. If the customer would prefer a call back, set a time that is convenient for the customer and that you know you will be able to call. Waiting for the customer to respond before placing him or her on hold is very important. The customer may be unwilling or unable to hold and may become angry or frustrated if he or she is not given an option. The customer may even hang up the call, and so you may waste time and effort trying to find a solution.

5. **Use the Hold button on your telephone to place a customer on hold.** Resist the temptation to simply set your headset or telephone down on the desk. The customer may want to read or think while on hold and may find the background noise distracting. The customer may also hear you asking questions or interacting with other customers or service providers who have come into your workspace and perceive that you are neglecting his or her incident or service request.

6. **When you return, thank the customer for holding.** Resist the temptation to say, "I'm sorry to keep you holding." Customers may consider such a comment insincere because if you were really sorry, you would not have kept them on hold in the first place.

The following example demonstrates how to use all of these points to put a customer on hold.

Tim, may I put you on hold for approximately 2 minutes while I obtain more information? (Wait for an answer.)

Okay, I will be back with you in a minute or two. (Forty-five seconds pass.)

Thank you for holding. What I have learned is that the next release of that application will be available in 2 months.

If you find it is going to take you longer than expected to handle a particular task, return to the customer and give the customer an update on your progress and the option of either continuing to hold or receiving a call back. The important thing is to stay in control and remain sensitive to your customer's needs.

Knowing When and How to Transfer Calls

You may need to transfer a caller to another person or group for a number of reasons. The customer may ask to speak with a particular analyst, have an incident or question that requires the help of a subject matter expert, or simply have called the wrong number and must be transferred to another department. Figure 3-7 lists different ways to transfer a caller. The method used will depend on the type of call and the needs of the caller.

- Hot transfer (conference call)
- Warm transfer
- Cold transfer

Figure 3-7   Telephone transfer techniques

A primary consideration of which technique to use when transferring calls is the amount of information you have received or given until the point when you determine a transfer is needed. The following examples demonstrate when and how to use the hot, warm, and cold telephone transfer techniques.

HOT TRANSFER (CONFERENCE CALL) A **hot transfer**, or conference call, occurs when you stay on the line with the customer and the service provider whom you are engaging in the call. A conference call may be appropriate when:

- You can continue to contribute to the resolution of the customer's incident.

- You can benefit from hearing how the incident is resolved by another service desk analyst or by a specialist from another group. For example, the incident being described by the customer has been occurring frequently, and you want to learn how to resolve it in the future.

- Time allows—that is, there is no backlog of incoming calls or work in the queue.

Before you establish a conference call, inform the caller that you want to engage another service provider and ask if it is okay. If the customer does not want to stay on the line, ask what he or she would prefer. If the customer would prefer to call back, save the information collected thus far and provide the customer a ticket number. If a call back is preferred, set a time that is convenient for the customer. Make sure you clearly communicate to the other service provider the customer's expectation of when he or she wants to be contacted.

When establishing a conference call, put the customer on hold and place a call to the person whom you want to engage in the call. Briefly explain the incident or service request to the service provider along with how you feel he or she can contribute to its resolution. Ask the service provider for permission to bring the customer on the line.

Use common sense when engaging another service provider. If the incident is critical and requires immediate attention, make sure the service provider knows that. If the incident is not critical, ask the service provider whether this is a good time or whether you could schedule a more convenient time for a conference call. Being considerate is in the best interest of your customer and will also enable you to maintain a good relationship with other service providers.

Many organizations designate on-call level two or level three service providers to ensure someone is always available to handle high-priority calls.

When permission is granted, bring the customer on the line and introduce the customer and the service provider. As a courtesy to the customer, explain the reason for the conference call and relay to the service provider any information the customer has given you thus far in the call. Include any problem determination steps you and the caller have already tried. Resist the temptation to have the customer repeat everything he or she has told you as this could leave the customer with the perception that you were not listening. You can, however, engage the customer in the call by asking him or her to let you know if you restated any information incorrectly. You can also encourage the customer to jump in if he or she would like to contribute additional information. Let the customer and the service provider know you plan to stay on the line. Stay on the line until the call is completed to the customer's satisfaction. Close the call as you usually would.

WARM TRANSFER A **warm transfer** occurs when you introduce the customer and the service provider to whom you are transferring the call but you do not stay on the line. A warm transfer may be appropriate when:

- There is no perceived value to be gained or given by staying on the line. This may be because you do not feel that you can continue to contribute to the resolution of the customer's incident. Or, you do not believe you can benefit from hearing how the incident is resolved by another service desk analyst or by a specialist from another group.

- Time does not allow you to stay on the line. This may occur when there is a backlog of incoming calls in the queue or you need to attend a meeting or leave for the day.

When transferring the customer to another department, let the customer know if there will be a wait in a queue or possibly a voice mailbox.

Before you warm transfer a call, inform the caller that you want to transfer him or her to another service provider and explain why. The service provider may be a subject matter expert who is best suited to answer the customer's question. Or, the service provider may be a security administrator who has the authority to provide the customer with the requested access to a confidential system. Ask the customer for permission to transfer him or her to the service provider, as shown in the following example.

> Mrs. Higgins, I understand your urgency in this matter. Would you mind if I transferred you to our security administrator for immediate assistance? (Wait for answer.) Great. Let me see if I can get her on the line.

If the customer does not want to stay on the line, ask what he or she would prefer. If the customer would prefer to call back, save the information collected thus far and provide the customer a ticket number. If a call back is preferred, set a time that is convenient for the customer. Make sure you clearly communicate to the other service provider the customer's expectation in terms of when he or she wants to be contacted.

Your company's policy and the role of the service provider to whom you are transferring the call will determine whether you place the customer on hold first or simply transfer the call. If there is a possibility that the service provider will either not be available or not be in a position to assist, put the customer on hold and place a call to the service provider to whom you want to transfer the call. Ask the service provider for permission to bring the customer on the line. When permission is granted, bring the customer on the line. If you know the service provider is available and in a position to assist the customer, simply bring the service provider on the line.

After you have both parties on the line, introduce the customer and the service provider. As a courtesy to the customer, explain the reason you are transferring the call and relay any information you have been provided thus far in the call. Include any diagnostic steps you and the caller have already tried and explain how you think the service provider can assist. As was the case when establishing a conference call, resist the temptation to have the customer repeat everything he or she has told you. This could leave the customer with the perception that you were not listening. You can, however, engage the customer in the call by asking him or her to let you know if you restated any information incorrectly. You can also encourage the customer to jump in if he or she would like to contribute additional information. Let the caller and the service provider know that you will not be staying on the line.

After you are confident that you have relayed all important information, and both the customer and the service provider have what they need to proceed, give the customer and the service provider the ticket number assigned to the customer's incident or service request for follow-up purposes. Encourage both the customer and the service provider to let you know if there is anything else that you can do, and then hang up.

COLD TRANSFER A **cold transfer** occurs when you stay on the line only long enough to ensure that the call has been transferred successfully. A cold transfer is appropriate when:

- The customer asks to be transferred.

- You *quickly* realize that the caller has dialed the wrong telephone number or that the caller should be transferred to another person or department.

A cold transfer is *not* appropriate when the customer has provided detailed information about the nature of the incident or service request. If a customer is upset and begins venting as soon as you pick up the telephone, you want to listen actively and collect as much information as you can. When the customer has provided detailed information, use either the hot or warm transfer technique described previously.

When a cold transfer is appropriate, acknowledge the customer's request to be transferred and let the customer know you are going to transfer him or her to the correct department, as shown in the following example.

> Please hold one moment while I transfer you to the Benefits department.

When appropriate, provide the customer with the telephone number of the person or group to whom you are transferring the call so that the customer can reach that person or group directly in the future. Many companies, particularly those that provide toll-free numbers, take this approach in an effort to manage the high cost of calls to the service desk. Make sure that providing a direct telephone number is, however, an acceptable policy at your company. Some companies prefer not to give out the direct telephone numbers of employees. Instead, customers are encouraged to contact a department, such as the service desk, when they need support.

 Dial carefully when transferring a call so the customer is not cut off. If time allows, attempt a warm transfer to mitigate the risk that the customer is transferred to the wrong extension.

Handling a customer call and placing a customer on hold or transferring a customer to another service provider requires an understanding of your company's telephone system, policies, and procedures. It also requires the use of common sense and sensitivity. Pay attention when you are the customer so you can gain an appreciation of how it feels when these techniques are and are not used appropriately. By applying these techniques appropriately, you can ensure every customer feels you have fully respected his or her time and needs.

To give real service, you must add something which cannot be bought or measured with money, and that is sincerity and integrity.

DONALD A. ADAMS

Fine-Tuning Your Telephone Skills

Telephone skills, like any other skills, need to be honed. You can always learn new techniques, and you can periodically rekindle your skills by attending a refresher course. New best practices are constantly emerging that you can use to improve your skills. Also, sometimes analysts just need to get back to the basics of excellent service: being responsive, demonstrating a caring attitude, and acknowledging the fact that customers are living, breathing human beings who have called because they need your help. This last point is particularly important when interacting with customers over the telephone, a technology that can be viewed as very impersonal.

CASE STUDY: Speakerphone Etiquette

© iStock.com/philsajonesen

*A **speakerphone** is a telephone that contains both a loudspeaker and a microphone. It allows several people to participate in a call at the same time without the telephone receiver being held. In some service desk settings, the use of speakerphones is discouraged for a number of reasons. First, many people do not feel comfortable talking on a speakerphone because they do not know who else may be listening. Second, the quality of some speakerphones makes it difficult for the customer and the analyst to understand everything that is being said. Last, speakerphones can be disruptive to coworkers and may make it difficult for them to hear other customers. There are times, however, when speakerphones are appropriate, such as when the team is working together to resolve an incident or when the team is holding an informal meeting to exchange new information or a new set of procedures. In these cases, steps can be taken to minimize the noise generated by the conversation being held via speakerphone. The following techniques can be used to minimize the negative effects of using a speakerphone:*

- *If possible, use the speakerphone behind closed doors.*
- *Ask all callers for permission before using a speakerphone.*
- *Introduce each person who is present.*
- *Briefly explain why each person is present.*
- *Participants who are speaking for the first time or who are unfamiliar to other callers may want to identify themselves before they speak.*

Speakerphones enable multiple people, regardless of their location, to work together. They minimize the problems that can occur when information is relayed second hand. Speakerphones also free people to use their hands to take notes, consult reference materials, and so forth. Used properly, speakerphones are an effective communication tool.

Continuously improving your telephone skills enables you to feel more comfortable and confident as a service provider, and also lets your customers know you care and sincerely want to help. As listed in Figure 3-8, you can use a number of techniques to fine-tune your telephone skills. Many of these techniques can be used to improve all of your skills—business, technical, soft, and self-management—not just your telephone skills.

- Self-study
- Monitoring
- Customer satisfaction surveys

Figure 3-8 Techniques to improve telephone skills

Self-Study

There are literally hundreds of books, videos, and podcasts available that you can use to improve your telephone skills and your skills in general. Occasional refresher courses and continuing education benefit even the most seasoned professionals. When you work in a service desk, take advantage of any training programs that are offered. Bring to the attention of your supervisor or team leader any training possibilities that you think will help. You can also engage in a self-study program by checking out books, CDs, or DVDs from your local library.

Appendix A lists books, magazines, and organizations you can use to obtain self-study training materials and additional information about the support industry in general.

Monitoring

A supervisor or team leader may monitor an analyst's interactions with customers to measure the quality of the analyst's performance. When monitoring, a supervisor or team leader may listen to a live or recorded call, observe an analyst's data entry and keystrokes during an email or chat session, or sit beside an analyst to watch an analyst interact with a customer. Used properly, monitoring is an excellent training technique because analysts receive specific feedback on how they can improve their contact handling. Monitoring also promotes the consistent handling of contacts and provides employees and supervisors specific guidelines to use when measuring performance. Some companies use monitoring only for training purposes. Others use monitoring both as a training tool and as a way of measuring performance.

Varying techniques and technologies are used to monitor service desk calls. Managers may simply walk around and observe calls being handled, or they may sit side by side with a particular analyst to monitor not only what the analyst is saying, but also how the analyst is following established procedures and using available systems. Some managers can plug in a headset when sitting next to an analyst, making it possible for them to hear the customer's side of the call along with the analyst's. Monitoring systems make it possible for managers to silently monitor calls from their office or review recorded calls at a later time or date. Voice and screen monitoring systems enable service desk managers to remotely review the conversation between a customer and an analyst as well as the keystrokes the analyst used while logging and handling the call. Voice and screen monitoring systems are highly complex and expensive. They are typically found in only large service desk and call or contact center settings.

To be effective, a monitoring program must be implemented carefully and analysts must perceive they are being given the opportunity to be successful. Most companies involve the service desk staff when designing their monitoring program so the staff is comfortable with the program and participates willingly. For example, management and staff may jointly define guidelines for how and when employees will be monitored. They may agree to monitor only recorded calls or to silently monitor live calls five times each month. Other guidelines include agreeing not to monitor partial calls or personal calls and placing a higher **weight**, or importance, on items in an effort to ensure analysts are focusing on the right things. For example, companies may assign a higher weight to delivering the correct solution than they assign to using a standard script to place a call on hold.

One key to a successful monitoring program is providing analysts with a checklist or scorecard that describes the specific criteria that supervisors or team leaders are using to measure the quality of a call. As shown in Figure 3-9, this checklist typically reflects all of the critical interactions that occur during the course of a telephone call. Checklist items may include using the service desk's standard script when answering the telephone or waiting for customers to respond before placing them on hold. Checklist items may also include items such as analysts' tone of voice, posture, use of knowledge resources, and so forth, as all of these items influence analysts' ability to deliver great service. Without a checklist, analysts are unsure what supervisors and team leaders are looking for when they monitor calls and, therefore, may perceive the results as subjective.

Used properly, monitoring enables you to put yourself in the customer's shoes and objectively assess the quality of your service from the customer's perspective. An effective monitoring program provides specific feedback that you can use and apply day to day.

MONITORING CHECKLIST

❑ Use standard greeting:
  • Service desk. This is Andy. How may I help you?

❑ Listen actively:
  • Respond to the customer (uh-huh, I see, I understand).
  • Ask questions.
  • Verify understanding (state back, paraphrase).
  • Listen to *what* is being said and *how* it is being said.

❑ Demonstrate a *can do* attitude:
  • Be positive and caring.
  • Avoid negatives (such as I can't, We don't, etc.).

❑ Build rapport:
  • Use the customer's name (including titles when appropriate, such as Dr., Professor, etc.).

❑ Ask skill-assessing questions (when appropriate).

❑ Collect required information (that is, to log the call):
  • Verify existing information when available (vs. asking the customer to provide information you already have).
  • Ask for information in the same order every time.

❑ Diagnose the incident:
  • Use diagnostic scripts and problem-solving checklists.
  • Use available systems (such as incident management systems, knowledge management systems, etc.).

❑ If the incident must be escalated:
  • Determine the priority.
  • Recap next steps.
  • Provide an incident number.
  • Provide a workaround (if possible).

❑ If a solution can be provided:
  • Deliver the solution at the customer's skill level.
  • Explain any self-service options the customer can use in the future (when appropriate).

❑ Verify customer satisfaction.

❑ Use standard closing:
  • Ask if there is anything else you can do.
  • Thank the customer for calling.
  • Let the customer hang up first.

Figure 3-9 Sample monitoring checklist

Customer Satisfaction Surveys

A necessity for the service desk is to solicit feedback from customers by conducting customer satisfaction surveys, which provide the customer's *perception* of the support services they received. The two most common customer satisfaction surveys are event-driven surveys and overall satisfaction surveys. **Event-driven surveys** are customer satisfaction surveys that ask customers for feedback on a single, recent service event. **Overall satisfaction surveys** are customer satisfaction surveys that ask customers for feedback about all contacts with the service desk during a certain time period.

 Event-driven and overall satisfaction surveys may be used to measure satisfaction with all contact types including telephone calls, email, chat, and web forms. These surveys are often sent to customers via email and may include a link to a web-based survey.

Service desk managers use survey responses to measure the performance of the service desk team and to identify improvement opportunities. Survey responses, particularly responses to event-driven surveys, can also be used to measure individual performance and identify training needs. The feedback that customers provide via event-driven surveys is particularly useful to individual analysts because it represents feedback about a specific event that the analyst handled. Analysts can use this feedback to improve their telephone skills.

If the service desk where you work does not have a monitoring program or it does not conduct customer satisfaction surveys, you can still receive feedback. You can listen actively to your customers when you are providing support. For example, if a customer begins to raise his or her voice, check your tone of voice to ensure you are remaining calm and making positive statements. You can also ask a trusted coworker or your team leader to provide feedback. Ask for feedback not only when you need to improve, but when you handle a situation efficiently and effectively as well.

 One of the best ways to improve your telephone skills is to record and review your calls. If the technology is available, ask to review recorded calls on a periodic basis. If not, place a recording device on your desk and record your calls so you can hear how you sound and determine ways to improve.

Regardless of the method used to obtain feedback, analysts can use the feedback their customers and coworkers provide to identify their weaknesses and determine ways they can improve. It is important to remember that your recollection of an event and another's perception of an event may represent different perspectives. When working in a service desk, you must follow the policies of your company while being sensitive to the needs of your customers, other service providers, and coworkers. If a customer perceives that you were rude or disrespectful, you must accept that and determine a more positive way to communicate in the future. If a service provider perceives that you did not relay all important information before you transferred a call, you must accept that and vow to slow down and be more thorough in the future. By working hard, being consistent, and keeping a positive attitude, you can let your caring attitude shine through.

INTERVIEW WITH...

Courtesy of Benjamin Compton

BENJAMIN COMPTON
TECO ENERGY
IT SERVICE QUALITY ANALYST
www.tecoenergy.com
The TECO Energy Service Desk supports 5,000 internal customers located in 34 offices in Florida and five offices in Kentucky.
The service desk has a total of eight analysts that handle level one
support, along with an IT service quality analyst, a manager, and
a director. The TECO Energy Service Desk is the proud recipient
of the 2009 HDI Team Excellence Award for internal support.

Question: What is your background, and how did you become an IT service quality analyst?

Answer: I have 20 years experience in IT and spent many of those years in application
development. I also have a background in organizational learning and was involved in helping
an organization achieve ISO 9000 certification. ISO 9000 is a family of International Standards for Quality Management Systems. I realized that I enjoyed helping people more than
writing code and joined the service desk in 2007. My job is to help improve the performance
of our people, processes, and technology while also creating a culture that is engaging and
growth promoting. The management team at TECO Energy is committed to helping people
succeed by ensuring they know what is expected of them and that they have the tools to do
their job.

Question: What channels are used to receive contacts at the service desk?

Answer: The primary channel is the telephone. We also have a self-service tool that
customers can use to report incidents and service requests via the service desk's web site. We
eliminated email as a channel after realizing that it was difficult to manage and measure. It
often delayed service by requiring multiple exchanges to deliver a solution. We developed a
communication plan to help customers transition from email to the web self-service site. The
change has not affected our customer satisfaction. In fact, customer satisfaction has gone up
since we made the change.

Question: How is the service desk structured?

Answer: We have eight analysts who report to the service desk manager. On a rotation basis,
one analyst is always in the field providing desk side support and another analyst handles
tickets submitted via the service desk's web site. The remaining analysts handle telephone
calls.

Question: How do you measure team and individual performance?

Answer: Our team and individual performance metrics are the same and are linked to the
IT department's goals, which are linked to business drivers. We periodically hold customer
focus groups and regularly survey our customers to ensure we're focused on helping the

company achieve its goals. Our key performance indicators (KPIs) are divided into two categories: cost and quality. We set targets for each KPI and then measure individual and team performance on a daily and monthly basis. For cost, we measure call answer rate and strive to answer 95 percent of calls presented. We measure average speed of answer and are just under our target of answering all calls within 40 seconds. We measure mean time to resolve incidents and have targets that reflect the priority and nature of the incident. For quality, we measure both first contact and first level resolution. Our target is to resolve 72 percent of incidents on first contact (while the customer is on the telephone). We are exceeding our target to resolve 75 percent of contacts "at the desk," which means that while we weren't able to deliver a solution via the telephone, we were able to resolve the incident using only the service desk's resources.

Question: What techniques do you use to measure customer satisfaction?

Answer: This is our most important metric. We have a goal of 96 percent customer satisfaction. We are achieving 98 percent. To measure customer satisfaction, we send customers a survey via email for every fifth call handled on first contact and for every contact that is not solved on first contact. The results are compiled weekly and provided, along with comments, to each individual analyst. I personally follow up on any negative comments to determine how we can satisfy that customer and how we can improve. Also, all calls are recorded along with screen captures and we randomly monitor calls for quality. In addition to ensuring analysts are following procedures such as always asking for permission before placing a customer on hold, we use monitoring to identify lessons learned and opportunities to improve. We provide individual coaching as needed, review individual performance metrics with each analyst every month, and periodically compile generic feedback for the entire team.

One of the critical factors for determining customer satisfaction is focus groups. Focus groups allow customers to tell us directly whether or not we are meeting their expectations. A transactional survey (related to a ticket) tells the story of a single experience. A focus group tells a much broader and more poignant story. Focus groups provide us the type of feedback that allows for transformational change.

Question: Are there performance metrics that you only use internally?

Answer: Yes. For example, we measure daily (but don't publish) cost per contact to ensure our services are cost-effective and in line with industry norms. We also measure analyst utilization (time spent on the phone working with a customer). We publish a team utilization rate internally and provide individuals their results via an individual scorecard. These measurements are not part of our goals, and we do not use them for coaching. They simply help the service desk analysts see the business side of their work.

Question: What techniques do you use to capture quality data and produce meaningful metrics?

Answer: That is a great challenge. Metrics are a slippery duck. If you're just starting out, it will take much iteration before you get them right. We start by focusing on what customers have told us is important to them in focus groups. Then, each metric goes through a vetting process to ensure we are capturing the right data, not double dipping and counting the same data twice, and creating the right formula.

Question: What techniques do you use to help analysts understand how their performance is being measured?

Answer: Analysts are provided the equations used to measure performance and are also given training on how to correctly use their tools to collect quality data. We also provide analysts with a booklet, called *"The Story Behind the Numbers"*, that explains what is being measured and why. Analysts also review their performance metrics on a monthly basis with the service desk manager. Questions about metrics can be asked and resolved in those meetings.

Question: Congratulations on achieving the HDI Team Excellence award. Is benchmarking your performance important?

Answer: It is because benchmarking our performance against other organizations is another way that we can identify opportunities to improve. We also participate annually in a consortium that enables us to benchmark our performance against our peers in the utility industry.

Question: Have you adopted any industry frameworks or standards to guide your improvement efforts?

Answer: Yes. We've adopted the ITIL framework and are using it to improve all areas of IT. Using ITIL really helped elevate the importance of the service desk and enabled people to understand the important role it plays in the incident management process. More than 80 percent of our customer's perception of IT comes from what the service desk does, and so we've got to take it seriously. ITIL helps us understand how to improve our processes and how to measure our performance. It also emphasizes holding people accountable for their efforts.

Question: It seems you use performance measures in a very positive way.

Answer: We do. A key to our success is that the entire management team is extremely focused on people. I would estimate that 45 to 50 percent of our management team's time is devoted to helping people succeed. We are constantly looking for ways to help people get better at doing their job. We don't want to hear excuses. We want people to be accountable for their performance and accept reality. Once people accept reality we can help them improve. Performance measures provide both the team and individuals with opportunities to improve. They enable analysts to build confidence and to develop a story they can use to help progress their careers. We let analysts know that if they don't hit their numbers for a given period of time, it's okay. If they do the right things and focus on improving, the numbers will follow.

Letting Your Caring Attitude Shine Through

It is difficult to handle incidents and enthusiastically answer questions day in and day out. Some days it seems as if you have to drag the facts from customers who want their incidents solved NOW! It is even harder to be "up" for each call, but that is what is required if your goal is to be excellent. Providing superior customer support is a habit—a state of mind that requires enthusiasm and passion. You have to work at it every day, and you have to take care of yourself in the process. Practice relaxing, and surround yourself with positive reminders of your commitment to customer satisfaction.

Using scripts is an excellent habit-building technique and ensures a consistent experience when customers call the service desk. Scripts are not meant, however, to make you behave like a robot, never deviating from predefined remarks. Try to avoid rushing through scripts or using a tone of voice that implies tedium or boredom. When appropriate and allowed, change the phrasing of your script slightly to make it sound fresh and enthusiastic. For example, rather than always saying, "Feel free to call us if you need help in the future," you can say, "Give us a call if there is anything else you need." What you say is important, and the words you use must be positive, but *how* you say it is equally as important. Be enthusiastic!

Become familiar with all of the scripts used at the service desk where you work and, when needed, suggest additional scripts.

It is also important to remember that service desks that respond to calls in a *consistent* manner are perceived as more professional than those that do not. When service desk analysts respond to calls in different ways, customers may be uncomfortable during the call-handling process, or they may begin to mistrust the responses they receive. When working in a service desk, you must understand your company's policies and resist the temptation to deviate from those policies, even when you perceive that doing so is in your customer's best interests. If you feel a policy needs to be changed, provide your team leader or supervisor with the reasons why you believe a change is needed and suggest reasonable alternatives. Until the policy is changed, be a team player, and support the policies of your company in a positive way that acknowledges the needs of your customers.

Remember that there is always something you *can do*.

Chapter Summary

- The telephone is one of the most common ways that businesses and customers communicate. Telephone technologies used by service desks range from simple voice mailboxes and fax machines to highly complex technologies, such as Voice over Internet Protocol (VoIP), automatic call distributors (ACDs), and voice response units (VRUs). When implemented properly, these technologies benefit customers and service desk analysts.

- To be excellent, service providers must see each and every customer encounter as critical to the success of the organization. Critical interactions that occur in the course of a typical service desk call include answering the call, taking a message, and closing the call. Handling calls about unsupported products is also important and represents an excellent opportunity to demonstrate your *can do* attitude.

- Two things that frustrate customers most are being placed on hold for an extended period of time and being transferred repeatedly. Placing customers on hold or transferring them to another service provider requires an understanding of your company's telephone system, policies, and procedures. It also requires the use of common sense and sensitivity. You can minimize customer frustration by listening to your customers' preferences and carefully managing their expectations.

- Telephone skills, like any other skills, need to be honed. Techniques you can use to fine-tune your skills include self-study, monitoring, and customer satisfaction surveys. You can use each of these techniques to obtain feedback that you then can use to improve your skills. You can also record and listen to your calls, or you can ask a trusted coworker or your team leader for feedback. Ask for feedback about what you do well along with what areas you can improve.

- Providing superior customer support is hard work. You have to work at it every day, and you have to develop good habits. Scripts are an excellent habit-building technique and ensure consistency when customers call the service desk. It is also important to take care of yourself, stay relaxed, and let your caring, *can do* attitude shine through!

Key Terms

announcement system—Technology that greets callers when all service desk analysts are busy and can provide valuable information as customers wait on hold.

automated attendant—An ACD feature that routes calls based on input provided by the caller through a touch-tone telephone.

automatic number identification (ANI)—A service provided by a long-distance service provider that discloses the telephone number of the person calling.

available state—An ACD state that occurs when an analyst is ready to take calls.

best effort—A policy that states analysts do their best to assist a customer within a predefined set of boundaries, such as a time limit.

caller identification (caller ID)—A service provided by a local telephone company that discloses the telephone number of the person calling and, where available, the name associated with the calling telephone number.

cold transfer—A way of transferring a telephone call when you stay on the line only long enough to ensure that the call has been transferred successfully.

computer telephony integration (CTI)—The linking of computing technology with telephone technology to exchange information and increase productivity.

event-driven survey—A customer satisfaction survey that asks customers for feedback on a single, recent service event.

fax—An image of a document that is electronically transmitted to a telephone number connected to a printer or other output device; short for *facsimile*.

hot transfer—A way of transferring a telephone call when you stay on the line with the customer and the service provider whom you are engaging in the call; also known as a *conference call*.

impact—A measure of the effect an incident, problem, or change is having on business processes (ITIL definition).

off-the-shelf—A personal computer software product that is developed and distributed commercially.

overall satisfaction survey—A customer satisfaction survey that asks customers for feedback about all contacts with the service desk during a certain time period.

priority—A category that defines the relative importance of an incident, problem, or change and that is based on impact and urgency (ITIL definition).

queue—A line; can be used to refer to a list of calls, tickets, email messages, or chat requests waiting to be processed.

recording system—Technology that records and plays back telephone calls.

screen pop—A CTI function that enables information about the caller to appear, or pop up, on an analyst's monitor based on caller information captured by the telephone system and passed to a computer system.

script—A standard set of text and behaviors.

skills-based routing (SBR)—An ACD feature that matches the requirements of an incoming call to the skill sets of available analysts or analyst groups; the ACD then distributes the call to the next available, appropriately qualified analyst.

speakerphone—A telephone that contains both a loudspeaker and a microphone.

target resolution time—The time frame within which the support organization is expected to resolve an incident.

ticket—A term commonly used to describe a record stored in a database that contains the details of a customer contact; also known as *case*, *incident*, *log*, *record*, and *service request*.

urgency—A measure of how long it will be until an incident, problem, or change has a significant impact on the business (ITIL definition).

voice mail—An automated form of taking messages from callers.

Voice over Internet Protocol (VoIP)—A technology that translates voice communications into data and then transmits that data across an Internet connection or network.

voice response unit (VRU)—A technology that integrates with another technology, such as a database or a network management system, to obtain information or to perform a function; also called an interactive voice response unit (IVRU).

warm transfer—A way of transferring a telephone call that occurs when you introduce the customer and the service provider to whom you are transferring the call but you do not stay on the line.

weight—A rating scale of importance.

workaround—A temporary way to circumvent or minimize the impact of an incident.

wrap-up mode—A feature that prevents the ACD from routing a new inbound call to an analyst's extension.

Review Questions

1. What do professional telephone skills ensure?

2. Why is it important that calls are handled consistently?

3. List four factors that influence the telephone technologies used by a service desk.

4. Describe the benefits of VoIP in a service desk setting.

5. What two things must be done for customers to view voice mail positively?

6. Do you need to log customer incidents and service requests that are received via voice mail and fax? Explain your answer.

7. List four of the capabilities that ACDs provide.

8. How is skills-based routing different from normal ACD routing?

9. A VRU integrates with another technology to do what? Provide one example.

10. How does a VRU obtain information?

11. What is a screen pop?

12. Describe three of the benefits that service desk analysts receive when telephone technology is implemented properly.

13. List four critical interactions that influence a customer's perception of your professional telephone skills when handling a telephone call.

14. How can scripts be used by service desk analysts?

15. What are two techniques you can use *before* you answer the telephone to ensure you are ready?

16. What three pieces of information should you provide or ask when answering the telephone?

17. It is always acceptable to use a customer's first name. True or False? Explain your answer.

18. Why should you ask customers for the information you need to log calls in the same order every time?

19. When there is more than one person in the service desk, why should you avoid encouraging customers to speak with only you?

20. Why are service desks able to deliver high-quality support for supported (versus unsupported) products and services?

21. Describe four pitfalls of assisting customers with incidents relating to unsupported products.

22. What should you do if a customer asks to speak with an analyst who is unavailable?

23. What are four important pieces of information that you should obtain when taking a message?

24. List the seven steps you should follow when closing a call.

25. How long should customers be kept on hold?

26. What is an important point to remember before you put customers on hold?

27. Briefly describe the differences between hot, warm, and cold transfers.

28. When using the hot or warm technique to transfer a call, why should you resist the temptation to have customers repeat everything they already told you?

29. List two ways you can improve your telephone skills through self-study.

30. What does monitoring promote?

31. What can you learn from customer satisfaction surveys?

32. What three things can you do to obtain feedback if your company does not have a monitoring program or it does not conduct customer satisfaction surveys?

33. How might customers respond when analysts handle calls inconsistently?

34. What do you do when there is nothing you can do?

Discussion Questions

1. Generally speaking, do companies that use sophisticated telephone technologies implement them in a way that benefits the company, its customers, or both? Explain your answer.

2. A customer calls on a cell phone and you can barely hear her. What should you do?

3. Monitoring calls can be perceived positively or negatively by analysts. Some analysts feel it is a form of spying, or a way to catch them doing something wrong. Other analysts feel it is an excellent way for them to receive feedback and improve their skills. What factors do you think influence how an analyst feels about monitoring? How do you feel about monitoring?

Hands-On Projects

1. **Track telephone technology usage.** For 1 week, keep a record of every time you encounter telephone technology when conducting personal or work-related business. Jot down the name of the company, the technology that you encountered (if you can tell), and a grade (such as A, B, or C) that reflects how well you perceive the company used the technology and the techniques discussed in this chapter. For example, if you

were prompted to leave a voice mail message, were you given an indication when your call would be returned? Briefly comment on any ways these companies could improve their use of telephone technology. Summarize the results in a report.

2. **Discuss the pros and cons of VRUs.** Assemble a team of at least three classmates or use your school's online message or discussion board. Discuss the different ways you use VRUs in the course of going about your day. The indicator that you are using a VRU is having to input information by using the keys on your touch-tone telephone or speaking into the telephone. For example, you may use a VRU at your bank to determine your current balance or whether a check has cleared. Or, you may use a VRU to register for classes at your school. Develop a list that describes the positive benefits of using this technology and the negative or frustrating experiences that you and your teammates have had. As a class, prepare a brief summary of your conclusions.

3. **Answer the telephone with a smile.** It has been said that if you do something for 21 days, it becomes a habit. For the next 21 days, practice putting a smile on your face before you answer the telephone, both at work and at home. To remind yourself to smile, place a note or mirror by your telephone. Strive to convey energy and enthusiasm in your tone of voice. Share with your classmates any feedback you received from callers.

4. **Explain an analyst's absence in a positive way.** Review the following phrases and suggest ways the statements can be made more positive. Prepare a list of revised statements along with a brief explanation of your suggested revision.

   a. I don't know where Jim is. I'll have him call you when he gets back.

   b. I think she has gone to the restroom. Can I have her call you back?

   c. He's probably still at lunch. Do you want to try back in a while?

   d. I think Louisa is coming in tomorrow. I'll have her call you if she does.

   e. Judy went home early today. Can I have her call you tomorrow?

   f. Mr. Sanchez has not come in yet. Would you like to try again in an hour or so?

   g. Deborah is really busy right now. Would you like to leave a message?

5. **Take complete messages.** When you are required to take a message for someone, whether at work or at home, collect all of the information discussed in this chapter. Ask the recipient of the message for feedback on the completeness of your message. Assess your ability to take complete and accurate messages.

6. **Look for a "thank you."** For the next 24 hours, note how many service providers and customers thank you for your business or help. Service providers can include the clerk at a local retail store or the waiter at a restaurant where you dine. Customers can be internal or external to the company where you work, or they can be coworkers or classmates that you are helping with a project. Write a brief summary of your observations.

7. **Pay attention when you are the customer.** Over the course of several telephone calls, pay attention any time you are put on hold or transferred to another person or group. Note any situations wherein you experience frustration as a result of the way your call was handled or any times you were cut off. If your call was transferred, determine whether a hot, warm, or cold transfer was used. Note whether you were asked to repeat any information when your call was transferred. Write a brief summary of your experiences.

8. **Learn about the importance of telephone skills.** Interview a friend, family member, or classmate who uses the telephone extensively at work. (It does not have to be a service desk.) Ask this person the following questions:

   a. Which telephone technologies are used at your company?

   b. How do you perceive the effectiveness of each of these technologies?

   c. Do you use scripts when answering the telephone, placing customers on hold, and so forth? If yes, what are the scripts?

   d. What techniques do you use to improve your telephone skills?

   e. What techniques are used to measure your telephone skills (for example, monitoring or customer satisfaction surveys)?

   f. In what ways do you find the feedback derived from these techniques useful?

   g. What habits have you developed that enable you to have positive telephone interactions with customers?

   Write a brief report that summarizes what you learned from this person. Present your conclusions to the class, or share your conclusions via your class message board.

Case Projects

1. **WRK Systems, Inc.** You have been hired as a consultant to help a new service desk develop scripts and call-handling procedures. The service desk has an incident management system that uses the customer's product number to retrieve the customer's profile. The service desk manager wants analysts to request this information when answering the telephone. Develop a script that analysts can use when answering the telephone. Propose the script to the service desk manager, and explain the benefits of having analysts say what you are suggesting.

2. **Shoe String Budget.** The service desk you work for has a very limited budget. Your boss asked you to determine what self-study aids can be used to improve the telephone skills of your team. Go to your local library or search the web to prepare a list of available books, CDs, DVDs, online videos, and podcasts you would recommend. Explain why you selected each one.

3. **Miller Brothers, Inc.** You are the supervisor for a service desk that supports the internal customers of Miller Brothers, Inc., a small manufacturing company that has recently opened a new facility in a different state. Other than the Benefits department, the service desk is the only department that has a toll-free telephone number. As a result, you are beginning to see an increase in the number of transferred telephone calls. Develop a set of step-by-step instructions that your staff can use to perform cold transfers.

CHAPTER 4

Technical Writing Skills for Support Professionals

In this chapter you will learn:

◎ The impact of technology on the service desk and its customers

◎ The role of the service desk analyst in a technology-centric world

◎ The most common documents used by service desks to convey information

◎ The characteristics of good technical writing

◎ Proven techniques to improve your writing skills

The technical support industry has undergone a dramatic change in the past decade in how it collects information and delivers support. Most companies have implemented incident management systems that enable service desk analysts to log and manage customer incidents and service requests. Technologies such as the Internet, email, instant messaging (IM), and chat are complementing the telephone and on-site services as ways to communicate with customers and other support professionals. Support professionals use and develop online wikis and knowledge bases that contain answers to FAQs, solutions to known errors, and policies and procedures that customers can use as well. All of these changes have prompted the need for support professionals to add technical writing to their list of required skills. **Technical writing** involves writing documentation that explains technical issues in ways that nontechnical people can understand. Technical writing includes following any documentation standards that have been put in place to increase the consistency and readability of documents. Technical writing also promotes compliance with existing policies, such as service management and information security policies.

Good writing skills enable you to communicate technical information accurately, completely, and comprehensively to customers, managers, and coworkers. These people have varying skill levels, and good writing communicates information in a way that each can understand. Because written communication conveys emotion just like verbal communication, your tone of voice is important when you write, just as it is when you speak. It is also important to be concise and consistent so readers can quickly obtain the information they need.

Technology-Delivered Support

Historically, customers called the service desk on the telephone or perhaps walked in to the service desk area when they needed assistance or information. Although that still happens, companies now provide additional ways for customers to obtain support, all of which require effective writing skills. Customers may send an email message or use chat to communicate. Many companies offer self-services via their web sites that customers can use to obtain support without having to wait to speak with a service desk analyst. Self-services may include accessing a knowledge base of solutions, a menu of service requests, or a list of FAQs. Often these sites use social media channels such as forums, wikis, blogs, micro-blogs such as Twitter, social networks such as Facebook and Myspace, and video and podcast sharing sites such as YouTube to keep customers informed and aware of their options. Technology-delivered support services enable the service desk to anticipate and proactively meet its customers' needs. These alternate ways of delivering support enable the service desk to accommodate its customers' preferences in terms of how they obtain support, better prioritize and manage its workload, and, ultimately, improve service desk services. They also enable the service desk to reduce the overall cost of delivering support. The key is to ensure that technology-delivered services are quick, convenient, and useful for customers, not just cost-effective for the company.

Successful companies understand that effective use of the Internet, email, and other technologies is not just a matter of installing hardware and software or implementing applications. It also requires that these companies diligently capture and deliver high-quality information. For most service desks, this means rethinking not only the skills that service desk analysts must possess, but also the skills and knowledge that customers must possess.

Used effectively, technology empowers both customers and service desk analysts. Used improperly, technology can frustrate everyone and alienate customers. Telephone, Internet, email, IM, and chat technologies all play a role in customer support. Moving forward, no single technology will replace all of the others. Technologies such as the telephone, IM, and chat provide immediacy and the ability to interact with a human being. Customers will continue to use these technologies when they do not want to wait for an email response or do not have the ability or the desire to access web-based services. For example, customers will use the telephone, IM, or chat when they are experiencing a high-priority incident or when they have questions that need to be answered before they order a new product. They may also turn to the telephone or IM when web-based services are not available or the network is down. And, they may rely on IM or chat when a dial-up service being used to connect to the Internet is tying up their telephone line.

Alternately, email provides the ability to send and receive detailed information. Customers will continue to use email when they want to submit an inquiry outside of normal service desk hours, when they do not require an immediate response, or when they want a written reply. For example, customers use email when they want a detailed set of instructions or when they have a general inquiry, such as when the next release of a product is due out.

Web-based services provide customers with the ability to perform functions, such as filling out forms, resetting passwords, and downloading software, in addition to interacting with service desk analysts. Web-based services will continue to be used by those customers who feel comfortable with web technology and by those who find it helpful. For example, customers use the web when they need to submit a form to have a workspace set up for a new employee or when they want to obtain answers to FAQs. Customers who want to work at their own pace and on their own schedule also will rely on web-based services. Service desk analysts must feel comfortable communicating via all of these methods and must possess or develop the different skills that each of these technologies requires.

The Service Desk Analyst's Role in a Technology-Centric World

The availability of technology has dramatically changed the role of the service desk analyst. Analysts must be extremely flexible in their ability to continuously learn new technologies and adapt those technologies to their work. They need to understand and use a myriad of technologies, including the telephone, email, and web-based services, to support their customers and communicate with their coworkers. Also, analysts are required to record the results of their efforts, typically in an incident management system. The incident management system may be part of an integrated ITSM solution that is also used to record information about problems, changes, and so forth. **Integrated ITSM solutions**, sometimes called enterprise solutions, are a suite of systems that companies use to manage their incident, problem, knowledge, change, service asset and configuration management, and request fulfillment processes.

All of these technologies extend the service desk's ability to gather, organize, and use data and information. **Data** is a set of raw facts that are not organized in a meaningful way. Data becomes information when it is organized in a meaningful way.

 Data analytics is the science of examining raw data with the goal of finding meaningful patterns, unknown correlations, and useful information. The use of data analytics helps companies and organizations make better business decisions and improve the quality of their services.

Data and information are part of what is known as the data-information-knowledge-wisdom (DIKW) hierarchy, which is illustrated in Figure 4-1. **Knowledge** is the application of information along with people's experiences, ideas, and judgments. **Wisdom** is the judicious application of knowledge. Wisdom enables people to answer the questions "Why?" and "When?" Wisdom is created when people have the knowledge and experience to make sensible decisions and judgments. Wisdom generally deals with the future and is uniquely a human characteristic that cannot be automated. In other words, using tools and databases to collect and use data, information, and knowledge enables people to make wise decisions.

Figure 4-1 Data-information-knowledge-wisdom (DIKW) hierarchy

The best companies view information as an extremely valuable resource. They rely on their service desk analysts to **capture**, or collect, the high-quality data needed to create accurate and useful information. Consequently, service desk analysts must recognize and embrace the important role they play in capturing data, producing information, and sharing knowledge. Gone are the days when simply resolving an incident is good enough, or when people in a service desk setting could hoard their knowledge or relay knowledge by word of mouth. Today, service desk analysts must capture data that can be reused by customers and other analysts to solve similar incidents, and that can be used to produce the information needed to prevent incidents and problems from recurring. At a minimum, analysts must capture the data needed to reduce the time it takes to resolve incidents if they recur.

Some organizations use reputation-based rewards and gaming techniques, such as points and badges, to encourage knowledge capture and sharing.

Analysts are expected to log tickets, document solutions, develop procedures, and exchange information in a way that can be easily used by customers, managers, and coworkers. As a result, writing skills and typing (or keyboarding) proficiency are important assets in the service desk. People with good writing and keyboarding skills can quickly and easily capture needed data. People with good writing skills also understand the importance of complying with applicable documentation standards and as a result can capture data that is accurate and consistent.

Because people with good writing skills are more proficient at quickly capturing accurate and consistent data, they may be given a wider range of responsibilities and offered greater opportunity. For example, they may be asked to prepare recommendations that lead to product improvements, or they may be asked to manage or contribute content to the service desk's web site. By developing good writing skills, you can position yourself to seize these opportunities when they arise. After all, good writing skills not only enable you to communicate efficiently and effectively with customers, they enable you to communicate your abilities to management as well.

Many companies require job candidates to submit a writing sample or complete a writing test as a part of the interview process. Good writing skills make a positive impression.

Enabling Customer Self-Service

People regularly use self-services, such as vending machines, voice mail, ATMs, online banking or banking by telephone, and self-checkout at stores. A **self-service** is a service that enables customers to help themselves. Customers appreciate services that enhance their self-sufficiency and enable them to accomplish tasks at their own pace. When given proof that a new way of obtaining service works, customers will embrace and then demand services that free up their most valued commodity—time. Enabling self-service for technical support is no different.

Service desks use technologies such as automated email response management systems and web technology to provide self-services. Customers use these technologies to order products, obtain product information, and find solutions to incidents without speaking with a service desk analyst. Software publishers and application developers often include features in their products that enable and encourage self-service. Many companies provide robust and interactive online help with their software and application programs that customers can then access and use to answer questions and obtain step-by-step assistance. Hardware manufacturers and software publishers also embed diagnostic software in their products that customers can use to troubleshoot and potentially resolve incidents on their own.

Both customers and service desk analysts benefit from self-services. Customers benefit from self-services, such as lists of FAQs, because they do not have to speak with an analyst to receive the information they need. When lists of FAQs are published, service desk analysts are free to work on more complex incidents and contribute to projects. Simple self-services, such as providing customers with the ability to submit incident and service requests via email or a web form, are appreciated by customers because customers can use a familiar tool to request service. These simple self-services also reduce the time it takes analysts to handle incidents and service requests—and therefore reduce the cost to handle incidents and service requests—because customers are documenting preliminary data, such as customer and incident data, themselves (often by using online forms provided by the service desk). This data then is or can be logged automatically into the company's incident management system.

Customers have come to expect self-services. Customers appreciate self-services that save them time and reduce their frustration. In fact, customers often view companies that fail to provide self-services as out of touch and inefficient. For example, most people would be surprised to call a company and have the telephone ring unanswered. We expect to interact with some technology. At a minimum, we expect to hear a message with the company's business hours. Additionally, we want the ability to leave a voice mail message. We mistrust the legitimacy or professionalism of companies that do not provide this basic service. Customers also expect companies—particularly companies that provide technical support—to use web technology to enable self-services.

Customer Support via the Internet

The Internet has dramatically changed the way customers expect support services to be delivered. Customers expect external service desks to have a web site they can reach via the Internet. The **Internet** is a global collection of computer networks that are linked to provide worldwide access to information. Some companies that provide external support may give customers access to secured information via an extranet. An **extranet** is a web site that is accessed via the Internet—that is, it can be accessed by the general public—but that requires a password to gain entry to all or parts of the site. Internal service desks often enable their customers to access a web site via their company's intranet. An **intranet** is a secured, privately maintained web site that serves employees and that can be accessed only by authorized personnel. In other words, an intranet is a secured portion of the Internet that cannot be accessed by the general public.

Self-services that service desks may offer customers via their web sites include:

- Answers to FAQs

- Tips, techniques, and helpful hints

- Schedules for company-sponsored training classes

- Instructional videos and online demonstrations

- Information about new and planned products and services

- The ability to update customer profile information, such as address information and customer preferences
- Online forms to submit incidents and service requests
- Current status reports (available without calling the service desk)
- A current list of standard products
- A catalog of services
- Purchasing policies and information
- A knowledge base of solutions that customers can use to resolve incidents on their own
- The ability to download software, software patches, and upgrades
- The ability to reset or change a password
- Email links to submit service requests and comments such as compliments or complaints
- A link or pop-up providing access to live text chats with service desk analysts
- An icon to request a call back
- A forum to submit questions and exchange ideas with other customers
- A link or pop-up providing access to customer satisfaction surveys
- Links to other useful web sites

Hyperlinks, or **links**, are text or graphics in a hypertext or hypermedia document that allow readers to "jump" to a related idea. Clicking a link might open a pop-up window with a definition, instructions, a still picture, or an animated picture. A link can also run an audio or video clip, or jump to a web page. Hypermedia and hypertext are interactive storage methods. **Hypermedia** stores information in a graphical form. **Hypertext** stores information in a nongraphical form. Both enable users to access the information in a nonlinear fashion using hyperlinks.

Functionality and ease of use are the keys to a successful service desk web site. When accessing a support web site, customers are not looking for a simple billboard with a telephone number to call for support. They are looking for a way to obtain the information they need, when they need it. Figure 4-2 shows a sample service desk web site.

Well-designed web sites offer customers a variety of options, including a searchable knowledge base, FAQs, tutorials, and troubleshooting wizards. When customers cannot find the information they need, they want to obtain assistance easily. A well-designed web site clearly communicates additional ways that customers can obtain support, including the telephone, email, chat, and user forums. The best sites offer customers the ability to personalize their support experience by, for example, specifying a language, creating personalized home pages, and signing up for email alerts and blogs or newsletters.

Figure 4-2   Sample service desk web site

Web sites enable companies to cost-effectively deliver support to their customers 24 hours a day, 7 days a week. Even when the service desk is closed, a web site can offer access to frequently requested information and basic services such as FAQs and knowledge bases, and the ability to contact the company via email.

Using Email Effectively to Communicate with Customers

It is fairly common for service desk analysts to use email to communicate with their coworkers and managers. Service desks may use email internally to communicate the status of projects and promote awareness of changes to existing procedures, or they may use email to communicate schedule changes and notify staff of upcoming system changes.

Companies use email in a variety of ways to communicate with customers. Some companies use email simply to inform customers about the status of outstanding incidents and service requests, while encouraging customers to submit those incidents or service requests via the telephone or their web site. Often, these companies provide online forms that prompt customers for information specific to their concern. They may also use email to automatically acknowledge that the customer's contact—regardless of the channel used to make contact—has been logged and assigned a tracking number. Many companies use email to conduct customer satisfaction surveys. Customers either respond to the email or use a link provided in the email message to access a web-based survey. Email can also be used to simultaneously inform large numbers of customers about a virus, product change, or new release that might affect them.

According to HDI, just over than 89 percent of service desks use email to receive incidents from customers (2013 Support Center Practices and Salary Report, HDI). For many organizations, this is an informal channel that customers are encouraged to use only for lower-impact incidents that do not require an immediate response. For example, according to the same HDI study, only 75 percent of organizations measure incidents received through email, and only 17 percent of companies respond to emails in less than 15 minutes. Most companies respond to incidents submitted via email in anywhere from 15 minutes to 4 hours, while 12 percent respond in more than 4 hours. Although such a delayed response may be appropriate in some cases, such as very low-impact incidents or service requests, customers—even those who choose to avoid the telephone—often seek a more immediate response via a technology such as chat.

It is important to remember that although email is an easy way to communicate with customers, it does not provide many of the capabilities that an incident management system provides. For example, email cannot be used to automatically create trend reports, and it cannot be used as a knowledge base. For this reason, service desk analysts typically log all email requests received from customers in their company's incident management system. Analysts must also record all status updates related to a customer's incident or service request in the incident management system, not in email messages that may be lost or forgotten.

Companies that use email and the web as their primary communication channels with customers often use email response management systems. Email response management systems such as emailtopia (*www.emailtopia.com*), Kana (*www.kana.com*) and RightNow (*www.oracle.com*) enable service desks to manage high-volume chat, email, and web form messages in much the same way that ACDs enable service desks to handle telephone calls. For example, these systems enable service desks to route messages to queues; run real-time reports to determine such statistics as how many emails are received per hour, per day, and so forth; prioritize messages; and categorize messages so service desks can report on the types of messages being received. These systems also provide analysts with the ability to search and review customer messages and view a history of a customer's activities on the support web site. In other words, service desk analysts can see the different web pages, FAQs, and so forth that a customer examined prior to submitting his or her message.

Whether an email response management system is available or not, many incident management systems now integrate with most standard email packages to allow automation of common tasks. Email messages from customers can be automatically logged as tickets. The incident management system can then automatically send a return email message to inform customers that their contact was logged and to provide a ticket number. Some companies automatically send email messages to customers each time the status of their incident or service request changes. Other companies automatically send email messages with a detailed description of the final resolution when the ticket is closed. A link to a customer satisfaction survey requesting feedback may accompany the final resolution.

One downside of email is that it can be perceived as impersonal. Another downside is that analysts sometimes find that using email lengthens the problem-solving process. If the service desk receives an email that does not contain sufficient information, the analyst needs to send a return email. The analyst must then wait for a response before being able to resolve the incident. If the analyst does not communicate effectively and the customer misunderstands the analyst's message, the problem-solving process may take even longer and require even more exchanges. In the context of email, an **exchange** is when one email is received and another is sent. On average, two to three exchanges are required to resolve an incident in a typical service desk setting. Few organizations resolve incidents in one exchange.

To minimize downsides such as email being perceived as impersonal and inefficient, service desk analysts must use common sense and courtesy when communicating with customers via email.

The effective use of email will gain you the respect of customers and coworkers, and, like excellent telephone skills, will serve you well throughout life. Common sense, care, good judgment, and good writing skills will enable you to make the most of this powerful communication tool. These same characteristics will enable you to effectively use tools such as IM and chat.

 The section "Email Best Practices" in this chapter provides specific techniques for using email effectively.

Using Instant Messaging and Online Chat to Facilitate Communication

IM and online chat are quickly surpassing email as a preferred method of communication in the business world, where an immediate response is often required. This is because both are cost-effective, simultaneous ways to communicate. Unlike email, where there can be a delay of several minutes or more between when a message is sent and received, IM and online chat are instantaneous. They are essentially text versions of a phone call.

Instant Messaging

Instant messaging involves a text-based conversation between two people, although the two people can invite others to join in. **Instant messaging systems** enable two or more people to communicate in real time over the Internet. People can send an IM by typing on a computer keyboard or on a wireless device such as a cell phone, a smartphone, or a tablet. Unlike email, where you can send a message even if a recipient is not online, IM requires that all parties be online at the same time. Popular IM services are AIM (AOL Instant Messenger), Google Talk, MSN Messenger, and Yahoo! Messenger.

In a service desk setting, analysts typically use IM primarily to communicate with each other or with level two service providers about an ongoing incident or service request. For example, a field service representative may use IM to inform a service desk analyst that he or she has arrived at a customer site to begin work on a high-priority incident. Or, a service desk analyst may use IM to communicate with a member of the network support group about a network outage.

Because IM does not provide the capabilities of an incident management system, and because there may be security concerns in terms of the data being transmitted, most service desks currently limit IM communication with customers. A service desk analyst may use IM to communicate the status of an incident to a customer who has an outstanding (logged) incident. Or, a service desk analyst may use IM to communicate with a customer whose telephone line is in use by a dial-up service. Analysts must then record these IM communications with customers in the service desk's incident management system. Following this procedure ensures that all parties who access the incident management system—not just the parties who are sending and receiving messages—have the latest information.

Online Chat

A **chat**, or online chat, is a simultaneous text communication between two or more people via a computer. According to HDI's 2013 Practices and Salary Survey, more than 46 percent of its members use chat. An additional 21 percent plan to add this capability within the next 12 months. A variety of factors are causing companies to look more closely at using chat to communicate with customers. These factors, which benefit both the company and customers, include:

- Satisfying and retaining customers who increasingly demand alternatives to the telephone and real-time communication
- Creating a competitive advantage
- Reducing the overall cost of delivering support
- Eliminating the need for customers to incur long-distance telephone charges
- Eliminating the need for customers to subscribe to an IM service
- Improving the quality of communications via standardized responses
- Providing a live communication channel when a telephone connection is unreliable or unavailable

- Being able to create a documented transcript of contacts
- Being able to integrate technologies such as the web and the company's incident management and email management systems
- Increasing the efficiency of analysts through the use of simultaneous chat sessions

Analysts also benefit when chat technology is used. Benefits to analysts include:

- Minimizing language barriers that can occur when speaking via the telephone
- Breaking up the monotony of being on the telephone
- Being able to multitask and handle a variety of chat sessions at the same time
- Being able to easily provide customers with documents, links, and other information such as commands that can be used to resolve the incident or service request
- Having access to a documented transcript that can be used to review steps taken or to evaluate analyst performance
- Receiving contacts appropriate to their skill set when skills-based routing is available

Companies are integrating chat with other systems such as incident management systems, email response management systems, and web-based knowledge management systems. This integration allows service desk analysts to simultaneously use these resources when interacting with customers. A service desk analyst may, for example, use chat to send the answer to an FAQ or send the customer a link to a solution in the company's knowledge base. This integration also enables the service desk to keep a record of and monitor these transactions for quality purposes.

Companies that do business via the Internet primarily use channels such as chat, email, and online help to interact with customers. Integrating these channels maximizes the companies' technological resources while reducing the overall cost of delivering support.

Although the benefits of IM and chat are compelling, most companies work hard to establish guidelines for IM and chat usage in an effort to manage customer expectations. These guidelines address factors such as the cost, legal, security, training, and management challenges that companies face as they implement these technologies. For example, companies must spell out the types of interactions that are appropriate for IM and chat. Failing to do so could result in customer dissatisfaction or, worse, a lawsuit. Companies must also staff these channels appropriately. Failing to do so could result in customers waiting in a queue to chat with an analyst just as they currently wait to speak with an analyst on the telephone. Companies must also ensure they can create a written transcript of communications between analysts and customers. This written transcript ensures that important customer data is captured, and it provides the ability to monitor IM and chat communications for quality.

INTERVIEW WITH...

NANCY FLYNN
FOUNDER AND EXECUTIVE DIRECTOR
THE ePOLICY INSTITUTE
COLUMBUS, OHIO
www.epolicyinstitute.com
Instant messaging brings many costly business and legal challenges to the workplace. Nancy Flynn, author of *Writing Effective Email, 3rd Edition* (AXZO Press, Crisp Series 2014), answers a few questions about IM in the workplace and how employers and employees can make the most of this popular tool. Nancy Flynn is founder and executive director of The ePolicy Institute and the author of *Instant Messaging Rules, Social Media Rules, The ePolicy Toolkit, The ePolicy Handbook*, and several other books. She has been featured in *U.S. News & World Report, Fortune, The New York Times*, and *The Wall Street Journal*, and on CNBC and National Public Radio.

Courtesy of Nancy Flynn

Question: Why is instant messaging so popular?

Answer: Instant messaging is popular because it delivers speed. Email is a powerful communication tool, but it simply isn't speedy enough for fans of instant messaging. Instant messaging appeals to users who want to communicate instantaneously with colleagues, clients, and other third parties. Instant messaging can do anything email can do, including transmit text, images, and files. It also offers a few capabilities that email does not, such as chat rooms and web conferencing, screen sharing and whiteboards, access to content, and the ability to multitask.

Question: Is instant messaging being used in business?

Answer: Absolutely. While email remains the electronic communications tool of choice in offices worldwide, many organizations have added IM to their electronic business communications toolkits. In addition to the organizations that are formally engaged in some level of instant messaging for internal and external communications, millions of employees are instant messaging on public networks without management's knowledge or authorization. That makes instant messaging risky business.

Question: What are the risks of using instant messaging in business?

Answer: Instant messaging poses a broad range of potential risks to employers. The greatest IM challenges are controlling security system breaches, monitoring written content, retaining and archiving business records, ensuring employee productivity, and managing user IDs. Security is a top concern as a significant amount of corporate use takes place across public networks, which lack built-in safeguards against Trojan horses, worms, viruses, and other destructive and malicious intruders. This makes sensitive business information vulnerable to malicious hackers, identity thieves, and eavesdroppers. The greatest risks, however, fall under the categories of content concerns and records retention. Because of its instantaneous nature, many business users think instant messaging—more so than email—is a throwaway medium that permits casual off-the-cuff content. On the contrary, IM can create business records that must be retained by the organization for legal, regulatory, and business purposes. Unfortunately for users, personal, nonbusiness-related IM chat may be retained alongside business records, often without employees' knowledge. The fact that instant messages may be considerably more casual and conversational than traditional paper records does not diminish their significance in the eyes of litigators, regulators, and the courts. All electronically stored information creates potential evidence, which holds as much legal weight as paper records.

Companies must teach all employees to distinguish electronic business records (IM or email) that must be saved, stored, and produced in the event of a subpoena from transitory (insignificant, personal, and nonbusiness-related) messages that can be deleted. They must inform employees about the potentially costly risks the organization faces when IM, email, and other electronic business records are not retained and preserved in a legally compliant fashion. Employees must also understand that they should not reasonably expect privacy when it comes to instant messages, email messages, and other electronic content created, stored, transmitted, or received using company resources. Electronic systems, accounts, and tools—including instant messaging—belong to the employer, not the employee. Most companies monitor IM and email transmissions to ensure they adhere to the organization's ePolicies and rules governing content, use, and other issues.

Question: What is appropriate content for business IM transmissions?

Answer: In the workplace, IM content should be business-appropriate. In other words, it should be professional, polite, and polished. Best practices call for companies to implement written policies that instruct employees to compose instant messages that adhere to guidelines such as the following:

Employees must abide by the Company's IM content and language guidelines. Using language that is obscene, vulgar, abusive, harassing, profane, suggestive, intimidating, misleading, defamatory, or otherwise offensive is a violation of the Company's instant messaging policy and can lead to disciplinary action or termination. Jokes or inappropriate commentary related to ethnicity, race, color, religion, sex, age, disabilities, physique, or sexual preference are also prohibited.

Such guidelines help employers keep their organizations out of harm's way, while giving employees access to a cutting-edge, productivity-enhancing tool. Employees must guard their own privacy as well. As part of their employee education efforts, many companies suggest that employees protect themselves, their families, and friends by strictly separating their business and personal lives. In other words, save your personal messaging for home.

Question: What advice can you offer to people using instant messaging in the workplace?

Answer: The most effective tone for electronic business correspondence is professional, yet conversational. To achieve that tone, I suggest you take the colleague, customer, and competitor test. Imagine that you are in an elevator crowded with colleagues, customers, and competitors. What tone would you use? What would you say? What information would you reveal, and what would you keep under wraps? If you wouldn't say it aloud while sharing close quarters with the people you work for, with, and against, don't write it in an instant message, which might be retained and later revealed publicly—to the embarrassment of you and your employer.

Using and Creating Knowledge Bases

Technologies such as email, IM, and online chat are fast and easy ways for customers to contact the service desk with incidents and service requests. Knowledge bases make it possible for service desks to quickly and consistently respond to customers' incidents and service requests.

Few, if any, companies have the resources to re-create a solution each and every time an incident or problem occurs. Also, because technology is increasingly complex and changing very rapidly, many companies are unable to give analysts adequate training. When training is provided, it may not occur when analysts need it most—*before* the technology is introduced. Consequently, just as customers can use self-services to help themselves, analysts must help themselves by learning to use and create online knowledge bases. Although the contents will vary from one organization to the next, knowledge bases typically provide access to information sources such as customer information, documents, policies and procedures, and incident resolutions.

A knowledge base can be built using sophisticated technology or it can simply be a collection of books and documents used to resolve incidents. For example, most service desks make available the following knowledge resources:

- Class notes obtained in training classes

- Internet sites that analysts can access via bookmarks

- Online help

- Product manuals

- An incident management system for looking up similar or related incidents

- Coworkers and subject matter experts

Referring to class notes and product manuals can be time consuming, particularly if they are disparate or unorganized. Consulting coworkers and subject matter experts can be costly as these individuals are being pulled away from other tasks, perhaps to answer questions that have been answered many times before or are documented in procedures. Consequently, companies are trying to consolidate their knowledge resources and maximize their human resources by implementing knowledge management systems. These systems capture human knowledge and organize it in a way that it can be easily accessed and used consistently by people who are involved in handling incidents and service requests.

 Most hardware and software vendors post FAQs and solutions to known errors on their web sites. Many service desks add links from the service desk web site to vendor web sites, so analysts and customers can quickly access the vendor information.

Knowledge management systems benefit service desk analysts considerably because the information they need is available online whenever they need it. They do not have to wait for a coworker to get off the telephone or for a subject matter expert to return from vacation or training to access that person's knowledge. Many knowledge management systems can also lead an analyst through troubleshooting steps that help resolve complex incidents, which then improves the analyst's problem-solving skills.

The practice of building a knowledge management system and using all available knowledge resources is not meant to imply that humans are unimportant and unnecessary. In fact, it is quite the opposite. Companies want to free human resources to work on unique and complex incidents rather than wasting time answering routine questions. Furthermore, most people prefer to work on interesting new incidents rather than handle the same boring incidents over and over.

As artificial intelligence matures and avatars become more cost-effective, organizations will increasingly use both in conjunction with knowledge management systems to provide some basic customer services, often more quickly than a live analyst. Live analysts will handle new and more complex inquiries.

Some people resist contributing to knowledge management systems and believe this gains them "job security" as they are the only one who has needed information. Given the rapid pace of change in the business world, withholding knowledge or continuing to hold on to knowledge that may soon be obsolete is one of the worst things analysts can do. By contributing to and using their company's knowledge management system, analysts can improve their reputation as team players. Analysts can also expand their knowledge and free themselves to learn new skills.

Much of the flexibility and power of a knowledge management system comes from the many search-retrieval technologies available. These retrieval technologies allow users to specify search criteria, which are then used to retrieve relevant information. **Search criteria** are the questions or symptoms entered by a user. Some of these retrieval technologies do very simple data matching, whereas others use highly sophisticated artificial intelligence.

Commonly used search retrieval technologies include:

- **Case-based reasoning (CBR)**—A searching technique that uses everyday language to ask users questions and interpret their answers. CBR finds perfect matches based on user queries but also retrieves cases that are similar to the perfect match. Possible solutions are ranked in order of probability from most likely to least likely to resolve the incident.

- **Decision tree**—A branching structure of questions and possible answers designed to lead an analyst to a solution. Decision trees work well for entry-level analysts because they can walk through a methodical approach to solving incidents.

- **Fuzzy logic**—A searching technique that presents all possible solutions that are similar to the search criteria, even when conflicting information exists or no exact match is present. Fuzzy logic requires that some part of the search criteria specified is valid.

- **Keyword searching**—The technique of finding indexed information by specifying a descriptive word or phrase, called a **keyword**. Keywords must be indexed to be located and an *exact* match must be found.

- **Query by example (QBE)**—A searching technique that uses queries, or questions, to find records that match the specified search criteria. Queries can include **search operators**, connecting words such as AND, OR, and NOT. QBE can also find records that *do not* contain the search criteria or that contain a value less than, greater than, or equal to the specified search criteria, such as a date range.

These search retrieval technologies have value only if the data stored in the knowledge management system is complete and accurate. The expression "garbage in, garbage out" is appropriate: If inaccurate or incomplete information (garbage) is stored in the knowledge base, then inaccurate or incomplete information will be delivered when a search is performed.

To maintain these systems, most companies designate a knowledge engineer or knowledge base administrator (KBA) who develops and oversees the knowledge management process and ensures the information contained in the knowledge management system is accurate, complete, and current. It is the knowledge engineer's responsibility to ensure all available information sources are added to the knowledge management system and made available to the service desk. The knowledge engineer may provide training in an effort to ensure analysts can quickly and easily retrieve information when needed. The knowledge engineer is also involved in developing documentation standards to ensure that the information stored in the knowledge management system can be easily retrieved, is readable and complete, and is compliant with and promotes applicable policies.

A knowledge engineer does not create and maintain all of the knowledge. That is the responsibility of many people in an organization including service desk analysts.

In smaller companies, a service desk analyst with excellent writing skills may perform this role on a part-time basis. Larger companies may have one or more full-time knowledge engineers. In larger companies, these individuals are often degreed technical writers. Organizations that have adopted Knowledge-Centered Support (KCS) often establish roles such as KCS Candidate, KCS Contributor, KCS Publisher, KCS Coach, and Knowledge Domain Expert. These roles represent increasing levels of competency and responsibility relative to the KCS methodology.

A premise of KCS is that individuals assigned to any of these roles can use and contribute knowledge. That knowledge is made available to the support organization immediately in draft form in an effort to avoid "reinventing the wheel." Although the knowledge may be improved as it is reused, once evidence of demand for knowledge is established (e.g., the knowledge is used several times to handle incidents), then the article is subjected to more formal technical and compliance reviews. Once such reviews are complete, the article may be published to self-service and made available to customers.

KCS users often adopt the refrain "UFFA," which stands for use it, flag it, fix it (if you have the authority), add it.

This demand-driven approach to knowledge article review is different than the traditional knowledge engineering approach to knowledge management, which tends to take a formalized approach to publishing any and all knowledge. This more formalized approach can cause a delay and may mean that knowledge is not available when it is needed most, as incidents are being reported.

Regardless of the approach adopted, the steps taken to implement and administer a knowledge management system are similar to those taken when implementing and administering a content management system. Simply put, a **content management system (CMS)** is software used to manage the content of a web site. As is the case with knowledge management, the software is only one small part of what goes into publishing useful information via the Internet. Both knowledge management and content management involve collecting, editing, formatting, and publishing information in a way that enables the target audience to quickly and easily locate and use it.

Companies want people who share their knowledge, cross-train their coworkers, and continuously develop new skills. Companies also want people who comply with existing policies and procedures and who deliver information in a consistent way. Storing knowledge online enables analysts to achieve all of these goals. In addition, it reduces the time that service desk analysts spend answering routine and repeated questions. Analysts are then free to work on more complex incidents and pursue new skills, such as improved writing skills.

Writing Service Desk Documents

The amount of writing done by service desk analysts varies from one company to the next. However, a number of documents are common to all service desks. Figure 4-3 lists some of the most common documents service desk analysts prepare. Each document has a different audience and purpose. Before writing a word, it is a good practice to ensure you understand the audience's needs and how they plan to use the information, along with any documentation standards that have been established for the document you are producing.

- Tickets
- Email messages
- IM and chat messages
- FAQs
- Knowledge management system solutions
- Blogs
- Scripts
- Reports
- Procedures

Figure 4-3 Common service desk documents

It is also important to understand the etiquette, or rules governing the level of professionalism expected when producing work-related documents. These rules vary from one organization to the next. Using "chat speak" may or may not be viewed as appropriate when communicating with coworkers via an informal channel such as email, IM, or chat, but it is typically considered inappropriate and unprofessional when preparing formal documents and when communicating with customers or superiors. **Chat speak** is a term for the abbreviations and slang commonly used in email, IM, and chat messages for brevity or due to a limitation on the number of characters that can be used when sending messages. Abbreviations such as *LOL* (laugh out loud) are often used within sentences or alone as shorthand. When communicating for business, remember that recipients may not understand what you are trying to communicate or they may misinterpret your message. Furthermore, some popular acronyms for email, IM, and chat are simply not appropriate for business communications.

Regardless of the type of service desk document, the primary goal of service desk writing is to accurately convey technical information in an interesting way that can be understood by readers.

The amount of documentation analysts write depends on the technology available to their service desk and the size of their service desk. Analysts at most service desks log incidents and service requests (i.e., tickets), and send and receive email messages. They may also be asked to prepare other documents such as FAQs, reports, policies, and procedures. On the other hand, some service desks have technical writers who prepare these documents and analysts have little involvement.

The section "Improving Your Technical Writing Skills" later in this chapter provides best practices you can use when you prepare these service desk documents.

Tickets

Service desk analysts typically log tickets in an incident management system at the time the request is received. Figure 4-4 shows a sample data entry screen that service desk analysts may use to log an incident or service request. Well-written tickets provide other analysts and service providers with the information they need to handle incidents and service requests quickly. They also provide a historical accounting of the steps taken to solve an incident or service request.

When documenting incidents in a ticket, analysts should clearly record all of the information the customer provides. They should also include *all* of the steps they have taken to diagnose and resolve the incident. Analysts sometimes leave out problem-solving steps that they perceived to be obvious. Unfortunately, if an action is not explicitly stated, coworkers or other service providers have no choice but to assume the step was not taken. For example, if a ticket does not mention that you verified the customer's monitor was powered on, and then you escalate the incident, the field service engineer will most likely ask that question before going on-site. This not only wastes the field service engineer's time, but it can also frustrate and even anger the customer who must answer the same question multiple times. Sometimes all of the problem-solving steps are part of an existing checklist or model. In that case, it is appropriate for analysts to simply state that they completed the checklist and then summarize the results. Well-documented incidents and service requests will include details such as who, what, when, where, and how.

Figure 4-4   Sample ticket entry screen

Most tickets are made up of two basic parts: data fields and text fields. A **data field** is an element of a database record in which one piece of data is stored. Most systems can validate data as it is entered into data fields and enforce a standard in terms of what data is entered. This means the system can ensure that a Date field accepts only correctly formatted dates, as opposed to words. In the United States and Canada, dates typically conform to the MM/DD/YYYY format (for example, 11/27/2014). In many European countries, dates typically conform to the DD/MM/YYYY format (for example, 27/11/2014). In many Asian countries, dates typically conform to the YYYY/MM/DD format (for example, 2014/11/27). Again, when data fields are used, the system enforces the standard in terms of how the data is entered. A **text field** is a field that accepts free-form information. Text fields are used to collect detailed information such as descriptions, status updates, and solutions. Text fields cannot typically validate data as it is entered in the system. In other words, the system cannot enforce a standard in terms of what data is entered.

Reports are usually created using the data entered into data fields because the data can be validated. As a result, the person creating the report can predict what data will be present in a data field.

Many companies establish standards for how to enter certain words or phrases into text fields. For example, a standard may direct analysts to use the term *reboot* as opposed to *cold boot*, *warm boot*, or *power off and on*. Although the system cannot enforce the use of these standards in a text field, the presence of the standard helps analysts write more consistently and minimizes the confusion that can result from inconsistent terms.

When working in a service desk, strive to understand how the data you collect is being used. This helps you to better understand why it is important to enter information as accurately as possible. For example, many incident management systems have a category or type field. This field reflects the category or type of incident being reported and is often used to search a knowledge management system, determine priority, and determine the appropriate level two support group to contact in the event the service desk is unable to resolve the incident. Many incident management systems also have a Date Resolved field. Analysts sometimes simply enter the current date and time, even though the incident was resolved earlier in the day or week. Accuracy is important, however, and takes only a few seconds more. The Date Resolved field, for example, is often used to determine whether the incident was resolved within the target resolution time. If an inaccurate date and time are entered, this ticket appears on a report as missing the SLA or late, even though it may not have been.

Another reason accuracy is important is that service desks are increasingly providing their customers with the ability to check the status of outstanding tickets, usually through the service desk's web site. This customer access has heightened awareness within the support industry of the need to document requests accurately and professionally, and maintain tickets on as close to a real-time basis as possible. Remember that even when customers cannot access tickets directly, the ticket data is often automatically forwarded to the customer in an email message, so it is important to be accurate and professional.

The data documented in tickets is also used by other service desk analysts and other service providers to diagnose and solve incidents, and by management to create reports and analyze trends. Effective trend analysis can eliminate recurring incidents, thus saving valuable time and, ultimately, increasing customer satisfaction. Many companies use the data captured in their incident management system to justify resources and to measure the performance of both the service desk team and individual analysts. You may perceive that it takes too much time to create complete and accurate tickets. Remember, however, that management analyzes ticket data to more fully understand your workload and your contributions. They also rely on this information to institute improvement opportunities that may save time in the long run.

Email Messages

Every day, service desks use email to communicate internally or with customers. Well-written email messages are as clear and concise as possible while conveying a positive, friendly tone. When email messages are too long, readers may become bored or miss an important detail. When email messages are too succinct or impersonal, readers may consider the messages abrupt or even rude.

Ultimately, email messages should provide as much of the needed information as possible the first time and not prompt additional messages to be sent back and forth. Try to anticipate follow-up questions a coworker or customer may ask and volunteer the information. If a lengthy discussion is needed, it may be best to make a telephone call or schedule a meeting.

IM and Chat Messages

Like email messages, IM and chat messages are documents in that they form a record of a communication. They can be saved, cut and pasted into other documents, and even used as evidence in a dispute. Service desk analysts must understand their company's policies regarding the use of IM and chat, particularly in terms of the audience for each. Some companies prohibit the use of IM when communicating with customers as it is difficult to enforce standards and ensure messages are captured in the company's incident management system. However, these companies may permit analysts to use IM to communicate with other service desk analysts or with subject matter experts. In such cases, analysts must understand and comply with the policies and etiquette of using IM in the workplace, or risk appearing unprofessional.

Companies that offer online chat to their customers typically do so via a formal set of procedures. Also, these companies typically have the ability to record a transcript of the chat, which can then be automatically captured in the company's incident management system. Because this is a channel used to communicate with customers, service desk analysts are often provided scripts that can be used to ensure communications are professional and also to increase efficiency.

Because there is typically a limitation placed on the number of characters that can be used when sending IM and chat messages, they must be as clear and concise as possible. As is the case with email messages, IM or chat messages must convey a positive, friendly tone, or they may be considered rude. They must also provide as much of the needed information as possible the first time and not prompt additional messages to be sent back and forth. If a lengthy discussion is needed, it may be best to make a telephone call or schedule a meeting.

FAQs

A common business practice that is particularly relevant to service desks is publishing lists of **frequently asked questions (FAQs)**, written answers to the most common customer queries. These answers are then made available to customers. They can be posted on a company's web site, published in the service desk's newsletter, incorporated into documentation such as a user's manual, or distributed at a training class. Some companies list the top 10 FAQs for a given month, for a specific product, or for a certain type of user, such as those who are new to a product.

 It is important to update FAQs regularly as issues become obsolete, new topics arise, and best practices evolve.

The key to a well-written FAQ is to state both the question and the answer clearly and in a language that is appropriate to the audience. In other words, phrase the question the way that customers do when they contact the service desk, then explain the answer in language that customers can understand. It is okay to use jargon and technical terms in the answers as long as the terms are appropriate for the reader's presumed level of skill and you define those terms for the reader.

FAQs are a basic self-service and enable service desks to proactively address their customers' needs. Analysts can also develop FAQs that provide their coworkers with answers to common questions about their area of expertise. FAQs satisfy coworkers and customers because these people are able to find solutions and answers to questions on their own. Many people prefer FAQs because they can find answers to questions they may be reluctant to ask or they think may seem silly.

Knowledge Management System Solutions

Knowledge management systems have value only if the information stored in the knowledge base is accurate and complete. Unfortunately, if analysts perceive the information in a knowledge management system is inaccurate or incomplete, they become hesitant to use the system and may return to the practice of seeking out a human who can assist. To be effective, a knowledge management system must be carefully developed and maintained.

An effective knowledge management system serves as a repository for reusable resolutions to incidents and service requests that are developed by analysts and service providers, such as the network management group and development groups. A **resolution** is a definitive solution to an incident or service request, or a proven workaround. In most systems, resolutions are stored as records in a separate file from tickets. This enables the use of one resolution to solve many incidents or service requests (referred to as a **one-to-many relationship**), as illustrated in Figure 4-5. In other words, the same resolution can be used each time an incident recurs without being retyped or cut and pasted into each ticket.

Resolutions do not describe things to *attempt* when diagnosing incidents or responding to inquiries. Checklists and tip sheets can be used to provide this type of information. A resolution represents the known solution to an incident or service request. Resolutions also do not contain the details of a single specific incident or service request, such as names and dates. These specific data elements would make the resolution unusable if the same incident happens in the future. By developing a generic resolution—one that does not contain specific details—the resolution is reusable. Thus, one resolution can be used to solve many incidents.

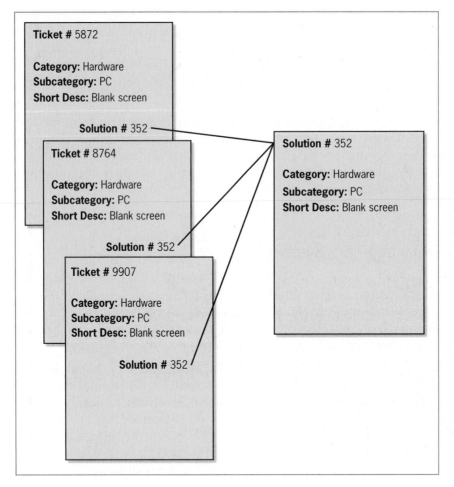

Figure 4-5 One solution to many incidents or service requests

Many service desks develop standards that describe how to write resolutions. Creating a standard resolution format serves many purposes. Analysts with varying skill levels can obtain information at the level of detail that they need. Resolutions are presented in a consistent format, so the human mind can quickly and easily pick out key data elements, such as commands and variables. A standard resolution format also makes the writing process easier because analysts know how to present information when documenting resolutions. For example, analysts know how to specify words or phrases that may be similar or confusing, such as *monitor* as opposed to *screen*. Figure 4-6 shows a sample format for a standard resolution.

Standard resolutions contain two types of information:

1.   Fields that are used to index the resolution and link it to the type of incident or service request being solved

2.   Text that describes the resolution

Sample Standard Resolution Format

Consider the following guidelines when creating resolutions:

Category: Use care when specifying this field. Specifying a very generic category can result in a resolution being presented a greater number of times than is appropriate.

Subcategory: Use care when specifying this field. Specifying this field in too detailed a fashion can result in the resolution rarely being presented.

Resolution Short Description: Provide a brief, symptom-oriented description of the resolution that is not incident specific.

Resolution Description: Provide a reusable description of the resolution. *Reusable* means that details relating to a single specific incident such as names and dates are not included in the resolution. Although the need for those details may be referenced in the resolution, the actual details should reside in the ticket. Include:

- A technical resolution that offers an experienced technician a brief summary
- A detailed resolution that offers a less experienced technician a more step-by-step approach

The following documentation standards have been developed in an effort to achieve consistency when documenting Resolution Descriptions:

- Enclose variable data in brackets; for example, **[xxxxxx]**.
- Enclose specific commands in quotation marks; for example, **"xxxxxx"**.
- When attaching another document, specify
  See *att:document.docx* **for additional information**.
  where *att:document.docx* represents the name of the attachment.
- When referencing a manual or user's guide, specify
  Refer to the *Word User's Guide* for additional information.
  where *Word User's Guide* represents the complete and accurate name of the reference document. Include the manual's release, version, or volume number when appropriate.
- When appropriate, indicate customers or other service providers to be notified when this resolution is implemented.

Figure 4-6 Sample standard resolution format

The description of a resolution may contain links to online documents, or a multimedia presentation of some kind, such as a video or audio clip. This enhances the usability of the information and enables people who are visual learners to receive the information in a meaningful way. Figure 4-7 shows a resolution that was written using a standard format.

Technical Solution	Detailed Solution
Delete print jobs with SunOS lp commands	1. rsh as root to the server where the print queue resides
	2. Type **lpq-P[xxx]** where xxx is the queue name
	3. Find the print job to kill, note the job # and the username
	4. Type **lprm-P[xxx] [job#] [username]**
	5. Use the line printer control (lpc) utility to bring the queue down, restart it, and bring it back up again as follows: **lpc down [xxx]** where xxx is the queue name **lpc restart [xxx]** **lpc up [xxx]**

Figure 4-7   Resolution with a standard format

When working in a service desk, strive to use all available knowledge resources and contribute to the creation of your company's knowledge management system. By doing so, you can considerably expand your ability to resolve incidents and you can help others resolve incidents by sharing what you know. Respect the fact that your coworkers and other service providers are just as busy as you are. Rather than interrupting their work to ask a routine question, look in the knowledge base for the answer. If you have difficulty finding a resolution or using your company's knowledge management system, seek help from someone who is involved in administering or maintaining the system.

Blogs

A blog is an effective way for a service desk to engage with its customers and to establish a social media presence. A **blog**, or web log, is a journal kept on the Internet. Blogs are typically updated frequently and display entries in reverse chronological order. They often contain links to other useful sites. Blogs are a great way for service desks to make announcements, share tips and tricks, promote services, and share statistics, trends and accomplishments.

One reason to blog is put a human face on the service desk. To accomplish this, include author photos in your blog header or with each post.

The most effective blogs are based on a strategy aimed at a specific target audience. An editorial policy can be used to determine the range of topics to be included in the blog, how frequently information will be posted and the blog's style. Blogs tend to be written in a more informal style as if the author were speaking directly to the audience. The content and audience will dictate the service desk's editorial policy.

Blogs are an excellent way for the service desk to engage with its customers by enabling and encouraging readers to respond with comments and to share the blogs with others. Service desks can share and provide readers the ability to share and comment on blogs via social networking sites such as Facebook, Google+, Twitter, LinkedIn, Yammer, and Chatter. If the content is informative and relevant to the target audience, readers are likely to spread the word and return for future editions.

Scripts

Another common way that service desks use social media is via media or video sharing sites such as YouTube and Vimeo. These sites can be used to upload videos that provide, for example, information about the service desk, how to contact the service desk, how to demonstrations, and informal training videos. The best videos begin with a script, which is where writing skills come into play.

Developing scripts for successful videos is in some ways the same as writing for a print media. The video must have a specific purpose and address the needs of a designated target audience. With videos, however, simplicity is key. The shorter the video, the more likely people will watch the entire video. The video must provide a clear opening statement that grabs people's attention and states the benefits of watching the video, optimally within the first 15 seconds. When developing a script, it is best to use simple language and shorter sentences that are easy for the audience to absorb. Such an approach enables the presenter to speak as if the audience is a friend or coworker. An effective script tells a story in that it has a beginning, middle, and end. An effective script also states a problem, provides a solution, and then encourages action. An effective script also maximizes the ability to include pictures, charts, and diagrams to help deliver the desired messages.

Common practice is to keep the length of a video between two to three minutes. If a video is interesting, however, length is not as important.

Reports

Entry-level analysts do not typically prepare reports, but senior analysts and managers often do. Although in smaller service desks, where analysts tend to be jacks-of-all-trades, anyone may be asked to prepare a report. Reports may be statistics or detailed accountings that are produced from the data collected in an incident management system. Creating this type of report requires knowledge of the system, the available data, and knowledge of the reporting package used to pull the data out of the system. Reports may also reflect the results of a study, the status of a project, or the analysis of statistics. For example, a report may describe why the volume of calls goes up on Thursdays, or why the number of PC-related incidents has gone down in the past 2 months. Preparing these reports requires writing skills and an understanding of the recipient's expectations. Some common reports a service desk analyst may create include progress reports, requirements reports, and business cases.

Progress Report

A progress report provides an update on activities, such as a project. Typically a progress report states:

- Activities completed during the current period (such as this month)
- Activities to be completed during the next period (such as next month)
- Activities that are overdue and why those activities could not be completed on time
- Considerations and concerns that require management attention

Management usually designates the time frame of progress reports.

Requirements Report

A requirements report typically provides:

- An assessment of the current environment
- A description of requirements that will result in an improved environment
- Considerations and concerns that require management attention
- Recommendations

A **requirement** is something that is necessary or essential. For example, a customer requirement is a service that customers expect the service desk to offer. Requirements can also be associated with technology. For example, a company must identify its requirements for a new incident management system before it begins looking for one. Without determining the requirements, the selected system most likely will not meet the company's needs in the long term. Gathering and documenting requirements is usually the first step taken at the start of a new project.

Business Case

A business case explores a proposed project such as implementing a new system or offering a new service, and typically provides:

- The viability of the proposed project
- The risks and benefits of starting or continuing with the project
- Possible alternatives

The first time you are asked to prepare a certain type of report, find out exactly what is expected in terms of format and content. Ask to see a copy of a similar report that you can use as an example. Prepare an outline of the report you plan to prepare, and then ask for feedback and approval of the outline before you begin preparing the actual report. These are all ways you can avoid wasted time and effort. Also, be open to feedback. Few reports are perfect the first time. Ask for specific, constructive feedback so you can continuously improve.

How to prepare a business case is discussed in Chapter 7.

Procedures

Companies more than ever are involving the service desk staff in the development of procedures. These procedures may be used by customers, the internal support organization, or simply within the service desk. A **procedure** is a step-by-step, detailed set of instructions that describes how to perform the tasks in a process. Many companies develop a standard format, or template, as illustrated in Figure 4-8, that is used to prepare procedures. This ensures that procedures have a consistent look and feel and are therefore easier to read.

When writing procedures, you must state every step explicitly. Do not assume readers know that they have to log on to the network before they can retrieve their email. Although a step may seem obvious to you, it may not be at all obvious to all readers. To keep procedures succinct, some companies embed links in procedures that readers can click to obtain a definition or more detailed instruction. This allows a single procedure to be relevant to readers of varying skill levels.

It is also a good idea to state the result readers can expect when a task is complete. For example, let readers know that they can proceed when the message "Logon Complete" appears. You can also let the readers know what to do if the message does not appear.

Insert Procedure Title

Introduction	Insert description of procedure.

Special Instructions Insert any special instructions or information to be considered before users begin performing this procedure.

- First consideration
- Second consideration
- Third consideration

⊃ **Note:** Use the Note icon to highlight pertinent or key information about a procedure.

⊙ **Important:** Use the Important icon if you want to emphasize, qualify, or clarify information.

🖉 **Warning:** Use the Warning icon to highlight actions that can result in a loss of data.

✪ **Best Practice:** Use the Best Practice icon to highlight a particular procedure as the most beneficial or efficient.

Procedure Follow these steps to [insert actual procedure].

1. Step One
2. Step Two
3. Step Three

Figure 4-8   Sample standard procedure format

If any single force is destined to impede man's mastery of the computer, it will be the manual that tries to teach him how to master it.

WILLIAM ZINSSER

When writing procedures, it is appropriate to include information about what *not* to do. For example, you can inform customers that restarting their PC may not be the best way to resolve an incident. Explain that it could result in the loss of data or it could erase the conditions needed to diagnose an incident. Another good practice is to include detailed warnings as needed that communicate important instructions. Figure 4-9 shows a sample warning message.

WARNING: Email attachments can contain viruses that can infect computer files and have harmful side effects. Before opening an attachment, scan the attachment by saving it to your computer and then scanning the attachment with antivirus software.

Figure 4-9   Sample warning message

Many service desks create and maintain a Service Desk Analyst's Guide. Some service desks refer to this document as a Technician's Guide, a Procedures Guide, or Standard Operating Procedures (SOPs). Figure 4-10 shows a sample table of contents for a Service Desk Analyst's Guide.

A Service Desk Analyst's Guide spells out the policies and procedures of the service desk and contains information that service desk analysts need to do their work. A Service Desk Analyst's Guide ensures the knowledge and experience of service desk management and key service desk staff members is available, even when the managers or staff members are not. In other words, analysts can first consult this guide to determine how they should handle a given situation. A Service Desk Analyst's Guide is often used to help new service desk staff members obtain an understanding of the service desk's policies and procedures. A Service Desk Analyst's Guide should be considered a "living" document that is updated regularly. Many organizations maintain this guide online to make it more accessible and easier to revise. Service desk analysts often help to create the Service Desk Analyst's Guide because they are the ones who will be using it day in and day out. Helping to create a Service Desk Analyst's Guide is an excellent way to practice and improve your writing skills.

Service Desk Analyst's Guide
Table of Contents

Service Desk Mission x
Service Desk Mission x
Service Desk Operating Objectives x
Service Desk Analyst's Personal Objectives x

Training/Development x
Service Desk Training Plan x
Training Objectives x
Training Activities x
Training Schedule x
References (Books, CDs, Magazines, etc.) x
Current Skills Inventory Matrix x

Call Management x
Scripts x
Answering the Phone x
Terminating a Call x
Miscellaneous Customer Ser
Important/Emergency Phone Numbers

Customer Profiles . . . .

Incident Management . . . .
Incident Management Introduction . . .
Incident Management Process Owner .
Incident Management Indicators and Ol
Incident Management Roles and Respo
Incident Management Process Flow. . .
Incident Escalation/Notification Guideli
Incident Management Related Procedu
Adding an Incident Record . .
Assigning an Incident. . . . .
Resolving an Incident. . . . .
Verifying Customer Satisfact
Closing an Incident . . . . . .
Incident Management Reports (Daily, W

Change Management x
Change Management Introduction x
Change Management Process Owner. x
Change Management Indicators and Objectives x
Change Management Roles and Responsibilities. x
Change Management Process Flow x
Change Categories x
Change Flow by Category x
Change Management Related Procedures x
Change Management Reports (Daily, Weekly, Monthly, etc.) x

Inventory Management x
Standard/Recommended Hardware and Software x
Keyboard Mappings x
Obtaining Inventory/Configuration Information. x

After-Hours Procedures. x
After-Hours Call List x
Determining What Is an Emergency x

Disaster Recovery x
Incident Management System x
Phone System x
Workstation (Toolkit) x

Vendor Management. x
Service Contract Specifics x

Appendix A: Glossary of Terms and Acronyms. x

Appendix B: Frequently Asked Questions. x

Appendix C: Troubleshooting Tips and Techniques x

Appendix D: Service Level Agreements x

Figure 4-10 Sample table of contents for a Service Desk Analysts Guide

Each of the service desk documents discussed in this section have a specific purpose and a target audience. To prepare these documents, you must adapt your writing to the style of the document and to the needs of the target audience. Learning the rules of writing will provide you with the foundation needed to write any document and to make a positive impression with your writing.

Improving Your Technical Writing Skills

No matter what type of service desk document you are writing, the quality of your writing is important. Well-written materials are simpler to comprehend, provide needed information, and leave a good impression. Writing, like any other skill, improves and becomes easier with practice. Another way to hone writing skills is by paying attention when you are reading, just as you can improve your customer service skills by paying attention when you are the customer. Also, a number of excellent books and classes are available. In fact, many universities and community colleges offer classes in technical writing.

Technical Writing Best Practices

Service desk analysts need good writing skills whether they are logging a ticket in the company's incident management system, sending an email, preparing a report, posting a blog, or preparing content for the service desk's web site.

Regardless of the type of document, good technical writing requires a coherent, precise style. The best practices listed in Figure 4-11 will help you develop an effective writing style and improve your writing skills.

- Select an appropriate style.
- Select a narrative mode.
- Know your audience.
- Use the active voice.
- Use simple language.
- Be concise.
- Be specific.
- Avoid or define jargon, technical terms, and acronyms.
- Break up your writing with lists and short sections.
- Be consistent.
- Check your work for accuracy and completeness.
- Check your grammar, punctuation, and spelling.

Figure 4-11   Technical writing best practices

These best practices become second nature when used consistently. After mastering these principles, you can focus on the important part of writing—your content.

Select an Appropriate Style

Many organizations develop documentation standards that guide people creating documents. These standards are often referred to as style guides. A **style guide** is a set of standards for designing and writing documents.

Some organizations adopt a commercially available style guide such as *The Chicago Manual of Style* or *The Elements of Style.* These texts provide generic guidance on topics such as punctuation and grammar usage. Organizations may also develop one or more corporate style guides that offer more specific guidance. A corporate style guide typically describes characteristics such as:

- Document format (such as whether and how to specify headers and footers)

- Narrative mode (such as second-person narrative)

- How terms are defined

- How figures are presented

- How documents are secured (based on their target audience)

- How the company's brand and intellectual property rights are protected (such as through the use of copyright symbols, trademark symbols, and so forth)

Corporate style guides may direct writers to reference a particular commercially available style guide for more generic guidance (such as for matters involving punctuation), and then focus only on those areas that are unique to the organization. As the guidance varies slightly from one publication to the next, selecting a single commercially available publication for use by all of a company's employees or contractors ensures consistency.

Keep in mind that documentation standards vary from one organization to the next, and may vary from one document to the next. Therefore, it is important to become familiar with any applicable standards before you begin writing. Failing to do so will typically result in rework.

Appendix A lists several books and style guides you can use as references and to improve your writing skills.

Select a Narrative Mode

Selecting a narrative mode involves determining the perspective, or point of view, to be used to present information. The narrative can be identified by looking at the pronouns used in the text. Third-person narrative, shown in the following example, is generally considered a more formal style of writing and is commonly used in technical writing. Third-person narrative uses pronouns such as *he, she, it,* and *they.* To avoid gender-specific pronouns (*he* and *she*), you can avoid pronouns altogether or use third-person plural pronouns such as *they* and *their.*

Third-person narrative: This section describes technical writing best practices.

Third-person narrative: Service desk analysts can improve their writing skills by using the best practices in this section.

First-person narrative is typically considered inappropriate in technical writing. First-person narrative uses the pronouns *I* and *we*. Text written in first-person narrative puts the focus on the writer, as shown in the following example, and can be perceived as subjective or egotistical.

First-person narrative: In this section, I am describing technical writing best practices.

Second-person narrative is typically avoided in technical writing because it is directed at a single reader and can be perceived as commanding. Second-person narrative, as shown in the following example, uses the pronouns *you* and *your*. Second-person narrative is appropriate only when you want to leave no doubt about who should perform an action or take responsibility for a task. For instance, second-person narrative may be appropriate for informal documents such as emails to coworkers.

Second-person narrative: You can use this section to learn about technical writing best practices.

A key to successful writing is to select a narrative mode and then use that mode consistently. Generally, it is best to use third-person mode when preparing technical documents. If using the first-person narrative makes the information more understandable to the reader or lends more credibility to the document, then go ahead and use the first-person mode. If you want to speak directly to the reader, use the second-person mode.

Know Your Audience

To communicate clearly, you must determine the skill and education level of the intended readers. This is particularly true with technical subjects. Service desk analysts typically prepare written materials that are geared to a particular audience. For example, analysts may use email messages to communicate with customers, tickets to communicate with coworkers, and reports to communicate with management. Customers, coworkers, and managers all have varying skill and education levels, and your writing must address each reader's needs.

Ultimately, every reader should be able to understand your main ideas. Regardless of the document and its intended audience, it is appropriate to use technical terms as long as you define those terms the first time you use them. Strive to strike a balance between a very simplistic writing style and one that is highly technical. Either extreme can alienate your audience.

When preparing documents, it is also important to know how much information your reader wants and needs. This is particularly true when preparing reports and other potentially lengthy documents. For example, when presenting a business case to the requesting committee, you need to provide all available details. However, it is common to also prepare a summary, or executive summary, of the report for management. The summary typically refers the reader to the actual study for any details he or she may choose to review.

Use the Active Voice

Active voice is when the subject of a sentence causes or does the action. When you use active voice, it is clear who is doing the action. Passive voice is when the person or thing performing the action is acted upon. When passive voice is used, it is unclear who is doing the action. Active voice makes your writing style seem more vigorous and your sentences more concise. Active voice also creates the impression the activity is ongoing. The difference between active and passive voice is shown in the following example.

Passive voice: Our web site is updated every day.

Active voice: Analysts update our web site daily.

Use Simple Language

Simple language communicates more efficiently and effectively than complex language laced with technical terms. It is becoming more acceptable to use a relaxed, conversational style with customers and coworkers. But, if you would not use a phrase during a normal conversation, do not use it in written documents. Keep it simple. Remember that the ultimate goal is to communicate, not confuse. Different language styles are shown in the following example.

Complex: By applying the enclosed instructions, you can remedy the situation.

Simple: You can use these procedures to resolve the incident.

Formal: It is unfortunate that I was unavailable when you visited the Service Desk 2 days ago.

Informal: I'm sorry I missed you the other day.

Be Concise

The fewer words you use, the better. Unnecessary words waste space, take more time to read, and inhibit comprehension. Reread your first draft, and eliminate any words, sentences, or phrases that do not add value to your meaning. The following example shows a wordy sentence that has been edited to be more concise.

Wordy: Apparently, this incident has happened before and was not resolved correctly. Repeated attempts to resolve the incident have not been successful.

Concise: Attempts to resolve this recurring incident have not been successful.

Be Specific

By its very nature, technical writing must deal in specifics, not generalities. When customers and managers read an incident description or report, they seek detailed information, such as facts, figures, data, recommendations, and conclusions. Being vague can severely weaken the impact of your writing and the value of the information you are producing. Do not be content to say something is good, bad, fast, or slow when you can say *how* good, *how* bad, *how* fast, or *how* slow. Use words that are specific and concrete, as shown in the following example.

Vague: We respond to email messages as quickly as possible.
Specific: We respond to email messages within 4 hours.

Avoid or Define Jargon, Technical Terms, and Acronyms

Good technical writers use terminology that is compatible with their readers' technical background, as shown in the following example. If a technical term is appropriate and most readers will understand it, use the term. But avoid jargon and technical terms when a simpler word will do just as well. If you must use technical terms or if you want to introduce an acronym, define the term or acronym the first time you use it.

Technical: Maximize the visible spectrum on your LED.

Nontechnical: Turn up the brightness on your monitor.

Undefined acronym: Many service desks use an ACD to manage incoming telephone calls.

Defined acronym: Many service desks use an automatic call distributor (ACD) to manage incoming telephone calls.

Break Up Your Writing with Lists and Short Sections

Readers want to acquire needed information quickly and tend to have short attention spans. Short sentences and paragraphs help them read and grasp information rapidly. Numbered sequences or lists arranged in a logical order also work well, as shown in the following example.

Numbered sequence:

Check the following when a customer has a blank screen:

1. Is the monitor plugged in?
2. Is the monitor powered on?
3. Is the screen saver turned on?

Bulleted list:

Consider the following when establishing a service desk:

- Your company's goals
- Your customers' expectations
- Your commitment to customer satisfaction

 Use numbered sequences only when a specific order is required.

Be Consistent

In fiction, varying word choice is appropriate. In technical writing, however, inconsistencies cause confusion. To avoid confusion, once you have used a name or title for something, do not use a different name or title to refer to the same thing, as shown in the following example.

Inconsistent: A field service representative will be on-site tomorrow afternoon. The technician will fix your printer and your monitor.

Consistent: A technician will be on-site tomorrow afternoon to fix your printer and your monitor.

To increase the readability of a list, use the same grammatical construction for each item in a list. When lists are presented in a consistent way, readers find them easier to understand and remember, as shown in the following example.

Inconsistent grammatical construction:

Reasons companies establish a service desk include:

- To provide customers a single point of contact
- Minimization of support costs
- Minimize the impact of incidents and changes
- Increasing end-user productivity
- Customer satisfaction enhancement

Consistent grammatical construction:

Companies establish a service desk to:

- Provide customers a single point of contact
- Minimize support costs
- Minimize the impact of incidents and changes
- Increase end-user productivity
- Enhance customer satisfaction

Check Your Work for Accuracy and Completeness

Accuracy is extremely important in technical writing because people use the answers, solutions, and procedures to do their work, to use software and applications, and to operate hardware. Inaccurate or incomplete information may cause your customers or coworkers to waste time or experience additional incidents. When documenting solutions and procedures, include each and every step a customer or coworker must follow, even ones that seem obvious or intuitive to you. Ask a coworker or subject matter expert to review complex documents for accuracy and completeness. They can catch typographical errors and may question invalid assumptions you have made in the document.

Check Your Grammar, Punctuation, and Spelling

Grammar, punctuation, and spelling are important. As a final step, proofread every document to eliminate any grammar, punctuation, and spelling errors. Readers may catch errors you missed and perceive that you are lazy or uncaring when it comes to your work. The time it takes to make your documents free of errors pays off in the reader's trust of the information and leaves the reader with a positive perception of you and your company.

Many technologies provide spelling- and grammar-checking utilities that catch some errors. However, still reread your documents. Some words may be spelled correctly but used inappropriately. For example, the words *knew* and *new* are frequently confused as are the words *their*, *there*, and *they're*.

When in doubt about grammar, punctuation, or spelling rules, check a style guide or dictionary, or ask an experienced coworker for feedback.

Good writing skills will serve you well regardless of the technology you are using, the type of document you are preparing, or the audience you are trying to reach. Good writing skills also enable you to promote your ideas and enhance your opportunities by completing a greater variety of assignments.

 To improve your writing skills, write regularly, ask for feedback on your writing, and identify and work to fix your writing weaknesses.

Email Best Practices

Email has transitioned from an informal way to communicate to a serious business tool. This is evident by the overwhelming volume of email that companies receive on a daily basis and the pressure placed on companies to respond to emails quickly and professionally. Email also absorbs a significant amount of time during the typical workday. An email is a written document, and so the technical writing best practices discussed in the previous section apply. The best practices listed in Figure 4-12 provide additional techniques you can use to make the most of this tool at the service desk.

- Manage customer expectations.
- Acknowledge the person.
- Be practical and be patient.
- Check your grammar, punctuation, and spelling.
- Be forgiving.
- Avoid lengthy discussions and debates.
- Avoid negative and derogatory comments.
- Use special characters, emoticons, and acronyms appropriately.
- Use forms and templates to save time.
- Verify your distribution lists periodically.
- Standardize your signature.

Figure 4-12   Email best practices for service desk analysts

Manage Customer Expectations

Some service desks view the telephone or chat as the primary way of receiving customer contacts. Because email is a secondary method, they check it infrequently and sporadically, or they check it only periodically, such as twice per day. Other companies view email as their primary communication channel and check continuously for new messages. If customers do not know how the service desk treats email messages, they may be disappointed with the service desk's response. Therefore, it is important that the service desk communicate its email policies to customers. The service desk must indicate the priority it places on email requests and the time frame within which email requests will be addressed. These terms may be dictated by a Service Level Agreement.

Whatever your service desk's policy is, communicate it *clearly* to customers so they know what to expect. Some companies publish a service desk quick reference card or newsletter that communicates their email policy. A service desk quick reference card can also spell out the information that customers must provide when using email to submit a request. Figure 4-13 shows a sample service desk quick reference card. This card or newsletter may be made available to customers via hard copy, an email, or the web.

Service desks must refine their email policy as needed to meet their customers' needs. As service desks see an increase in the volume of email requests, analysts need to check for new messages regularly throughout the day as opposed to just periodically. The key is to respond promptly.

 Some service desks automatically inform users that their email has been received and provide a time frame within which the users can expect a response. Some service desks also automatically log emails in their incident management system.

It is also important for analysts to encourage customers to send messages to the service desk's email box, not their personal email box. This helps to ensure that every email request is logged and addressed in a timely fashion, regardless of an individual analyst's workload or schedule.

Acknowledge the Person

Because email supports a level of anonymity, people sometimes say things in an email message that they would never say in person. Other times they ignore email messages or fail to respond in a timely fashion. Remember, however, that when you send or receive email, you are conversing with another person. Think about and acknowledge that person just as you would if you were interacting in person or over the telephone. Be considerate. Be respectful. Include only those things you would say if that person were standing in front of you.

Service Desk
Quick Reference Card

This handy booklet explains the services provided by the service desk and also suggests better ways to interface with the service desk.

Give Us a Call
(800) 555-7890

Please be advised that our peak times are 8–9:30 a.m. and 1:30–2:30 p.m. During peak times, call volumes are greater and you may encounter a delay before reaching an analyst.

Send Low-Priority Email
Messages to
service.desk@example.com

We guarantee a response to all email messages within four hours.

24 Hours
Monday through Friday

Note: Coverage provided on weekends by data center operations.

What Services Does the
Service Desk Provide?

The service desk:
   Monitors all systems and
 • network lines to ensure availability

- Serves as a central point of contact for you to report any hardware or software incidents
- Assists with your user ID–related tasks (cancel, print, status, routing, etc.)
- Broadcasts information about upcoming changes and scheduled or unscheduled system outages
- Logs all incoming contacts and facilitates incident resolution to your satisfaction
- Contacts the proper source to correct any problems that we cannot solve directly and provides you with a solution in a timely manner
- Communicates with all IS departments to maintain a high level of system availability

When Contacting
the Service Desk

- Please give us your name and extension.
- Identify the PC you are working at by reading the number on the white label in the lower-right corner.
- Check your screen for any error messages that may help us determine the source of the incident.

- Give us an estimated time factor when you are experiencing a response time problem (10 seconds, 2 minutes, none).
- Indicate which system or application you are encountering a problem with (Payroll, Word, etc.).
- Give the model number of the failing device for hardware-related incidents.

How Does the Service Desk
Manage Calls?

The service desk manages calls in accordance with their business impact or priority.

Priority definitions are:

1 – System or component down, critical business impact, no alternative available, notify management immediately, bypass/recover within 4 hours, resolve within 24 hours

2 – System or component down or degraded, critical business impact, alternative or bypass available, resolve within 24 hours

3 – Not critical, deferred maintenance acceptable, circumvention possible with no operational impact, resolve within 72 hours

Figure 4-13   Sample Service Desk Quick Reference Card

Remember, too, that writing an email to a customer is different than writing an email to a friend or family member. Figure 4-14 shows an email that is so succinct, it will likely be perceived as terse.

> To: joe.smith@example.com
> From: jlk_customertechsupport@example.com
> Subject: Re: #63476
>
>
> Joe, go to http://66.182.92.20 to download the correct drivers
> Thanks for contacting Technical Support

Figure 4-14 Poorly written email message

In business, it is best to take a more formal approach. This includes using a meaningful subject line as well as personalizing your response and closing.

Use a Meaningful Subject Line

Recipients typically scan the subject line and determine if they should open, forward, save, or delete an email message. An email with a generic subject line such as "Important, Read Immediately!" may get mistaken for **spam**, an unsolicited email, and be deleted either by the recipient or by an automated email filter. A subject line such as "RE: #335262" does not tell the recipient what the message is about. A clear and meaningful subject line, as shown in the following example, lets the customer know right away that the message is a response to his or her inquiry.

RE: Backing up your data (ticket 335262)

Personalize Your Response

Use the customer's name respectfully. It is best to use a more formal greeting such as "Dear Mr. Lenox" rather than "Hi Vincent" or "Hi Vinny." Recall that if a customer uses a title, such as Professor, Dr., or Ms., address the customer using that title until the customer gives you permission to use a first name or nickname, as shown in the following example.

Dear Ms. Boyet
Dear Professor Levy
Dear Rae

When in doubt, use the exact name the customer provides in his or her closing. If a customer signs the message "Chris" and it is unclear whether Chris is a male or female, the greeting "Dear Chris" is appropriate.

Personalize Your Closing

When closing a message, use a positive tone and make it easy for the customer to obtain additional assistance in the future. Unless your company's policy directs otherwise, always include your full name and department. The following example shows an appropriate closing.

Your ticket number is 58026. Please refer to that number if you need to contact us again concerning this matter.

If we may be of further assistance, please contact us by email or by phone at 1-800-555-4567 between 7 a.m. and 9 p.m. Central Standard Time.

Sincerely,
Karen Dingman
Customer Support Service Desk

Personalizing emails does not mean that each and every email is 100 percent unique. Most service desks provide prewritten responses and closings that can be used to save time and ensure consistency. These prewritten responses and closings can then be edited to avoid sending customers a generic response that does not acknowledge their specific incident or service request. Figure 4-15 shows the email from Figure 4-14 presented in a more formal, professional manner. Although the message in Figure 4-15 is still succinct, it is much more positive and personal.

To: joe.smith@example.com
From: jlk_customertechsupport@example.com
Subject: Re: Driver not found (Ticket # 63476)

Dear Mr. Smith,

We are sorry that you were unable to locate the correct drivers for your external CD-RW drive.

Please go to www.example.com/hernandezcdcompany/support/drivers to download the correct driver.
Click the link next to the make and model of the drive you purchased. Follow the instructions
on your screen to download and install the driver.

Once the driver is installed, we suggest you uninstall and reinstall the software that came with
your drive. When you reinstall the software, the driver will be located automatically.

You can use the manual that came with the product or you can visit www.example.com/
hernandezcdcompany.com/support/usersguide to learn how to use your new drive.

If you need additional assistance, please do not hesitate to contact us by email or by phone at
1-800-555-1234 between 8 a.m. and 9 p.m. Eastern Standard Time.

Sincerely,

Bill Richards
Technical Service Desk

Figure 4-15   Well-written email message

Be Practical and Be Patient

Email is not always the best way to communicate. Use common sense. If a customer immediately
needs information that you have, pick up the telephone and call him or her. Even if you prefer to
send an email message because the information is detailed, consider calling or sending an instant
message to let the customer know it is on the way. Remember, too, that not everyone is online
throughout the day, so a customer may not respond immediately to an email message. Also, if you
send a message to someone in another country, it may be delivered outside of business hours or
during a holiday in that person's country. If you do not receive an immediate response to an email,
be patient. Resist the temptation to resend the message or perceive you are being ignored. If an
immediate response is needed, email may not be the way to go.

Check Your Grammar, Punctuation, and Spelling

Unless you are corresponding with a friend or family member, form and accuracy both matter.
The quality of an email message constitutes a first impression. People will judge the appearance
of your email messages just as they would your appearance if you were standing in front of them
and form an opinion about your competence. Remember, every message you send to a

customer also represents your entire company. Take care to avoid errors that will reflect poorly on you or your company or leave a bad impression. Resist the temptation to hastily send a response without regard for grammar and punctuation. *Always* check your spelling. Customers may mistrust or discount an entire response if they find typographical errors.

Proofread every message twice before you send it. For an important message that contains detailed or complex information or a message going to many people, ask a coworker to also proofread the message.

Be Forgiving

Just as you do not want someone to misjudge you if they find a typographical error in one of your messages, be forgiving when you find errors in others' messages. If you believe that you misunderstand the person's point or that you need additional information, simply ask for clarification or for the missing details. If you receive a copy of a message that a coworker sent to a customer or manager that contains an error that you feel could damage the reputation of your coworker or the company, tactfully bring the error to your coworker's attention and suggest specific ways the coworker can improve the message.

Avoid Lengthy Discussions and Debates

Email communication sometimes requires sending several messages back and forth to resolve an issue. This can be compounded if one of the parties is not "listening" or misunderstands the information.

When writing emails, it is best to limit the number of subjects in the message, or clearly distinguish a change in subjects, such as by leaving a blank line or by numbering the items. This is particularly important when you are requesting responses to different subjects. For long messages, consider listing your requests at the beginning of the message so the recipient does not need to continuously reread the message to uncover your questions or requests.

Conversely, respond carefully when replying to an email message. Verify that you have answered *all* of the customer's questions in the order they were presented. You may want to restate each question and follow it with the answer. Optimally, anticipate any additional questions the customer may ask and provide the information needed to fully satisfy the customer's request.

It is best to avoid attachments unless they are essential for a number of reasons: (1) They can transmit viruses. (2) They take time to download. (3) They take up space on the recipient's computer. (4) Increasingly, companies are blocking incoming email messages that contain attachments and may remove prohibited attachments before allowing outgoing email messages to be delivered. Some Internet service providers (ISPs) simply delete incoming email messages that contain attachments without informing the sender or the recipient. If detailed information must be sent, let the recipient know how to retrieve the information. A common practice is to include a link to a directory or web site.

At times, direct conversation is needed. If a lengthy discussion or an intense problem-solving session seems necessary, pick up the telephone or schedule a meeting. Remember that when communicating with customers, it is your responsibility to communicate clearly and effectively. If a customer misunderstands you, it is *you* who must clarify your position or clear up the misunderstanding.

Avoid Negative and Derogatory Comments

What you say and how you say it is just as important when using email as it is when communicating in person or over the telephone. Perhaps it is even more so with email because customers may misinterpret your words or interject an inappropriate emotion. In other words, they may *perceive* that you are being rude, even though that is not your intent. Furthermore, if you are rude, they can forward the message to your boss or print it out and hold you accountable. You also want to avoid saying negative things about your coworkers or your company. Again, email messages can be easily forwarded, and you may find that negative comment making its way to someone whom you would prefer not see it. If you do not want the world to see something, do not put it in an email message. Let your caring, *can do* attitude shine through and you cannot go wrong.

Watch what you say via social media as well. Accordingly to a 2013 FindLaw survey, 29 percent of young social media users fear their posts could cause an employer to turn them down for a job or fire them.

Use Special Characters, Emoticons, and Acronyms Appropriately

Relaying emotion and emphasizing a point are two of the most difficult things to do when communicating in the written form. Special characters and **emoticons**, symbols used to convey feelings, can help when used appropriately. In the absence of formatting features such as bold and underline, you can use special characters, such as asterisks surrounding a word as shown in the following example, to emphasize a point.

Passwords must be at least six characters long and *are* case sensitive.

Capital letters emphasize a point, but try not to overdo it. CAPITALIZING MANY WORDS OR AN ENTIRE SENTENCE IS GENERALLY PERCEIVED AS SHOUTING. It is best to follow standard capitalization rules.

Include emoticons such as a smiley face—☺—or a frowning face—☹—sparingly, and take care to use them appropriately. The following example lists appropriate and inappropriate uses of emoticons.

Appropriate: Placing a smiley face at the end of a message that indicates you are looking forward to meeting a customer at next month's user group meeting

Inappropriate: Placing a smiley face at the end of a message that delivers bad news

Resist the temptation to be overly cute or to use obscure emoticons or acronyms. Furthermore, some popular acronyms for IM, chat, or email are simply not appropriate for business communications. When in doubt, leave out special characters, emoticons, and acronyms.

Use Forms and Templates to Save Time

Service desks often use forms and templates to customize their email messages and to distribute and collect information electronically. These forms may be used to request information, report incidents, request new products and services, and so forth.

A **form** is a predefined document that contains text or graphics users cannot change and areas in which users enter data. Forms save time for customers and analysts. Customers save time because they know what data they must provide to submit their incident or service request. Analysts save time because they get the data they need to begin working on the incident or service request. Forms often correspond to the ticket entry screen of the incident management system so that analysts have the data needed to quickly log customer contacts. Some email and incident management systems interface and log contacts automatically.

A **template** is a predefined item that can be used to quickly create a standard document or email message. Templates save analysts time because they can save text and items such as custom toolbars and links to web sites, and quickly reuse those items to create documents and email messages. The time it takes to create forms and templates pays off in time saved down the road.

Verify Your Distribution Lists Periodically

Checking for new email messages and responding to messages you receive on a daily basis can be a challenge. Receiving unnecessary email can be frustrating. To avoid being a source of frustration for your customers, periodically verify your distribution lists. This ensures you do not send a message to someone who no longer works for a company or who has moved into a new position and no longer uses your company's products or services. Conversely, a person who should be receiving your information may not be on the list. Make sure you are sending messages to the correct recipients.

Email users have seen a tremendous increase in the amount of spam they receive in recent years. Companies that send legitimate emails, such as to announce the release of new products or to inform customers about viruses, must diligently manage their distribution lists in an effort to maintain customer goodwill. Many companies provide easy ways for customers to opt out of mailing lists and specify their preferences with regard to marketing emails and technical alerts. Many companies are also rethinking the practice of having customers use their email address to log on to their web sites because customers are increasingly hesitant to post their email address online, where it may fall into the hands of spammers.

Standardize Your Signature

Most email packages provide the ability to automatically insert a signature into an email message. A good practice for a service desk is to use a standard format for all analysts' signatures that includes all the ways to contact the service desk. This consistency lends a professional air to messages and ensures customers know alternate ways to get help. Figure 4-16 shows a sample service desk email signature.

Remember to put the service desk's telephone number and email address in your signature, as opposed to your personal telephone number or email address, so customers cannot contact you directly. Although it may seem you are providing personalized service by having customers

```
Mary Jane Smith
Service Desk Analyst
The Super Software Company
"Working hard to keep you working!"
Web: www.example.com
Email: service.desk@example.com
Phone: (816) 555-HELP (4357)
Fax: (816) 555-3255
```

Figure 4-16   Sample service desk email signature

contact you directly, you are actually doing your customers and coworkers a disservice. You may be out of the office on a day when a customer needs assistance and the contact will go unanswered. Furthermore, you fail to leave customers with the impression that anyone at the service desk can assist them.

Writing for a Global Audience

Technology makes it possible for service desks to interact with customers worldwide at any time of the day or night. When writing for global customers, it is important to remember that how you use expressions, dates, times, and even numbers can confuse your customers. Figure 4-17 lists two techniques you can use to minimize any confusion.

- Avoid idioms.
- Internationalize dates, times, and numbers.

Figure 4-17   Writing techniques for a global audience

Avoid Idioms

When writing for a global audience, it is best to avoid idioms. An **idiom** is a group of words whose meaning is different than the meanings of the individual words. In other words, an idiom is a phrase or expression that cannot be taken literally. Idioms may be derived from historical references, sports, books, television, or movies—all of which tend to be culturally specific. For example, the expression "Let's touch base in a couple of days" is a reference to the American sport of baseball.

Many idioms have become so commonplace that we use them without realizing they may be confusing to someone from another country. A person in the United States may say that he was "blown away" by the new technology introduced at a trade show, meaning that he was amazed or astonished by the technology. If you look at the words literally, however, you can understand how a nonnative English speaker may be confused.

Strive to edit idioms out of your documents and emails to avoid any confusion. Rather than say a service request has "fallen through the cracks," simply say that it was misplaced. Although telling a customer that you will "bend over backwards" to help may make sense to you, stating that you will do your best to help will make sense to everyone.

Internationalize Dates, Times, and Numbers

Dates, times, weights, measurements, and temperatures are expressed differently from one country to the next. The international standard for expressing dates is year/month/day. In the United States, however, the date is typically expressed as month/day/year. Most countries other than the United States use the metric system. Many countries use the Celsius temperature scale, as opposed to the Fahrenheit temperature scale used in the United States.

Strive to remember these differences when communicating with global customers. To avoid confusion, be specific. When you give someone the hours that the service desk is available, make sure you specify the time zone. You may also want to consider giving measurements and temperatures in all applicable forms. For example, "the daily temperatures at the conference are expected to be around 60° Fahrenheit (15° Celsius)."

Remember that whether your customers are in another part of the country or on the other side of the world, learning about and respecting their culture will always serve you well. It is also best to use plain language and a polite, positive tone.

Writing is an acquired skill that becomes easier when you know the rules. If you do not enjoy writing, consider taking a technical writing class so that writing becomes easier. You may find that you enjoy it more. If nothing else, you will be able to write faster and thus have more time for the things you do enjoy. The ability to write well is an important skill that technical professionals must possess. In today's digital age, good writing is quickly becoming a critical success factor. Remember that all it takes is practice, practice, practice.

Chapter Summary

- Technologies such as the Internet, email, and chat complement the telephone and on-site services as a way to communicate with customers. These technologies extend the service desk's ability to gather, organize, and use information. They also enable companies to provide self-services that customers can use to obtain the information they need, when they need it. Information is an extremely valuable resource, and people with good writing skills are able to capture it easily and accurately.

- When working in a service desk, good writing skills are needed to log tickets; send email, IM, and chat messages; develop answers to FAQs and knowledge base solutions; prepare reports; or prepare policies and procedures. When preparing these documents, always be aware of the document's target audience and purpose. Before you write a word, ensure you understand the audience's needs and how it plans to use the information. As you write, be sure to comply with applicable documentation standards so documents are accurate and consistent. Learning the rules of writing will provide you with the foundation needed to write any document and to make a positive impression with your writing.

- Writing, like any other skill, improves and becomes easier with practice. It also helps to know the rules. Technical writing best practices help you develop an effective writing style and improve your writing skills. Email best practices help you use email in a consistent, professional manner. The ability to write well is an important skill that technical professionals must possess. In today's digital age, good writing is quickly becoming a critical success factor. Remember that all it takes is practice, practice, practice.

Key Terms

blog—A journal kept on the Internet; short for *web log*.

capture—To collect.

case-based reasoning (CBR)—A searching technique that uses everyday language to ask users questions and interpret their answers.

chat—A simultaneous text communication between two or more people via a computer; also called *online chat*.

chat speak—A term for the abbreviations and slang commonly used in email, IM, and chat messages for brevity or due to a limitation on the number of characters that can be used when sending messages.

content management system (CMS)—Software used to manage the content of a web site.

data—A set of raw facts that is not organized in a meaningful way.

data analytics—The science of examining raw data with the goal of finding meaningful patterns, unknown correlations, and useful information.

148 **data field**—An element of a database record in which one piece of data is stored.

144 **decision tree**—A branching structure of questions and possible answers designed to lead an analyst to a solution.

175 **emoticon**—A symbol used to convey feelings.

134 **exchange**—An email transaction in which one email is received and another is sent.

134 **extranet**—A web site that is accessed via the Internet—that is, it can be accessed by the general public—but requires a password to gain entry to all or parts of the site.

176 **form**—A predefined document that contains text or graphics users cannot change and areas in which users enter data.

150 **frequently asked questions (FAQs)**—Well-written answers to the most common customer queries.

144 **fuzzy logic**—A searching technique that presents all possible solutions that are similar to the search criteria, even when conflicting information exists or no exact match is present.

135 **hyperlink**—Text or graphics in a hypertext or hypermedia document that allow readers to "jump" to a related idea; also called a *link*.

135 **hypermedia**—A storage method that stores information in a graphical form so users can access the information in a nonlinear fashion using hyperlinks.

135 **hypertext**—A storage method that stores information in a nongraphical form so users can access the information in a nonlinear fashion using hyperlinks.

178 **idiom**—A group of words whose meaning is different than the meanings of the individual words.

139 **instant messaging system**—Technology that enables two or more people to communicate in real time over the Internet.

131 **integrated ITSM solution**—A suite of systems that companies use to manage their incident, problem, knowledge, change, service asset and configuration management, and request fulfillment processes; sometimes called *enterprise solutions*.

134 **Internet**—A global collection of computer networks that are linked to provide worldwide access to information.

134 **intranet**—A secured, privately maintained web site that serves employees and that can be accessed only by authorized personnel.

144 **keyword**—A descriptive word or phrase.

144 **keyword searching**—The technique of finding indexed information by specifying a descriptive word or phrase, called a *keyword*.

132 **knowledge**—The application of information along with people's experiences, ideas, and judgments.

(135) **link**—*See* hyperlink.

(151) **one-to-many relationship**—One resolution that resolves many incidents or service requests.

(157) **procedure**—A step-by-step, detailed set of instructions that describes how to perform the tasks in a process.

(144) **query by example (QBE)**—A searching technique that uses queries, or questions, to find records that match the specified search criteria; can include search operators.

(156) **requirement**—Something that is necessary or essential.

(151) **resolution**—A definitive solution to an incident or service request, or a proven workaround.

(144) **search criteria**—The questions or symptoms entered by a user.

(144) **search operator**—A connecting word such as AND, OR, and NOT.

(133) **self-service**—A service that enables customers to help themselves.

(171) **spam**—Unsolicited email.

(162) **style guide**—A set of standards for designing and writing documents.

(130) **technical writing**—A technique that involves writing documentation that explains technical issues in ways that nontechnical people can understand.

(176) **template**—A predefined item that can be used to quickly create a standard document or email message.

(148) **text field**—A field that accepts free-form information.

(132) **wisdom**—The judicious application of knowledge.

Review Questions

1. Describe four ways that technology-delivered support services benefit the service desk.

2. What role do technologies such as the telephone, IM, and chat play in delivering support?

3. What role does email play in delivering support?

4. What role does the web play in delivering support?

5. How are data and information different?

6. How do good writing and keyboarding skills benefit people working in a service desk?

7. Describe five ways that companies such as hardware manufacturers and software publishers are enabling customers to help themselves.

8. Explain how intranets and extranets are different than the Internet.

9. What are the keys to a successful service desk web site?

10. List four ways that companies can use email to communicate with customers.

11. You can send an instant message even if a recipient is not online. True or False? Explain your answer.

12. Why do most service desks currently limit IM interactions with customers? Explain your answer.

13. List three reasons why analysts must learn to use and create knowledge bases.

14. What factors influence the amount of documentation that service desk analysts write?

15. Should you include all of the steps you have taken to diagnose an incident when creating a ticket? Explain your answer.

16. How is a data field different than a text field?

17. Name four users of the data entered in a ticket.

18. What is the key to a well-written FAQ?

19. What is a reusable resolution?

20. List three benefits of having a standard format for resolutions.

21. What should you do if you are asked to write a type of report that you have never written before?

22. What is a "living" document?

23. List three techniques you can use to improve your technical writing skills.

24. What is a style guide?

25. What do you need to know about your readers to communicate clearly?

26. When should you define a technical term or acronym?

27. When should you use a numbered list?

28. Name two things that customers need to know about a service desk's email policy.

29. Why is it important to check your grammar, punctuation, and spelling when sending an email message?

30. What should you do if you want to send a customer detailed information via email without using an attachment?

31. Why is it important to carefully choose your words when communicating in writing?

32. Why do you want to avoid capitalizing entire sentences in an email message?

33. A(n) _____ is a predefined item that can be used to quickly create a standard document or email message.

34. Should you put the service desk's telephone number or your personal telephone number in your standard signature? Explain your answer.

Discussion Questions

1. What are the pros and cons of using IM to communicate with customers?

2. Companies that offer web-based support services increasingly are making it difficult for customers to contact the company via the telephone. For example, some companies do not have a telephone number listed on their web site or they charge a fee for telephone-based support. Very often, the company's perspective is that it has made a tremendous investment in its web site and wants to maximize that investment. What is your perspective as a customer?

3. Prepare a list of the various channels that service desks use to deliver support services such as the telephone, email, and chat. Prepare a second list that represents the various situations in which customers need support. For example, they are unable to access an application, they are having trouble using a software package, or they want to order a new hardware device. For each situation in which customers need support, discuss what would be the most appropriate channel from the customer's perspective and then from the service desk's perspective.

Hands-On Projects

1. **Identify support options.** Select an application or device that you use regularly. Identify all of the ways you can obtain support from the vendor by answering the following questions. Prepare a short summary of your findings.

   a. Is telephone support available?

   b. During what hours is telephone support available?

   c. Is email support available?

   d. Does the vendor guarantee a response to emails within a stated time frame? If yes, what is the time frame?

   e. Does the vendor have a web site?

   f. Are FAQs available on the web site?

   g. Is chat available on the web site?

   h. What other ways, if any, can you obtain support?

2. **Document an incident and its resolution.** Briefly describe an incident that you recently encountered or were asked to help with. Include details such as who, what, when, where, and how. Document the incident and its resolution using the guidelines described in this chapter.

3. **Prepare a list of FAQs.** Prepare a list of at least five questions that you are frequently asked about an aspect of your life, such as school, your job, a hobby, or a sport that you enjoy, along with the answers to those questions. Prepare the FAQs using the guidelines described in this chapter.

4. **Prepare a progress report.** Prepare a brief progress report about an important activity you are involved in, such as a project at school or at work, or an upcoming event that you are planning, such as a wedding or a vacation. Prepare the progress report using the guidelines described in this chapter.

5. **Write a procedure.** Write a procedure for a simple task, such as tying a shoe or brushing hair. Pair up with a classmate, and then have the classmate follow your procedure exactly to see if he or she can successfully complete the task. Ask the classmate to give you feedback on your writing. For example, is the procedure accurate, complete, and easy to understand? Refine your procedure based on any observations you made while your classmate was following the procedure and based on his or her feedback. Have the classmate follow or review your refined procedure and provide any additional feedback.

6. **Assess your writing skills.** Select a report or paper that you have written recently. Read through the report and, given the technical writing best practices you have learned in this chapter, note any changes you could make to improve the quality of the report. Briefly summarize your findings.

7. **Examine a style guide.** Select a commercially available style guide or obtain a copy of any documentation standards that are published by your school. Read through the report you selected in Hands-On Project 6. Note any changes you could make in terms of style to improve the quality of the report. Briefly summarize your findings. Rewrite the report or a few pages of the report using the technical writing best practices you have learned in this chapter and the documentation standards that you have adopted. Read through the report again. Briefly summarize how the changes you have made improve the readability of the report.

8. **Develop a standard signature.** Using the format suggested in this chapter, develop a standard email signature. Use telephone numbers and addresses related to your job or school.

9. **Substitute idioms with less confusing expressions.** Conduct a class brainstorming session or use your school's online message or discussion board. Prepare a list of at least 10 idioms used in everyday language. Replace each idiom on the list with a less confusing expression.

Case Projects

1. **Requirements Report.** Your school's service desk manager has hired you as a consultant. The manager wants to enhance the service desk's web site and provide students with the ability to use self-services. Your job is to determine the students' requirements for an improved web site. Ask three to five of your classmates how the school's web site can be improved in an effort to provide self-services. Using the guidelines described in this chapter, prepare a one-page requirements report that describes your findings.

2. **Research Script Writing Best Practices.** You work as a service desk analyst for a growing law firm and believe the service desk can enhance its services by using short how-to videos to supplement classroom training. Use the web to research script writing best practices for use when creating the videos. After you finish your research and analysis, prepare a script that can be used to describe your findings. Include the following information in your script:

- Benefits of using video to provide ad-hoc training to your customers
- Five tips for creating an effective script for a how-to video
- Two to three steps the viewer can take to get started on an effective script.

Finally, prepare a 2 to 3 minute video that presents the findings in your report, and share the video with your class.

3. **Unsupported Product.** Your company is discontinuing support for a software program that is still supported by the software publisher. Create a template that can be used to respond to customers who request support for this product. Use the tips and techniques discussed in this chapter, and do not forget your *can do* attitude.

CHAPTER 5

Handling Difficult Customer Situations

In this chapter you will learn:

- ◎ The power of a positive attitude
- ◎ Why customers sometimes behave in challenging ways
- ◎ Proven techniques to handle irate, difficult, and demanding customers
- ◎ How to respond, not react, to difficult customer situations
- ◎ Positive steps you can take to stay calm and in control

Most customers are pleasant, calm, and appreciative of analysts' efforts. Unfortunately, there are times when customers become upset, angry, and demanding. These difficult situations can be extremely stressful. As a service desk analyst, you cannot control your customers' behavior. However, you *can* control your response to their behavior, and you *can* develop the skills needed to handle even the most difficult situations.

When handling difficult customer situations, it is important to be empathetic to each customer's needs. This means you must listen actively and try to understand why the customer is upset or angry. You must then acknowledge and address the customer's emotional state before you begin trying to resolve the customer's incident. You must also remember that you cannot take difficult situations personally. You must learn to maintain a positive attitude, manage your stress, and stay calm and in control.

The Power of a Positive Attitude

It would be nice if day in and day out people were pleasant and agreeable. The reality, though, is that we all have bad days. We all can become upset or even angry when things are not going our way—particularly when dealing with technology. For many people, it seems that the closer the deadline or the greater the importance of an assignment, the bigger and more frustrating a technical problem becomes. Murphy's Law—anything that can possibly go wrong will go wrong—seems particularly relevant when dealing with technology. Technology can be frustrating, but remember that when customers are having a problem using technology, it is your job as an analyst to help.

Most of the time, customers who contact the service desk are reasonable, pleasant, and grateful for your help. Some customers have a great sense of humor and are fun to work with. Some customers are very interesting and knowledgeable, and enjoy collaborating with you to resolve an incident. Some customers may even teach you a thing or two, if you are open and willing to learn. However, other customer situations are more challenging. A customer who is upset may need a caring ear and a calm helping hand. A customer may be angry and want to hear an apology followed by a swift and sound resolution to his or her incident. A customer may even be demanding, perhaps unrealistically so, and insist that you satisfy his or her needs—*now!*

Although difficult customer situations are the exception, not the rule, anyone who interacts with customers must be prepared to assist customers who are upset, angry, or demanding. A skilled professional faces these situations with tact, diplomacy, and a positive attitude. A positive attitude is a key characteristic of professionalism, and it is important to recognize that your attitude is your choice. Choosing a positive attitude enables you to focus on what you can do—versus what you cannot do—to assist customers. Focusing on what you can do greatly increases your chances of gaining the customer's trust and willingness to work toward a solution. Choosing a positive attitude also enables you to focus on customers' needs, not their angry or frustrated tone of voice. Such an approach enables you to remain empathetic and in control of your response.

When you choose to be pleasant and positive in the way you treat others, you have also chosen, in most cases, how you are going to be treated by others.

ZIG ZIGLAR

Because they are so stressful, difficult situations can affect your attitude and even your interactions with other customers. If you receive a call, an IM, or an email message from an irate customer first thing in the morning, it can ruin your entire day—if you let it. That is why it is important to avoid the temptation to make sweeping statements, such as "Why is everyone being so difficult today?" or "Why are all of these customers so nasty?" These pessimistic generalizations can cause you to lose your perspective and can even influence your coworkers' attitudes. A coworker who has been having a great day may begin to view things negatively.

Although it is sometimes hard to do, try to consider and treat each customer and each situation as unique. Try to put yourself in your customers' shoes, and strive to fully understand their needs. This perspective will not do anything to change the behavior of angry or demanding customers, but it will enable you to control how you respond to your customers' behavior.

Negative attitudes are contagious and can be detrimental to your career. A courteous, respectful, and positive *can do* attitude will serve you well both in business and in life.

Understanding Customer Behavior

To understand customer behavior, you must strive to empathize with what customers are experiencing. **Empathy** involves identifying with and understanding another person's situation, feelings, and motives. Being empathetic does not mean you are responsible. If a customer is screaming at you because he cannot print his report and it is going to be late, you are not responsible for the late report. The customer may have procrastinated writing the report until the deadline was reached, or he may have known there was a problem with the printer and failed to report it to the service desk. Regardless, it *is* your responsibility to acknowledge the fact that the customer is upset and do everything you can to help him get the report printed. Is that not what you would want if you were the customer?

People working in a service desk often know shortcuts or have access to experts that customers do not, and so they do not always fully appreciate a customer's experience. Make an effort to use the products your service desk supports, and try to experience your service desk's services. For example, rather than going directly to an expert when you have a question about how to use a new software package, call or contact the service desk as a customer would and request service. Put yourself in your customers' shoes, and try to relate to the confusion and frustration everyone feels at times when dealing with technology.

Keep in mind that the frustration customers experience when dealing with an incident may be compounded when they try to obtain support. Customers who have spent a considerable amount of time trying to fix an incident on their own, perhaps by searching the service desk's web site, may become frustrated and perhaps even angry when they are required to wait an extended period of time in a queue. Figure 5-1 lists some of the situations that may cause customers to become frustrated or angry when trying to obtain support.

- Broken promises
- Long wait times
- Confusing telephone menus
- Confusing user instructions or online help
- Unmet expectations
- Having to call or email repeatedly
- Having to repeat details previously provided
- Looming deadlines
- Negative phrases, such as "That's not our policy" or "You're wrong"
- Poor product quality
- Rude analysts
- Being placed on hold without being asked
- Being placed on hold for an extended period of time
- Web sites that are difficult to navigate, inaccurate, or incomplete
- Having to use the telephone to obtain support (no other channels to obtain support)

Figure 5-1   Situations that may frustrate or anger customers

Be aware that your company or department may be responsible for some of these situations. If a customer is angry because past promises have been broken, it is imperative that you keep your promises. If a customer is confused and you realize during your conversation that a solution posted on the service desk's web site is incorrect or incomplete, it is important that you immediately apologize for the customer's inconvenience and thank the customer for bringing the discrepancy to your attention. Work with the customer to resolve the incident, and then do all you can to ensure the solution is corrected on the web site as quickly as possible.

 Best practice frameworks such as ITIL help organizations establish customer-focused processes and technologies in an effort to minimize difficult customer situations.

Remember that you can always do something. If customers are complaining that your company's telephone menus or web site are confusing or they had to wait too long to get through on the telephone, you can pass each complaint on to your team leader or supervisor. You can also tell customers about any shortcuts they can use to move more quickly through the telephone menus or web site.

Unmet expectations are a major source of customer frustration or anger. The service desk can minimize this frustration by setting and managing customer expectations. Many service desks use SLAs to set customer expectations and to communicate the service desk's policies and procedures. If customers are regularly complaining about a particular policy, take the time to document their concerns and communicate that information to management. It may be time to change the policy!

In the middle of every difficulty lies opportunity.

ALBERT EINSTEIN

Do not think that because you have reported a customer complaint once, you do not need to report that same complaint again. You should report each instance, particularly if you are hearing the same complaint repeatedly. Management may not act on a single complaint but often will respond when it receives the same complaint from a number of customers. Take the time to document each and every customer complaint so management has an accurate picture of the problem.

On any given day, everyone has more or less patience, awareness, and persistence. The presence or absence of these qualities affects your ability to solve problems. Give your customers the benefit of the doubt. They may just be having an exceptionally bad day, or you may be the one having the bad day. Be honest. Do not blame your customers for your lack of patience or for your negative attitude. Strive to be positive and professional at all times.

It also helps to pay attention when you are a customer. Consider how you feel when you receive service from someone who is having a bad day. Consider how you feel when a service provider complains to you about how busy he is or how difficult her job is. Do you care? Typically, no. You just want service. Remember that it is not your customer's fault that you are having a bad day.

INTERVIEW WITH...

Courtesy of Bill Clement

BILL CLEMENT
TECO ENERGY
BUSINESS COMPUTING ANALYST
www.tecoenergy.com
The TECO Energy Service Desk supports 5,000 internal customers located in 34 offices in Florida and five offices in Kentucky. Bill is one of eight analysts that handle level one support. Bill is the proud recipient of the 2009 HDI Tampa Chapter Analyst of the Year award.

Question: How did you come to work in a service desk?

Answer: I've been in the computer industry for 22 years and have worked in the service desk for several different companies. I've also been a network manager and a messaging administrator, but I seem to always gravitate back to customer support. I've been in my current position for the past 6 years.

191

Question: What do you do in a typical day?

Answer: I always arrive early so I can organize my day and log in to our telephone and computer systems before customers start calling at 7:00. Another team in Information Systems provides basic services overnight such as resetting passwords, contacting an on-call analyst in the event of an emergency, and logging tickets into the queue for the morning. On a rotation basis, one person handles the tickets in the queue each day. Our primary responsibility, however, is to be on the phone. We take calls one at a time, but also watch for any trends that could indicate a systemwide incident. Within the service desk, we use an instant messaging service to communicate with our teammates while continuing to work with customers. When we receive a call for assistance, whenever possible we take remote control of the customer's desktop (after requesting permission) to help us resolve the incident. This helps to avoid the confusion and frustration that can result from having customers with varying computer aptitudes attempting to describe what is occurring on their end. It also gives the customer an opportunity to "watch and learn" while we resolve the issue. Whenever possible, even if it takes a few minutes more during the call, we offer to teach the customer how to resolve an incident through self-help. For example, we may teach a customer how to use an available utility to reset their own password or assign a printer as their default printer. Most customers prefer to learn these techniques, as it helps them to resolve incidents more quickly if they recur. This also benefits the service desk because it reduces our call volume in the future.

Question: What aspects of your job do you enjoy?

Answer: I enjoy helping people. I've had other jobs that involved just supporting technology, but it suits my personality to interact with people. I also enjoy the teamwork. Our management team constantly challenges us to grow as a team and work together toward our goals. We have monthly one-on-one call reviews to critique and refine our skills. Management also takes advantage of these reviews by observing each of our individual strengths and passing on tips and techniques to the rest of the team to help us to all grow stronger. Because we're constantly improving, each of us is happier in our job. This is reflected in the way we interact with each other, our customers, and members of other teams within IT. The structure on which we base our technical knowledge base is crucial to our strength as well. We've adopted the Knowledge-Centered Support (KCS) methodology, which ensures we capture and share what we learn as a team, rather than having each team member constantly rediscover resolutions that others already spent time resolving. Communication is key. If I don't document what I've learned or if I keep it to myself, it hurts the entire team. If I share what I've learned, our first contact resolution statistics go up, we're able to handle calls more quickly, and our relationships with teammates improve as well.

Question: What challenges do you face, and how do you overcome them?

Answer: Some of the most challenging situations come from working with different types of people, some of whom may be distraught or upset when they call for help. Listening skills are critical and help you determine how best to communicate to the customer that you care and will resolve their incident. Some people are demanding or may request more than we are allowed to give, such as granting rights to unauthorized services or installing software that we don't own. Others don't care about building a relationship—they just want their problem fixed. Regardless of the situation, you've got to listen carefully not only to what is being said, but also to how it is being said. You've got to adapt to people's personalities and state of mind, and figure out how to gain their trust in a short period of time, which isn't always easy. When you listen carefully, you can hear if a person is smiling. You can hear if he or she is upset, anxious, or angry. You need to be receptive to these cues and respond with not only the resolution to the incident, but also with the type of empathy and concern that the customer needs or expects.

Knowing how to set expectations and negotiation skills are important as well and help you give customers what they need, even if you can't give them what they want. You've also got to present yourself in a way that fosters respect. Customers may occasionally berate you or curse at you due to their frustrations or the pressures they may be under. They may feel threatened by their boss, or they may just need to vent. In those situations, you must remember the customers' emotions aren't directed at you and you must not take the situation personally. You need to let these situations roll off your shoulders and focus on giving customers what they need—both emotionally and technically. You've got to ensure customers that if you can't help, you will get them to someone who can.

Challenging situations are inevitable, and you need to learn to control your emotions. It's something you have to think about before you start your day and be prepared to deal with. If you get upset because of something a customer says during an interaction, you're only hurting yourself. If you stay in control, everyone wins. Be empathetic. Tell the customer that you understand how frustrating this can be. Then make a "hero statement" such as "I'm sure we can fix this." You will usually hear your customer take a deep breath and relax when they realize that they are in good hands, that you care, and that you will do whatever it takes to help them resolve the incident so they can get back to doing their job.

Question: What do you do following a particularly difficult call?

Answer: Sometimes I just take a deep breath, compose myself emotionally, put a genuine smile on my face, and get ready for the next call. If I feel that I've offended the customer or made a mistake in some way, I bring the call to my manager's attention. This gives my manager the opportunity to contact the customer and determine if we need to follow up. This reassures the customer that we care about them and builds the customer's confidence and respect for our team. Sometimes we may go back and listen to the recorded call to figure out what we can learn from the situation and how we can improve.

Question: What advice would you give someone pursuing technical customer support as a career?

Answer: It's important to have an understanding of technology along with troubleshooting skills. You must also be able to understand the dynamics of working in a team setting. Most importantly you have to be a good listener. Careful, perceptive listening enables you to determine the customer's personality and state of mind, and then how to approach the call. It is a skill that requires patience, daily practice, and review to develop and maintain. In time, you'll learn to hear a customer's disposition and needs, and quickly determine how to respond appropriately. You must also realize that intuitive communication is a two-way street. When customers call, they need your help so they can get back to doing their job. If you have just completed a difficult call with an abusive customer, the new caller still deserves to be greeted by a strong, happy analyst who conveys confidence and concern for his or her needs. The new caller shouldn't be able to tell that you are having a bad day or that you've just handled a difficult call. Learn first to keep yourself happy and positive, and make the choice each day not to let difficult customer situations rule your emotional state. Take a deep breath. Put a smile on your face and in your voice. Listen carefully so you can understand and empathize with your customers' needs. In this job, you need to be technically competent, but it is just as important to build strong relationships with both your customers and your team.

Winning Over Difficult Customers

Working with difficult customers requires patience and composure. How you respond to these customers, particularly during the early moments of your conversation, greatly influences their perception and willingness to work with you. If a customer is confused or upset, you can make the situation worse by failing to listen or by failing to empathize with the customer's situation. If a customer is frustrated, you can cause the customer to become even more frustrated or even angry by failing to communicate with positive statements. Figure 5-2 lists a step-by-step approach you can use to handle even the most difficult situation.

Step 1: Get focused.

Step 2: Let the customer vent.

Step 3: Listen actively.

Step 4: Acknowledge the customer's emotional state.

Step 5: Restate the situation and gain agreement.

Step 6: Begin active problem solving.

Figure 5-2 Technique for handling difficult customer situations

Step 1: Get Focused

If you sense that an interaction with a customer is going to be difficult, get yourself focused. Take a deep breath. Make sure you have a smile on your face or that you appear eager and caring. Sit or stand up straight, and get ready to take notes. These are preparatory steps that you should be following prior to each customer interaction—whether on the phone or face to face—but they are sometimes overlooked. You may be particularly busy or you may be relaxed and joking with coworkers when you answer the phone without thinking. Before you know it, the pressure is on. Rather than plowing forward unprepared, take a few seconds to relax and get focused.

Step 2: Let the Customer Vent

An upset or angry customer has a story to tell, and you must let the customer tell that story from beginning to end without interruption. If you interrupt the customer at any time, it is likely that he or she will start the story over. Or, the customer may have rehearsed what to say and written down several points that he or she wants to make. Until each point is made, the customer cannot calm down. This venting is necessary for the customer's well-being. Your challenge is to listen actively and look for cues that the customer is ready for you to begin taking control of the interaction. Customer cues include a deep sigh or a challenging statement such as "...and what are you going to do about it?"

Customers may occasionally call with a story that you have heard many times before. It is important to remember that although you have heard the story before, this particular customer is telling it for the first time and wants to be heard. Be patient and understanding. Use the opportunity to practice your active listening skills. You may hear something you did not expect.

Step 3: Listen Actively

Recall that active listening involves participating in a conversation and giving the speaker a sense of confidence that he or she is being heard. When a customer is venting, resist the temptation to ask questions, but still communicate the fact that you are listening. Nod your head or use acknowledging and encouraging verbal phrases at appropriate points in the conversation, as shown in the following example, to let the customer know you are listening.

> Uh-huh.
> Go on.
> I see.
> I understand.

Remember also to pay attention to *what* is being said and *how* it is being said. Listen carefully for the central theme of the customer's incident or complaint. In other words, listen for the "real" problem in the customer's story. Try not to get bogged down by a customer's angry words or by what may be exaggerated statements. Take notes, and be prepared to restate the customer's incident or complaint.

Step 4: Acknowledge the Customer's Emotional State

An upset or angry customer needs to feel that you care and that you fully understand the situation before he or she can calm down. If you fail to acknowledge the customer's emotional state, that customer is likely to perceive that you were not listening and become even more upset. You must acknowledge the customer's emotion, even if you do not understand why the customer has that emotion. Try to empathize with the customer or at least accept that this customer may be having a really bad day and needs your help. This is also an excellent time to build rapport by respectfully using the customer's name and communicating your willingness to take responsibility and do all you can. In other words, let the customer know you are there to help resolve his or her incident or handle his or her complaint to the best of your ability. When appropriate, sincerely apologize to the customer for any inconvenience your company may have caused, as shown in the following examples.

> Miss Navarro, I'm sorry our field service engineer did not arrive at the promised time. Let me find out what happened. Would you like to hold while I contact his office, or would you like me to call you back?
>
> Mr. Boyet, I'm sorry there is a problem downloading software from our web site. Let me walk you through the procedure.

It is imperative that you be respectful and genuine at this point of the interaction. If you use a snide or derogatory tone of voice when using the customer's name, the customer will most likely be offended. If you use an insincere tone of voice when apologizing, the customer will doubt your apology. If you do not feel that you can apologize using a sincere tone of voice, you must at least acknowledge the customer's emotion and let the customer know you will do all you can to help, as shown in the following examples.

> Mr. Sheng, I understand that you are very upset. I will do everything I can to get this laptop problem resolved right away.
>
> Mary, I appreciate your frustration and I want to help. Help me understand the problem you are having with your tablet.

Step 5: Restate the Situation and Gain Agreement

It is imperative that you gain the customer's agreement that you fully understand the situation and manage the customer's expectations about when a solution will be delivered. Fixing the wrong incident or promising the incident can be resolved in an unrealistic time frame just makes the situation worse. Many organizations have SLAs in place that dictate the time frame within which incidents will be resolved based on their priority. Analysts must be aware of these time frames and avoid making promises that cannot be met. Begin, when possible, by restating the incident in the customer's exact words. This lets the customer know that you were listening. Ask the customer to verify your understanding of the incident. Use a simple verifying statement, such as the ones in the following example, to obtain agreement from the customer that you have heard the point he or she is making.

> Is that correct?
>
> Did we cover everything?

It may not always be possible or practical to restate the incident in the customer's exact words. Customers can sometimes be vague when describing an incident, and symptoms can have multiple interpretations. In these situations, gain customer agreement by paraphrasing. When you finish paraphrasing the incident, ask the customer to verify your understanding of the situation.

There may also be times when you need to let the customer know that you do not understand the information that he or she is providing. When doing so, avoid negative phrases that have an accusatory tone. A better approach is to ask the customer to help you understand. The following example shows how a negative phrase can be reworded in a positive way.

Negative words: You're not making any sense. You're confusing me.

Positive words: I'm sorry, I'm confused. Could you repeat…

Step 6: Begin Active Problem Solving

If you have been patient, clearly communicated that you care and sincerely want to help, and gained agreement from the customer that you understand the situation, the customer should now have calmed down. This means that you can begin diagnosing the incident and developing an action plan or solution. This does not mean you can lose your focus. It is likely that the customer is still fragile, and you may have to repeat some or all of these steps for handling a difficult customer situation before the incident is resolved fully.

Many analysts want to go straight to problem solving when a customer is upset or angry. Their thinking is that the best and fastest way to calm down the customer is to resolve the incident. Solving the incident is important and will be the final outcome, but assisting and satisfying the customer is the ultimate goal. This requires that you strive to understand, acknowledge, and address the customer's emotional needs as well as the customer's technical needs.

 Remember that you are supporting people—living, breathing human beings with feelings and emotions—not just technology.

Note that each step applies to handling difficult email messages from customers as well. It is sometimes tempting to scan a customer's message and quickly send off a response. With email, however, you do not have to reply instantaneously as you do when handling a telephone call. You can read and reread the message before formulating a reply. If the email is particularly lengthy, you can print the message and underline or highlight each of the customer's questions or complaints to ensure each is addressed in your reply. Or, you can state, "See responses below," and then type your replies in a different color font after each of the customer's questions or complaints. If a customer's description of an incident is unclear, you can paraphrase the situation, provide a solution based on your understanding, and encourage the customer to reply if you misinterpreted the situation.

Although it is important to respond promptly to all email messages, take the time you need to (1) calm down, and (2) draft a positive, professional response. A good technique is to draft a reply, reread the customer's email to ensure you did not miss or misinterpret any details, and then fine-tune your reply. When in doubt, ask a coworker or team leader to read the customer's email and verify that your response is appropriate.

Calming Irate Customers

Customers do not start out being irate. Typically, people first experience a lesser emotion, such as frustration or confusion, which builds to anger. In most cases, these emotions can be avoided by using the technique for handling difficult customer situations previously discussed, and by the proper handling of situations such as placing customers on hold, transferring customers, and so forth. At times, however, people run out of patience or take offense to a situation and become angry. Incorrectly labeling or commenting on an emotion that the customer is not conveying can also escalate emotions. For example, telling someone who is merely frustrated to "calm down" can make them angry.

People experience varying degrees of anger. Some people are very slow to anger. Others seem to become enraged by the slightest inconvenience. If a customer's incident or concern is addressed quickly by using the technique for handling difficult customer situations previously described, he or she may not become irate. On the other hand, bypassing one or more of the steps in this technique can cause the customer to become increasingly upset or angry. It is important to listen carefully so you can accurately assess and address a customer's level of emotion.

Initially, a customer describes the inconvenience of the incident being experienced, or his or her frustration with the current situation. By acknowledging the customer's frustration and communicating that you will do all you can to remedy the situation, as shown in the following example, you can calm the customer and gain the customer's confidence.

Customer: I've had to wait 20 minutes to get through. Why can't you people learn to pick up the telephone?

Analyst: I'm sorry to keep you waiting. How can I help you?

Customer: This is the third time I've called about this printer this week. Why can't you get someone out here who will fix it right?

Analyst: I'm sorry that your printer is still not working correctly. Let me pull up a history of the problems that you have been having so we can determine the best course of action.

If you fail to acknowledge the customer's emotion or the source of frustration, the customer may become even angrier, as shown in the following example. Very often a customer becomes angrier because he or she perceives that you do not understand and are not addressing his or her concerns. In other words, the customer perceives that you are not listening.

Customer: You're not listening. Let me say it again.

Customer: I don't seem to be getting anywhere with you. Let me talk to your supervisor.

At this point, the customer may be starting to mistrust you. Even though you may have been listening very carefully, you have not *communicated* that fact to the customer. You may have acknowledged *what* the customer said, but not *how* the customer said it. The customer is going to either give you one more chance or ask to speak with someone else. Make sure you understand how to engage help at this point, if you need it. Some telephone systems have a "panic" button that analysts can press to get their team leader's or supervisor's attention. Some analysts stand up and wave or somehow signal to a coworker or team leader that they need assistance. Do your best to handle the call, but do not be afraid to ask for help when you need it.

 Be aware of your company's policies regarding dealing with upset and angry customers. Know what you can and cannot do to assist these customers as well as when and whom to ask for help.

One situation where analysts may need help is when a customer is using particularly offensive or abusive language. Most companies have policies that dictate how to handle this type of situation. Many companies coach their analysts to determine if the customer is using foul language in reference to a situation or against the analyst personally. If the customer is using foul language in reference to a situation, it is up to individual analysts to determine their tolerance level for the language. Analysts are encouraged to remember that customers will often stop using foul language after they have had a chance to vent and the analyst acknowledges the customer's emotional state (as previously discussed). If the customer is using foul language against the analyst personally or the analyst is uncomfortable with the language, most companies advise analysts to progressively ask the customer to speak in a professional manner, as shown in Figure 5-3.

1. Let the customer know that you want to help. "I am sorry that there has been a problem. I will do everything I can to assist you."

2. If after venting, the customer continues to use offensive language, ask the customer to speak in a professional manner. "I'm trying to assist you. Could you speak in a professional manner?"

3. If the customer continues to use offensive language, let the customer know that you are going to take action if the language persists. "I appreciate your frustration [anger, concern], and I'm trying to assist you. If you cannot speak in a professional manner, I will have to transfer you to my supervisor."

4. If the customer cannot speak in a professional manner, take action. "As you are unable to speak in a professional manner, please hold while I transfer you to my supervisor."

Figure 5-3   Technique for handling offensive or abusive language

In today's society, swearing or cursing is increasingly commonplace. In some cases, customers may not even be aware that their language is potentially offensive. Analysts must strike a balance between empathizing with the fact that the customer is upset while giving the customer a chance to calm down, and taking abuse. Accepting foul language, whether from customers or coworkers, in essence, gives the person permission to continue using the language. If you find a person's language offensive, do not be afraid to speak up. It is important to do so, however, in a professional manner that is in keeping with your company's policies.

Watch *what* you say and *how* you say it whether you are communicating in person, over the telephone, or in writing.

Finally, some customers will become irate even if you have done your best. Remember that some people have unrealistic expectations or they may be trying to manipulate you in order to get their way. Sometimes customers are simply under so much stress that they are incapable of calming down. Your challenge is to ensure your actions do not drive customers to their irate state. It is very important to understand that customers may be responding to your behavior, or what they perceive is your behavior, when they become increasingly angry. For example, you may be using negative phrases, such as "That's not our policy" or "We don't support that," without offering the customer any options or alternatives. Keep it positive, and focus on what you *can* do.

CASE STUDY: Customers' Complaints and Social Media

The Internet and social media channels make it possible for customers to voice their opinions and complaints to a wide audience any time of the day or night. Social media channels include Internet forums, blogs and microblogs such as Twitter, wikis, social networking sites such as Facebook and Myspace, and video-sharing sites such as vimeo and YouTube. According to a 2013 study conducted on behalf of global insurer XL Group, half of 18–34 year olds say they are more likely to complain about a product on social media than they were a year ago. According to a 2012 Edison Research survey, 42 percent of customers complaining in social media expect a response with 60 minutes. According to the same survey, 57 percent of respondents who have attempted to contact a brand, product, or company through social media for customer support, expect the same response time at night and on weekends as during normal business hours.

Because these technologies often offer a perceived layer of anonymity, customers can be quick to judge and can be brutal with their criticism. Successful companies understand that this feedback can reach millions of people, and they work hard to ensure customer complaints are handled quickly and professionally.

Some companies have proactively joined these various channels and use them to communicate with customers, monitor customer complaints, and identify improvement opportunities. According to a 2011 Martiz Research study, 29 percent of respondents who lodged a complaint via Twitter were contacted by the companies in question. This is smart business as, according to the same study, 83 percent of the complainants that received a reply liked or loved the fact that the company responded.

Other companies use social media channels to market their companies and promote their brand, but they fail to view these channels as ways to improve customer service. These companies can only react when a customer complaint, viewed by millions via the Internet, causes negative publicity and drives away customers.

Savvy consumers increasingly research companies' customer service reputation online prior to purchasing products and services at least some of the time. Companies that respond quickly, and publicly, to customer complaints—even minor complaints—are viewed as responsive and customer focused. Companies that fail to respond, or respond only once complaints gain widespread publicity, are viewed as uncaring and untrustworthy.

Most companies have policies regarding employees' use of social media channels. Some prohibit such use altogether. Others encourage their employees to reach out to customers who post complaints or express dissatisfaction or confusion regarding the company's products and services. Employees using social media must understand that they are acting on behalf of their company and so must take responsibility for what they write and exercise good judgment. These employees must also understand that their employers often monitor social media channels and so are aware of what employees are saying, even when away from the office. The best companies view complaints as a valuable opportunity to improve and strive to handle complaints before they go viral. These companies understand that customers whose complaints have been resolved swiftly and fairly will not only become loyal customers, they will often refer other customers to the company—hopefully via the Internet.

Repairing a Damaged Customer Relationship

Even the most dissatisfied customers will continue doing business with a company if their incidents and complaints are *consistently* handled quickly and cheerfully. Companies that provide world class customer service understand this fact and work hard to establish policies aimed at maintaining their customers' good will, even in difficult situations.

Realistically speaking, however, sometimes there is nothing you can do for a customer. The customer may simply have unrealistic expectations. Or, the customer may believe that a product is broken, when, in fact, the product was simply not designed to perform the function the customer requires. In this type of situation, a positive vocabulary is extremely important. Let the customer know what you can do or what the product can do. When possible and appropriate, describe to the customer any alternate ways to meet his or her needs. If the customer is still dissatisfied, let the customer know that you will document the complaint and pass it on to management. When appropriate, ask your team leader or supervisor to assess the situation and speak with or contact the customer.

As a service desk analyst, the best thing you can do is stay focused on what you can do for the customer. The worst thing you can do is make promises that you cannot keep.

You cannot assume that you have regained a customer's trust just because that customer seems to be happy when you complete a contact. Customers often feel they have to fight for their rights, and even the slightest misstep can cause a customer to once again become defensive and distrusting. Patience and consistent follow-through are required to repair a damaged relationship. **Follow-through** means that you keep promises, including getting back to the customer when you said you would—even if you do not have a resolution to the incident. If letting the customer know that you have not forgotten about him or her is the best you can do, it is better than the customer hearing nothing. Follow-through means that a field service engineer arrives on-site when promised or within the time frame specified in the company's SLA—or calls *before* the engineer is late to arrange a new arrival time. The key here is to keep customers informed and be sure they know and are comfortable with exactly what is being done to resolve their incident or complaint.

Consistent follow-through builds trust. Companies that keep their customers informed, keep their customers!

Proactive communication is an extremely effective way to prevent or minimize customer dissatisfaction. The best companies proactively communicate by, for example, broadcasting a message when customers can expect a longer than usual wait time when calling. Some companies send letters or emails to customers informing them of a problem with the company's web site or about a product recall. Most customers appreciate being informed of an incident before they discover it for themselves.

After the incident has been resolved, it is important that you or someone from your service desk or company follow up to ensure the customer is fully satisfied. **Follow-up** means that a service desk or company representative verifies that the customer's incident has been resolved to the customer's satisfaction and that the incident has not recurred. Some companies have the service desk manager or the customer's sales representative contact a dissatisfied customer in an effort to show that the company values the customer's business. In some cases, you may be the company representative contacting the customer.

Although you may feel uncomfortable following up with a customer who was very angry and, from your perspective, perhaps unreasonable, it is the only way to repair the relationship. Repairing the relationship enables both you and the customer to feel comfortable when working together in the future. Furthermore, some analysts report that when they have called or emailed angry customers to follow up, the customers apologized for their behavior. A customer may indicate that he was getting pressure from his boss or she was having one of those days when nothing seemed to go right. When difficult situations are handled properly, even the most disgruntled customer can become the service desk's greatest advocate.

Your most unhappy customers are your greatest source of learning.

BILL GATES

Keeping Yourself in Control

Difficult situations are inevitable when interacting with customers, so it is important to be prepared. By practicing the techniques listed in Figure 5-4, you will gain the confidence needed to stay calm and in control. By responding to difficult situations in a positive, professional manner, you will gain personal confidence as well as your customers' trust and respect. Remember that you are a professional, and your job is to serve and support your customers.

- Learn to respond, not react.
- Stay calm under pressure.
- Get ready for your next contact.

Figure 5-4 Techniques for staying in control

These techniques for staying in control are life skills that you can apply to any difficult situation, professional or personal. When you master these skills, difficult situations become less stressful as you develop a track record of handling them successfully.

204

Learn to Respond, Not React

Reacting is easy, especially in a difficult customer situation. Without thinking, you say or do the first thing that comes to mind. Very often, you mirror the behavior, even bad behavior, of your customer. If a customer shouts, your instinct may be to shout back. If a customer is rude, you may be tempted to be rude in return. When you react without thinking, situations can quickly spiral out of control and you may say or do things you will later regret.

Responding involves making a conscious choice to control *your* behavior. As a professional, it is your responsibility to act in a positive, constructive way, regardless of the customer's behavior. Try to remember that a customer who is angry or upset needs your assistance just as badly as a pleasant customer who asks you nicely for help. Try to think rationally about what the customer needs, and respond calmly to that need.

Practice using the proven techniques discussed in this chapter to get and keep even the most difficult situation under control. Recall that getting focused is the first step in handling a difficult customer situation. It is easy to lose your focus, so take a few seconds to calm yourself any time you feel that you are losing control. By thinking rationally and staying calm at all times, you can *respond*, rather than react, to your customers.

One reason that service providers may react negatively in difficult customer situations is that they feel defensive and take the situation personally. You may think or even say, "It's not my fault—," and you are right. It typically is not your fault, and even if it is your fault (for example, you made a mistake), you cannot take the situation personally. An effective way to deal with a difficult customer situation is not to worry about who is at fault. Simply ask the customer to give you the opportunity to assist and then focus on what you can do. Do your best, learn from your mistakes, and take satisfaction in knowing that most customers appreciate your efforts.

Stay Calm under Pressure

People experience stress and pressure differently. Some analysts can remain relaxed in stressful situations and rarely become upset. Other analysts feel threatened and may panic when facing even a slightly difficult situation. Learning to stay calm under pressure requires that you learn to control *your* behavior. It is your job to stay in control and handle even the most difficult situations in a professional, positive manner.

Difficult situations are tough. As a human being, you can lose control of your emotions on any given day in much the same way that your customers can lose theirs. This is because different sides of our brains handle logic and emotion. As is illustrated in Figure 5-5, the left side of our brain absorbs memorized data and handles linear and logical thinking. The right side of our brain handles emotion.

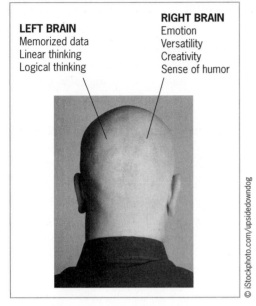

LEFT BRAIN
Memorized data
Linear thinking
Logical thinking

RIGHT BRAIN
Emotion
Versatility
Creativity
Sense of humor

© iStockphoto.com/upsidedowndog

Figure 5-5   How our brains handle logic and emotion

The two sides of our brain work together. Though in most people one side dominates the other. When we are extremely upset or angry, however, the right brain takes over. You may have heard the expression "he's not in his right mind," which implies that someone is not thinking clearly. Well, the truth is that when we are extremely upset or angry, we *are* in our right mind. As a result, we are incapable of thinking logically as that is an activity handled by our left brain.

Given the way our brains work, you can understand why you must avoid the temptation to focus only on problem solving when someone is in an emotional state. In other words, you must resist the temptation to engage the customer in left-brain activities when the customer's right brain is in control. You must first acknowledge the customer's emotional state and let the customer know that you empathize and understand his or her needs and expectations. Then, and only then, will the customer regain the capability of his or her left brain and as a result be ready to respond logically and rationally.

Determining the dominant side of your brain may be helpful to you as a service desk analyst. If you are predominantly a "left-brained" person, you will tend to be a very logical thinker and may have a difficult time understanding why other people become emotional. As a result, you may try to go straight to problem solving without addressing the customer's emotional needs. Remember, this can cause the customer to become even more upset because the customer may perceive that you are not listening. Predominantly left-brained thinkers must learn to listen for and acknowledge emotion.

If you are a very "right-brained" person, you may find that you become emotional fairly quickly in a difficult situation. You may find that you tend to become upset or angry when you encounter someone who is upset or angry. Remember that reacting in a negative way can cause a difficult situation to quickly escalate out of control. Predominantly right-brained thinkers must learn to control their own emotions.

Whether you are left- or right-brained, it is important that you remain calm and in control at all times. This is essential when you are interacting with a customer who is extremely upset or irate. In other words, you must maintain control of your ability to think logically. If you become upset or enraged, then neither you nor the customer is going to be able to bring the situation under control or solve the problem. One way to remain calm and in control is to learn the symptoms that you experience when you are getting upset or angry, such as the ones listed below.

- Clenched jaw
- Concentration loss
- Grinding teeth
- Headache
- Nausea
- Neck and shoulder tension
- Rapid heart rate
- Reddening face
- Shallow breathing
- Strained tone of voice
- Sweating

When speaking to a customer on the phone or face to face, the customer may notice these symptoms, and the customer's perception of these symptoms could, in fact, make the situation worse. If your voice becomes strained, the customer may perceive that you are raising your voice or shouting, or the customer may perceive that you are being rude or curt and begin to respond in a similar manner. Condition yourself to stay focused on what you have to do, and not how you feel. Figure 5-6 lists some of the techniques you can use to stay calm under pressure. Each technique has a different benefit, so you may want to use two or more of these techniques in combination.

- Take a deep breath.
- Sip water.
- Use positive imagery.
- Use positive self-talk.

Figure 5-6   Calming techniques

Take a Deep Breath

Tension causes your chest to tighten, which in turn causes your breathing to become shallow. This can also affect your voice, which may become high pitched or raspy. Taking a deep breath or a series of deep breaths will lessen the tension and enable you to resume a normal breathing rate. Breathe in deeply—inhale—through your nose so that you fill your lungs and feel the release of tension, then breathe out—exhale—fully through your mouth. Remember, however, not to exhale audibly or the customer may perceive your deep breath as a sigh of weariness or a sign of frustration. You may want to mute the telephone for a second or two while you take your deep breath, or, when facing a customer, you may want to take a series of smaller, less obvious breaths.

Sitting or standing up straight is another way to improve your breathing. Poor posture—caused by slumped shoulders, slouching, or an ill-fitting chair—makes it difficult to breathe deeply. Shallow or restricted breathing will, in time, reduce your energy and affect your attitude. Sitting up straight enables you to fully inflate your lungs and release nervous energy.

Sip Water

Taking a sip of water lubricates your throat and helps restore your voice to its normal pitch. It will also buy you the few seconds you may need to calm yourself before you speak. Sipping water is comparable to the practice of counting to three before you speak.

Use Positive Imagery

Positive imagery is the act of using mental pictures or images to influence your thinking in a positive way. Some analysts envision themselves standing next to the customer, looking at the incident. Rather than negatively imagining that you are pitted against the customer, this positive image enables you to remember that you and the customer are pitted against the incident, as shown in Figure 5-7. Some analysts replace the image of an angry customer with the image of someone they love and care about. Analysts who use this technique find that it enables them to remain empathetic and to better understand their customer's perspective.

Use Positive Self-Talk

Positive self-talk is the act of using words to influence your thinking in a positive way. The words people use, even when they are talking to themselves, influence their thoughts and attitudes. It is normal for people to talk to themselves throughout the day. Whether people are conscious of it or not, the words people use affect how they think about themselves and how they experience situations. By watching the words that you use, you can begin to notice which of your thoughts are positive and which are negative. Once you become aware of how your self-talk sounds, you can practice eliminating negative thoughts and attitudes by using positive words, as shown in the following example.

Figure 5-7 Negative versus positive imagery

Negative words: I can't handle this.

Positive words: I know what to do.

When facing a difficult customer situation, use positive self-talk to remind yourself that you cannot take this situation too personally. Tell yourself that you know what to do, and coach yourself to use the proven techniques discussed in this chapter to calm your customer and begin resolving the incident. Train yourself to replace negative thoughts about the customer with positive thoughts. Try to maintain a positive perspective, as shown in the following example.

Negative perspective: What a jerk.

Positive perspective: This person is really upset. What can I do to help?

Practice will enable you to make each of these calming techniques a habit that you will do without conscious thought. Techniques you can use to practice staying calm under pressure include role-playing with another analyst or with your supervisor or team leader. You can also record your calls and listen to them afterward, listen to other analysts' calls to learn what you can, and review a difficult call in a staff meeting to see how it could have been handled better.

Remember, too, that difficult situations do not occur only when you are at work. Practice these techniques any time you find yourself losing control. If someone is rude to you or you find yourself becoming angry, think about how you are feeling and make a conscious effort to calm yourself and regain control. The more you practice these techniques, the more confidence you will have when handling difficult customer situations.

Customers tend to respond positively when you are calm, confident, and in control. Learn to control your own emotions so you can focus on meeting your customers' needs. Remember, you must meet your customers' emotional needs as well as their technical needs, which requires active listening and empathy.

Get Ready for Your Next Contact

It is likely that you will find some difficult situations more draining than others. The time of day the situation occurs, your level of preparedness, and even your personal mood all influence your ability to recover from a difficult situation. Take the time you need to compose yourself before answering your next call or chat, handling your next email, or meeting your next customer. Give yourself the opportunity to let your positive, *can do* attitude shine through. In most cases, you may just need to stand up, take a deep breath, and stretch a bit. Then you will be ready to go. In some cases, however, you may need to follow all or some of the techniques listed in Figure 5-8. You need to follow these techniques only when you feel a situation has been particularly upsetting.

- Inform your team leader or supervisor.
- Take a short break.
- Avoid caffeine or other stimulants.
- Employ stress-coping mechanisms.

Figure 5-8 Techniques for recovering from a particularly upsetting situation

Inform Your Team Leader or Supervisor

If you are upset, it is likely that the customer may still be upset. Your team leader or supervisor needs to be informed to determine what, if any, additional steps should be taken to satisfy the customer. This also lets you present the facts of the situation from your perspective, enabling your team leader to have a balanced view in case the customer perceives the situation differently.

Take a Short Break

Leave the area, and catch your breath for a few moments. Take a short walk outside if you can to get some fresh air, or to the water cooler to get a drink of water. If a walk is not possible, take a minute to look out the window and observe nature. If the day is dismal, look at art or go someplace where you can hear music. Engage as many senses as you can and try to clear your mind of negative thoughts.

Avoid Caffeine or Other Stimulants

Caffeine is a stimulant and can increase your anxiety or exacerbate your feelings of frustration or anger. Caffeine is found in coffee, tea, cola, and chocolate. If you feel compelled to eat or drink something after a difficult situation, keep it simple. Drink a big glass of water or eat a simple snack, such as whole wheat crackers or a small handful of nuts. Give your body the time and fuel it needs to unwind.

Employ Stress-Coping Mechanisms

Just as people experience stress in different ways, people also employ varying techniques to manage and cope with stress. Some analysts keep a stress ball at their desk. Some service desks have a punching bag that analysts can use. Some analysts turn to a coworker or seek out a friend whom they can talk to about the situation. Try these or other stress-coping mechanisms.

 Chapter 9 explores the causes of stress and ways to minimize its negative effects.

Finding the humor in a situation is an excellent stress-coping mechanism. Having a sense of humor is not just about telling or laughing at jokes. It is a perspective on life that allows you to maintain a positive outlook. Laughter is a great release, and people with a sense of humor tend to be more flexible and less anxious. Used inappropriately, however, humor can make a situation worse. Take care to avoid even the appearance of laughing at a customer or belittling his or her concerns. When in doubt, keep your humorous thoughts to yourself.

Remember that each and every difficult situation you handle will increase your confidence and your ability to handle future situations. As time passes, you will find these situations less stressful because you have developed the skills needed to calm your customers and gain their confidence. You will also have learned how to take care of yourself and prepare yourself for the next customer. Difficult situations are inevitable. By practicing the techniques discussed in this chapter, you can handle these situations with confidence.

Chapter Summary

- Most customers are pleasant, calm, and appreciative of your efforts, but there are times when customers become upset, angry, and demanding. A skilled professional faces these situations with tact, diplomacy, and a positive attitude. A positive attitude is a key characteristic of professionalism, and it is important to recognize that your attitude is your choice. Choosing a positive attitude enables you to focus on what you can do—versus what you cannot do—to assist customers. Choosing a positive attitude also enables you to focus on the customers' needs, not their angry or frustrated tone of voice. Such an approach enables you to remain empathetic and in control of your response.

- Proven techniques enable you to understand, acknowledge, and address the emotional needs of your customers as well as their technical needs. Consistent follow-through and follow-up enable you to maintain your customers' goodwill and repair a damaged relationship. When difficult situations are handled properly, even the most disgruntled customer can become the service desk's greatest advocate.

- Difficult situations are inevitable, so it is important to be prepared. By thinking rationally and staying calm at all times, you can learn to respond, not react, to these situations when they occur. One way to stay calm and in control is to learn the symptoms such as headaches, nausea, or neck and shoulder tension that you experience when you are under pressure. You can then use techniques such as taking a deep breath or sipping water to relieve these symptoms, enabling you to focus on meeting your customers' needs. Taking the time to compose yourself before you answer a new call, handle a new email, or meet with the next customer is also important.

- Each and every difficult situation you handle will increase your confidence and your ability to handle future situations. In time, you will find these situations less stressful because you have the skills needed to calm yourself and your customer and to stay in control at all times.

Key Terms

empathy—The act of identifying with and understanding another person's situation, feelings, and motives.

follow-through—The act of keeping promises, including calling the customer back when you said you would—even if you do not have a resolution to the incident.

follow-up—The act of having a service desk or company representative verify that the customer's incident has been resolved to the customer's satisfaction and that the incident has not recurred.

positive imagery—The act of using mental pictures or images to influence your thinking in a positive way.

positive self-talk—The act of using words to influence your thinking in a positive way.

Review Questions

1. You can control your customer's behavior. True or False? Explain your answer.

2. List three characteristics skilled professionals must display when facing difficult customer situations.

3. Why is it important to avoid the temptation to make sweeping negative statements about your customers?

4. What is empathy?

5. Being empathetic means that you are personally responsible for another person's situation. True or False? Explain your answer.

6. What influences an upset or angry person's willingness to work with you?

7. What are four preparatory steps you can take prior to each customer interaction in order to get focused?

8. Why is it important to let an angry customer vent?

9. What should you be listening for when a customer is venting?

10. What can happen if you do not acknowledge a customer's emotional state?

11. What tone of voice is appropriate when you are using a customer's name or when you are apologizing to a customer?

12. When handling a difficult situation, when can you begin active problem solving?

13. Briefly describe the three stages customers go through on the way to becoming irate.

14. How can you ensure your behavior is not driving a customer into an irate state?

15. How do customers want their incidents and complaints to be handled?

16. Describe two ways to regain a dissatisfied customer's trust and repair a damaged relationship.

17. How is *responding* to a difficult situation different than *reacting* to it?

18. What are two things you must do in order to respond, rather than react, to difficult customer situations?

19. What do you need to do if you are a predominantly left-brained service provider?

20. What do you need to do if you are a predominantly right-brained service provider?

21. What symptom that you are upset or angry is it possible for a customer to notice when you are talking on the telephone?

22. What symptom that you are upset or angry is it possible for a customer to notice when you are face to face?

23. List four techniques a person can use to stay calm when facing a difficult situation.

24. What physical benefits do you derive from taking a deep breath when under pressure?

25. What benefits do you derive from taking a sip of water when under pressure?

26. What is positive imagery?

27. What kind of words can you use to eliminate negative thoughts and attitudes?

28. Why is it important to inform your team leader or supervisor that you have just handled a particularly difficult situation?

29. Why should you avoid caffeine after a stressful situation?

30. What are three things you can do in an effort to find difficult customer situations less stressful?

Discussion Questions

1. Some people believe that they must be aggressive when interacting with service providers or they will not get what they want. How do you think they came to feel that way? Are they right?

2. In some organizations, management directs service desk staff to apologize any time a customer is dissatisfied—even when the customer is wrong. In other organizations, management feels that although service desk staff must always be empathetic when a customer is dissatisfied, it is only necessary to apologize when the company has clearly made a mistake. What are the pros and cons of these two scenarios? What, if any, impact could these policies have when analysts are handling difficult customer situations?

3. A common customer complaint is that a support organization failed to follow-through on promises made or follow-up to ensure a customer's satisfaction. What are some potential causes for a support organization's failure to communicate?

Hands-On Projects

1. **Practice being empathetic.** For the next week, note any situations you encounter or observe where someone becomes upset, angry, or demanding. Then, try to think of situations you were involved in that enable you to relate to what the people who have become upset, angry, or demanding are experiencing. For example, if the driver behind you beeps the horn as soon as the traffic light turns green, try to think of a situation when you may have been late for work or school and as a result experienced frustration with the driver in front of you. The point of this project is to simply acknowledge the fact that we are all human and we can all lose our cool on any given day. Briefly summarize the situations you observed and the personal experiences you used to empathize with each situation.

2. **Discuss situations that cause frustration or anger.** Assemble a team of two or three classmates or use your school's online message or discussion board. Discuss the list of situations presented in this chapter that may cause customers to become frustrated or angry. As technology users—and therefore, at times, customers yourselves—discuss these situations and answer the following questions, and then present your ideas to the class:

   a. What other situations that cause frustration or anger can your team add to this list?

   b. From the expanded list, what are the top five situations that cause technology users frustration?

   c. Select the three situations that your team feels are the greatest causes of frustration.

   d. Brainstorm a list of ways that companies can minimize the frustration that customers may experience when facing these situations.

3. **Discuss a difficult customer situation.** Assemble a team of three to five classmates or use your school's online message or discussion board. Ensure that you or one classmate on your team has, as a service provider, faced a difficult customer situation. For example, a team member may have encountered a difficult customer situation in his or her workplace. Or, a team member may have done work for a family member or neighbor who was dissatisfied. Have the classmate describe the difficult situation to the best of his or her recollection. Discuss and document your team's answers to the following questions:

   a. What emotion was the customer experiencing?

   b. How, if at all, can you empathize with the emotion the customer was experiencing?

   c. Constructively assess the response of your classmate (the service provider) to the customer's emotional state.

   d. What, if anything, could have been done to prevent this situation?

   e. Given what you learned in this chapter, what can you learn or what conclusions can you draw from this scenario?

4. **Explore the role of social media in customer service.** Explore popular social media channels such as Facebook, LinkedIn, Myspace, Twitter, YouTube, vimeo, and so forth. Select a company you do business with regularly or that you admire, and then evaluate its use of social media channels. Answer the following questions:

   a. Briefly describe how this company uses social media channels to communicate with customers. For example, does the company use the channels to market its services, solicit customer feedback, and acknowledge and handle customer complaints?

   b. Describe whether and how this company's use of social media influences your perception of the company.

5. **Become aware of broken promises.** It is not uncommon for service providers to make promises to their customers they cannot realistically keep. A waiter in a restaurant may tell you he or she will be "back in a second" with your check. Realistically, that is impossible because the "second" is up before the waiter has even turned to retrieve your check. For the next week, pay attention to the promises that service providers make to you. Select two or three situations, and briefly note your perceptions in terms of the following:

   a. When the promise was made, did you consider it realistic?

   b. Was the promise kept?

   c. How did you feel when the promise was or was not kept?

   Given what you have learned in this chapter, what conclusions can you draw from this exercise?

6. **Learn the predominant side of your brain.** Use the following two exercises to learn whether you tend to be predominantly left-brained or right-brained. The first exercise is simple; the second is more comprehensive.

Exercise One—Simple Left-Brain, Right-Brain Exercise

This exercise uses the relationship between your thumbs and your brain to determine if you tend to be left- or right-brained.

   a. Fold your hands together with your fingers intertwined (the way people often do when they are preparing to pray).

   b. Look at your thumbs and determine if your left or right thumb is resting on top.

If your right thumb is resting on top, it is likely that you are predominantly right-brained. If your left thumb is resting on top, it is likely that you are predominantly left-brained. A fun way to validate this preference is to reverse your thumbs. That is, put the thumb that had been resting on the bottom on the top. You will typically find that it feels uncomfortable.

Exercise Two—Comprehensive Left-Brain, Right-Brain Exercise

This exercise uses your answers to a series of questions to determine if you tend to be left- or right-brained (*Brain Builders!*, 1995, pp. 332–3). Check one answer for each question.

Question	Answer	Score
1. In your opinion, *daydreaming* is (a) a waste of time; (b) an amusing way to relax; (c) helpful in solving problems and thinking creatively; (d) a good way to plan your future.		
2. What's your attitude about *hunches*? (a) Your hunches are strong and you follow them. (b) You are not aware of following any hunches that come to mind. (c) You may have hunches, but you don't trust them. (d) You'd have to be crazy to base a decision on a mere hunch.		
3. When it comes to *problem solving*, do you (a) get contemplative, thinking it over on a walk, talking with friends; (b) make a list of alternatives, determine priorities among them, and take the one at the top; (c) consult the past by remembering how you handled something similar to this situation before; (d) watch television, hoping the problem will go away?		
4. Take a moment to relax, put this book down, close your eyes, and put your hands in your lap, one on top of the other. Which hand is on top? (a) your right hand; (b) your left hand; (c) neither, because they are parallel.		
5. You are goal oriented. (a) True; (b) False.		
6. When you were in school, you preferred algebra to geometry. (a) True; (b) False.		
7. Generally speaking, you are a *very organized* type of person, for whom everything has its proper place and there is a system for doing anything. (a) True; (b) False.		
8. When it comes to speaking or writing or expressing yourself with words, you do pretty well. (a) True; (b) False.		
9. When you're at a party, you find yourself more natural at listening rather than talking. (a) True; (b) False.		
10. You don't need to check your watch to accurately tell how much time has passed. (a) True; (b) False.		
11. When it comes to athletics, somehow you perform even better than what you should expect from the amount of training or natural abilities you have. (a) True; (b) False.		
12. If it's a matter of work, you much prefer going solo to working by committee. (a) True; (b) False.		
13. You have a near photographic memory for faces. (a) True; (b) False.		
14. If you had your way, you would redecorate your home often, take trips frequently, and change your environment as much as possible. (a) True; (b) False.		
15. You are a regular James Bond when it comes to taking risks. (a) True; (b) False.		
Total Score		
Score divided by 15		

Scoring Key:

1. (a) 1 (b) 5 (c) 7 (d) 9
2. (a) 9 (b) 7 (c) 3 (d) 1
3. (a) 7 (b) 1 (c) 3 (d) 9
4. (a) 1 (b) 9 (c) 5
5. (a) 1 (b) 9
6. (a) 1 (b) 9
7. (a) 1 (b) 9
8. (a) 1 (b) 7

9. (a) 6 (b) 3
10. (a) 1 (b) 9
11. (a) 9 (b) 1
12. (a) 3 (b) 7
13. (a) 7 (b) 1
14. (a) 9 (b) 1
15. (a) 7 (b) 3

a. Score each answer using the scoring key.

b. Total your points.

c. Divide your total points by 15.

The lower the number, the more left-brained you are. The higher the number, the more right-brained you are. A score of 1 indicates that you are exceptionally left-brained. A score of 8 indicates you are exceptionally right-brained. A score of 5 indicates that regular traffic flows between your left and right brain.

7. **Learn the symptoms you experience under pressure.** For the next week, record the symptoms you experience any time you are upset or angry at home or at work. Remember that you do not have to be extremely upset or irate to experience symptoms. You may simply be frustrated or perhaps confused. Keep a log of the situations you encounter and the symptoms you experience. Also, note on your log any ways you may be exacerbating these symptoms, for example, by consuming an excessive amount of caffeine. Assess how you relieve these symptoms, and identify any techniques you can use to stay calm in these situations. Share your experiences with your classmates, and discuss how you can use the techniques discussed in this chapter to stay calm and in control.

8. **Assess your habits.** Staying calm when faced with a difficult situation requires that you have good habits in place for dealing with pressure. Briefly describe a technique or techniques you use to calm yourself when facing a difficult situation. For example, is it your habit to take a deep breath or use positive self-talk? Briefly describe the benefits you derive from this habit. Given what you have learned in this chapter, what additional techniques can you incorporate as a habit?

Case Projects

1. **Customer Service Script.** You have been hired as a consultant to a company that wants to (1) improve its customer service, and (2) reduce the stress its staff experiences when handling difficult situations. Drawing from your experiences both as a customer and as a service provider, develop a script that illustrates a difficult situation. Prepare a series of questions you can use to prompt empathy for the customer's situation, constructive feedback for the service provider's handling of the situation, and tips and techniques for handling this situation better in the future.

2. **Training Class: Respond Positively to an Angry Email.** Your boss has asked you to develop a handout for a training class about how to respond positively to an angry email. He wants this handout to contain a customer email with an obvious angry tone and several complaints that must be addressed. He also wants the handout to contain a response to the customer's email that acknowledges what the customer said and how he or she said it..Prepare the handout for his review.

3. **Difficult Customer Situation.** A coworker has just had to handle a difficult customer situation. She thinks she could have handled the situation better and has asked for your feedback. Also, the customer hung up, in disgust, before the analyst was able to assist, and she does not know what to do. Here is how your coworker describes the call to you:

Customer: This is Jane Apponte. Let me talk to Suzie Peters.

Analyst: I'm sorry, Ms. Apponte. Suzie is on another call right now. Is there something I can do to help you?

Customer: No, I can't wait. Interrupt her and tell her that I am waiting to speak with her.

Analyst: I can't do that, ma'am, but I can take your telephone number and have her call you back when she gets off the phone.

Customer: That's not good enough. I have been waiting two hours for someone to get out here and fix my PC.

Analyst: Did you call the service desk about your PC?

Customer (becoming irritated): Of course I called the service desk. Suzie told me a technician would be here within the hour and no one has shown up or called. I have a meeting in 10 minutes, and I want this taken care of before I leave. You need to get someone out here right now!

Analyst: Do you know your ticket number?

Customer (shouting now): I don't care what the ticket number is. Get someone out here now!

Analyst: Ms. Apponte, there is nothing I can do until I know your ticket number. Please hold while I look it up. [Places customer on hold.]

Customer: [Hangs up in disgust.]

First, write out the steps that must be taken immediately to address this customer's concern. Then, write out a sample script that shows how the analyst could have handled the call better. Include in the script examples of how analysts can let their *can do* attitude shine through. Share and discuss your recommendations with your classmates.

6

Solving and Preventing Incidents and Problems

In this chapter you will learn:

◎ How to use processes to resolve incidents and problems

◎ Proven techniques you can use to methodically resolve incidents

◎ How and when to take ownership of ongoing incidents

◎ How to keep management and customers informed about the status of incident resolution activities

◎ Ways to manage your workload and maintain a positive working relationship with other support groups

◎ How to use the problem management process to focus on finding root causes and preventing problems

To be successful, service desk analysts must be able to resolve incidents efficiently and effectively. Common incidents include broken devices, error messages, or system outages. Resolving incidents efficiently and effectively involves more than simply searching a knowledge base for known solutions. It requires a methodical approach, or process, through which analysts gather all available data, determine the probable source of an incident, and then decide on a course of action that restores service to the customer. When incidents are resolved quickly and correctly, the negative effects on the business are minimized and customer productivity is enhanced.

Service desk analysts must also be able to detect and help resolve problems, which are the cause of incidents. Common problems include chronic hardware failures, corrupt files, software errors or bugs, and human error. Resolving problems also requires a methodical approach, or process, through which analysts gather all available data, determine the root cause of a problem, and determine both temporary and permanent resolutions that work around or eliminate the root cause. The **root cause** is the most basic reason for an undesirable condition or problem, which, if eliminated or corrected, would prevent the problem from existing or occurring.

This chapter provides a brief overview of the incident and problem management processes, but it focuses on problem-solving skills. **Problem-solving skills**—also known as **troubleshooting skills**—are the thinking skills used to answer a question or resolve a difficult situation. In this phrase, the term *problem* refers in a broad sense to any question that needs to be answered or difficulty that needs to be resolved.

Service desk analysts need effective questioning skills and superior listening skills to be good problem solvers. Persistence is also important because proficient problem solving requires going beyond the quick fix to find a permanent solution. By analyzing trends and suggesting ways to eliminate the root cause of problems, analysts can help reduce the number of incidents that customers experience and even prevent incidents altogether. Problem solving is an innate skill, but it is also a skill that can be improved with practice. Improved problem-solving skills enable analysts to resolve more incidents and problems, resolve them more quickly and accurately, and, ultimately, satisfy more customers.

INTERVIEW WITH...

Courtesy of Lori Smiley

LORI SMILEY
METRO GOVERNMENT OF NASHVILLE
IT SERVICE MANAGER
www.nashville.gov

The Metro Government of Nashville Technology Services Support Center (TSSC) is part of the Information Technology Services (ITS) department. The TSSC supports 19,000 internal employees located in over 255 physical locations. The TSSC has nine analysts, a manager, and an application administrator, and it provides support 24 hours a day, 7 days a week, 365 days a year.

Question: What role does the service desk play at Metro Government of Nashville?

Answer: The TSSC serves as the single point of contact for ITS users. We also serve as the first point of contact for many of the applications maintained and supported by other IT groups throughout Metro such as the Police department and the Finance department. We handle on average 8,000 contacts per month submitted via the telephone, email, and fax. We resolve 35 percent of all contacts at the TSSC, which includes both incidents and service requests. We escalate those we cannot solve to other groups such as e-messaging, desktop support, network support, network security, and so forth. We follow up on escalated contacts to ensure they are resolved in a time frame that reflects the priority of the incident or service request, and we ensure that our customers are satisfied with the resolution.

Question: What characteristics do you look for when hiring people for service desk positions?

Answer: The TSSC serves as the customer advocate, so customer service skills are critical. Although a broad technical background is a plus, we are more focused on a person's ability to learn new skills and to learn them quickly. This ability is crucial as technology is constantly changing and becoming more complex. We also look for people who have great planning and organization skills. These skills are needed to handle the ever-changing procedures and pace at which things move in the TSSC.

Question: What techniques do you use to enhance the problem-solving capabilities of your team?

Answer: The TSSC is constantly receiving new and updated procedures for the new and ever-changing systems and technologies that we support. Finding a way to organize that information and make it easily accessible is a constant challenge. We use Microsoft SharePoint to organize our procedures, troubleshooting tips, workarounds, FAQs, and so forth. We use the SharePoint blog feature to collaborate within the TSSC and with the desktop support team when incidents occur that require advanced troubleshooting. The blog and the SharePoint calendaring feature also help us keep track of ongoing issues and the availability of technicians at any given point in time. Additionally, we can easily search our incident management system for error messages and symptoms to locate resolutions to past incidents. We recently completed a project to refine the subject tree that we use to log and categorize incidents and service requests in our incident management system. We have embedded some procedures and checklists into the subject tree to also help our analysts. The application administrator oversees all aspects of our incident management system, including maintaining the application (e.g., upgrades), account management, ensuring data quality, and reporting.

Question: How do you see the service desk changing in the next 5 years?

Answer: Service desk trends reflect many of the trends we see around us every day—a fast-food culture, people living and working longer, people needing constant stimulation to fend off boredom, and having to constantly do more with less. Our culture is a fast-food culture in that our customers want it all, they want it *now*, and they want it their way. The service desk must recognize that customers are increasingly more technically savvy. These technically savvy users want to interact with technologies that enable them to access the answers and information they need in a quick, easy, and friendly way. At the same time, people tend to be working longer and, believe it or not, there are still people out there who do not have email addresses or computers in their homes and who are just learning to use computers. These customers often want to interact with a human being and want more of a personal touch. They demand our patience and soft skills such as listening and empathy. Ensuring service desk analysts have the skills needed to adapt to these changing customer requirements is a challenge and will continue to be a challenge in the years to come. Keeping people with strong technical skills engaged and interested only adds to this challenge.

The service desk has historically been viewed as an entry-level position, and there is a perception that analysts are simply waiting for an opportunity to move into another position. We need to change that perception and recognize the service desk as the profession that it has become. We must communicate the value of the service desk to our customers, other teams within IT, and within the service desk itself. We've got to give people incentive to stay in the service desk through higher salaries, higher job grades, and so forth. We've got to provide incentives for other teams to respect and work more closely with the service desk. We've got to find creative ways to keep technically savvy analysts with good troubleshooting skills engaged and inspired in the service desk setting, often by engaging them in projects aimed at ensuring that the service desk is involved early when new or changed technologies are being introduced. Projects may also be focused on improving the capabilities of the service desk. Doing so requires helping analysts develop the required planning and project management skills in addition to the technical skills.

Last but not least, as the economy continues to wax and wane, the need to do more with less continues. One way to do more with less in the service desk is by incorporating the different tiers, or levels, of support into the service desk, and the service desk into those different tiers of support. In other words, we've got to have interchangeable parts. Traditional level two roles such as desktop and network technicians will be expected to spend time in the service desk as staffing and training needs arise. Service desk analysts will rotate into desktop and network support roles to both enhance their skills and fill staffing voids in those areas. All must remember that at the end of the day, the goal is to satisfy our customers, and customers really don't care who resolves the incident, they just want quality service.

Question: What advice would you give someone who is currently working in a service desk?

Answer: I encourage analysts to understand how critical what they do is to both the organization, and to their careers. I also encourage analysts to appreciate the tremendous opportunities they get by working in a service desk. They get to see every aspect of IT—applications, the network, security—and they can then choose where they want their career to go. They can also acquire skills, such as problem-solving, project management, teamwork, and communication skills, that will serve them well regardless of what opportunities come their way in any career. They just have to be willing to learn! Analysts should think of every incident they log as a resume. They are being judged on how accurate and complete that incident is, how well they diagnosed the incident, and, when needed, how well they worked with other members of the service desk team and other support groups to get the incident resolved. Most importantly, they are being judged on whether they have done everything needed to satisfy the customer—something we've got to do to survive and thrive in today's competitive business world.

Using Processes to Resolve Incidents and Problems

Most service desks use processes and procedures to ensure incidents and problems are handled quickly, correctly, and consistently. Each activity, or task, in a process has a procedure that describes how to do that task. In other words, processes define *what* tasks to do, and procedures describe *how* to do the tasks. When multiple groups are involved in resolving an incident or a problem, processes and procedures provide the framework that enables each group to understand its role and responsibilities—that is, what to do and how to do it.

 Clearly defined and documented processes and procedures are critical as they ensure needed data is gathered, important problem-solving steps are not forgotten, and incidents and problems are handled in a consistent manner.

Flowcharts are often used in business to outline processes. A **flowchart** is a diagram that shows the sequence of tasks that occur in a process. Table 6-1 describes the purpose of some common symbols used in flowcharts. Flowcharts are a good way to show how all the procedures involved in a process are interconnected.

Symbol	Name	Purpose
(A)	On Page Connector	Represents an exit to, or entry from, another part of the same flow chart.
Task	Task	Shows a single task or operation.
Predefined Process	Predefined process	Represents another process that provides input or receives output from the current process.
Decision	Decision	Represents a decision point and typically has a "yes" branch and a "no" branch.
— No →	No result	Used in conjuction with a decision to show the next task or decision following a "no" result.
Yes	Yes result	Used in conjuction with a decision to show the next task or decision following a "yes" result.
Start/Stop	Start/Stop	Shows the starting point or stopping point of a process.

Table 6-1 Flowchart symbols

Processes and procedures are particularly important in the fast-paced service desk setting, where the bottom line is always to meet or exceed customer expectations. A successful service desk must perform several tightly integrated processes to achieve customer satisfaction. These processes are integrated because the output produced by one process might be used as input to another process. Two of the most common processes found in service desks are incident management and problem management.

ITIL views the incident management and problem management processes as separate and distinct. **Incident management** is the process responsible for managing the lifecycle of incidents. The objective of incident management is to restore service as quickly as possible in an effort to minimize the impact of incidents that affect a company's systems, networks, applications, and products. **Problem management** is the process responsible for managing the lifecycle of problems. The objectives of problem management are to minimize the impact of incidents, eliminate recurring incidents, and prevent problems and their resulting incidents from occurring.

One reason these processes are viewed as separate and distinct is that performing root cause analysis often prolongs the restoration of service. **Root cause analysis** is a methodical way of determining why problems occur and identifying ways to prevent them. In this day and age when outages can cost companies millions of dollars, most organizations strive to first restore service—via incident management—and then later determine the root cause. This is like a firefighter who first puts out a fire and then calls for an arson inspector to determine the root cause. Another reason to keep the two processes separate is that not all incidents require root cause analysis. In some cases, the root cause is obvious, such as in the case of a device that was dropped or damaged. In other cases, root cause analysis may not be justified, such as in a situation where an easy-to-use and viable workaround exists.

Although these processes have different objectives, at their most basic level they involve a similar set of activities. These basic activities include:

- **Identification**—Detecting and identifying incidents or problems through monitoring, trend analysis, and observation. **Trend analysis** is a methodical way of determining and, when possible, forecasting service trends.

- **Logging**—Reporting the incident or problem and logging relevant information, typically in an integrated IT service management tool. Logging includes categorizing the incident or problem and assigning a priority.

- **Investigation and diagnosis**—Using available resources and proven problem-solving techniques to determine what has gone wrong and how to correct it.

- **Resolution**—Performing the corrective action that repairs, replaces, or modifies the source of an incident or eliminates the root cause of a problem.

- **Closure**—Verifying that the corrective action was successful, that the incident or problem was resolved to the customer's satisfaction, and that all incident and problem details are recorded accurately and completely.

Although these basic activities are similar, the techniques used to investigate and diagnose incidents and problems are different.

Solving Incidents Methodically

Studies indicate that a high percentage of technical incidents are recurring in nature. In other words, the same incidents are repeatedly reported to the service desk either by different customers or by the same customer if they are not resolved correctly the first time. As a result, plenty of information is available for finding solutions to incidents. As a service desk analyst, you can draw from personal experience; access available knowledge bases, scripts, and checklists; or use tools such as remote control and diagnostic systems in an effort to find a solution. You can also engage other analysts or level two service providers who may have experienced the same or similar incidents in the past via the incident management process.

Incident management is one of the most common service desk processes and involves logging, tracking, and resolving incidents. Figure 6-1 shows a fairly simple incident management process. This process varies from one company to the next and may be much more complex.

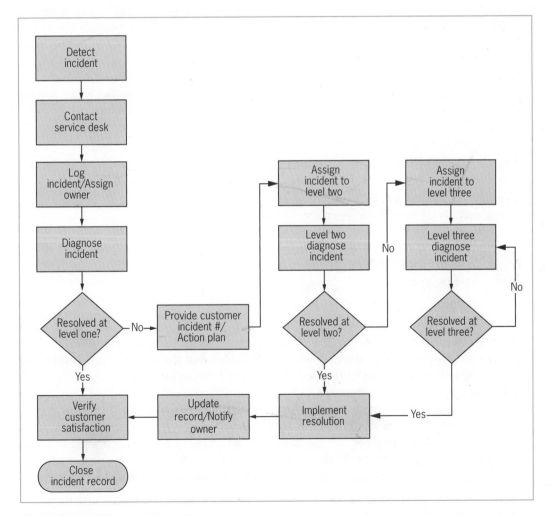

Figure 6-1   Incident management process

The incident management process begins when an incident is recognized. More specifically, it begins when a symptom is detected. A **symptom** is a sign or indication that an incident has occurred. The probable source of the incident must then be identified before problem solving can begin. The **probable source** of the incident is the system, network, application, or product that is most likely causing the incident. The incident management process ends when a corrective action repairs, replaces, or modifies the source of the incident to the customer's satisfaction.

 Incident management does not include identifying the incident's root cause. That is the responsibility of problem management.

It is important to distinguish the symptom and the probable source of an incident from the root cause. Each can be different. If a customer contacts the service desk and indicates an error message occurs each time she tries to print a report, the error message is the incident symptom. The analyst may determine that the probable source of the customer's printing incident is the software package being used to print. The analyst could determine this by personally routing a report to the printer to see if it prints. If it does, the analyst can eliminate the printer as the probable source. Further discussion with the customer may lead the analyst to conclude that the root cause of the problem—that is, the cause of the incident—is not, in fact, the software package that the customer is using, but the incorrect set of procedures that she is using to issue the print command.

The terminology used to describe the incident management process can vary from one organization to the next, just as the process can vary. The terms *fault* and *error* are sometimes used to describe incidents. These terms generally imply a condition that is causing a component to fail to perform the required function.

 ITIL defines a **known error** as a problem that has a documented root cause and a workaround. Known errors are identified and managed via the problem management process.

The incident management process typically also includes answering customers' questions and inquiries. **Questions** such as "How do I...?" are customer requests for instructions on how to use a product. Questions occur when a product is not broken, but the customer simply needs help using it. Questions can often be resolved by using self-help technologies such as online help, FAQs, or a knowledge base. **Inquiries** such as "When will my equipment arrive?" are customer requests for information. Inquiries, like questions, usually occur when the product is not broken, but the customer wants a current status report. Customers can often obtain answers to inquiries about orders or a new release of software by accessing a company's web site. Other inquiries, such as a request for the status of an outstanding incident, may require the assistance of an analyst who performs a lookup in a database or obtains a status from another group.

Most companies distinguish between incidents, questions, and inquiries because they represent varying degrees of impact and customer satisfaction—or dissatisfaction—with the performance of a product or company. For example, a customer calling to inquire about the date for the next release of a software package may not be dissatisfied with the existing product—he or she is just looking forward to the new version. On the other hand, a customer who gets error messages or loses data when trying to use a software package is clearly dissatisfied, and the company must try to resolve the incident quickly or risk losing that customer. Distinguishing between incidents, questions, and inquiries also enables companies to report on these different types of contacts and determine which are most common. Companies can then ensure that there are processes and technologies in place for resolving each type of contact in the most efficient, cost-effective way possible.

 Many companies also distinguish between incidents and service requests, which are user requests for information, advice, or standard changes. A different process, the request fulfillment process, is typically used to handle service requests.

The incident management process describes the overall approach to be used when handling incidents within a company. Within the boundaries of the incident management process, analysts need problem-solving skills to investigate and diagnose each incident. The most efficient and effective way to find a solution to any given incident is to take a methodical approach. Figure 6-2 lists the basic steps to follow when investigating and diagnosing incidents.

Step 1: Gather all available data and create information.

Step 2: Diagnose the incident.

Step 3: Develop and execute a course of action.

Figure 6-2   Steps for investigating and diagnosing incidents

Analysts with strong problem-solving skills condition themselves to gather and analyze all available data before drawing a conclusion.

Step 1: Gather All Available Data and Create Information

How well you gather all available data and create information greatly influences your ability to quickly find the correct solution, or a viable workaround. It takes time and effort to capture the data needed to create accurate information. It is not enough to gather and store data in your head. You must log the data accurately and completely in an incident management system so managers, other service desk analysts, level two service providers, and customers can use the data.

Information is a valuable resource, and the most efficient and effective service desks use comprehensive incident management systems to capture as much data as possible. They can then use this data to create the information needed to justify resources, increase customer satisfaction, enhance productivity, improve the quality of products and services, deliver services more efficiently and effectively, and create new products and services. On the other hand, some service desks are so overwhelmed with their responsibilities, or so understaffed, that they capture little or no data. As a result, they have trouble creating the information needed to measure their performance and make improvements. The information needs of the service desk where you work and the complexity of the incident influence the amount of data you are required to gather.

Service desks that capture data typically divide the data into various categories. These data categories tend to be similar from service desk to service desk because most service desks perform similar processes. Each service desk captures additional data categories specific to its business or industry. Figure 6-3 lists the most common data categories captured by service desks.

- Customer data
- Incident data
- Status data
- Resolution data

Figure 6-3   Common data categories

This data, typically captured through fields in the service desk's incident management system, enables service desks to track incidents and service requests; measure team, individual, and process performance; and perform trend and root cause analysis.

Customer Data

Customer data, the identifying details about a customer, includes the customer's name, telephone number, email address, department or company name, physical address or location, and customer number, employee number, or user ID. All of the data and text fields that describe a single customer are stored in a **customer record** in the incident management database. A **record** is a collection of related fields. When customer data is stored in a customer record, analysts do not have to request and key in this information every time a customer contacts the service desk. Instead, the analyst can access this information and simply verify key data elements such as the customer's telephone number, email address, or physical address as needed.

Customer records are linked to incident records, which are also stored in the incident management system, by a unique *key* field such as customer name, customer number, employee number, or user ID. These fields can be used to quickly identify a customer contacting the service desk and to research a customer's history of incidents.

The actual field names used in the data categories vary from one service desk to the next.

Incident Data

Incident data is the details of an incident or service request. Incident data includes incident type (such as an incident or request), channel used to submit (such as telephone, email, or web request), category (such as hardware or software), affected service, system, or device (such as a printer or monitor), the symptom, the date and time the incident occurred, the date and time the incident was logged, the analyst who logged the incident, the incident owner, a description, and a priority.   .

Incident priority typically remains the same throughout the life of an incident. This ensures the incident is resolved in the proper time frame and that it is not forgotten or neglected. However, obtaining new information such as a higher impact or decreased urgency could prompt a change in the priority.

Incident data is stored in fields, and all of the fields that describe a single incident are stored in an **incident record** in the incident management system. These fields can be used to search the knowledge base for solutions, track incidents, research and track trends, or identify problems.

Incident records typically contain a Type field that is used to specify the type of incident being reported, such as incident, question, and so forth. Organizations that use the same tool to handle incidents and service requests may also use the Type field to distinguish the two. The data fields that analysts are required to enter may vary based on the incident type specified. For example, fewer data fields may be required when an answer to an FAQ is provided or an incident is resolved quickly using a solution from the service desk's knowledge management system. Conversely, more data fields may be required for an incident escalated to level two support.

One piece of information analysts must always collect from customers is a description of the incident. Many service desks capture two types of incident descriptions: a short description and a detailed incident description. A **short incident description** succinctly describes the actual results a customer is experiencing, as shown in the following examples.

> Error msg H536 displays when customer is logging on to accounting system.
> Customer is bounced back to main logon screen.
> Spreadsheet package fails when customer runs new macro.

Stating the short incident description is an excellent way to obtain agreement from customers that you understand the incident they are experiencing. The short incident description is often used in reports or online queries to provide a brief overview of the incident. Part or all of the short incident description may also be used to search a knowledge base for workarounds or solutions.

Be succinct when creating the short description, but not to the point of making it incomprehensible. Avoid abbreviations, acronyms, and jargon unless they are well known to the audience. Eliminate words such as *and* and *the* unless they contribute considerably to the readability of the short description.

A **detailed incident description** provides a comprehensive accounting of the incident and the circumstances surrounding the incident's occurrence. The detailed incident description should contain a number of items, including:

- The result the customer expects. For example, the customer expects a report to appear on the printer.

- The actual result the customer is experiencing. For example, the report is not printing despite the fact that the printer is turned on.

- Steps the customer took to get the result. For example, the customer issued a print command.

- The history or pattern of the incident. For example, this is a new report and the customer has never tried printing it before. To determine the history or pattern of the incident, you can ask the customer questions such as:

  ◆ Does the incident occur every time the customer performs this step?

  ◆ Does the incident only occur in certain circumstances? What are those circumstances?

  ◆ Does the incident only occur intermittently? Under what conditions?

- Whether the incident is part of a larger incident. For example, the printer is attached to a portion of the network that is currently down.

Notice that one of the first parts of the detailed incident description is the result the customer expected. Problem solving involves asking questions until you determine *why* the customer's expected result did not happen.

Status Data

Status data is details about an incident that are used to track the incident throughout its lifecycle. Status data includes incident status (such as assigned, awaiting parts, resolved, closed), the person or group assigned, and the date and time assigned. This data is stored in fields in the incident record in the incident management system. After an incident record is created, that record is continuously updated as new data—such as status data—becomes available.

These fields can be used to report on the status of outstanding incidents and to monitor SLA attainment. Figure 6-4 shows a sample incident aging report that is used to ensure that outstanding incidents are being resolved within their target resolution time. Many companies use this type of report to monitor adherence to an SLA goal, such as "Resolve 95 percent of incidents within their target resolution time."

Assigned To	<1 Day	2–3 Days	4–5 Days	6–10 Days	>10 Days	% Within Target
Field Services	24	6	3	1	2	98
Network Support	54	23	15	9	13	94
Development	76	54	8	2	1	87
Vendor	93	27	3	4	12	75

Figure 6-4 Sample incident aging report

Resolution Data

Resolution data is details that describe how an incident was resolved. These details include the fields required to track service level compliance and perform trend analysis, such as the person or group who resolved the incident, resolution description, date and time resolved, customer satisfaction indicator, date and time closed, and possible cause. This data is stored in fields in the incident record in the incident management system. After an incident record is created, that record is continuously updated as new data—such as resolution data—becomes available.

 The root cause is typically not recorded in the incident record. When justified, a problem record is created and used to investigate and, ultimately, eliminate the root cause.

Typically, after required customer and incident data has been collected, you can begin diagnosing the incident. An initial status such as "open" is often assigned automatically by the incident management system.

Step 2: Diagnose the Incident

When diagnosing an incident, you are trying to determine the probable source of the incident and a corrective action that can be used to restore service. Determining the probable source of an incident can be extremely difficult, particularly when dealing with complex technology, such as the technology found in a client/server or cloud computing environment. **Client/server** is a computing model where some computers, known as clients, request services, and other computers, known as servers, respond to those requests. Consider the earlier scenario where the customer issued a print command and the report did not appear. Figure 6-5 illustrates all of the computing components that must be working correctly for the customer's report to print. This is, of course, a very simple diagram, but it shows that any number of potential points of failure may need to be considered when determining the probable source of an incident.

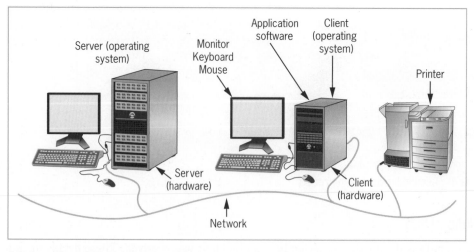

Figure 6-5 Components of a client/server computing environment

Many techniques are used to diagnose incidents and determine the probable source. Figure 6-6 lists the most common of these techniques. Each technique is useful, and you may use more than one technique in the course of diagnosing an incident.

- Ask questions.
- Simulate the customer's actions.
- Use diagnostic tools.

Figure 6-6 Incident diagnostic techniques

Ask Questions

Asking questions is an extremely effective way to diagnose incidents. Asking questions enables you to continue gathering the data needed to identify a solution. You gain insight as to why the incident is occurring. You also gain insight about the customer. For example, the customer's ability to answer your questions and use of terminology when answering will provide you with insight about the customer's skill level.

When asking questions, you must listen actively to both the response your customer is giving and the emotion with which your customer is giving that response. Remember that you must acknowledge and address any strong emotions before you begin or continue actively diagnosing the incident. Remember, too, that your questions must be appropriate to the customer's communication style. Keep in mind that you can ask open-ended questions to obtain more detailed information, and you can ask closed-ended questions that prompt short answers such as *yes* and *no* to take control of the conversation.

To become an efficient problem solver, you must condition yourself to ask and obtain answers to a basic set of questions. These basic questions can help you isolate the probable source of the incident. Figure 6-7 lists these basic questions and provides a series of additional questions that you can use to obtain the data you need.

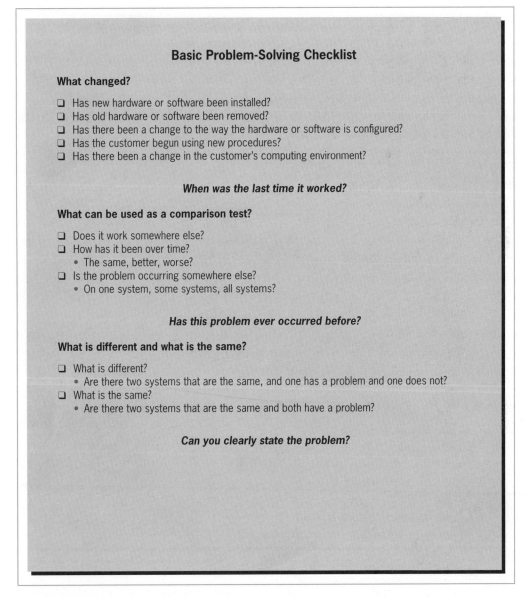

Basic Problem-Solving Checklist

What changed?

❑ Has new hardware or software been installed?
❑ Has old hardware or software been removed?
❑ Has there been a change to the way the hardware or software is configured?
❑ Has the customer begun using new procedures?
❑ Has there been a change in the customer's computing environment?

When was the last time it worked?

What can be used as a comparison test?

❑ Does it work somewhere else?
❑ How has it been over time?
  • The same, better, worse?
❑ Is the problem occurring somewhere else?
  • On one system, some systems, all systems?

Has this problem ever occurred before?

What is different and what is the same?

❑ What is different?
  • Are there two systems that are the same, and one has a problem and one does not?
❑ What is the same?
  • Are there two systems that are the same and both have a problem?

Can you clearly state the problem?

Figure 6-7 Basic problem-solving checklist

Time may not allow you to ask all of these questions in the course of diagnosing an incident. Usually you will not have to. The goal is to condition your mind to run through these questions as the customer is relaying information. In other words, you may not need to actually ask a question to receive an answer. The customer may simply provide the answer while describing the incident. You then need to ask only those questions that have not yet been addressed but still need to be answered, up until the point where you are able to isolate the probable source of the incident.

Brainteasers and puzzles are an excellent way to improve your problem-solving skills. They teach you to ask questions, view incidents and problems from many different angles, and go beyond the obvious in search of a solution.

In addition to these basic questions, many service desks provide checklists that present questions more specific to actual incidents. Figure 6-8 shows a problem-solving checklist that can be used to diagnose printer incidents.

Printer Problem-Solving Checklist

✓ Have you ever had this problem before?	Yes/No
✓ Have you ever been able to use this printer before?	Yes/No
✓ Is this a network printer?	Yes/No
✓ Is your device properly attached to the network printer?	Yes/No
✓ Have you checked the print queue status?	Yes/No
✓ Has the printer been moved recently?	Yes/No
✓ Is the printer plugged in?	Yes/No
✓ Is the printer powered on?	Yes/No
✓ Do you see a power indicator light?	Yes/No
✓ Do you see an online indicator?	Yes/No
✓ Does the printer have paper in it?	Yes/No
✓ Does the printer have an error code?	Yes/No
✓ Have you ever successfully printed this report?	Yes/No
✓ Has it ever printed on this printer?	Yes/No
✓ Can you route the report to another printer?	Yes/No

Figure 6-8   Printer problem-solving checklist

These checklists may be developed by level two or level three service providers and made available via a knowledge management system, or you and other service desk analysts may develop checklists for the different types of incidents you encounter. For example, you may have a checklist for each software package or application you support or for each type of hardware you support, such as monitors, printers, and so forth. These checklists will help you avoid letting customers lead you to an incorrect course of action. If a customer calls and indicates his printer will not print and he has powered it on and off and checked the paper and toner, you might assume a hardware failure has occurred and escalate the incident to the field services group. By asking additional questions, you may learn the customer was routing his report to a different printer.

 Because a high percentage of incidents are caused by change, asking, "When was the last time it worked?" is often a good place to start when diagnosing an incident. The customer may even volunteer this information when describing the incident, and so it is important to listen carefully.

Some of the questions in this chapter may seem obvious and almost too simplistic. However, it is often the simple question that reaps the most information. If you ask a customer, "When was the last time the printer worked?" and she responds, "Yesterday, before I moved it," you may have a good lead on why the incident is occurring. Asking seemingly simple questions lets you quickly eliminate obvious causes before moving on to more complex diagnostics.

Simulate the Customer's Actions

Some service desks provide analysts access to the software packages or applications their customers are using. Some service desks also have lab areas where analysts can access systems that match customers' hardware and software configurations. Analysts can use these systems to simulate a customer's actions in an effort to determine the probable source of an incident. If an analyst can perform an action successfully that a customer cannot, then the probable source of the incident is more likely in the customer's computing environment. For example, if you can access the accounting system but the customer cannot, the accounting system can be eliminated as the probable source of the incident.

The usefulness of this technique depends on the access you have to the systems your customers use and on the policies of the company where you work. Some companies provide analysts with limited access to the systems and applications being used by customers, in which case analysts may not be able to fully simulate customers' incidents. Companies may limit access because customers are working with highly confidential information or because they are performing highly secure transactions. For example, a customer may be authorized to transfer funds in a banking setting or to change grades in an academic setting. In these situations, you may only be able to verify the system is up and running. If the system is up and running and you believe the incident is occurring within the system, your company's process may dictate you escalate the incident to a level two specialist who has the authority to perform further diagnostics within the system.

The policies of some companies include very strict standards that determine what technologies customers use. These standards influence what technologies the service desk supports along with what resources the service desk can use to simulate incidents. In an internal service desk setting, technology standards determine the technologies available to the company's employees. For companies putting BYOD policies in place, these standards determine the minimum requirements that must be met to ensure data confidentiality, integrity and accessibility. In an external service desk setting, these standards represent the minimum hardware and software requirements recommended to run a company's products without incurring incidents.

 Confidentiality, integrity, and accessibility (CIA) is an internationally recognized security model used to evaluate the information security of an organization.

It is not always possible for companies to establish or enforce technology standards. Some companies have customers with such diverse needs that standards would be prohibitive. Other companies, such as those that provide external support, may be contracted to support any systems their customers use. Efficient, effective incident management and knowledge management processes are always imperative, but they are particularly important in the absence of standards. A well-defined incident management process ensures that all incidents, even incidents with unfamiliar technologies, are handled quickly and consistently. A well-defined knowledge management process ensures solutions are captured for reuse.

The service desk is often involved in developing technology standards. As a result, the service desk can become very familiar with the technologies it supports. The service desk may be involved in testing and selecting the systems to be used within a company, so it will be familiar with the systems' strengths and weaknesses. It also typically receives copies of the systems, documentation, and training, so it can simulate and resolve incidents more quickly.

Some companies also establish standards that determine what changes customers can make to the systems they use. Such standards may not allow customers to change the way their systems are configured or install personal software, such as games, on their business computers. By tightly controlling the changes that customers make to systems, the company can prevent incidents that may occur as a result of an inappropriate change.

Without standards, customers may install equipment or software without the service desk's knowledge. As a result, the service desk does not have a copy of the system that can be used to simulate incidents. The installation of the new system may, in fact, be causing the incident. For example, a customer may download software from the Internet that contains a virus, which may corrupt files on the customer's PC or may even destroy portions of the customer's PC. Also, without standards, customers may be able to make changes to their systems that cause incidents. For example, a customer may change the PC's display settings in such a way that portions of the screen are no longer visible. Unfortunately, the customer may not remember making the change or may not recall exactly what change was made. In these cases, trying to simulate the customer's actions may be a waste of time or even impossible.

When technology standards exist, whether and how strictly those standards are enforced vary from one company to the next. Some companies encourage customers to comply with their standards by having the service desk provide a high level of support for standard systems and little or no support for nonstandard systems. In other words, customers who choose to use nonstandard systems may be on their own if they have questions or incidents. Although this policy of letting customers opt to use nonstandard systems without support may benefit the service desk—because it is not getting calls about nonstandard systems—the company rarely benefits in the long run. Incidents still occur—they are just not reported to the service desk. Furthermore, these incidents may be causing other incidents and problems that are difficult to detect because it is unclear what has changed in the computing environment. When standards are enforced, the productivity of all groups that use and support the systems improves. These standards benefit technology users because they receive the training they need and the number of incidents they encounter is minimized. These standards benefit the service desk and other support groups, such as level two service providers, because they are supporting a known set of systems and can acquire the training, tools, and talent needed to provide high-quality support.

CASE STUDY: Establishing Technology Standards

*Many companies establish standards that determine what hardware and software systems are used by their internal employees and, when appropriate, by their external customers. It is common for a committee to select the standard systems and define the policies that govern how the systems are used and supported. The committee typically is led by an IT planner and includes representatives from all of the groups that will use and support the standard systems: customers, the service desk, and any level two and three groups needed to support the systems. An **IT planner** produces and maintains the IT standards, policies, plans, and strategies that ensure the IT department's services meet the business' strategic needs.*

Systems undergo rigorous testing before they are selected to ensure they meet the selection criteria defined by the standards committee and to ensure the new systems are compatible with other standard systems. This testing also enables the standards committee to illustrate the benefits of implementing standard systems. Benefits of establishing technology standards include:

- ***The environment is less complex.** Rather than using two or more word-processing products, such as Microsoft Word and Corel WordPerfect, the product that best meets the company's needs is selected and implemented. As a result, customers, the service desk staff, and level two and three service providers can gain a high level of expertise in the chosen systems.*

- ***The ability to share data and exchange information is improved.** Rather than converting data from one system to another, such as a spreadsheet from Microsoft Excel to Lotus 1-2-3, a single system is used. As a result, many incidents and problems that can occur when converting data are prevented.*

- ***Effective training and self-help programs can be developed.** With fewer systems, companies have more resources available to develop and deliver high-quality training and self-help programs. The service desk receives the training and knowledge resources it needs to support the systems, and customers receive the training and knowledge resources they need to use the technology as efficiently and effectively as possible. Consequently, customers have fewer questions and incidents, and the service desk can quickly handle questions and incidents that do occur.*

- *Proactive support can be provided.* With fewer systems, the number of isolated random incidents decreases—because the number of potential points of failure is reduced—and more common, predictable incidents occur. By using trend and root cause analysis to proactively identify the likely source of potential incidents, the impact of incidents can be minimized. Or, incidents can be prevented.

- *Costs are controlled.* Companies that have standards can negotiate discounts with vendors because they are purchasing software licenses and hardware for a greater number of people. Companies can purchase a site license, which enables all users at a given location to use a software package, rather than purchasing more costly individual licenses. Companies can purchase on-demand licenses that they are only charged for when services are being used. Also, the costs associated with abandoning technology that does not work correctly are eliminated, as are the incidents that accompanied that technology.

- *The company is positioned to take advantage of state-of-the-art technology.* Allowing customers to use any system they want often makes it difficult for a company to implement new technology. For example, customers who use an older version of Windows must be transitioned to a newer generation Windows operating system before the company can implement the current release of Windows-based applications such as Word and Excel. Or, customers who use an older version of a browser must be transitioned to a newer browser before the company can implement a cloud-based application such as a customer relationship management system. Although the customers may be comfortable using the systems they have, those systems may not fit the long-term needs of the company and may be causing incidents. The standards committee stays on top of industry trends and selects systems that will benefit the company now and into the foreseeable future.

Users and people working in IT sometimes perceive that establishing technology standards decreases the user's ability to take advantage of the latest technology trends. Although that may be true to some extent, it is equally true that the latest technologies are often plagued with problems. Establishing technology standards enables companies to create a computing environment that is more stable and less complex. That is, they create a computing environment that has fewer incidents and is easier to change or upgrade and support.

Use Diagnostic Tools

In addition to providing systems that analysts can use to simulate a customer's action, some service desks provide analysts with tools, such as remote control systems, they can use to diagnose incidents. A **remote control system** is a technology that enables an analyst to view and take control of a connected device to troubleshoot incidents, transfer files, provide informal training, or collaborate on documents. Typically, the customer authorizes the analyst to access his or her system by keying a password. Because the analyst may be able to observe or access confidential information or transactions, some companies prohibit the use of these systems. When these systems are used, analysts can resolve many incidents that would previously have required a visit to the customer's site. Most customers appreciate this technology because they do not have to wait for a field service representative to arrive.

Not all customers feel comfortable with remote control technology, so it is important to ask permission and respect your customer's feelings on this matter. It is also important to be aware of any applicable security restrictions.

Additionally, most hardware and software systems manufactured today have built-in diagnostic tools. Many systems come with software that can be used to automatically schedule maintenance tasks that prevent incidents by cleaning up disk space and searching for and repairing data errors on the hard drive. Most systems also offer diagnostic programs customers can run if they encounter an incident. Some software packages include wizards that step customers through a series of diagnostic questions. Diagnostic tools can also be purchased. Popular PC utility packages such as Norton Utilities by Symantec or Systweak's Advanced System Optimizer provide the ability to schedule periodic system scans and updates in an effort to diagnose, prevent, and repair incidents. Service desk analysts can prompt a customer to use these tools either while they are working with the customer or, in some cases, before the customer contacts the service desk. The service desk can suggest on their Service Desk Quick Reference Card that customers use these tools, or customers can be prompted to use these tools when they access the service desk's web site. These tools can provide service desk analysts with the information they need to resolve an incident, but they also can provide customers with the ability to resolve incidents on their own. When customers resolve incidents on their own, service desk analysts are free to work on more complex and unique incidents.

Some companies are exploring the use of web-based digital agents, also known as intelligent agents or virtual agents, to diagnose and ultimately prevent incidents. A **digital agent** is a software routine that waits in the background and performs an action when a specified event occurs. For example, when a customer asks for help at a web site, a digital agent can interact with the customer and provide solutions in much the same way as a human. Digital agents can also take customers on a tour of a company's web site or escalate customers from self-service to assisted-service channels when needed.

Diagnostic tools are an effective way to diagnose incidents. Keep in mind that using these tools may not always be an option. If the network is down, access to a customer's system using a remote control system may not be possible. Or, if a hardware failure occurs, having a customer run a diagnostic program may not be possible. When diagnostic tools are not available, you can ask questions or simulate the customer's actions in an effort to identify the probable incident source.

Analysts often feel pressured to resolve or escalate incidents as quickly as possible. Because of this pressure, they may draw conclusions based on insufficient information or without understanding all of the facts. In other words, they may develop a course of action based on a symptom, rather than the actual probable source. You must take the time needed to fully diagnose the incident and identify the correct probable source. Otherwise, you can waste time developing a course of action that will not resolve the incident. Incorrectly identifying the probable source can also damage your relationship with level two service providers. A level two service provider who spends time diagnosing an incident only to learn that the incident should have been assigned to another group often resents the interruption and may mistrust you or the entire service desk in the future.

Step 3: Develop and Execute a Course of Action

After you have diagnosed the incident and identified the correct probable source, you can begin to develop a course of action or action plan. The course of action may involve researching the incident further, delivering a solution, escalating the incident to a level two service provider, or simply letting the customer know when to expect a status update. Note that the course of action taken will not be correct if an incorrect probable source was identified. When the correct probable source is identified, an analyst can do the following:

- Search a knowledge management system for solutions to known errors or for policies and procedures that can be used to develop a solution.

- Search the incident management system for past incidents that are similar or related to the current incident, which can then be used to further develop a course of action.

- Consult resources such as manuals, user's guides, procedures, online help, web sites, coworkers, subject matter experts, or the team leader in an effort to research the incident and identify a solution.

- Use personal knowledge to develop a solution.

- Use tools, such as remote control systems, to further diagnose the incident and identify a solution.

- Determine if a workaround is available that can satisfy the customer's immediate need.

The steps taken to execute the course of action will vary based on factors such as whether a solution was identified, how and by whom the solution will be delivered, and whether the customer is satisfied. Typically the course of action will involve:

- Delivering a solution by directing the customer to perform a procedure or series of procedures

- Directing the customer to a web site where the solution can be obtained

- Taking remote control and performing the repair

- Escalating the incident to the correct level two service provider or subject matter expert when a solution could not be identified or the service desk is unable to deliver the solution

- Logging a change record to have the corrective action performed via the change management process

The objective of incident management is to restore service as quickly as possible and so by using available resources, the service desk is often able to deliver a solution.

If the service desk is not able to deliver a solution, the incident is escalated to the next level of support. The level two service provider or subject matter expert uses his or her resources to continue determining a solution. Such resources may include more advanced skills or tools, greater authority, and physical proximity to the customer or device requiring repair. It is important to note that the service desk may have identified the solution, but it may not be able to actually deliver the solution. For example, the service desk may determine that a device requires an on-site repair and so escalate the incident to a level two service provider who can travel to the customer's location. Or, the service desk may escalate the incident to a level two group that has the authority to deliver the solution. In such cases, the service desk typically takes ownership and continues to follow up until the incident is resolved.

Prior to escalating an incident, the service desk determines the incident's priority based on its impact and the urgency with which a resolution is needed. This information is communicated to the level two service provider or subject matter expert to ensure the target time for an expected resolution—typically based on SLAs—is understood.

Some resolutions, such as completely replacing a piece of equipment, may be viewed as a change that must be handled via the company's change management process. In such cases, the service desk may create a request for change (RFC), or escalate the incident to a level two service provider who creates the RFC. A **request for change (RFC)** is a request to change the production environment. In the case of a **standard change**, which is a preapproved change that is low risk and follows a procedure, a service request may be used to trigger the change management process. A company's policies will specify when an RFC or service request is required to resolve an incident. The record ID of the RFC or service request is added to the incident record, and the incident remains open until the change is complete. This enables the service desk to "close the loop" and verify that the change resolved the incident to the customer's satisfaction.

Incident management is known as a **closed loop process**, which is a process that changes its output based on feedback. Incident management is a closed loop process because the customer who reports an incident must accept the solution before the incident can be closed.

Customers occasionally report incidents that are not actually incidents. Rather, they represent a desire on the part of the customer to change how the product functions. For example, a customer may report that a product cannot perform a particular function when, in fact, that function was intentionally left out when the product was designed, or, the customer must pay extra to gain access to the function. Conversely, that particular function may have been overlooked when the product was designed and, as such, represents a valid enhancement opportunity. Companies handle this type of situation differently. Some companies resolve the incident, create an RFC, and close the incident only when the change is completed. Other companies open an RFC and simply close the incident with a reference to the RFC. When the RFC is opened, ownership of the incident is transferred to the group responsible for completing the RFC.

When the service desk is unable to deliver a solution, it is important to review the course of action with the customer and ensure that the customer understands it and the time frame within which it will be executed. It is particularly important to let the customer know if the course of action or the time frame is dictated by an SLA. If the customer is dissatisfied, determine what the customer would prefer and, if possible, accommodate that preference. If you cannot accommodate the customer's preference, determine if there is an alternate course of action that will satisfy the customer's need in the interim. Record the customer's preference in the ticket and, when necessary, bring the incident to management's attention.

Make sure you understand your company's priorities and target resolution times so you can give customers an honest estimate of when to expect a resolution or status update. Promising a swift resolution that cannot be delivered creates dissatisfaction.

244

When the service desk *is* able to deliver the solution, it often does so by directing the customer to perform a procedure or series of procedures. Analysts must use their active listening skills to ensure the customer understands the procedure and is getting the desired result.

The service desk may also send the customer a link or direct the customer to a web site where the solution can be obtained and performed by the customer at his or her convenience. Such an approach typically involves the customer accessing a web site and following a procedure or downloading a fix such as a patch or a new release of software. The service desk may follow up to ensure service is restored, or it may provide the customer a ticket number and ask the customer to contact the service desk if additional assistance is needed.

When remote control technology is available, the service desk may deliver the solution by executing the procedure for the customer via remote control. Service desk policies will dictate when remote control technology is used and how to obtain permission for its use. Analysts using remote control technology must explain the steps they are taking and help customers understand if and how they can take such steps on their own in the future.

Knowing When to Engage Additional Resources

Most service desks strive to resolve as many incidents as possible at level one. At times, though, a level one analyst needs to consult a coworker or escalate an incident to a level two service provider. For example, a customer may be reporting a very complex or unique incident, or a customer may be having an incident with a product that you have not yet been trained to support. Your first course of action is to use resources such as a knowledge management system, online help, or product and procedure manuals. If these resources do not prove useful, you may turn to a coworker or level two service provider for help.

To ensure incidents are resolved as quickly as possible, many companies establish a **target escalation time**, which is a time constraint placed on each level that ensures incident resolution activities are proceeding at an appropriate pace. For example, a service desk's policy may state that level one should escalate incidents to level two within 30 minutes. Management typically asks analysts to exercise their best judgment in following this guideline. In other words, if an analyst feels that she is close to resolving the incident, she should proceed. On the other hand, if an analyst believes that he has exhausted his capabilities and that he has used all available resources, it is time to escalate the incident.

As an analyst, you should consider the following points as the target escalation time approaches but before you escalate the incident to another service provider:

- Do I have sufficient information to clearly describe the incident? Have I collected and logged pertinent details such as who, what, when, where, and how?

- Have I determined the probable source of the incident? Have I eliminated all other possibilities?

- Have I gathered and logged the information that is required by level two? If level two has provided a problem-solving checklist, has the checklist been completed and the results documented?

- What is the incident priority? Is this an incident that must be resolved right away or can the customer wait?

The service desk analyst and the customer usually work together to determine the priority of an incident. The incident priority typically dictates the target resolution time of the incident, and also identifies the order for working on incidents with the same priority. Factors that may influence the priority assigned to an incident include its impact on the business or on a customer's productivity, the number of times an incident has recurred, how long a customer's system has been down, the availability of a workaround, or the terms of a customer's SLA. For example, a customer, via an SLA, may be paying for premium service that requires a quicker resolution time. Management may also increase the priority of a incident when, for example, the customer affected is a company executive, the customer has had a similar incident before that was not resolved to the customer's satisfaction, or management simply makes a judgment call and prioritizes one incident over another.

Remember that when you consult with a coworker or escalate an incident to a level two service provider, that person will expect you to be able to provide the answers to the questions previously listed. If you cannot give these answers, you may need to ask a few more questions before you seek help. With the answers to just a few additional questions, you may be able to resolve the incident on your own.

Taking Ownership

Not every incident can be resolved immediately. Contrary to how it may seem at times, most customers *do* understand this fact. But when an incident cannot be resolved immediately, customers expect someone to take responsibility for ensuring the incident is resolved in the time frame promised. When a service desk analyst cannot resolve an incident in the course of the initial contact or an incident must be escalated to a person or group outside the service desk, an incident owner is designated. The **incident owner** is an employee of the support organization who acts as a customer advocate and ensures that an incident is resolved to the customer's satisfaction. When an incident owner is designated, the customer should not have to initiate another contact. Nor should the customer have to repeatedly contact the different groups involved in solving the incident to find out the incident's status or progress. The incident owner does that for the customer.

In many companies, the person who initially logs the incident is the owner. In other words, the service desk analyst who first handles an incident continues to follow up, even when the incident is escalated to level two or level three. This analyst (incident owner) may also be the only person who can close the incident and does so only after verifying that the customer is satisfied.

Many companies designate the service desk as the incident owner. This means that anyone in the service desk—not just the person who handled the initial contact—can perform the responsibilities of incident owner. These companies typically have robust incident management systems that are used to monitor and track incidents throughout their lifecycle. These systems may trigger an alert to indicate a predefined threshold is near and a status update is needed. These systems are used to maintain incident data, and so anyone accessing the system can see, at any time, an incident's current status. These systems often grant only a member of the service desk permission to close an incident. Typically the service desk does so only after verifying that the customer is satisfied. Figure 6-9 shows a sample escalation sequence where the service desk owns the incident throughout the incident lifecycle.

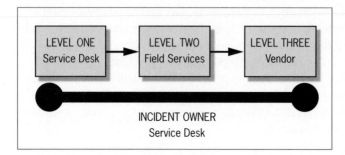

Figure 6-9 Sample escalation sequence with the service desk as the incident owner

In other companies, the incident owner changes as incidents are escalated from one level to the next. The person designated to work on the incident must accept responsibility and agree to assume ownership of the incident before the previous incident owner transfers responsibility (ownership) to him or her.

Regardless of how the incident owner is established, from a customer satisfaction standpoint, it is vital that for every single incident a designated representative of the support organization serves as an advocate for the customer. This practice ensures that incidents are not lost or forgotten and that customers' needs are considered at all times.

 Most organizations use surveys to measure and monitor customer satisfaction, solicit customer feedback, and continually improve service quality.

Incident Owner Responsibilities

Taking ownership of an incident comes with specific responsibilities. The incident owner accepts responsibility for proactively ensuring an incident is resolved to the customer's complete satisfaction, even though he or she may not actually develop or implement the solution. An incident owner:

- Tracks the current status of the incident, including who is working on the incident and where the incident is in the incident management process

- Proactively provides the customer regular and timely status updates

- When possible, identifies related incidents

- Ensures incidents are assigned correctly and are not passed from level to level or group to group without any effort being made to identify a resolution

- Ensures appropriate notification activities occur when an incident is reported, escalated, and resolved

- Ensures all problem-solving activities are documented

- Verifies that the customer is satisfied with the resolution

- Closes the incident ticket

To satisfy customers, each and every member of the service desk team must do all they can to ensure customer satisfaction. Sometimes that means sharing ownership responsibilities. In other words, analysts do the following:

- Monitor alerts and the status of outstanding incidents in the queue and follow up as needed.

- Help other analysts when they can. For example, an analyst may have recently been to a training class or may be a subject matter expert and can share his or her knowledge with others who may be following up on outstanding incidents.

- Update the ticket if a customer contacts the service desk to provide additional information or to obtain an up-to-date status. A good practice is to note in the ticket the date and time that the customer provided the information or requested a status update.

- Negotiate a transfer of ownership for any outstanding tickets if the analyst has been working on an incident but is going to be out of the office for an extended time, such as for training or vacation. A good practice is to ensure all tickets are up to date and all resolved tickets are closed before the tickets are transferred to another analyst or back to the service desk team.

Ownership is critical to the incident management process. Without it, incidents can be lost or forgotten and customer dissatisfaction invariably occurs. The concept of ownership ensures everyone involved in the incident management process stays focused on the customer's need to have the incident resolved in a timely fashion and to be informed when the incident requires more than the expected time to resolve.

Providing Status Updates to Management and Customers

An incident owner has the extremely important responsibilities of promoting awareness that an incident has occurred and regularly communicating the status of incident resolution activities. These activities are known as incident notification. **Notification** informs all of the stakeholders in the incident management process—including management, the customer, and service desk analysts—about the status of outstanding incidents. Notification can occur when an incident is reported or escalated, when an incident has exceeded a predefined threshold such as its target resolution time, or when an incident is resolved.

Notification to each of the stakeholders occurs at different points and has different goals. For example, *management* notification is appropriate when:

- The incident is extremely severe.

- The target resolution time or a predefined threshold has been or is about to be reached.

- Required resources are not available to determine or implement a solution.

- The customer expresses dissatisfaction.

In each of these cases, notification keeps management aware of incidents that might require management intervention. The goals of management notification are to ensure the following:

- Management knows the current status of incidents that are in an exception state, meaning that the incidents have exceeded a predefined threshold. For example, the target resolution time has been exceeded, or a level two support group is not acknowledging an incident that has been assigned to it within an agreed upon time frame.

- Management has the information needed to oversee incidents that involve multiple support groups. For example, resources from the network support and development groups are needed to resolve an incident.

- Management has sufficient information to make decisions (such as add more resources or reassign responsibilities), follow up with the customer, or call in other management.

- Management actions are recorded in the incident record so everyone affected by or involved in solving the incident knows what decisions management has made or what steps it took to follow up with the customer or involve other management.

These goals make sure the customer's incident is being addressed and responded to in an appropriate time and way.

Like management notification, *customer* notification is appropriate in specific situations, such as when:

- The analyst told the customer that he or she will provide a status at a given time, even if there has been no change in the incident's status.

- The target resolution time will not be met.

- Customer resources are required to implement a solution.

- The incident has a high priority and justifies frequent status updates.

- The customer was dissatisfied with earlier solutions.

Customer notification keeps the customer informed about the progress of the incident resolution. This lets the customer know the incident is being addressed and responded to in an appropriate time and way. The goals of customer notification are to ensure the following:

- The customer knows the current status of the incident.

- Customer comments or concerns are recorded in the incident record and addressed.

Three ways that service desks deliver value are by: (1) making it easy for customers to report incidents, (2) delivering solutions, and (3) taking ownership and ensuring that incidents that cannot be resolved immediately are addressed in the required time frame. One of the most common complaints service desks hear from customers is that they were not kept informed. It is important to remember that even bad news is better than no news at all. Contacting customers to let them know the target resolution time cannot be met, and perhaps explaining the reason for any delays (such as having to order parts), is far better than having the customers hear nothing.

Proactive communication is the most effective way to minimize negative customer reaction and instill customer confidence when incidents arise or when delays occur. Although customers may not be happy with a delay, they typically appreciate being kept informed. Customers may also accept explanations offered proactively as fact (we must order a part); whereas explanations offered in response to a customer inquiry about an overdue resolution may be viewed simply as an excuse (we are waiting on a part).

The service desk can notify management, customers, and others by telephone, in person, with an email or instant message, through a paging device, or automatically via the incident management system. How notification occurs and who is notified vary based on conditions such as the priority of the incident, who is affected by the incident, and when the incident occurs. Many service desks have documented procedures that spell out who to notify and how to notify them.

Building Good Relationships with Other Support Groups

Although most service desks strive to resolve as many incidents as possible at level one, there are times when a level one analyst needs to interact with people from other support groups, such as a field services group or a network support group. An analyst may need to escalate an incident to the support group or obtain a status update on a ticket previously assigned. The analyst may be asking for informal training or help developing a problem-solving checklist. A good relationship between the service desk and other support groups ensures that all groups can fulfill their roles and responsibilities.

It takes time and effort to build a strong relationship between the service desk and other support groups. Level one analysts must strive to continuously increase their knowledge and the efficiency and effectiveness of their problem-solving skills. This includes ensuring all available information has been gathered and logged, and all checklists have been completed and the results logged before an incident is escalated to level two. Level two service providers must respect the service desk's role as a front-line service provider. They must acknowledge the fact that the service desk's efforts are freeing them from the need to answer the same questions or resolve the same incidents over and over again. They must be willing to impart their knowledge to the service desk. This enables the service desk to resolve more incidents at level one, while also reducing the number of incidents the service desk escalates to level two. The service desk must be willing to receive that knowledge and seek assistance from level two only after using all other available resources, such as manuals, knowledge bases, and so forth.

The following techniques can be used to foster a strong relationship between the service desk and other support groups so all groups can reap the benefits.

Review and Understand Your Company's SLAs, OLAs, and Contracts

An organization may have SLAs with some or all of its customers, OLAs with internal (level two and level three) support groups, and contracts with external vendors. These agreements are critical in defining the roles and responsibilities of all of the support groups represented in the company's customer service value chain. These agreements contain information such as the services to be delivered, service hours, and performance metrics. These agreements are integral to the relationship that exists between customers, level one, and level two. For example, if a critical incident occurs and the company guarantees a customer in an SLA that the incident will be resolved in two hours, the OLA will specify that the service desk must notify level two immediately so the level two service provider has an adequate amount of time to respond. Conversely, the service desk must not insist that level two drop everything else to work on a noncritical incident that does not need to be resolved for several days. The service desk must resist the temptation to declare everything an emergency, or level two may become unresponsive. Understanding your company's SLAs, OLAs, and contracts is an excellent way to ensure everyone's expectations, including those of other support groups, are being met.

Provide Mutual Feedback

An excellent way to enhance the relationship between the service desk and other support groups is to ask the members of each group for feedback. You get more benefit from improving or addressing agreed upon issues than from addressing what you *think* the issues are. You can solicit feedback informally by getting feedback from someone in the support group that you know and that you trust will be constructive. The service desk team also can solicit feedback formally by, for example, preparing a survey, such as the one shown in Figure 6-10, that asks the members of other support groups for feedback. When the service desk is open to feedback, it will often find that other support groups begin to solicit and respond to constructive feedback in return.

Job Shadowing

Job shadowing involves working side by side with another person in an effort to understand and potentially learn that person's job. Job shadowing provides excellent benefits to both the service desk and support groups because each group is given the opportunity to walk in the other's shoes. This enables both groups to gain a better understanding of the other's perspective and priorities. Job shadowing is a particularly effective way to improve your problem-solving skills. For example, job shadowing may give you the opportunity to work with a specialist to resolve a complex or unique incident, or it may give you the opportunity to learn how to use new tools or to develop new checklists. As with providing mutual feedback, you can job shadow someone informally on your own, or your service desk may have a formal program in place.

Level Two Feedback Survey

The purpose of this survey is to solicit feedback that can be used to improve the quality of the services provided by the service desk. Please answer the questions below and provide constructive comments about how we can better work with your group. Your responses will help us in our ongoing effort to provide quality service to our customers and contribute to the success of the entire Technology Services organization.

Name (optional): _____

Department (optional): _____

1. How satisfied are you overall with the thoroughness and accuracy with which the service desk documents tickets assigned to your group? For example, incident description, steps taken to diagnose the incident, resolution steps attempted, and so forth?

    ❏ Very Satisfied   ❏ Somewhat Satisfied   ❏ Dissatisfied

    Please comment:

2. How satisfied are you overall with the service desk's ability to handle recurring incidents after you have given it training, documentation, solution information, and so forth?

    ❏ Very Satisfied   ❏ Somewhat Satisfied   ❏ Dissatisfied

    Please comment:

3. How satisfied are you overall with the accuracy with which the service desk determines the probable source of the incident and, as such, assigns tickets to your group?

    ❏ Very Satisfied   ❏ Somewhat Satisfied   ❏ Dissatisfied

    Please comment:

Page 1

Figure 6-10 Level two feedback survey

Level Two Feedback Survey

4. How satisfied are you overall with the service desk's efforts to diagnose the incident prior to seeking assistance from your group?

    ❑ Very Satisfied ❑ Somewhat Satisfied ❑ Dissatisfied

    Please comment:

5. How satisfied are you overall with the service desk's ability to record and assign the appropriate priority to the incidents that are reported to or discovered by it?

    ❑ Very Satisfied ❑ Somewhat Satisfied ❑ Dissatisfied

    Please comment:

6. How satisfied are you overall with the partnership that exists between your group and the service desk?

    ❑ Very Satisfied ❑ Somewhat Satisfied ❑ Dissatisfied

    Please comment:

7. Do you feel comfortable giving constructive feedback directly to the service desk in an effort to enhance the working relationship that exists between the two groups?

    ❑ Yes ❑ No

    Please comment:

8. What improvements have been made and what areas do you feel could be further improved between your group and the service desk?

    Please comment:

Thank you for taking time to complete this important survey.

Page 2

Figure 6-10 Level two feedback survey *(continued)*

Review Incident Management System Information

A common complaint from level two service providers is they cannot understand the information service desk analysts give in the tickets escalated to them, or they feel the information is incomplete. Conversely, service desk analysts often complain that level two service providers do not thoroughly document the steps taken to resolve an incident. As a result, the service desk is unable to reuse the resolution when a similar incident occurs. Periodic reviews of incident management system information by a team of level one and level two service providers can pinpoint areas that need to be improved. A good practice is to use real tickets during this review to illustrate and discuss examples of both poorly documented and well-documented tickets. The conclusions drawn during these reviews, and the examples of well-documented tickets can be used to create new or enhanced ticket-logging procedures and during training.

Communicate

When strained relations exist between the service desk and other support groups, it is often because of poor communication. The service desk and the support groups must make sure they communicate all appropriate information in a timely manner. For example, the service desk must let the support groups know when it typically receives its highest volume of contacts or when it is receiving an unexpectedly high volume of contacts. This information enables the support groups to understand the current capabilities of the service desk and the factors that influence its performance. Support groups must, in turn, let the service desk know when they are working on a large project or when they will be shorthanded. This information enables the service desk to appropriately manage its customers' expectations and may influence when and how the service desk escalates incidents.

 Everyone is busy in today's business world. Timely and regular communication will circumvent misunderstandings and promote a spirit of partnership.

Give Praise

One thing that makes working in the field of technical customer support so tough is that you rarely hear good news. In fact, for all intents and purposes, your job is to deal with bad news. Just as you hope to receive thanks for your efforts, you can let the people who work in other support groups know you appreciate the job they are doing. If a level two service provider develops a problem-solving checklist, a representative of the service desk can send an email message to the service provider's supervisor or team leader that expresses the team's appreciation. Some service desks maintain a drawer filled with snacks or toys, such as stress balls, that they can hand out to level two service providers who provide training or in some way go the extra mile. Although giving praise may seem like a small thing, it is easy to do, costs little to no money, and encourages continued goodwill. Giving praise also encourages praise in return. Praise is something we all appreciate.

Level one analysts and level two service providers must work together to ensure incidents are resolved quickly and accurately. All of the support groups within a company, including the service desk, have a role to play, and each must respect the other's role and responsibilities. Although it is the incident owner's responsibility to act as a customer advocate and ensure an incident is resolved to the customer's satisfaction, each and every member of the customer service value chain must do all they can to ensure incidents are resolved quickly and correctly.

Closing Incidents

After a solution has been identified and implemented, there are still questions that need to be asked and answered. These include:

- Did the solution resolve the incident?
- Is the customer satisfied?
- Has all pertinent data been recorded?

If the answer to any of these questions is "No," the incident cannot be considered resolved. At this point, the incident owner, assisted by coworkers, level two or level three service providers, and, when appropriate, management, must determine the next steps to take. If the answer to all of these questions is *yes*, the incident ticket can be closed.

 Most companies distinguish between resolving an incident and closing the incident. An incident is resolved when a service provider delivers a solution. The incident is closed only after the incident owner verifies that the customer is satisfied with the resolution.

Ensuring all pertinent data is recorded before an incident is closed is critical. Often incident management systems are configured to restrict who can close an incident—typically the incident owner—and the data fields that must be completed before the incident can be closed. Without this data, reports will be inaccurate and trend analysis cannot be performed.

Some service desks have highly skilled statisticians perform trend analysis. However, it is important to remember that any or all members of the service desk team can identify and analyze trends. Very often the front-line staff can identify trends simply by considering the contacts it is receiving. The service desk might notice it is receiving many contacts about a certain system or product and bring that fact to management's attention. A trend report can then be created to validate statistically the service desk's hunch. The trend can also trigger the problem management process, which is responsible for investigating and, where possible, eliminating the root cause.

When working in a service desk, do not hesitate to suggest ways that incidents can be eliminated. Be persistent and act on your hunches. Go beyond the quick fix, and take the time to resolve incidents correctly the first time. If, as an incident owner, you believe an incident has not been resolved, leave the incident ticket open and engage the resources needed to determine the correct solution. Your coworkers, managers, and customers will thank you.

If you don't have the time to do it right, when will you have the time to do it over?

JOHN WOODEN

Focusing on Prevention

Until the root cause of a problem is identified and eliminated, it is likely that incidents will recur. The problem management process identifies that root cause. The service desk typically contributes to and uses the problem management process through its integration with the incident management process. For example, many problems are detected by the service desk in the course of handling incidents or via trend analysis and are then logged as a problem and handled by the problem management process. Problem management uses incident-related data—much of which is recorded by the service desk—when investigating and diagnosing the root cause. In return, problem management identifies known errors and workarounds that the service desk can use to resolve and reduce the impact of incidents.

Senior service desk analysts, particularly those who are subject matter experts in a company's systems, networks, applications, and products may help investigate and diagnose problems. These analysts typically work with other technical specialists, vendors, and contractors. In the case of particularly complex problems, a team of experts work together under a problem manager. A **problem manager** coordinates all problem management activities and ensures problems are resolved within SLA targets. The problem manager makes sure the needed resources are available to analyze problems and to determine their root cause. The company can then take steps to prevent similar problems from occurring in the future.

The following sections describe common techniques used to diagnose problems. These techniques could be used to diagnose incidents. However, because they tend to be more time consuming and require greater skill, they are typically reserved for problem management.

Brainstorming

Brainstorming is a technique performed by a group of people that is designed to generate a large number of ideas for solving a problem. Keys to successful brainstorming include avoiding criticism, encouraging unusual ideas, encouraging everyone to contribute ideas, and compounding or combining ideas. During brainstorming, ideas should not be judged as good or bad. Participants must also resist the temptation to draw conclusions or make decisions during active brainstorming. After a complete list of ideas is generated, analysis can begin.

Five Whys

Five Whys is a technique that involves repeatedly asking the question "Why?" until the root cause of a problem is determined. For example, why do printers jam? If the answer is because the paper does not feed properly, ask why that is, and so on. The answer to one question leads to another question and eventually to the root cause. You may be able to ask fewer than five questions to determine the root cause.

Cause and Effect Analysis

Cause and effect analysis is a technique used to generate the possible causes of a problem or effect. This technique typically involves producing a chart or diagram to visually display the many potential causes for a specific problem or effect. A cause and effect diagram may be called a fishbone diagram because it often resembles a fishbone. This diagram may also be called an Ishikawa diagram because it was originally proposed by Kaoru Ishikawa, a professor in Japan, in the 1950s. Figure 6-11 shows a sample cause and effect diagram. In Figure 6-11, the effect being diagnosed is hardware failures. The vertical lines or "bones" of the diagram represent the major categories of problem causes. The horizontal lines are used to record the possible causes for each category. The possible causes may be determined by brainstorming, performing the Five Whys, or performing trend or root cause analysis. An effective technique is to transfer the identified causes to a Pareto chart for further analysis.

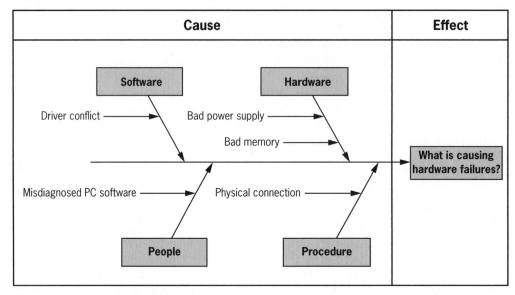

Figure 6-11   Sample cause and effect diagram

Pareto Analysis

Pareto analysis is a technique for determining the most significant causes from a list of many possible causes of a problem. Pareto analysis can be combined with the results produced from techniques such as brainstorming, Five Whys, and cause and effect analysis. This technique involves producing a bar chart that displays by frequency, in descending order, the possible causes of a problem—making it possible to identify the most significant of those causes.

 Pareto analysis reflects the Pareto Principle, also known as the 80/20 Rule, which, relative to problem management, means that 20 percent of the defects or failures that occur cause 80 percent of the incidents.

Figure 6-12 shows a sample Pareto chart. The left vertical axis of the chart represents the number of incidents the problems caused. The line graph shows the cumulative percentage associated with each problem cause. Figure 6-12 shows that cumulatively 84.2 percent of hardware incidents are caused by bad power supplies or bad memory modules. A conclusion that could be drawn from this chart is to select vendors that provide higher-quality components. Another conclusion could be to ensure power supplies and memory modules are kept in stock to minimize the time required to correct these failures. Providing training and diagnostic scripts to the service desk staff is also important so these incidents are quickly diagnosed and resolved.

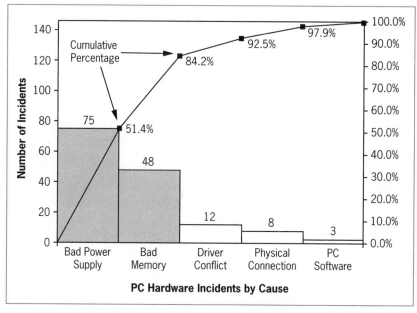

Figure 6-12 Sample Pareto chart

Kepner-Tregoe Problem Analysis

Kepner-Tregoe problem analysis is a proprietary problem analysis technique developed by Charles Kepner and Ben Tregoe. This technique involves defining and describing the problem, establishing possible causes, testing the most probable cause, and verifying the true cause.

Table 6-2 lists common root cause codes for technology-related problems. Notice that many of the root cause codes listed are not related specifically to hardware products or software systems. They are related to how people are implementing or using the technology. In many companies, the technology itself is actually quite stable. The bulk of the problems are caused by changes made to the technology or factors such as inadequate training and insufficient documentation.

Code	Description
Communications Failure	For example, network or telephone line down
Configuration Error	PC/system configured incorrectly
Database Problem	For example, database full or generating errors
Environment	For example, power outage
Hardware Failure	Hardware malfunction
Human Error	For example, procedures not followed or typing error
Incorrect Data	Incorrect input produced incorrect output
Incorrect Documentation/Procedures	Inaccurate or incomplete documentation/procedures
Incompatible Hardware	Incompatible/nonstandard hardware
Incompatible Software	Incompatible/nonstandard software
Installation Error	Hardware/software installed incorrectly
Insufficient Resources	For example, memory
Lack of Training	For example, for use with how-to type inquiries
Other	For use when no other response is appropriate
Planned Outage	Customer is unable to access a system due to a planned outage
Procedure Not Followed	Complete and accurate procedure not followed
Result of Change	Problem caused by a change to the system/device
Request for Information	For example, for use with inquiries
Software Bug	Incorrect software code
Unknown	Problem could not be duplicated

Table 6-2 Sample root cause codes

Most companies that use codes in fields such as root cause include an Other code that is used when no other response is appropriate. Misuse of this code can considerably reduce a company's ability to perform trend and root cause analysis. Constant monitoring of this code ensures the appropriate action is taken quickly to minimize misuse. For example, the best companies use the Other code to determine what, if any, additional codes are needed and what codes need further explanation. Excessive use of the Other code may also signal the need to provide additional training to a specific analyst.

 Some companies trigger an email message whenever the Other code is used. This email is sent to a system administrator or service desk team leader who can then determine what action to take.

Without accurate data captured by service desk analysts, problem management is not possible. When problem management is not performed, it is likely that resulting incidents will recur and that new incidents will appear. When problem management is performed, the organization is able to identify, eliminate, and ultimately predict and prevent problems' causes.

Given the rapid pace at which technology changes, it is unlikely that problem management will enable a company to prevent all problems. However, problem management will enable the elimination of common problems and the associated recurring incidents.

When working in a service desk, an understanding of your company's incident and problem management processes and strong problem-solving skills are essential to your success. The incident and problem management processes and the problem-solving process all require that you systematically gather data and information, use proven investigation and diagnostic tools and techniques, and, when necessary, engage additional resources. The incident management process focuses on restoring service and on ensuring that customers and managers are proactively kept informed about the status of incident resolution activities.

Handling incidents efficiently and effectively is important, but, ultimately, customers prefer that incidents be prevented. The problem management process focuses on minimizing the impact of incidents and preventing incidents by identifying and eliminating their root cause. Trend and root cause analysis can be used to prevent incidents, but only if you capture accurate and complete data. When incidents are prevented, you will have the opportunity to work on more complex incidents and pursue new skills.

Chapter Summary

- To be successful, a service desk analyst must be able to resolve incidents efficiently and effectively. Most service desks develop processes and procedures, such as the incident management process, in an effort to ensure incidents are handled quickly, correctly, and consistently. The goal of incident management is to restore service as quickly as possible in an effort to minimize the impact of incidents that affect a company's systems, networks, applications, and products.

- Within the boundaries of the incident management process, analysts use their problem-solving skills to handle each incident. The best problem solvers condition themselves to gather all available data, create information, and methodically diagnose the incident before developing and executing a course of action. Effective diagnostic techniques include asking questions, simulating the customer's actions, and using diagnostic tools.

- When incidents cannot be resolved immediately, customers expect someone to take responsibility for ensuring the incident is resolved in the time frame promised. The incident owner assumes that responsibility. The concept of ownership ensures everyone involved in the incident management process stays focused on the customer's need to have the incident resolved in a timely fashion and to be informed when the incident requires more than the expected time to resolve. Ownership is critical to the incident management process. Without it, incidents can be lost or forgotten and customer dissatisfaction invariably occurs.

- Once an incident is resolved, the customer is satisfied with the resolution, and all pertinent data is recorded, the incident can be closed. Ensuring all pertinent data is recorded is critical. Without this data, reports will be inaccurate and trend analysis cannot be performed.

- Problem management also uses this data to identify problems. Senior service desk analysts work with others to investigate and diagnose problems using techniques such as brainstorming, Five Whys, cause and effect analysis, Pareto analysis, and Kepner-Tregoe problem analysis.

- Without the data captured by service desk analysts, problem management is not possible. When problem management is not performed, it is likely that resulting incidents will recur and that new incidents will appear. When problem management is performed, the organization is able to eliminate the root cause of problems and, ultimately, prevent incidents. When incidents are prevented, you will have the opportunity to work on more complex incidents and pursue new skills.

- When working in a service desk, an understanding of your company's incident and problem management processes and strong problem-solving skills are essential to your success.

Key Terms

brainstorming—A technique performed by a group of people that is designed to generate a large number of ideas for solving a problem.

cause and effect analysis—A technique used to generate the possible causes of a problem or effect.

client/server—A computing model where some computers, known as clients, request services, and other computers, known as servers, respond to those requests.

closed loop process—A process that changes its output based on feedback.

customer data—The identifying details about a customer.

customer record—All of the data and text fields that describe a single customer.

detailed incident description—A comprehensive accounting of an incident and the circumstances surrounding the incident's occurrence.

digital agent—A software routine that waits in the background and performs an action when a specified event occurs.

early life support (ELS)—The stage in the service lifecycle that occurs at the end of a deployment and before the service is fully accepted into operation (ITIL definition).

Five Whys—A technique that involves repeatedly asking the question "Why?" until the root cause of a problem is determined.

flowchart—A diagram that shows the sequence of tasks that occur in a process.

incident data—The details of an incident or service request.

incident management—The process responsible for managing the lifecycle of incidents (ITIL definition).

incident owner—An employee of the support organization who acts as a customer advocate and ensures an incident is resolved to the customer's satisfaction.

incident record—All of the fields that describe a single incident.

inquiry—A customer request for information.

IT planner—The individual responsible for producing and maintaining the IT standards, policies, plans, and strategies that ensure the IT department's services meet the business' strategic needs.

job shadowing—Working side by side with another person in an effort to understand and potentially learn that person's job.

Kepner-Tregoe problem analysis—A proprietary problem analysis technique developed by Charles Kepner and Ben Tregoe that involves defining and describing the problem, establishing possible causes, testing the most probable cause, and verifying the true cause.

known error—A problem that has a documented root cause and a workaround (ITIL definition).

notification—The activities that inform all of the stakeholders in the incident management process (including management, the customer, and service desk analysts) about the status of outstanding incidents.

Pareto analysis—A technique for determining the most significant causes from a list of many possible causes of a problem.

probable source—The system, network, application, or product that is most likely causing an incident.

problem management—The process responsible for managing the lifecycle of problems (ITIL definition).

problem manager—An employee of the support organization who coordinates all problem management activities and ensures problems are resolved within SLA targets.

problem-solving skills—The thinking skills used to answer a question or resolve a difficult situation; also known as *troubleshooting skills*.

question—A customer request for instructions.

record—A collection of related fields.

remote control system—A technology that enables an analyst to view and take control of a connected device to troubleshoot incidents, transfer files, provide informal training, or collaborate on documents.

request for change (RFC)—A request to change the production environment.

resolution data—The details that describe how an incident was resolved.

root cause—The most basic reason for an undesirable condition or problem, which, if eliminated or corrected, would prevent the problem from existing or occurring.

root cause analysis—A methodical way of determining why problems occur and identifying ways to prevent them.

short incident description—A succinct description of the actual results a customer is experiencing.

standard change—A preapproved change that is low risk and follows a procedure.

status data—The details about an incident that are used to track the incident throughout its lifecycle.

symptom—A sign or indication that an incident has occurred.

target escalation time—A time constraint placed on each level that ensures incident resolution activities are proceeding at an appropriate pace.

trend analysis—A methodical way of determining and, when possible, forecasting service trends.

troubleshooting skills—See *problem-solving skills*.

Review Questions

1. Solving an incident involves determining its root cause. True or False? Explain your answer.

2. Define the term *root cause*.

3. Explain the relationship that exists between processes and procedures.

4. Draw the symbol that represents a task in a flowchart.

5. Draw the symbol that represents a decision point in a flowchart.

6. List and briefly describe the basic activities that the incident and problem management processes have in common.

7. A(n) _____ is a sign or an indication that an incident has occurred.

8. Why do most companies distinguish between incidents, questions, and inquiries?

9. List two types of data you must gather before you can begin diagnosing an incident.

10. What are two ways that a short incident description is used?

11. Briefly describe the items that should be included in a detailed incident description.

12. What are you trying to determine when diagnosing an incident?

13. List three benefits that are derived by asking questions.

14. List two ways that service desks provide analysts with the ability to simulate their customers' actions.

15. Describe two situations in which you may not be able to use diagnostic tools.

16. Why is it important to determine the correct probable incident source?

17. What typically dictates the target resolution time of an incident?

18. Why is incident management referred to as a "closed loop process"?

19. The incident owner is the person who develops and implements the solution to an incident. True or False? Explain your answer.

20. What can happen if no one takes ownership of an incident?

21. When can incident notification occur?

22. What are the goals of management notification?

23. What are the goals of customer notification?

24. What two things can service desk analysts do to build a strong relationship with their level two support groups?

25. What two things can level two support groups do to build a strong relationship with the service desk?

26. What three questions must be answered with *yes* before an incident can be closed?

27. List three ways you can help eliminate incidents when you work in a service desk.

28. Brainstorming involves identifying only the best ideas. True or False? Explain your answer.

29. What does an Ishikawa diagram display?

30. What are two ways that service desk analysts benefit when problems are prevented?

Discussion Questions

1. People with strong technical skills often feel that processes and procedures take too much time and stifle innovation. They like their freedom and feel that documenting their actions and results is a waste of time. Are they right? Discuss the pros and cons of processes and procedures versus independence and individuality.

2. In some organizations, an adversarial relationship exists between the level one service desk and some level two support groups. Discuss potential reasons for this adverse situation. Also discuss ways an adverse situation can be improved.

3. Most of us have experienced a situation where we had a fleeting thought—a hunch—that we ignored. Discuss the pros and cons of ignoring hunches. Also discuss how hunches can be used to prevent incidents.

Hands-On Projects

1. **Develop a process flowchart.** Assemble a team of three to five classmates. Develop a flowchart that shows all the steps for having a pizza delivered that contains the toppings the entire team agrees upon.

    a. Start the process with the decision to order a pizza, and stop the process by throwing the pizza box in the recycling bin.

    b. If you have access to flowcharting software, use it to construct and print your flowchart. The most popular flowcharting software is Microsoft Visio. SmartDraw.com also offers flowcharting software that you can download free of charge.

    c. Develop procedures for at least two of the steps in your process.

2. **Learn about the benefits of the ITIL incident and problem management processes.** Search the web using phrases such as "ITIL benefits incident management," "ITIL benefits problem management," and "ITIL benefits case studies." Prepare a two-page report describing the benefits of the ITIL incident and problem management processes. Include examples of companies that have implemented incident and problem management and the benefits they have realized.

3. **Tease your brain (part 1).** Brain teasers are effective ways to train your brain to solve problems. The following letters represent something that you learned early in life, most likely before you attended first grade. Add the next two letters to the sequence and explain how these letters fit into the sequence.

    O

    T

    T

    F

    F

    S

    S

    ?

    ?

4. **Tease your brain (part 2).** The first 10 letters of the alphabet have been divided into two groups.

   Group 1: A E F H I

   Group 2: B C D G J

   a. What pattern differentiates the two groups?

   b. Into which group would you put the letter *K*?

   c. Into which group would you put the letter *R*?

5. **Develop a problem-solving checklist.** Select a device or an application that you use regularly. Develop a problem-solving checklist that contains at least 10 questions that analysts can use to diagnose incidents customers may encounter when using the selected technology.

6. **Learn about remote control software.** Search the Internet and access the web site of two companies that manufacture remote control software (also known as remote support software). Some popular products include GoToMyPC, LogMeIn, pcAnywhere, ReachOut, and Timbuktu. For each of the two companies you select, summarize in a paragraph or two what you were able to learn about remote control software. Briefly describe the benefits of using these systems for both the customer and service desk analysts.

7. **Determine whom to notify.** A level two field service representative has just informed you that he will not meet the target resolution time for an incident because another incident he is working on is taking longer than expected. The only other person who could work on the incident is in training this week. As owner of the incident, briefly describe whom you would notify and how you would minimize customer dissatisfaction in this situation.

8. **Identify and prevent root causes.** Using your school's online message or discussion board or working as a class, use the brainstorming, Five Whys, or cause and effect analysis technique to determine the root cause of and ways to prevent the following problem: You are on your way to school and your car sputters to a stop on the side of the road. Why did your car stop?

Case Projects

1. **Mind Games.** You are the manager of a medium-sized service desk and have decided that you want your staff to have fun while improving its problem-solving skills. Go to the library, and look in books or magazines for brainteasers and puzzles that can be used to challenge your staff and encourage logical thinking. Select three brainteasers, and distribute them to your staff (choose three classmates). Discuss with your staff the techniques you learned in this chapter that could be useful in solving the brainteasers. What information is available? What is the expected result? What questions can you ask in an effort to determine the expected result?

2.   **Brownstein, Popp, and Hepburn.** You work for a small law firm and are part of a committee that is developing standards for the technologies the lawyers will be authorized to use. The lawyers where you work are very autonomous, and they resist any rules they perceive are unnecessary. For the first meeting, each attendee has been asked to prepare a list of benefits lawyers will derive as a result of establishing standards. The committee chair hopes that promoting the benefits will lessen resistance to the new standards. Prepare for the meeting by listing the benefits you perceive the entire firm, not just the service desk, will derive by establishing technology standards.

3.   **Eckes Office Supplies.** You have been hired as a consultant to help the internal service desk at Eckes Office Supplies improve the relationship it has with its level two support groups. In an effort to understand the dynamics of the current relationship, you will survey the service desk staff and members of the level two support groups. The service desk escalates a fairly high number of incidents to the network support group, so you have elected to work on that relationship first. Prepare a survey that can be used to solicit the service desk's perception of its relationship with the network support group. Your goal is to formulate questions that, when answered, will help you determine if the network support group is meeting the service desk's expectations. (*Hint:* Use the level two feedback survey presented in this chapter for ideas.)

Business Skills for Technical Professionals

In this chapter you will learn:

- ◎ How to acquire and use business skills in the workplace
- ◎ How to use business skills to identify and justify improvement opportunities
- ◎ How to use presentation skills to communicate
- ◎ Advanced business skills for technical professionals

In the support industry, technical professionals increasingly do more than simply support technology. They are being challenged to ensure that technology is useful and helps workers be productive. In other words, they are being challenged to ensure a company's technology enables its employees and customers to achieve their business goals.

To do this, technical professionals need business skills. These skills include the ability to understand and speak the language of business and the ability to analyze business problems and identify improvement opportunities. Merely identifying improvement opportunities, however, is not enough. Individuals must also be able to communicate the benefits of their ideas in financial terms and use presentation skills to market their ideas to management.

This chapter introduces some of the business topics and disciplines that technical professionals may encounter when they join the workforce. This chapter also describes business skills that managers are increasingly requiring technical professionals—particularly more senior technical professionals—to acquire and use, such as project management, cost-benefit analysis, and return on investment (ROI) calculations.

Acquiring and Using Business Skills in the Workplace

Whether a person works for a small company or a large corporation, some business skills are useful and required. The business world is extremely competitive. CIOs and hiring managers increasingly expect technical professionals to think like businesspeople and to possess at least some business skills. Also, difficult economic times along with trends such as automation and outsourcing mean companies have fewer job positions and can be very selective about whom they hire. People who have a mix of skills— including business, technical, soft, and self-management skills—create the greatest opportunities for themselves.

Obtaining Relevant Business Skills

Some business skills, such as those listed in Figure 7-1, are particularly relevant to technical professionals. It is important to note, however, that these skills are useful regardless of the profession you enter. You can acquire some business skills by simply observing and inquiring about the activities that occur where you work. Your business skills also grow as you acquire education and experience.

- Customer service
- Process management
- Listening and communication
- Writing
- Problem solving
- Financial management
- Making presentations
- Project management
- Conflict management
- Time management
- Human resources management

Figure 7-1   Business skills relevant to technical professionals

Customer Service

Skills such as understanding the importance of meeting customers' needs and knowing how to manage their expectations are imperative in today's competitive business world. The need for people who understand the characteristics of excellent customer service—responsiveness, a caring attitude, and skill—is great and such people are always in demand.

Process Management

Processes are an integral component of every service desk. Common processes such as incident and problem management, request fulfillment, knowledge management, and service level management are vital to the success of the service desk. People who understand processes can suggest improvements that save time and money by eliminating bottlenecks and unnecessary tasks. International acceptance of frameworks such as ITIL is also increasing the need for people who have experience developing, documenting, and continually improving and streamlining processes.

Listening and Communication

Listening and communication are two of the most basic skills needed in today's fast-paced business world. Knowing what to say and how to say it takes practice and a willingness to understand the varying communication styles of customers, managers, and coworkers. Good listening and communication skills benefit all areas of your life and can be improved with practice.

Writing

Writing is an increasingly important business skill. This is because an ever greater number of communications occur via technologies such as the Internet, email, IM, and chat. Service desk analysts are also regularly required to use writing skills to prepare documents such as tickets, knowledge articles, reports, policies, and procedures. The need for strong writing skills grows as a person advances in his or her career.

Problem Solving

Problem-solving skills are imperative in the support industry and valued regardless of a person's profession. Knowing how to methodically gather data, determine the probable source of problems, and develop solutions to problems are skills that improve with practice and experience.

Financial Management

Financial management skills range from being able to work within a budget—a must-have skill in the cost-sensitive business world—to preparing a business case and budget for a project or department. The need for these skills increases as technical professionals advance to team leader or supervisory positions. Financial management skills also include being able to communicate the financial benefits of improvement opportunities and using techniques such as cost-benefit analysis and ROI calculations. **Cost-benefit analysis** is a business calculation that compares the costs and benefits of two or more potential solutions to determine an optimum solution. **Return on investment (ROI)** is a business calculation that measures the total financial benefit derived from an investment—such as a new technology project—and then compares it with the total cost of the project.

Making Presentations

Using presentations to communicate is an important business skill because presentations are an accepted and effective way to communicate information and gain acceptance for ideas. Presentations are also an excellent way to build credibility. The use of presentations to communicate becomes increasingly important as a person advances in his or her career.

Project Management

Change is constant and imperative in the business world. As a result, most employees will be involved at some point with at least one project and often many projects at the same time. Technical professionals are often involved in projects such as hardware or software releases, or rollouts. An understanding of project management concepts makes it possible for a person to be effective whether he or she is a member of a project team or responsible for planning and managing a project.

Conflict Management

Conflict is a normal part of human interaction. Knowing how to manage conflict in a constructive way is an important skill, particularly when working in a team setting such as a service desk. Conflict management is an excellent life skill that can be improved with practice.

Time Management

Time management is a critical business skill that enables people to feel in control and stay motivated during these "do more with less" times. Good work habits, such as getting and staying organized, make it possible for people to feel job satisfaction and avoid stress and burnout. Like conflict management, time management is an excellent life skill that can be improved with practice.

Human Resources Management

Human resources management involves activities such as interviewing prospective employees, coaching team members, and conducting performance appraisals. In some team settings, team members provide feedback about their teammates' performance and may be involved in interviewing prospective employees. These skills become more important, and are typically required, as technical professionals advance to team leader or supervisory positions.

Many of these skills such as listening, communication, and writing are basic business skills that can be learned on the job, through self-study, or in the classroom. These skills, along with skills such as customer service, problem solving, project management, conflict management, and time management, are relatively universal and can be used regardless of a person's chosen profession. Skills such as financial management and human resources management are also important and become even more important as people advance in their careers.

CASE STUDY: Ethics in Business

An increasingly important business skill is having an understanding of ethics. **Ethics** *are the rules and standards that govern the conduct of a person or group of people. Such rules and standards dictate, or provide guidance about, what is considered right and wrong behavior. Ethical behavior is behavior that conforms to generally accepted or stated principles of right and wrong. The policies of a department or company dictate what is right and wrong behavior and may vary from one department or company to the next. For example, some companies permit limited personal use of the company's email system, whereas others restrict the use of email to work-related correspondences. Scandals in the business world and dilemmas such as the ease with which Internet sources can be plagiarized have prompted an increased awareness of the need for ethics in business.*

Obtaining Industry Knowledge

The business skills required for a service desk job vary depending on the industry in which the company is engaged and the job category (such as level one analyst, level one specialist, service desk supervisor, or service desk manager). The specific skills a company requires are determined by the company's job description.

Service Industry Knowledge

Most employers do not expect technical professionals to have fully developed business skills when they first join the workforce. Some basic knowledge, such as service industry knowledge, and a willingness to learn are viewed as a positive. **Service industry knowledge** is knowledge of the customer service and support industry. Companies that do not require this kind of experience at least consider it highly desirable. Many employers scan candidates' résumés for previous service experience or job experience that involves helping people. Relevant fields include teaching, sales, social work, and healthcare. These fields are relevant because people in these fields must be able to recognize they are delivering a service and their "customers" look to them for help.

Industry Knowledge

Some companies also desire business skills that are unique to the industry or profession the service desk supports, such as accounting or banking. These skills are called **industry knowledge**. Some service desks seek to hire people who understand the specific industry in which the company is engaged, such as manufacturing, retail, or financial. This industry knowledge makes it easier for an employee to understand the company's goals and contribute accordingly. Many service desks recruit from within the company to find candidates who are already familiar with the company and its goals. Service desks also often value candidates who have skills and knowledge that pertain to the product or service being sold. For example, a company that sells accounting software may seek service desk personnel who have an accounting background. Such knowledge enables the service desk analyst to understand the customer's needs and appreciate the impact on the customer's business when a product fails to perform properly.

Increasingly, managers are requiring technical professionals who want to advance in their careers to hone and use business skills. People applying for service desk management positions are also expected to have more advanced business skills and experience. The absence of business skills may not hinder a technical professional as he or she initially pursues a career, particularly if that person has strong technical, soft, and self-management skills. However, the presence of business skills will increase the opportunities available to a technical professional and speed up his or her advancement.

Employers often receive hundreds of résumés from people who have technical skills and certifications. Developing and demonstrating business skills are an effective way to differentiate yourself from the competition and increase your opportunities. Furthermore, if you are looking to advance your career, business skills are essential.

People who want to advance to a higher technical position or into a management role often find it difficult to give up their technical skills to acquire business skills. They are accustomed to being the experts and may enjoy having others look up to them and seek them out for assistance. In time, however, individuals who want to advance must move from knowing how to *fix* technology to how to *use* technology to achieve business goals.

Office suites such as Microsoft Office and OpenOffice.org are common business tools. Proficiency using these suites enables you to create and share professional-looking documents, spreadsheets, and presentations. Email, scheduling, and task management systems such as Microsoft Outlook also enable you to better manage your time and contact information.

Learning and mastering business skills takes time and training. Technicians who want to advance their ideas and their careers can begin by striving to understand their company's goals. They must then acquire the skills needed to understand and present in business and financial terms how technology can be used to achieve those goals. To do this, technical professionals must first learn to understand and speak the language of business.

In today's knowledge-based economy, what you earn depends on what you learn.

BILL CLINTON

Understanding and Speaking the Language of Business

The term *business* has many meanings and encompasses a broad range of disciplines. By definition, a **business** is a commercial enterprise or establishment. A commercial enterprise or establishment has profit as its chief aim. The term *business* may also be used to describe a person's occupation, work, or trade: "He is in the information technology business" or "She is in the accounting business."

The term *business within a business* is often used to describe a company's IT or Customer Service department. This term illustrates that although these departments may or may not have profit as their chief aim, they are responsible for delivering products and services to their customers in the most cost-effective way possible. Many companies that subscribe to the business-within-a-business concept challenge managers to think like entrepreneurs and run their departments as they would a small business.

Some companies are not commercially motivated. **Nonprofit** companies, also known as not-for-profit companies, are established for charitable, educational, or humanitarian purposes rather than for making money. Although the objectives of a nonprofit company are different than those of a for-profit company, the business skills required to work for both are similar.

A good way to learn more about business is to first learn about your company (or a company where you want to work), its mission, the industry that it is in, and its competitors. Study the words that are used to describe your company, its mission, and its goals. Gaining this "big picture" perspective will typically help you understand why, for example, certain technologies or data are viewed as highly important (strategic) or why certain projects are viewed as essential to the business (mission critical).

To learn more about a company, go to its web site and click the About link. The more you tap into *why* the company operates the way it does, the more successful you can be.

Companies are continuously striving to ensure information technologies support corporate goals and objectives, a process known as **business and IT alignment**. Learning about business in general, and your business more specifically, helps you as a technical professional to determine ways technology can help your customers achieve their goals. Admittedly, technology is critical to business. However, the focus of business continues to be on the business, not on the technology. Technical professionals who understand that focus can help business people understand available technologies and how best to use them. They can also ensure that new technologies, when introduced, offer real value to the business.

INTERVIEW WITH. . .

Courtesy of Jeffrey Brooks

JEFFREY BROOKS
GARTNER, INC.
RESEARCH VICE PRESIDENT
www.gartner.com

Organizations worldwide are transforming the IT service desk into a team that is focused on supporting the business rather than supporting just technology. Jeffrey Brooks, research vice president in the IT Operations Management team of Gartner, Inc., answers some questions about the changing role of the service desk. Gartner delivers technology research to global technology business leaders to make informed decisions on key initiatives. Jeffrey Brooks' research focuses on IT service management, including the service desk. Mr. Brooks has authored numerous publications, including coauthoring *The Help Desk Manager's Crash Course* (2009). He has received numerous individual and team awards, such as Customer Service Manager of the Year (2011) by the Stevie Awards for Sales & Customer Service, HDI Team Excellence Award for External Support (2010), and Customer Service Company of the Year (2009) at the NCTA 21 Awards.

Question: How is the role of the service desk changing?

Answer: Businesses are always going to have some form of a service desk or call center, at least for the near term. The days of the single point of contact where analysts are able to answer anything about any technology have, however, come and gone. This need is diminishing as people get comfortable with apps, mobile technologies, and web-based technologies. The traditional, reactive approach to support that is focused on the technology has to change. The service desk is moving to a more proactive approach. This includes getting service desk people out into the field so they can better understand the issues that are important to the business. They are building relationships and acting as trusted IT advisors by not only helping reactively when needed but by also looking for proactive opportunities such as preventative maintenance and informal training. Because younger people entering the workforce aren't inclined to pick up the telephone, the service desk must also offer options that may include walk-up services, such as an enterprise "genius bar," and search bar services that help users quickly and easily find the information they need, when they need it.

Question: How can the service desk help to increase business productivity?

Answer: In an enterprise setting, what the business needs is a business savvy IT resource that is focused on solving business problems. Going forward, the focus of the service desk should be on helping people be more productive in the workplace versus reactively fixing technology or even teaching people the basics of using technology. Many of these reactive activities can be handled via self-help or outsourced to companies that specialize in those services. The service desk—or even a technology such as an IVR—can act as a services broker on behalf of customers to get them to the resources or information that they need. This frees service desk analysts to become experts in particular areas of the business. To accomplish this, the service desk may establish "business productivity teams" as a complement to the existing service desk structure. These may be specialty teams within the service desk, or they may be teams that are embedded in business units. A **business productivity team (BPT)** has a singular focus on improving user productivity and business outcomes. This involves understanding what the business does and what is important to a given business unit.

The average IT organization is not aligned with the business and what the business thinks is important. Conversely, the business does not always understand the value of the IT organization and so may think that the entire department can be outsourced. Ninety percent of the impression that business users have of IT is based on how they interact with the service desk and so start there. Some organizations, for example, are using the BPT concept to provide executive support. Others are establishing BPTs to support a geographic region or location such as the corporate headquarters.

Question: How can the service desk demonstrate its value to the business?

Answer: An Infrastructure and Operations Business Value Dashboard (IOBVD) is an effective way to display value-based metrics. This includes monitoring and reporting on end-user productivity and the efficiency within which contacts and incidents are handled, in addition to traditional service desk metrics that focus on the productivity of the service desk itself. IOBVDs should show a well-balanced story that demonstrates the value the service desk provides to the business. For example, it's not enough to simply report on how many incidents the service desk handled and on the mean time to resolve (MTTR) those incidents. IOBVDs must explain how reducing the number of incidents means less disruption to the business and how reducing MTTR has increased business productivity. Other ways service desks can increase business productivity include looking for ways to reduce the impact of failed changes and the percentage of reopened incidents. Reopened incidents represent double disruption to the business. The key is to think in terms of business value and to demonstrate how efficiency and effectiveness increase productivity.

Question: How can service desks use best practices to improve their performance and better align their services with business needs?

Answer: A first step is to understand that frameworks and standards such as ITIL, DevOps, and the HDI Support Center Standard don't compete against one another, they can be combined. Also, organizations don't need to take an all or nothing approach. Rather, they can draw the greatest value from these frameworks and standards by putting the bits and pieces together a little at a time. One of the original purposes of ITIL was to establish a common vocabulary; to ensure there was a common understanding within organizations of what, for example, incidents, and problems, and changes are, and how these activities impact the business. Just having that common understanding is a benefit. When drawing from best practices, all along the way there is benefit but it's going to be slow. Culture change takes time and a willingness to follow established processes and procedures. Organizations can't expect improvement over night. The key is to base improvements on the needs of the business and on the maturity of the IT organization.

Using Business Skills to Identify and Justify Improvement Opportunities

People working in a service desk hear day in and day out from customers who are having trouble using technology. They have a unique opportunity to support the goals of business by working hard to eliminate or minimize the impact of technical problems and identify improvement opportunities. Service desk professionals can use data and techniques such as trend and root cause analysis to analyze these problems and identify improvement opportunities. They must also justify improvement opportunities by communicating the benefits of their ideas in financial terms.

To learn more about business skills, search libraries or bookstores for books on general topics such as *business* and *workplace skills* or specific topics such as *listening* and *time management*. Purchase books, CDs, and videos on the web from companies such as the American Management Association and Fred Pryor Seminars & CareerTrack.

Using Data to Identify and Quantify Improvement Opportunities

It is difficult to find a book or an article about service desks that does not describe the tools and technologies that enable service desk analysts and managers to do their work. Such tools and technologies are useless, however, if they do not provide and produce meaningful information. It is a waste of time for service desk analysts to log every incident in an incident management system if they cannot search the system in the future and retrieve historical information about the incidents they logged. Similarly, service desk managers and analysts and the problem manager must be able to use the incident management system to run reports and produce charts that show incident trends. These trends can then be used to identify opportunities to prevent incidents and problems and enhance existing products and services. Incident and problem trends also often influence future technology purchasing decisions.

Service desk analysts play an important role by collecting data on a daily basis that becomes information. This information is not just used to track outstanding incidents and service requests. It is also used to measure analyst's personal performance, the overall performance of the service desk, and, more importantly, customer satisfaction with the company. Failing to record events and activities accurately and completely can have very negative results for the company, the service desk, and the service desk employee. Figure 7-2 shows a sample of the types of data and information collected and used by service desks.

Common service desk team performance measures are discussed and defined in Chapter 8.

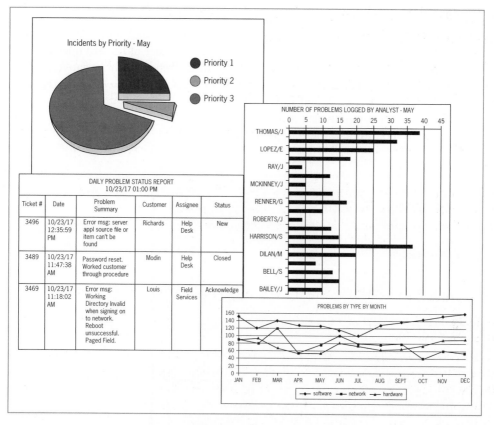

Figure 7-2 Data and information collected and used by service desks

Forward-thinking companies use the data they capture at the service desk to spot trends and discover the root cause of incidents. By getting a good grasp of incident trends and root causes, companies can increase customer satisfaction, enhance productivity, improve the quality of products and services, increase the efficiency and effectiveness with which services are delivered, and create new products and services.

People working in a service desk have the opportunity to continuously capture the data and information needed to determine customers' wants and needs. Successful service desks seize this opportunity by designing and implementing processes and technologies that enable them to capture and use customer information efficiently. People interested in a support-industry career must learn how to interpret data and share and add value to information. They can do this by learning to identify trends and the root cause of incidents.

Performing Trend and Root Cause Analysis

Simply capturing data does not prevent incidents or make it possible for companies to monitor and improve their services. To do so, analysts must study the data using techniques such as trend and root cause analysis.

Performing Trend Analysis

Trend analysis is a methodical way of determining and, when possible, forecasting service trends. Trends can be positive, such as a reduction in the number of how-to questions the service desk receives after an improved training program, or trends can be negative, such as a dramatic increase in incidents after a new product appears on the market. Trend reports provide service desk management and staff with the information needed to formulate improvement plans and communicate achievements. Figure 7-3 illustrates that trend reports can also be used to monitor and measure performance.

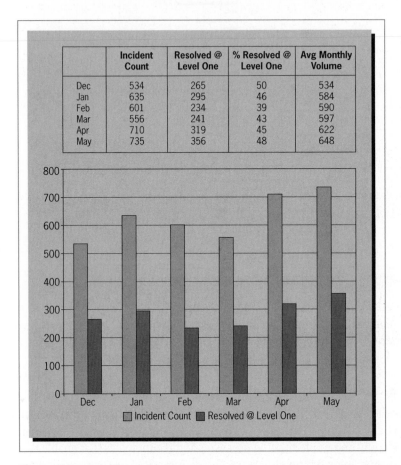

	Incident Count	Resolved @ Level One	% Resolved @ Level One	Avg Monthly Volume
Dec	534	265	50	534
Jan	635	295	46	584
Feb	601	234	39	590
Mar	556	241	43	597
Apr	710	319	45	622
May	735	356	48	648

Figure 7-3   Sample trend report

Charts and graphs are an excellent way to organize data and present information. They help the audience to visualize, compare and contrast, and analyze the information being presented.

The type of chart or graph selected depends on the data. Pie charts show how parts relate to a whole. A line or bar graph shows how data varies over time. Effective charts and graphs are easy to understand, visually memorable, and, most importantly, accurate.

This report shows a recent rise in the number of incidents logged by the service desk. A positive trend worth noting is that the service desk has increased the number of incidents resolved at level one, in keeping with the increase in its workload. This may be the positive result of recent training efforts, effective knowledge management, or the addition of improved diagnostic tools. If the percentage of incidents resolved at level one were decreasing, as opposed to increasing, it could mean that the level one service desk was understaffed and, as such, did not have adequate time to diagnose incidents. It could mean that a new product has been introduced and the service desk has not received adequate training. It could also mean that effective problem management has reduced the number of recurring incidents and the service desk is now being contacted about new, and perhaps more complex, incidents. Complementary reports, such as the types of incidents being reported to the service desk and the types of incidents that must be escalated to level two, can be used to validate analysts' findings and identify ways the service desk can continue to improve.

Used effectively, trend analysis involves looking at a set of data—such as the incidents reported during a given month—and viewing it from different angles in an effort to identify a trend. Figure 7-4 shows a breakdown of the top 10 hardware incidents for a given month by device. A comparable report could show a breakdown of incidents for a given month by application. Or, a report could show a breakdown of incidents reported by department or division.

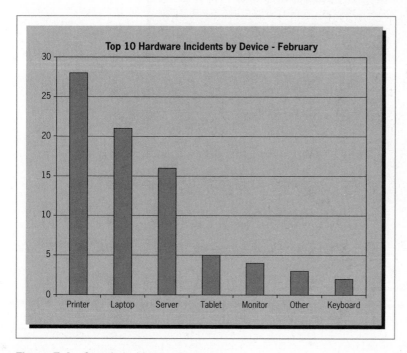

Figure 7-4   Sample incidents report

Many companies use top 10 reports to determine the types of incidents that require immediate action or warrant root cause analysis.

280

Trend reports make it possible to determine the most common and frequently occurring incidents and also make it possible for analysts to identify anomalies. An **anomaly** is a deviation or departure from the average or the norm. For example, printer incidents tend to be fairly common in most organizations. An exceptional number of printer incidents should, however, prompt additional analysis. In such a case, additional trend analysis or root cause analysis can be used to determine the cause of the anomaly.

Figure 7-5 shows a breakdown of the printer incidents identified in Figure 7-4 by root cause. This report reveals that a high percentage of printer incidents are caused by hardware failures. Such a statistic should prompt the company to revisit its product evaluation process and perhaps select a different brand of printer. This information can also be used to show printer manufacturers the extent of the incidents the company is experiencing. A complementary report might be arranged by model or manufacturer and show a breakdown of printer incidents caused by hardware failures. The company may also decide that additional root cause analysis is needed.

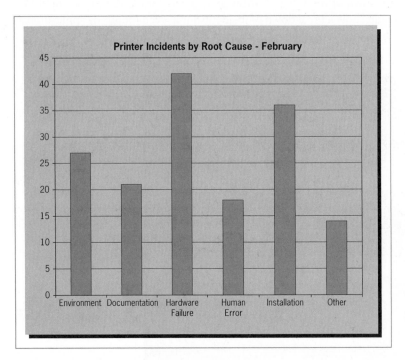

Figure 7-5   Sample incidents by root cause report

Performing Root Cause Analysis

Root cause analysis is used to determine *why* incidents are occurring so the company can take steps to prevent similar incidents from occurring in the future. When customers contact the service desk with an incident, they are typically experiencing a symptom. Using the information that the customer provides, the service desk analyst diagnoses the incident in an effort to determine the probable source and a possible solution.

Determining the root cause takes a little extra time and so does not occur during the incident management process. It is also not always necessary to determine the root cause. If the impact of an incident is very minor and either a viable workaround is available or the incident does not occur very often, root cause analysis may be deemed unnecessary. When root cause analysis is justified, a problem is created and problem management techniques are used to look beyond the obvious and seek an answer to the question, "Why?"

Some analysts think of the root cause only in terms of technology. If a customer experiences an incident using a word-processing package, the analyst may indicate that the probable source of the incident was software related. The actual root cause may be that the customer has not received adequate training and is using the word-processing package incorrectly. It is important to note this is not a user error. If the actual root cause is inadequate training, IT must take responsibility for eliminating that root cause by ensuring adequate training is provided. Until the root cause is identified and eliminated—that is, until the customer receives training—it is likely that the customer will continue to experience incidents.

The measure of success is not whether you have a tough problem to deal with, but whether it's the same problem you had last year.

JOHN FOSTER DULLES

The root cause is captured in a data field when problems are closed and is supplied by the person who identified the resolution. Root cause analysis enables organizations to examine this data to determine ways to reduce costs and prevent incidents by eliminating or correcting the real reason the incidents occur. As illustrated in Figure 7-6, many companies prepare reports that show the percentage of incidents that are caused by a particular root cause. This report shows a breakdown of incidents by root cause for a given month and is arranged by incident category. Such a report makes it possible for companies to focus on eliminating the incidents that are the most costly to the organization and that have the greatest impact on their customers.

	Closed Incidents by Root Cause From January 01 to January 31		
Category	Root Cause	Incident Count	% by Root Cause
Hardware	[All]	20	100%
	Hardware failure	14	70%
	Installation error	6	30%
Software	[All]	102	100%
	Insufficient resources	54	54%
	Configuration error	36	36%
	Incompatible software	10	10%
	Human error	2	2%

Figure 7-6   Sample root cause report

Trend and root cause analysis work hand in hand. They can be used together either reactively to minimize the impact of incidents or proactively to identify improvement areas. Service desks that use trend and root cause analysis only reactively rarely have the resources needed to handle incidents efficiently and effectively. They simply do not have the information needed to predict their workload. Service desks that use these analysis techniques proactively are able to justify and acquire the resources they need, when they need them. They are also able to better manage their workload, and even reduce their workload, by preventing incidents.

Root cause analysis is the more difficult of the two disciplines, so not all companies determine and document the root cause. These companies fail to take the extra time needed to determine *why* the incident occurred once they have fixed it. Unfortunately, by not capturing and then eliminating the root cause, these companies put themselves at risk for the incident to happen again. As a result, they may waste time rediscovering a solution or retrieving and implementing a solution from the knowledge management system. Remember, the fact that there is a solution in the knowledge management system does not make it okay for an incident to recur. Ultimately, customers would prefer that incidents be prevented.

To resolve incidents efficiently, effectively, and permanently, the service desk must be diligent in its efforts to capture and use information. This means that service desk analysts must log all incidents and capture accurate and complete data about those incidents, including, when appropriate, the probable root cause. Without the data captured by service desk analysts, trend and root cause analysis is not possible and so the actual root cause cannot be determined. When trend and root cause analysis is not performed, it is likely that existing incidents will recur and that new incidents will appear. When trend and root cause analysis is performed, recurring incidents are eliminated, incidents are predicted, and, in turn, incidents can be prevented. As a result, analysts are freed to work on more complex incidents and pursue new skills.

Given the rapid pace at which technology changes, it is unlikely that trend and root cause analysis enables a company to prevent *all* incidents. However, this analysis helps the service desk to eliminate common incidents and avoid major incidents by addressing incidents when they are minor. This analysis also aids the service desk in determining and communicating the cost savings that can occur when incidents are prevented.

Communicating the Financial Benefits of Improvements

Service desk managers are under constant pressure to demonstrate the value of service desk services and to justify the funds and resources the team needs to deliver those services. Service desk team members who have ideas about how to improve products and services will have those ideas adopted more quickly if they learn to justify and quantify the benefits of their ideas in financial terms.

Successful continuous improvement involves determining what improvements are needed, what improvements will enable the service desk to meet its goals, and what improvements can be made without depleting the current service desk budget. A **budget** is the total sum of money allocated for a particular purpose (such as a project) or period of time (such as a year). Good budgeting ensures the money does not run out before the goal is reached or the period ends.

Typically, the service desk management team prepares the service desk budget with input from the service desk team. The management team also obtains input from other departments because the service desk's budget is tied to other departments' initiatives. For example, in an internal service desk, if another department is installing a new software product, the service desk budget must reflect the tools, training, and so forth that analysts need to support that product. In an external service desk, if the company is introducing a new or enhanced product, analysts must have what they need to support that product as well. Individuals involved in preparing a budget rarely anticipate every expense that may arise in the course of a given period of time.

Circumstances change and opportunities are identified that can affect the budget. A business slowdown may prompt management to place a hold on nonessential spending. Conversely, a new technology may be introduced that could considerably benefit the service desk and its customers. When improvement opportunities such as a new technology are identified, they must be justified and prioritized in light of other budget expenditures.

Justifying improvement initiatives typically involves stating the expected benefits in the form of goals or objectives and expressing those goals as metrics. The metrics can then be used to compare the expected results of a project to the actual results to judge the success of a project. Metrics can also be used to demonstrate a project's ROI. Metrics typically assess characteristics such as:

- **Cost**—An amount paid or the expenditure of something, such as time or labor
- **Customer satisfaction**—A measure of the difference between how a customer perceives he or she was treated and how the customer expects to be treated
- **Efficiency**—A measure of the time and effort required to deliver services in relation to their cost
- **Effectiveness**—A measure of how completely and accurately services are delivered
- **Employee satisfaction**—A measure of how satisfied an employee is with his or her job
- **Quality**—A measure of how well products or services meet customer expectations

Some of these characteristics such as cost and efficiency are quite **tangible**, or capable of being measured precisely. In other words, it is possible to measure exactly how much something costs or how long it takes to complete a task. **Intangible** characteristics such as customer satisfaction, employee satisfaction, and quality are more difficult to measure precisely. This is because intangible characteristics reflect perception and are therefore more subjective. For example, customer satisfaction (or dissatisfaction) with a company's products and services can affect its bottom line. However, many other factors can also influence a company's bottom line, so the effect of customer satisfaction alone is typically hard to measure.

Employee satisfaction can be viewed as both tangible and intangible. Companies often focus on employee satisfaction in an effort to maintain a low turnover rate. **Turnover rate** is the ratio of the number of workers who had to be replaced in a given period of time to the average number of workers. Although some turnover is normal, an excessively high turnover rate can be quite costly. When costs such as lost productivity, recruitment, training, and new hire orientation are taken into consideration, the cost of turnover can equal 75 to 150 percent of an employee's annual salary. These costs are fairly easily measured and, therefore, tangible. On the other hand, the effect that employee satisfaction has on morale can be difficult to measure, but is no less important. Losing a key employee to a competing company can negatively affect the morale of an entire team. As a result, companies often work hard to retain peak performers. Conversely, losing a disruptive and unproductive employee can positively affect morale. As a result, companies must ensure an effective performance review program enables them to weed out poor performers.

Both tangible and intangible goals are important. As illustrated in Figure 7-7, goals can be like a seesaw. In other words, placing emphasis on one goal or taking emphasis away from one goal may cause a company's ability to achieve another goal to go up or down. When both tangible and intangible goals are established with goals such as quality and customer satisfaction as primary objectives, companies can achieve a more balanced, customer-oriented result.

Figure 7-7   Balanced service desk goals

Cost effectiveness, for example, ensures a proper balance between the cost of service on one hand and the quality of service on the other. Balanced goals are important because many performance goals influence each other. Placing too great an emphasis on any one goal can produce unintended results. For instance, emphasizing efficiency can reduce the average duration of calls but might cause customer dissatisfaction because customers feel they are being rushed off the phone. On the other hand, emphasizing effectiveness by having analysts devote an extensive amount of time to research may produce high-quality solutions, but might cause customer dissatisfaction because customers have a long average wait time for telephone calls.

When an improvement project begins, it is important to capture a starting point, or **baseline** metric, that can be used to demonstrate the success of improvement efforts. For example, prior to adding FAQs related to Wi-Fi networking to the service desk's web site, the service desk's incident management system can be used to create a baseline metric that shows the number of Wi-Fi networking how-to questions the service desk receives on a monthly basis. Six months after implementing the FAQs, the service desk can create a current metric. If the current metric indicates that the number of Wi-Fi networking how-to questions has gone down considerably, it can be surmised that the FAQs are a success. Although less tangible, the service desk could also show the number of **page hits**—web page visits—the FAQs are receiving, or use **exit polls** to show that the FAQs are being used and that customers consider them helpful. On the Internet, exit polls combine questions such as "Was this information helpful to you?" with a set of choices that customers can use to provide feedback. Choices may include Yes, Somewhat, and No buttons or a rating scale of 1 to 5 stars, for example. The service desk can also use social media as a measure by, for example, showing the number of people who Like the content on Facebook or share the content with others via social networking sites such as Facebook, Twitter, or Pinterest.

In many companies, improvement opportunities will never be acted on unless they are shown to have clear financial benefits, even if some of those benefits are intangible. Knowing a variety of ways to justify improvement opportunities helps the service desk gain acceptance for a greater number of ideas and more quickly obtain approval for ideas. Several techniques can be used to determine the cost of, or to show the cost savings realized by, an improvement initiative. Two of the most common techniques are to calculate a labor savings or to calculate and use cost per contact.

Calculating a Labor Savings

The expression "Time is money" is particularly true in the business world, where labor is often a company's single greatest expense. Labor and benefits usually represent 60 to 80 percent of a service desk's overall costs. Saving time such as by reducing the service desk's workload through automation or by providing self-services via the web, in turn, saves money.

Figure 7-8 illustrates the savings that can be realized by shifting calls from the service desk to web-based self-services. This example estimates that implementing an automated web-based system for password resets will result in a 75 percent reduction in the number of password reset requests made to the service desk via the telephone.

Cost/Data Element	Actual Data
Number of password reset requests	1,000/month
Average duration of calls requesting password resets	2 minutes
Total duration of calls requesting password resets (minutes)	2,000 minutes
Total duration of calls requesting password resets (hours)	33 hours
Average rate for level one analysts	$20.02/hour
Total cost of password resets via telephone (per month)	$660.66/month
Total cost of password resets via telephone (per year)	$7,927.92/year
Estimated percentage of password reset requests to be automated	75%
Labor savings by automating password resets	$5,945.94/year

Figure 7-8 Labor savings from automating password resets

This is, of course, a simplistic example. For the savings to be accurate, a cost-benefit analysis must be performed that considers the cost of implementing the web-based system, training the service desk staff and customers on how to use the system, marketing the service to customers, and so forth. When a quick estimate of labor savings is desired, however, this simple formula illustrates how a small set of data elements can be used to communicate a labor savings in financial terms.

According to HDI's 2013 Practices and Salary Survey, the median salary for a level one support technician is $41,635. The $20.02 average hourly rate used in Figure 7-8 is obtained by dividing this annual salary by 2,080 (52 weeks × 40 hours = 2,080 work hours per year).

When calculating savings, accurate data is important. When actual data is not available, companies often look for industry-standard metrics such as an hourly rate or cost per contact to use as a starting point for establishing goals and determining costs and benefits. Such metrics can be difficult to find, however, because no one organization represents the support industry as a whole. Organizations such as HDI, the Technology Services Industry Association, SupportIndustry.com, and Gartner, Inc., all provide their version of metrics such as cost per contact (some are free and others are fee based). Typically, they determine metrics by surveying their members or clients and by conducting surveys via the Internet.

Calculating and Using Cost per Contact

Cost per contact is a financial measure frequently used in the support industry. **Cost per contact**, historically called *cost per call*, is the total cost of operating a service desk for a given period (including salaries, benefits, facilities, and equipment) divided by the total number of contacts received during that period.

Contact volume is frequently used to calculate costs and create metrics such as cost per contact. **Contact volume** is the total number of contacts received during a given period of time. To obtain an accurate contact volume, service desks must implement technology that can be used to capture contact data. ACDs and email response management systems can capture the number of telephone calls, email messages, and chats received. In the absence of these technologies, service desk analysts must log all contacts in the service desk's incident management system. Logging all contacts provides the service desk with the data needed to produce meaningful metrics and to perform trend and root cause analysis.

Some companies also calculate **cost per unit**, the total cost of operating a service desk for a given period (including salaries, benefits, facilities, and equipment) divided by the total number of units (such as devices and systems) supported during that period. Table 7-1 shows the average cost per contact for telephone calls, emails, chats, and walk-ups according to HDI's 2013 Practices and Salary Survey.

Contact Type	Average Cost
Auto-logging	$11
Chat	$12
Email	$15
Telephone call	$17
Walk-up	$18
Web request	$14

Table 7-1 Average cost per contact

Cost per contact is an extremely useful metric that can be used in a variety of ways. Some companies use cost per contact to benchmark their services against other service desks or the industry average. **Benchmarking** is the process of comparing the service desk's performance metrics and practices to those of another service desk in an effort to identify improvement opportunities. Companies can use cost per contact to compare the cost of operating their internal service desk to the cost of an external supplier (outsourcer). Analysts can use cost per contact to quickly calculate the potential labor savings of a proposed project.

Meaningful goals and metrics, communicated in financial terms, enable the service desk team to justify opportunities and demonstrate improved performance. Presentations are often used to communicate the service desk's achievements and gain needed support and commitment for additional improvement initiatives.

Using Presentations to Communicate

Presentations are an important form of communication in the business world. They are used daily to convey information, promote the benefits of ideas and opportunities, and win approval for those ideas and opportunities. For professionals, presentations are an important way to build credibility, and the ability to make presentations can greatly influence a person's standing in his or her company, community, and industry.

For service desk professionals, presentations provide an invaluable opportunity to promote the service desk and communicate its value to the business. Presentations can be used to demonstrate the important role the service desk plays in terms of collecting, using, and disseminating data and information that can be used by the entire organization to continuously improve. Presentations are also often used to relay information during service desk team meetings or training sessions.

Designing and Making Presentations

Making a presentation is a great fear for many people. In fact, it has been said that some people fear making presentations more than spiders, snakes, and even death. Although making presentations can be nerve-racking, they are inevitable if you want to communicate your ideas and, more importantly, have those ideas accepted and acted upon. Presentations are a form of public speaking and are used in many different types of situations, such as:

- Facilitated workshops
- Meetings
- Sales presentations
- Seminars
- Speeches
- Training sessions
- One-to-one sessions

Although the settings in which these presentations are made may vary, they all have one thing in common: The audience members are being brought together for a reason. Their approval is needed to move forward on a project. Their input is needed to formulate an action plan. They need to be aware of something or learn something.

Just as the audience members are being brought together for a reason, there is a reason *you* are making the presentation. You have an idea that you want to advance. You have information that others want to hear. You have knowledge or skills that the audience members want to learn. Simply put, you are the expert.

Knowing the purpose of your presentation and repeating "I am the expert" may not eliminate the fear and anxiety that often accompany making a presentation. They are critical first steps, however, and cannot be overlooked. If you have great ideas, you must be willing to get up and communicate those ideas to other people. If you need people to commit resources to a project, you must be willing to ask for that commitment and explain the benefits to your audience. To be successful in the business world, you must communicate, communicate, communicate.

Although making a presentation is not an exact science, there are proven steps you can take to ensure success. The steps listed in Figure 7-9 represent a methodical approach that can be used whether you are making a 5-minute presentation or a 45-minute presentation. These steps can also be used regardless of the type of presentation you are making or the size of your audience. Completing these steps will give you the confidence needed to work through your fears and do your best.

> Step 1: State your objective.
>
> Step 2: Know your audience.
>
> Step 3: Design the presentation.
>
> Step 4: Rehearse the presentation.
>
> Step 5: Deliver the presentation.
>
> Step 6: Learn from the experience.

Figure 7-9 Proven steps for a successful presentation

Step 1: State Your Objective

A clearly stated objective has many benefits. Most importantly, it helps you to determine whether a presentation is needed. People often complain that they are asked to attend too many meetings. If writing a memo will meet your objective, do not ask people to take time out for a presentation. If a presentation is necessary, a clearly stated objective will help you focus your thoughts and the thoughts of your audience. A clearly stated objective also enables you and your audience to measure the success of your presentation. If you give a great presentation but fail to meet the stated objective, you may not obtain the results you seek and your audience will most likely be dissatisfied. In other words, a clearly stated objective enables you to set and manage your audience's expectations.

A single sentence should be all you need to state your objective, as shown in the following examples. If you need more than one sentence, you may be trying to achieve more than you can realistically accomplish in a single presentation. The exception to this rule would, of course, be extended presentations such as seminars and training sessions. The key is to be realistic about the results you are trying to achieve. Persuading people to radically change their work habits or to adopt an expensive new technology may require more than one presentation.

Obtain approval from management to assemble a team and explore the use of remote control technologies.

Inform service desk analysts about new procedures for handling chat contacts.

Communicate the status of a project, and obtain management commitment to dedicate resources to upcoming activities.

290

Step 2: Know Your Audience

This step is critical and greatly influences all future steps. Making a presentation to a group of your peers is different than speaking to a group of managers or to a group of customers. This step requires you determine what is important to your audience members. Do they want you to get to the point quickly? Do they want you to back up your material with statistics? Do they want you to cover a subject in-depth? If you do not know your audience, you cannot answer the questions that audiences most often ask: "How does this affect me?" and "How does this benefit me?"

Knowing your audience also involves understanding the background of your audience. If you are giving a technical presentation and your audience is not technical, you will have to use basic terminology or define the terminology you are using. If part of your audience's primary language is not the language you speak, you may need to adapt your vocabulary, slow your rate of speech, or have a translator available. It is also a good idea to avoid idioms and speak in relatively short sentences that are limited to single ideas.

When in doubt, ask. Ask the person who entrusted you to make the presentation about your audience. Ask people who have made a presentation to your audience in the past to give you their advice. One size does not fit all when making presentations. The more you know about the needs of your audience, the greater your success.

Learning about your audience may prompt you to rethink or refine your objective and vice versa. For example, presenting an in-depth overview of a new process to management is typically not a good idea. Management will want a summarized view with a statement of benefits. Conversely, making a presentation to your peers that is aimed at obtaining funding for a new project will not produce the desired result. Your peers will want to know how much of their time the project will take and whether the project has management's commitment.

Step 3: Design the Presentation

Designing a presentation is like writing a story. It needs to have a beginning, a middle, and an end. In presentation terms, these components are referred to as the introduction, the body, and the closing. One of the best ways to design a presentation is to begin with an outline that includes a timeline. Preparing an outline will help you organize your thoughts and develop a logical flow of ideas. Including a timeline ensures the presentation you design can be completed within the allotted time frame.

When demonstrating a system, such as a new incident management system, begin with a description of the system's uses and its benefits. Technical professionals sometimes dive straight into a system demonstration without selling its benefits. Even when your objective is to teach people *how* to use a system, begin with an explanation of *why* to use the system.

After you have an outline, research the topic and collect facts that support your objective. Showing that you have done your homework builds credibility with audience members. Be specific. Quote sources. Include current statistics. Incorporate into your presentation stories that show your experience and knowledge of the topic. When appropriate, include the findings of other experts in the field.

When your research is complete, you can begin to develop visual aids that support and communicate your ideas. Visual aids are important, but they should not be the only content that you present. People quickly become bored when a presenter stands in front of a room and simply reads the presentation word for word from the slides. The audience wants you to share (depending on the nature of the presentation) your knowledge, experience, observations, or recommendations, and back that up with visual aids.

An effective technique is to anticipate the questions your audience may ask and use visual aids to answer those questions. Common questions include:

- **Who?**—Use organization charts or *correct* department or division names to communicate who, for example, will benefit from a new technology or be affected by a new system.

- **What?**—Use bullets or numbered lists to answer questions such as "What are the risks?" and "What are the benefits?"

- **When?**—Use Gantt charts to communicate schedules or a sequence of events. A **Gantt chart** is a type of bar chart that is often used to illustrate a project schedule.

- **Where?**—Use maps or drawings of buildings to communicate the scope of a project, system, or service.

- **Why?**—Use bullets or numbered lists to answer questions such as "Why is a new system needed?" or "Why is it a good time to offer new services?"

- **How?**—Use tables, charts, and graphs to answer questions such as "How much?" and "How many?"

Figure 7-10 shows the various visual aids that can be used to answer these questions.

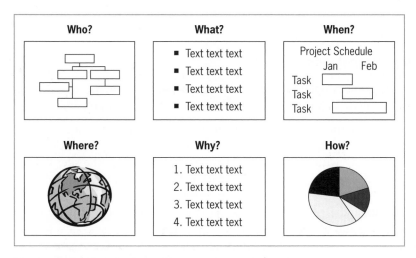

Figure 7-10 Sample visual aids

When your visual aids are completed, conduct a preliminary walk-through of your presentation. This enables you to fine-tune the sequence of your visual aids and the timing of your presentation. You may also decide you need more, or fewer, visual aids for the time allotted. The most successful presenters use their oral or storytelling skills to transition seamlessly from one visual aid to the next.

Step 4: Rehearse the Presentation

There is an old expression: "Practice makes perfect." Rehearsing your presentation is a critical step. This helps ensure you can cover your material in the time allotted. Your audience will quickly lose interest or may have to leave if you run over the time allotted. Your audience typically expects you to leave time for questions as well. What this means is that you must fine-tune your presentation until it is just right. Not too long. Not too short. This is not an easy task, but it does get easier with practice.

It is better to have your presentation run a little short than a little too long. Preparing a shorter-than-needed presentation ensures you can cover all your material in the allotted time and also allows time for questions and answers. When rehearsing, time your presentation so you know where you should be at the halfway point of your allotted time. That way, if you are running behind while delivering your presentation, you know to pick up the pace a bit and make up for lost time. If you are running ahead of schedule, you can add an example or two, which you prepared during your rehearsal, to elaborate on points along the way.

Keep in mind that rehearsing is different than memorizing. Although you may want to memorize your introduction and your closing because they are critical to setting audience expectations, it is better to memorize only the key points you want to make during the body of your presentation. Some people write their key points on a piece of paper or on index cards so they have them to refer to if they need a reminder. If you try to memorize every word, you may become flustered if you are interrupted by a question or forget a key point. Furthermore, you may bore people if you do nothing but read from your notes or visual aids. Rehearsing your presentation several times will give you confidence in your knowledge of the material and enable you to fine-tune your notes and visual aids to the point where they are most effective.

Step 5: Deliver the Presentation

This is the scary part for some people. Although making a presentation may seem scary, it is not a life-or-death situation. It is, however, a situation for which you can prepare.

Before your presentation, take the time to make a final check of your equipment and the site. If you need a laptop or tablet to make your presentation, make sure one is available or that your personal device will work with any audiovisual equipment already at the site. Verify ahead of time that any cables needed to connect your device to the equipment already at the site will be available or bring your own cables. Back up your presentation to a portable storage device such as a flash drive, and carry it with you as an extra safety measure. Arrive at the site as early as possible to set up and test your equipment. If you need other visual aids, such as a flip chart or a whiteboard, make sure those are available. Make sure water is available that you can use to calm your nerves and lubricate your throat during your presentation. There is nothing worse than walking into a room 5 minutes before making a presentation and realizing the site is not ready. Do yourself a favor and double-check every detail. That way you can spend the 5 minutes prior to your presentation greeting your audience and using calming techniques such as deep breathing and positive self-talk: "I am the expert!"

Keep in mind that for many people, delivering the presentation is actually the fun part. These people often admit they were scared the first time they made a presentation. They may even still become a bit anxious prior to a particularly important presentation. For people who are willing to take the risk, however, the rewards are worth it. Remember, the audience wants to hear what you have to say, and you are the best person to say it.

When making a presentation, be confident. After all, you have done your homework. Also, be enthusiastic. Know that if you do not appear to be confident in your recommendations or excited about the benefits of a project, you cannot expect your audience to be either. Look from one audience member to the other. In even the toughest rooms, you will find people who are nodding in agreement with your message or listening closely to what you have to say. When people smile in response to your enthusiasm, smile back.

Standing stiffly behind a microphone or lectern will magnify your nervousness. Although you want to avoid pacing back and forth, move around a bit and interact with your visual aids and the audience. Try not to stand in front of your visual aids or turn your back to the audience.

For many presenters, handling questions is the most challenging part of making a presentation. One reason is that answering questions in the course of a presentation can throw off your timing. If this is a concern, and time is a considerable constraint, politely ask your audience members at the start of the presentation to hold their questions until the end, as in the following example.

Ladies and gentlemen, in the interest of time, please hold all of your questions until the end.

If you run out of time for questions at the end, let the audience know that you will be happy to respond to their questions offline. The following example shows one way to do this.

I'm sorry we ran out of time for questions. I am happy to stay and answer your questions. Or, my email address is on your handout.

When possible, try to handle questions when they are asked. Remember, however, to answer the question asked and only the question asked. Then get back to your presentation. If an audience member asks a complex question that you know you are going to answer shortly, politely ask the audience member to hold his or her question until the appropriate point in your presentation, as shown in the following examples.

> That's a great question, and I'm going to cover the answer shortly.
>
> Could I ask you to hold that question and I'll come back to it shortly?

When possible, acknowledge the person's question when you get to the appropriate point in your presentation and stay with the question until you know it is answered fully. The following examples show a couple of ways to do this.

> Here's the answer to Jane's question about metrics.
>
> As I recall, there was a question about the project schedule. Here is the schedule....

Handling questions when they are asked can be challenging. People sometimes ask questions that seem irrelevant or perhaps even hostile. Do your best to answer all questions politely and briefly. If necessary, remind the audience of the presentation objectives and any time constraints you may be facing. It is your responsibility to keep the presentation on track.

 An effective technique is to use a flip chart or whiteboard to create a "parking lot" for questions, ideas, and suggestions. Recording this information and keeping it visible makes it easier for audience members to focus on your presentation as they can see that they have been heard.

Audience members usually expect to receive a handout. The handout may simply be a copy of your presentation that audience members can download from a web site or that is sent via email. The handout may also be a report. When appropriate, provide a simple handout that includes web links that audience members can use to obtain additional details.

Presenters often distribute handouts at the start of their presentation so audience members can follow along and take notes. However, there are situations where presenters may opt to distribute the handouts at the end of the presentation, such as when the handout is a comprehensive report that you want audience members to read offline. The key is to let audience members know when and if they will be receiving a handout so they can take notes accordingly.

Step 6: Learn from the Experience

Many lessons can be learned from making presentations. Most people who have made more than two presentations will tell you sometimes they go well and sometimes they do not. Most of the mistakes that occur when making presentations are the result of overlooking one of the steps discussed earlier. Take time after each presentation to evaluate your performance and determine how you can improve. If audience evaluations are provided, view the feedback you receive as constructive and figure out what you can do to improve.

Presentation evaluations can be harsh, and you may be blamed for factors out of your control. For example, people may complain that the room was too hot or too cold or that there was not enough coffee. Accept responsibility for what you can change and pass other feedback on to the appropriate party. Do not take it personally!

Some people are born communicators and find making presentations invigorating. Others may not enjoy making presentations at first, but find they do get easier in time. Whether or not you enjoy making presentations, presentation skills are essential if you want to educate, inform, obtain information from, build consensus with, and communicate with others.

Author Susan Jeffers wrote a great book called *Feel the Fear and Do It Anyway* (Jeffers Press, 2007). Although her book is not specifically about making presentations, the sentiment very much applies. The only way to overcome your fear of making presentations is by getting up and making presentations. The good news is, the more often you present and the more varied the setting, subject matter, and audience are, the more comfortable you will become.

Making presentations is an important business skill—one of the many business skills you must acquire if you want to get ahead in the competitive workplace.

Advanced Business Skills for Technical Professionals

Advanced business skills such as managing projects, conducting a cost-benefit analysis, and calculating ROI are critical skills for more senior technical professionals. Although the need for these skills may vary from company to company, having even a basic understanding of these concepts enables you to make the most of learning and growth opportunities. For example, you can learn about managing a project by participating on a project team. Or, you can gain a better understanding of techniques such as cost-benefit analysis and ROI by simply learning to communicate costs and benefits in financial terms.

Like technical skills, business skills training is only effective when it is reinforced in the workplace. Understanding how to do something is not the same as actually doing it. Many technical professionals acquire their business skills on the job. They may participate on a project team and learn about managing projects. Or, they may be asked to justify an idea and learn how to compare the costs and benefits of a proposed solution. To excel at advanced business skills, technical professionals require a blend of formal training and experience. In other words, simple observation is not enough. Some study, even if only self-study, is needed along with experience. This is particularly true in the case of a skill such as project management.

Managing Projects

In the business world, change is constant and it is occurring at an increasingly rapid pace. This means that people working in a service desk are continuously exposed to projects. According to *A Guide to the Project Management Body of Knowledge (PMBOK® Guide)* published by the Project Management Institute, a **project** is a temporary endeavor undertaken to create a unique product, service, or result. Projects can be small, such as installing a new computer, or quite large, such as moving a team of people from one office to another or developing and installing a new business application.

Service desk professionals may complete projects by, for example, creating a set of new FAQs for the service desk's web site. Or, they may support the end product of a project, such as a new or enhanced system. Service desk professionals may also initiate projects. To initiate projects, analysts must first sell their ideas to management using the techniques previously discussed such as using data and information to quantify their ideas, communicating the benefits of their ideas in financial terms, and using presentations to market their ideas to management.

For larger projects, a business case is often used to justify the initiation of a project. A **business case** is a report that describes the business reasons that a change is being considered, along with its associated costs, benefits, and risks. Typically, a business case provides a description of the current ("as is") environment along with an assessment of what is right about the environment and what needs to be improved. A business case also describes a proposed future ("to be") environment along with a roadmap of changes that must be made to achieve the desired state. It also discusses the risks of both maintaining the current environment and pursuing the proposed environment. A business case is typically prepared by a business analyst. A **business analyst** is an individual who is skilled at working with end users to determine their needs. A business analyst may be an employee of the company or an independent consultant.

To be successful, technical professionals must understand project management concepts and tools. As working on a project usually involves working on a team, they must understand the roles that people play within a project and they must understand how to work successfully with others on the project team.

Chapter 8 discusses teamwork and the service desk.

Early in their careers, service desk analysts are typically on the receiving end of projects. In other words, they learn about the project when it is nearing completion. For example, the service desk learns about a new accounting system when the Development organization is preparing to install the system and deploy it to the Accounting department. Or worse, it learns about the system the day after it is installed and customers start calling the service desk for assistance. Because they have not been involved in the project since its inception, service desk analysts sometimes find it difficult to understand why a project is being managed in a certain way. Learning about project management concepts enables you to better understand how projects are managed and the critical factors that enable project success.

Best practice frameworks such as ITIL recommend involving the service desk early in the project planning process. Such an approach ensures that the service desk's requirements are considered and that the service desk is prepared when the product or service is deployed.

Project management is the process of planning and managing a project. All projects, regardless of their size, require some planning and have the following elements:

- A clearly defined scope
- Well-defined deliverables
- Clearly defined acceptance criteria
- An established start date
- An established end point

Project planning begins with a written definition of the **project scope**, which is a description of the work to be done in a project. The project scope serves as an agreement between the customer of the project and the supplier about the project's end product and includes a description of the acceptance criteria to be used to evaluate the project's success. **Acceptance criteria** are the conditions that must be met before the project deliverables are accepted.

Failing to clearly define and manage project scope is one of the most common reasons that projects fail. Managing customer expectations when working on a project is just as important as it is when delivering customer services. Failing to manage customer expectations can lead to scope creep and ultimately customer dissatisfaction. **Scope creep** describes unplanned changes to a project's scope. Some scope creep is normal and beneficial. Left unchecked, however, scope creep can quickly exhaust a project's financial, human, and technological resources and extend its schedule.

To minimize scope creep, many companies have a project change control process in place for reviewing and approving scope changes. This is particularly important when scope changes result in the need for additional resources, such as time and money.

In the case of small projects, the project scope may be as simple as a change that is submitted and approved via the company's change management process. For larger projects, the project scope is typically defined by a project planning committee made up of project stakeholders. A **project stakeholder** is a person or group that is involved in or may be affected by project activities. For larger projects, the project scope is documented in the following areas:

- **Project overview**—A summary of the project and of the business need driving the project

- **Project deliverables**—The items to be delivered as a result of the project, such as products, systems, services, reports, and plans

- **Project objectives**—The measurable goals in terms of time, money, and quality that the project must achieve to be considered successful

- **Considerations and concerns**—A description of all considerations and concerns identified during the development of the project scope

- **Change control plan**—A description of how the project scope will be managed and how agreed upon changes will be incorporated into the project deliverables

Once documented, the project scope must be approved by the project sponsor. The **project sponsor** is the person who has ultimate authority over the project. The project sponsor provides or secures funding for the project, provides high-level guidance and direction to the project team, resolves issues when necessary, approves scope changes, and approves major deliverables. The project sponsor is responsible for ensuring the project is aligned with the organization's business goals, but he or she is not typically involved in the day-to-day activities of the project. That is the responsibility of the project manager.

The **project manager** is the person who leads the project team and is assigned the authority and responsibility for overseeing the project and meeting the project's objectives. The project manager is typically selected after the project scope is defined and approved.

A **project charter** is a short document that formally authorizes the project and gives authority to the project manager.

Not all projects require a team. Some projects, particularly smaller projects, may be completed by a single individual. In such cases, that individual is the project manager. He or she may not be assigned that title, but that individual assumes the responsibilities of a project manager. The individual's manager will typically serve as project sponsor, although, again, he or she may not be assigned that title. Project manager responsibilities include:

- Developing and maintaining a project plan

- Directing project activities

- Creating project status reports

- Preparing and participating in project reviews

- Resolving project plan deviations

- Resolving and escalating to management, if necessary, issues that pertain to the project

- Administering project change control (that is, managing changes to the project scope)

One of the project manager's most important responsibilities is developing and maintaining a project plan. A **project plan** is a summary document that describes the project, its objectives, and how the objectives are to be achieved. For smaller projects, the project plan may consist of scheduling a change via the organization's change management system and documenting a simple to-do list in the change record.

If you are failing to plan, you are planning to fail.

TARIQ SIDDIQUE

Larger projects require a much more formal approach. An important component of the project plan for larger projects is a task-oriented breakdown of the work to be done, also known as a **work breakdown structure (WBS)**. As illustrated in Figure 7-11, the work breakdown structure is used to logically arrange the tasks to be completed and define milestones. A **milestone** is a key or important event in the life of a project. The work breakdown structure is also used to assign resources to tasks, create schedules, and estimate costs.

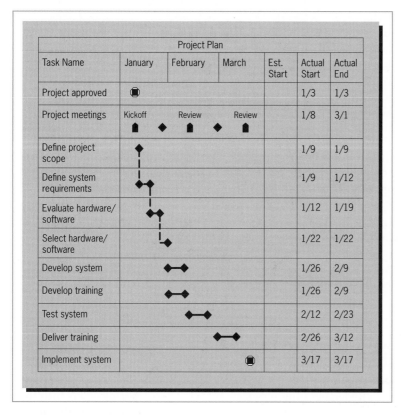

Project Plan						
Task Name	January	February	March	Est. Start	Actual Start	Actual End
Project approved	◉				1/3	1/3
Project meetings	Kickoff ⬛ Review ⬛ Review ⬛				1/8	3/1
Define project scope	◆				1/9	1/9
Define system requirements	◆◆				1/9	1/12
Evaluate hardware/ software	◆◆				1/12	1/19
Select hardware/ software	◆				1/22	1/22
Develop system	◆—◆				1/26	2/9
Develop training	◆—◆				1/26	2/9
Test system	◆—◆				2/12	2/23
Deliver training		◆—◆			2/26	3/12
Implement system			◉		3/17	3/17

Figure 7-11 Sample project plan

Many software products are available that can be used to create and manage project plans. Some of the most popular products include Milestones Simplicity by KIDASA Software, Inc., TurboProject by IMSI, Microsoft Project by Microsoft, and SureTrak Project Manager by Primavera Systems. These products provide the ability to create project plans along with reports and charts to communicate project status.

A critical project manager responsibility is communicating on a regular basis with the project sponsor, project stakeholders and their management, project team members and their management, and all other interested parties. Project status reports are an important communication tool and typically include the following:

- Accomplishments this period

- Accomplishments planned next period

- Resources required next period

- Considerations and concerns

- An updated project plan

With smaller projects, project status may be reported via the change management system. For larger projects, status reports are typically submitted in writing and periodically via presentations.

Ongoing communication is critical to a project's success. Communication must occur before, during, and after the project to ensure stakeholders and all parties affected by a project understand its purpose and goals. This is sometimes a difficult concept for technical professionals to understand. A busy technical professional may think, "I'm getting the work done. I don't have time to do a bunch of paperwork about it." Failing to communicate, however, almost always results in mismanaged expectations and dissatisfaction.

People with strong technical skills are sometimes assigned the role of project manager because their skills are highly important to a project. The fact that a person is highly technical does not mean that he or she knows how to be a good project manager. Furthermore, not all technicians enjoy doing the work that project managers are required to do, such as developing project plans and communicating project status. Some people prefer to serve as a project team member, rather than as project manager. Other people enjoy the project manager role and strive to continuously improve their project management skills.

Learning about project management concepts and tools will enable you to assess your abilities and determine how you can best contribute to a project team.

You can learn a lot about project management by simply observing how projects are run and by trying to understand the keys to project management success. You can also learn a lot by being an active participant when working on a project team. Rather than simply focusing on your assigned tasks, try to understand the bigger picture and how your piece fits into the puzzle. Try to understand the constraints that may be placed on the project by the project's scope and how the project manager is containing that scope.

If you are interested in being a project manager, take advantage of any training that is offered where you work or seek out self-study opportunities. You can also ask a seasoned project manager to serve as your mentor. Many project managers hone their skills by serving as a deputy, or assistant, to another project manager. This technique enables you to gain an understanding of how projects are run without you bearing all of the responsibility. Once you have a better understanding of how projects are run, you can begin initiating projects aimed at implementing your ideas.

Project management certification programs enable people to enhance and demonstrate their project management skills. The most recognized and valued certification programs are the Project Management Professional (PMP) certification offered by the Project Management Institute (PMI) and the Project+ certification offered by CompTIA.

Conducting a Cost-Benefit Analysis

Senior technical professionals, service desk team leaders, and service desk managers are often required to quantify proposed projects using a cost-benefit analysis. Cost-benefit analysis can be as simple as deciding to replace a desktop computer with a laptop. Although the cost of the laptop may be greater than that of the desktop computer, the benefits such as mobility and a smaller footprint justify the cost for many people, particularly when the user travels for work or wants a less cluttered workspace. In this example, after the decision is made to purchase a laptop, a second cost-benefit analysis must be performed to compare available laptops. That analysis must take into consideration factors such as the reputation of the manufacturer and the size and weight of the laptop. Once the costs and benefits are compared, a specific laptop is selected.

A cost-benefit analysis can also be quite complex and require considerable time and skill. This is particularly true when a proposed solution represents a significant investment, such as implementing a new service, or making a significant culture change, such as adopting ITIL. Because of the time and skill required, the cost of performing a complex cost-benefit analysis can be considerable. As a result, companies typically offer guidelines that determine the level of detail required in a cost-benefit analysis. These guidelines consider factors such as the size, cost, and impact of the proposed solution.

In its simplest form, a cost-benefit analysis uses only financial costs and financial benefits. Financial costs may be one-time (nonrecurring) costs or they may be ongoing (recurring). Figure 7-12 shows sample costs and benefits.

Many of the costs and benefits reflected in Figure 7-12 are expressed in monetary values and can be measured precisely. However, a more sophisticated approach to cost-benefit analysis attempts to place a financial value on intangible costs and benefits. This can be highly subjective. For example, what is the value of increased customer satisfaction? Although companies may be able to demonstrate increased customer satisfaction such as by surveying customers, showing its connection to the company's bottom line can be difficult.

As shown in Figure 7-12, some companies assign a numeric value (nv) to intangible benefits. For example, maximum benefit may be assigned a value to 3, average benefit a value of 2, and nominal benefit a value of 1. This numeric value can then be used for comparison purposes.

Costs	Alternative 1	Alternative 2
Personnel costs such as payroll costs including overtime benefits and expenses *Note:* Nonrecurring costs include activities such as project planning and management, solution design, development, and implementation. Recurring costs include end-user education and training, end-user support, and system maintenance activities.	$	$
Hardware costs such as computing devices, mobile devices, peripheral devices such as printers and scanners, and network devices *Note:* Hardware costs include the one-time cost of purchasing equipment as well as recurring maintenance and upgrade costs.	$	$
Software costs such as operating system software, application software, productivity tools, and monitoring tools *Note:* Software costs include the one-time cost of purchasing software as well as recurring maintenance and upgrade costs.	$	$
External services such as outsourcing services, voice and data communication services, and professional services (consultants) *Note:* External services costs may include the one-time use of consultants as well as recurring services such as outsourcing services.	$	$
Facility costs such as office space, security, and utilities *Note:* Facility costs may include nonrecurring costs such as temporary quarters for the project team as well as recurring costs associated with housing personnel and equipment.	$	$
Total Costs	$	$
Benefits		
Increased profits	$	$
Decreased costs	$	$
Total Benefits	$	$
Net Benefits (Total Benefits – Total Costs)	$	$
Intangible Benefits	Numeric Value (NV)	
Increased customer satisfaction	NV	NV
Improved communication	NV	NV
Net Intangible Benefits (Total Numeric Value (TNV))	TNV	TNV

Figure 7-12 Sample costs and benefits

Intangible benefits are important and must be taken into consideration. This is particularly true in the support industry where intangible benefits, such as those listed in Figure 7-13, can determine whether a service desk succeeds or fails.

- Better information
- Improved communications
- Improved customer relations
- Increased customer satisfaction
- Improved employee morale
- Increased knowledge
- More accurate solutions
- More proactive service

Figure 7-13   Sample intangible benefits

If insufficient data prohibits expressing an intangible benefit in financial or numeric terms, the judgment and experience of the individual or team performing the cost-benefit analysis are used to determine the value of intangible benefits. When estimating benefits, care must be taken to identify the benefits for all recipients of a proposed solution and for any organizations involved in delivering or supporting the proposed solution. For example, implementing a new remote control system will benefit service desk customers, service desk staff, and level two service providers.

The end result of a cost-benefit analysis is the identification of the best solution to a business problem, given two or more proposed solutions. Simply put, it answers the questions:

- Which of the proposed solutions is the best solution?
- Is the proposed solution worth the cost?

The key to whether a solution is worth the cost lies in the goals of the organization. Each company must decide what the benefits (tangible and intangible) are worth to its organization.

Calculating Return on Investment

Another technique used to assess the worth of a project is to calculate its return on investment (ROI). The following is the standard formula used for simple ROI calculations.

ROI = Net Benefits / Project Investment

Like a cost-benefit analysis, ROI in its simplest form uses only financial costs and benefits. Figure 7-14 illustrates the estimated cost savings to be realized when a service desk that handles 24,000 contacts per year transitions customers away from 100 percent phone-based services to a combination of phone, email, and self-services via the web. Industry-standard metrics are used to illustrate the expected savings. To achieve these cost savings, and to provide flexibility to its customers, this service desk plans to implement a $75,000 upgrade to its existing incident management system. The upgrade provides features such as an automated email interface, a web-based self-help tool, and an automated password management system.

Contact Method	Usage Percentage	# of Contacts	Cost per Contact	Cost
Pre-Investment				
Phone	100%	24,000	$28.19	$ 676,560
Post-Investment				
Phone	65%	15,600	$28.19	$ 439,764
Email	25%	6,000	$20.66	$ 123,960
Self-service	10%	2,400	$ 8.25	$ 19,800
Total Costs				$583,524
Total Annual Savings				$ 93,036
Total First Year Investment (upgrade to existing incident management system)				$ 75,000
Total First Year Benefits in Savings				$ 18,036
Annual ROI Percentage (Benefits / Investment * 100)				124%

Figure 7-14   Sample ROI calculation (incident management system upgrade)

In this simple example, the cost savings realized by reducing the cost per contact more than justify the investment. However, it is likely that additional benefits could be quantified, such as reduced abandon rate, faster average speed of answer, and reduced average wait time. **Abandon rate** is the percentage of abandoned calls compared to the total number of calls received. An **abandoned call** is a call where the caller hangs up before an analyst answers. **Average speed of answer (ASA)** is the average time it takes an analyst to pick up an incoming call. **Average wait time**—also known as **average queue time**—is the average number of seconds or minutes a caller waits for an analyst after being placed in the queue by an ACD.

As shown in Figure 7-14, ROI typically states the return on investment in percentage terms.

ROI% = Net Benefits / Project Investment × 100

Calculating ROI can be much more complex, however, because benefits can also be intangible. As with performing a cost-benefit analysis, intangible benefits can be difficult to define and express in financial terms. They are important though and must be taken into consideration.

Consider the case of a small five-person service desk. The service desk supports customers at both the corporate headquarters where the service desk resides and a second office across town. At least weekly, a member of the service desk team drives to the remote office to diagnose and repair incidents that could not be diagnosed over the telephone or via email. Customers are frustrated by the time it takes to have their incidents resolved. The service desk team is frustrated because the drive to the remote office is time consuming and stressful. The drive is through a high-traffic area and on average takes 2 hours (round trip). Driving to the remote office is also costly, and team members are spending an average of $40 per month on gas and tolls. In such a scenario, the tangible and intangible benefits of implementing a $200 remote control software package are considerable. As illustrated in Figure 7-15, a quick calculation of time savings and expenses shows that a return on the $200 investment could be realized within months.

ROI Calculation	Cost
Monthly travel time per analyst (2 hours @ $19 per hour × 4 trips)	$ 152.00
Monthly expenses per analyst ($40 per trip × 4 trips)	$ 160.00
Total monthly expenses	$ 312.00
Eliminating one trip per month (total monthly expenses / 4)	$ 78.00
Total annual savings (one trip per month × 12)	$ 936.00
Total first year investment (remote control software cost)	$(200.00)
Total first year benefits in savings	$ 736.00
Annual ROI percentage (Benefits / Investment * 100)	368%
Payback period (Investment / Benefits * 12)	3.3

Figure 7-15   Sample ROI calculation (remote control software implementation)

This is, of course, a simplistic example. For the ROI to be accurate, other costs and benefits should be considered, such as the costs associated with implementing the system and the benefits in terms of increased productivity realized by customers and service desk staff, increased first contact resolution, and decreased average time to resolution.

In this scenario, intangible benefits such as increased customer satisfaction and improved employee morale are not reflected in the ROI calculation. These benefits are important, however, and may outweigh the financial benefits. Customer and employee complaints, customer and employee satisfaction surveys, and judgment and experience on the part of decision makers can be used to quantify these intangible benefits.

As shown in Figure 7-15, some companies also determine the time it takes to recover an investment when calculating ROI. The period of time over which the benefits of an investment are received is known as the **payback period**.

Payback Period = Project Investment / Net Benefits × 12 Months

Some companies establish guidelines relative to the use of the payback period when making purchasing decisions. For example, if the payback period is less than 6 months, purchase the product immediately. If the payback period is greater than 6 months, consider the purchase in light of other budget expenditures. If the payback period is greater than 1 year, consider the purchase in a future budget.

Calculating ROI has many benefits, including greater credibility for IT and better business and IT alignment. ROI can be a complex and time-consuming calculation and is therefore typically reserved for larger technology investments. In its simplest form, however, ROI is a useful way to communicate the worth of even a small investment. Simply put, ROI answers the questions:

- What do I get back (in return) for the money I am being asked to spend (invest)?

- Is the return worth the investment?

IT professionals and business analysts are regularly challenged to answer the question, "What is the ROI?" In practice, this is a difficult question to answer. The answer becomes easier, however, as you develop the business skills needed to identify and communicate costs and benefits in financial terms.

The business world has changed and technical professionals must change as well. By acquiring and using business skills, technical professionals can expand their opportunities and have more control over their careers. Rather than always being told what to do and how to do it, technical professionals with business skills can propose new and better solutions and participate fully in bringing their ideas to life.

Chapter Summary

- Whether a person works for a small company or a large corporation, some business skills are useful and increasingly required. Many business skills relevant to technical professionals such as listening, communicating, and writing are basic business skills and can be learned on the job, through self-study, or in the classroom. These skills, along with skills such as customer service, process management, problem solving, project management, conflict management, and time management, are relatively universal and can be used regardless of a person's chosen profession. Skills such as financial management and human resources management are also important and become more important as people advance in their careers.

- People working in a service desk hear day in and day out from customers who are having trouble using technology. As a result, they have a unique opportunity to support the goals of business by using what they learn from customers to eliminate or minimize the effect of incidents and identify improvement opportunities. To do this, technical professionals must learn to use data to identify and quantify improvement opportunities, and to use techniques such as trend and root cause analysis. They must also learn how to use goals and metrics, communicated in financial terms, to state the expected benefits of their ideas and to justify improvement initiatives.

- Presentations are an important form of communication in the business world. Although making presentations can be nerve-racking, they are inevitable if you want to communicate your ideas and, more important, have those ideas accepted and acted upon. Making a presentation is not an exact science, but there are proven steps that can be taken to ensure success. The more often you present and the more varied the setting, subject matter, and audience, the more comfortable you will be.

- Advanced business skills such as managing projects, conducting a cost-benefit analysis, and calculating return on investment (ROI) are increasingly critical skills for more senior technical professionals. Although the need for these skills may vary from company to company, even a basic understanding of these concepts will enable you to make the most of learning and growth opportunities. To acquire these skills, some study, even self-study, is needed, along with experience.

- The business world has changed, and technical professionals must change as well. By acquiring and using business skills, technical professionals can expand their opportunities and have more control over their careers. Rather than always being told what to do and how to do it, technical professionals with business skills can propose new and better solutions and participate fully in bringing their ideas to life.

Key Terms

abandon rate—The percentage of abandoned calls compared to the total number of calls received.

abandoned call—A call where the caller hangs up before an analyst answers.

acceptance criteria—The conditions that must be met before the project deliverables are accepted.

anomaly—A deviation or departure from the average or the norm.

average queue time—See *average wait time*.

average speed of answer (ASA)—The average time it takes an analyst to pick up an incoming call.

average wait time—The average number of seconds or minutes a caller waits for an analyst after being placed in the queue by an ACD; also known as *average queue time*.

baseline—A metric used to show a starting point.

benchmarking—The process of comparing the service desk's performance metrics and practices to those of another service desk in an effort to identify improvement opportunities.

budget—The total sum of money allocated for a particular purpose or period of time.

business—A commercial enterprise or establishment; also used to describe a person's occupation, work, or trade.

business analyst—An individual who is skilled at working with end users to determine their needs.

business and IT alignment—A process aimed at ensuring that information technologies support corporate goals and objectives.

business case—A report that describes the business reasons that a change is being considered, along with its associated costs, benefits, and risks.

business productivity team (BPT)—A team that has a singular focus on improving user productivity and business outcomes (Gartner definition).

change control plan—A description of how the project scope will be managed and how agreed upon changes will be incorporated into the project deliverables.

considerations and concerns—A description of all considerations and concerns identified during the development of the project scope.

contact volume—The total number of contacts received during a given period of time.

cost—An amount paid or the expenditure of something, such as time or labor.

cost-benefit analysis—A business calculation that compares the costs and benefits of two or more potential solutions to determine an optimum solution.

cost effectiveness—A metric that ensures a proper balance between the cost of service and the quality of service.

cost per contact—The total cost of operating a service desk for a given period (including salaries, benefits, facilities, and equipment) divided by the total number of contacts received during that period; historically called *cost per call*.

cost per unit—The total cost of operating a service desk for a given period (including salaries, benefits, facilities, and equipment) divided by the total number of units (such as devices and systems) supported during that period.

customer satisfaction—A measure of the difference between how a customer perceives he or she was treated and how the customer expects to be treated.

effectiveness—A measure of how completely and accurately services are delivered.

efficiency—A measure of the time and effort required to deliver services in relation to their cost.

employee satisfaction—A measure of how satisfied an employee is with his or her job.

ethics—The rules and standards that govern the conduct of a person or group of people.

exit poll—A measurement technique that, on the Internet, combines questions such as "Was this information helpful to you?" with a set of choices that customers can use to provide feedback.

Gantt chart—A type of bar chart that is often used to illustrate a project schedule.

industry knowledge—Business skills that are unique to the industry or profession the service desk supports.

intangible—A characteristic that is difficult to measure precisely, such as customer satisfaction, employee satisfaction, and quality.

milestone—A key or important event in the life of a project.

nonprofit—A company established for charitable, educational, or humanitarian purposes rather than for making money; also known as *not-for-profit*.

page hit—A web page visit.

payback period—The period of time over which the benefits of an investment are received.

project—A temporary endeavor undertaken to create a unique product, service, or result (Project Management Institute definition).

project charter—A short document that formally authorizes the project and gives authority to the project manager.

project deliverable—An item to be delivered as a result of a project, such as a product, system, service, report, or plan.

project management—The process of planning and managing a project.

project manager—The person who leads the project team and is assigned the authority and responsibility for overseeing the project and meeting the project's objectives.

project objective—A measurable goal in terms of time, money, and quality that the project must achieve to be considered successful.

project overview—A summary of the project and of the business need driving the project.

project plan—A summary document that describes a project, its objectives, and how the objectives are to be achieved.

project scope—A description of the work to be done in a project.

project sponsor—The person who has ultimate authority over a project.

project stakeholder—A person or group that is involved in or may be affected by project activities.

quality—A characteristic that measures how well products or services meet customer expectations.

return on investment (ROI)—A business calculation that measures the total financial benefit derived from an investment and then compares it with the total cost of the project.

scope creep—A term used to describe unplanned changes to a project's scope.

service industry knowledge—Knowledge of the customer service and support industry.

tangible—A characteristic that is capable of being measured precisely, such as exactly how much something costs or how long it takes to complete a task.

turnover rate—The ratio of the number of workers who had to be replaced in a given period of time to the average number of workers.

work breakdown structure (WBS)—A task-oriented breakdown of the work to be done.

Review Questions

1. List two reasons that business skills are useful and increasingly required.

2. What are two factors that influence the business skills and knowledge required for a service desk job?

3. Describe three ways that people can learn business skills.

4. Individuals who want to advance in the support industry must move from knowing how to _____ technology to how to _____ technology to achieve business goals.

5. What is business and IT alignment?

6. List the four most common data categories captured by service desks.

7. How are customer records linked to incident records?

8. Describe two ways that customer data is used.

9. Describe two ways that incident data is used.

10. Describe two ways that status data is used.

11. Describe two ways that resolution data is used.

12. Define the term *trend analysis*.

13. Trends can be positive or _____.

14. Why is it important to eliminate the root cause of problems?

15. What is a budget?

16. Quality is a tangible characteristic. True or False? Explain your answer.

17. Why are intangible characteristics difficult to measure?

18. Why is having a balanced set of goals important?

19. How do you calculate an hourly rate from an annual salary?

20. Define the term *cost per contact*.

21. What are three benefits of having a clearly stated objective when designing and making presentations?

22. What do you need to know about your audience when designing and making presentations?

23. Rehearsing a presentation involves memorizing every word you want to say. True or False? Explain your answer.

24. What are two ways to handle questions when making a presentation?

25. Understanding how to do something is the same as actually doing it. True or False? Explain your answer.

26. What is a business case?

27. List five elements that all projects share regardless of their size.

28. What is scope creep?

29. What are two of the project manager's most important responsibilities?

30. What is a cost-benefit analysis?

31. A cost-benefit analysis answers what two questions?

32. The key to whether a solution is worth the cost lies in _____.

33. Define the term *ROI*.

34. ROI answers what two questions?

Discussion Questions

1. How important is it for technical professionals to acquire business skills? What skills are most important? What skills are most transferable from one job to another?

2. Consider the characteristics typically used to create metrics: cost, customer satisfaction, efficiency, effectiveness, employee satisfaction, and quality. Which of these characteristics are tangible, and why? Which are intangible, and why? Which are the easiest to measure, and why?

3. Technical professionals often have a "just do it" philosophy. Discuss and debate whether project management skills and a disciplined approach to projects are really needed in today's fast-paced business world.

Hands-On Projects

1. **Learn about business skills.** Interview a friend or family member who is in a senior technical or management position. Ask this person how he or she developed business skills such as understanding and speaking the language of business, using data to solve business problems, making presentations, managing projects, and conducting a cost-benefit analysis. How important does this person feel it is to have business skills? What other skills does this person feel are needed to be successful in the business world? Summarize what you learned from this interview in two or three paragraphs.

2. **Learn about the language of business.** Visit the web site of the company where you work or where you would like to work, and click on the About Us link (or a comparable link such as Welcome or Corporate Information). What language does the company use to describe its mission and its goals? Is the company not-for-profit or for-profit? What can you learn about the industry that the company is in and its vision for the future relative to that industry? What, if any, industry-specific terms are used to describe the company? Summarize what you have learned about this business in two or three paragraphs.

3. **Learn how data is captured and used.** Go to the web site of one of the popular incident management systems listed below. Download and install a demonstration or trial version of the system to learn more about data fields captured by service desks. Explore the web site and demonstration version of the system you select, and then prepare a table or spreadsheet that shows what data fields the system collects for each of the data categories: customer data, incident data, status data, and resolution data. Also, provide a paragraph or two describing how the data is used—for example, the types of reports that can be created, the types of metrics that can be produced, the types of knowledge base searches that can be performed, and so forth.

Product and Vendor
assyst by Axios Systems
HelpSTAR by Help Desk Technology International Corporation
HEAT by FrontRange Solutions
Remedy by BMC Software
Track-It! by Numara Software

4. **Evaluate and debate performance characteristics.** Choose two classmates to work with either in teams or via your school's online message or discussion board. Each person should select one of the following performance characteristics: efficiency, effectiveness, or quality. List the pros and cons of focusing on this single performance characteristic. For example, list the pros and cons of focusing only on how efficiently the service desk is performing while ignoring its effectiveness or the quality of its services. Debate these characteristics by having each team member present the merits of a single performance characteristic and state why he or she believes that characteristic is more important than the others. End the debate by summarizing the pros and cons of focusing on a single performance characteristic.

5. **Report on a trend.** Everywhere you look, studies are being conducted that produce a trend. It seems you cannot watch a television news show or read a magazine without hearing or seeing the phrase "Studies show that...." Select a topic in which you are interested—sports, cooking, gardening, the Internet, and so forth. Search for

and explore a web site or read a magazine that specializes in the subject you have selected and find a trend. Prepare a brief report that describes the trend and explains your perspective on factors that are influencing the trend.

6. **Identify presentation tips and techniques.** Assemble a team of at least three classmates or use your school's online message or discussion board. Discuss the topic of using presentations to market your ideas. Develop a list of reasons why people fear making presentations. Using your list, prepare a second list of 10 practical tips and techniques that people can use to minimize the anxiety associated with making presentations. Share your tips and techniques with the class.

7. **Present the status of a project.** Practice makes perfect. To practice your presentation skills, prepare and present to the class a brief (5-minute) presentation that provides the status of a project in which you are currently involved. The project could be acquiring and preparing a new tablet for school or work, an upcoming celebration (such as a wedding or graduation), or moving into a new home. Use the format of a project status report as your outline.

8. **Learn about project management software.** Go to several web sites of the project management software vendors mentioned in this chapter. Download demonstration or trial versions for two systems. Complete the demonstrations or explore the trial versions. Prepare a table or spreadsheet that compares the features and benefits of the two products you have selected.

9. **Perform a cost-benefit analysis.** Many people who perform a cost-benefit analysis on a regular basis tend to call it "shopping around." Think of an acquisition you have been considering. For example, you may be thinking about acquiring a digital camera, a mobile device such as a tablet, or a fairly expensive gift for a friend or family member. Complete the following steps:

   a. Document the goal you are trying to achieve.

   b. Produce a table that shows all of the costs (purchase price, monthly service fee, time to set up, and so forth) and benefits of two or more of the products you want to purchase.

   c. Analyze the costs and benefits (tangible and intangible), and select a product.

   d. Document the reason for your decision.

Case Projects

1. **Root Causes of Browser Problems.** You are the team leader at a service desk that recently installed a new integrated service management tool. This system provides the ability to log and capture the root cause of problems. You decided to begin by tracking the root cause of browser-related problems. Prepare a list of root causes for browser-related problems. For each root cause, identify at least one proactive way to prevent this type of problem from recurring.

2. **Tips for Effective Charts and Graphs.** You want to begin using charts and graphs to communicate ideas you have for improving service desk capabilities and performance. Search the web or go to your local library and learn more about how to effectively use charts and graphs to present information. For example, how can you use color to enhance your charts and graphs? How can you use labels to provide additional information about the data being presented? Prepare a list of 10 tips for creating effective charts and graphs.

3. **ROI Presentation.** Your team leader wants you to help prepare a presentation aimed at convincing the service desk manager to invest in remote control software. Prepare three slides that show the tangible and intangible benefits of remote control software to customers, the service desk team, and level two service providers. (*Hint:* Refer to the section "Technical Writing Best Practices" in Chapter 4 for practical tips and techniques for writing with lists and being consistent.)

8

Teams and Team Players in a Service Desk Setting

In this chapter you will learn:

- ◎ The characteristics of a successful team
- ◎ The stages of growth that teams go through
- ◎ How successful teams manage the inevitable and normal conflict in a team setting
- ◎ How to understand your role in the service desk and in your company's support organization
- ◎ How to contribute to your team's goals
- ◎ The skills needed to have positive working relationships with your teammates

In the frenetic setting of a technical service desk, no single person can know everything about all the products supported and provide all the support that customers need. The demands are too great. As a result, the members of the service desk must work together as a team. A **team** is a group of people organized to work together toward the achievement of a goal. To be successful, all team members must understand how their efforts contribute to the attainment of that goal.

Working in a group that calls itself a team does not make a person a team player. A **team player** is a person who contributes to the team's success by cooperating freely and communicating openly with his or her teammates. An effective team is made up of team players who contribute special skills or a unique personal style to the team. To be a team player, you must understand your role in the service desk and your role in the company's support organization. You must know how you can contribute to your team's goals, and you must support and respect the abilities of other team members and acknowledge their contributions.

Working as a Team

Not all work requires the efforts of a team. For example, the sales profession usually requires an individual endeavor. Although a salesperson's efforts may benefit the sales team or company, the salesperson's compensation is typically based on personal achievements. As a result, a company's salespeople often compete with one another to enhance their personal standing. In a team setting, competition is eliminated and team members work together toward a common goal.

Technical support lends itself to a team setting for a number of reasons, including:

- **The sheer number of available products.** The technology marketplace is jammed with vendors looking to sell their products and become a market leader. Users or potential users may be tempted to say, "A printer is a printer," but each product has unique features and functionality that a service desk analyst must understand in order to support it. Although an analyst may be able to become proficient in a single product line or family of products, no one can master all of the products available today.

- **The integration of products and systems.** A dramatic increase in the number of integrated products and systems makes it even more difficult for analysts to diagnose and determine the probable source of incidents. The Microsoft Office suite, which integrates products such as Word, Excel, Access, PowerPoint, and Outlook, is just one example of how tightly integrated products can be. The integration of a company's web site with its customer management, knowledge management, and order management systems is another example. The challenge facing service desks is compounded by the fact that many of these products and systems may be supported by different level two groups, or even by different external vendors (as is often the case with cloud computing). As a result, the service desk must interface with multiple groups or organizations when the source of an incident is unclear.

- **The constant and pervasive rate of technological change.** It has become virtually impossible for a single individual to be aware of and understand the changes occurring within a single market segment, such as hardware-, software-, application- or network-related products, much less the integration of these products throughout an entire company. Simply reading and assimilating all of the information offered in trade magazines, in electronic magazines (usually called e-zines), and on web sites could constitute a full-time job. This does not even include putting that information into action.

- **The need for business knowledge.** Technical support is about helping people use technology to achieve business goals. Service desk analysts must understand the business goals of their customers so they can help their customers use technology to achieve those goals. This means, in addition to technical skills, analysts may possess skills and knowledge that are unique to the profession they support, such as accounting skills or banking knowledge. It is not possible or practical for all members of the service desk team to acquire every business and technical skill needed to support their customers. Rather, team members typically specialize in different areas of the business and then work together to solve incidents that span multiple specialty areas.

- **The increasing complexity of the business world.** Service desk analysts work with people of varying skill levels, education levels, and generational and cultural backgrounds. Furthermore, service desks often partner with vendors and suppliers in the course of delivering services. For example, many companies outsource some service desk activities in an effort to deliver high-quality support services at a reduced cost. It would be extremely difficult for one service desk analyst to manage these diverse relationships and speak the many technical and nontechnical languages associated with them.

- **The need to use resources efficiently and effectively.** Managers demand high productivity and high quality. Service desk analysts must handle service requests and solve incidents correctly the first time because little to no time exists to do things over. Also, analysts who lack the skills or training to perform a task that their job requires do not have the time it would take to figure things out on their own. As a result, service desk analysts must collaborate with teammates and other service providers to get the job done as quickly and correctly as possible.

Technical support lends itself to a team setting because the demands of the environment are simply too great for a single analyst. Instead, the members of the service desk need to work together as a team. Each analyst must maintain a high level of knowledge about the products and systems for which he or she is recognized as an expert, and at the same time show respect and support for the other members of the team. In other words, a member of the service desk team who is highly skilled in one particular product cannot discount the efforts of another team member who is not familiar with that product. That other team member may be highly experienced in another product or may have business skills, soft skills, or self-management skills that contribute to the goals of the team.

Characteristics of a Successful Team

Just as working in a group that calls itself a team does not make a person a team player, assembling a group of team players does not make a successful team. To be successful, a team must share the characteristics listed in Figure 8-1. Teams that do not exhibit these characteristics are often ineffective and suffer negative side effects, such as low morale, low productivity, and high stress.

- A clear sense of purpose
- Shared leadership
- Diversity
- Openness and trust
- Positive relationships with other support groups

Figure 8-1 Characteristics of a successful team

A Clear Sense of Purpose

For a service desk to be successful, the mission and goals of the team must be clearly defined and accepted by all of the team members. A **service desk mission** is a written statement describing the customers the service desk serves, the types of services the service desk provides, and how the service desk delivers those services. In other words, a mission defines *who* the service desk supports, *what* it supports, and *how* it provides that support. The mission then determines the type, size, and structure of the service desk.

 It is important that employees understand the service desk's mission and how it fits into the company's mission. Companies whose employees understand both the company mission and their department mission attain considerably higher customer satisfaction rates than companies whose employees do not.

Service desk goals are measurable objectives that support the service desk mission. Most service desks establish specific goals each year in an effort to clarify what analysts are supposed to focus on, eliminate conflicting goals, and encourage analysts to produce the desired results. Individual performance goals further define how service desk analysts contribute to their team's goals. **Individual performance goals** are measurable objectives for analysts that support the service desk mission. Because individuals contribute to teams in different ways, individual performance goals may vary from one person to the next. However, all individual performance goals will support the service desk's goals.

 Without a clearly defined mission and goals, a service desk can fall prey to the "all things to all people" syndrome, which can quickly stretch its resources too thin and make its team spirit quickly decline.

Shared Leadership

Having a formal team leader to whom members are loyal is another characteristic of a successful team. Although a successful team can work around a poor team leader, an effective leader enables the team to achieve its full potential by removing obstacles and by sharing leadership responsibilities as needed to get the job done.

Team leader roles and titles may reflect a person's position within an organization such as supervisor or manager, or they may reflect a temporary assignment, such as project manager or committee chairperson. Team leaders are typically held accountable for a team's success and may be given authority over many of the team's actions. Ineffective team leaders take advantage of this authority by telling the team what to do and how to do it, without seeking input.

319

A more effective approach is to share leadership responsibilities. Such an approach ensures each team member feels responsible for meeting the team's goals. Shared leadership also ensures that each team member's strengths are used to the fullest when needed and that the team stays focused, even in the team leader's absence.

Although the formal team leader may be solely responsible for certain administrative responsibilities, such as setting team goals and monitoring and measuring performance, effective teamwork requires the active participation of each team member. It is the team leader's responsibility to encourage team members to assume leadership roles such as planning and coordinating team activities and identifying solutions to team problems. The most effective leaders (whether the formal team leader or not) make suggestions, remain open to ideas, and encourage others to do the same.

In the workplace, many people work in **virtual teams**, which are groups of people who work across time, space, and organizational boundaries. With virtual teams, the team leader and team members may physically reside anywhere in the world and may, in fact, never actually meet in person. A benefit of virtual teams is that the individuals best suited to fill the team's needs can be engaged, regardless of their physical location. In such situations, shared leadership is critical. Team members must hold each other accountable and must lead by example by completing tasks as assigned and by assisting others as needed.

The achievements of an organization are the result of the combined effort of each individual.

VINCE LOMBARDI

Diversity

A common misconception is that to be successful, all team members must be alike, agree on everything, and get along at all times. The reality is that the most successful teams are made up of people who have unique skills and exhibit varying approaches to teamwork. In a baseball team, for instance, each player performs a different task. One plays first base, another specializes in pitching, and so on. Each player has an area of expertise and may actually not perform well in an area other than his or her specialty. (Pitchers, for example, are notoriously poor batters.) Each player must also at times be a leader and at other times follow the leader. What makes these people with varying talents a team? It is their desire to play together in order to win the game. In business terms, team players must be willing to work together to achieve the team's mission and goals.

A common challenge that business teams face is age diversity. One workplace might include four generations:

- **Seniors**—people born before 1945
- **Baby Boomers**—people born between 1945 and the early 1960s

- **Generation X**—people born between the early to mid-1960s and the late 1970s

- **Generation Y**—people born after the late 1970s; also referred to as Millennials

These groups of workers have very different views about issues such as work ethic, respect for authority, management style, dress code, and work schedules. Seniors tend to value teamwork and loyalty and often believe the team is more important than the individual. Baby Boomers tend to value teamwork and loyalty but are also comfortable seeking individual success. Generation X tends to believe a high-performing team is composed of strong members who focus on delivering individual results. These workers tend to be more oriented toward achieving personal goals. Generation Y tends to thrive on teamwork and collaboration. These workers are much more apt to question authority and will stay with an employer only when they are being offered a variety of experiences. These workers also seek a balance between work and their personal lives. They require flexibility.

Depending on their age, workers have different views about how to approach teamwork. For example, a team of Seniors and Baby Boomers tends to meet face to face, at least occasionally, to ensure the team is clearly focused on its goals. Generation X resists constant meetings, preferring to remain focused on individual tasks. Generation Y is quite content to meet virtually. For these workers, collaboration is much more instantaneous and often occurs via technologies such as email and IM.

Teams may be composed of individuals from a single generation, or they may be multigenerational. Each team must determine how best to accommodate each generation's preferences to maximize productivity.

Depending on their age, workers also have very different views about technology. Seniors, Baby Boomers, and Generation X have watched technology dramatically change the way people work. Generation Y workers, on the other hand, have never known a time when technology was not used in the workplace. In the case of technology, Generation X and Generation Y workers are often the ones who introduce communication and collaboration technologies to the team setting.

A key to success for multigenerational teams is valuing the contribution of each generation. Many companies provide managers and team leaders with age diversity training aimed at treating workers from each generation the way they want to be treated, and using the talents of each generation to achieve team goals. These companies are able to retain experienced employees while also attracting new employees who bring fresh ideas, talents, and skills.

Diversity: the art of thinking independently together.

MALCOLM FORBES

When team-oriented companies consider a prospective employee, they look at the individual's personality and willingness to work in a team setting and toward team goals, as well as the person's business and technical skills. They want to ensure the new hire will fit into the company's corporate culture and into the culture of the hiring team. Cultures vary from company to company and team to team, just as they vary from one country to the next. Some companies have a hierarchical culture where layers of managers coordinate and control the work of their employees. Other companies have more of a participative culture where self-directed teams coordinate and control their work with support from a team leader when needed. Furthermore, the culture of teams within a company can vary. In a company with a hierarchical culture, a particular manager may encourage a participative work environment. Both companies and employees benefit when an employee's personality is compatible with a team and company's culture. This is particularly true in organizations that do not have formal management chains and strictly defined job descriptions.

Together Everyone Achieves More.

AUTHOR UNKNOWN

Openness and Trust

Communication within a team setting is just as important as communicating with customers. Team members must be willing to share their knowledge, give and receive constructive feedback, and freely express their feelings. Effective communication requires that team members are not only willing to talk, but also willing to listen. If a team member does not understand a point a coworker is making, that person must ask for clarification on, paraphrase, or summarize his or her teammate's point of view to ensure understanding. Team members must also be able to rely on each other to get the job done. Although it is human nature to have a bad day now and then, team members must not impose their personal moods and problems on their coworkers. This does not mean that team members should not ask for help when they need it. In the most effective teams, members feel comfortable stating their weaknesses and looking to teammates for strength.

Personal and professional insecurities on the part of individuals can stand in the way of teamwork. A person who is insecure about his standing in a team may be hesitant to voice his opinion or share his knowledge. Or, a person who is insecure may become defensive, uncooperative, or angry when questioned about her work. People who experience insecurities must work hard to overcome their fears and have confidence in their abilities and in the abilities of others. Techniques such as positive self-talk and assertiveness training can help people overcome their insecurities and establish positive working relationships with their teammates.

To deal with an insecure person, listen to and try to understand him or her. Treat him or her with respect and interest. A positive approach may prompt the person to become more open and trusting.

Positive Relationships with Other Support Groups

When working in a team, members are accountable not only to the other members of their team, but also to the "greater team," which constitutes the customer service value chain within their company and includes external suppliers. Successful teams have positive working relationships with other groups, including level two support groups, the training group, the Sales and Marketing departments, and external suppliers. The service desk must rely on these groups to provide knowledge, tools, and credibility. When the service desk lacks credibility, customers may contact these groups directly, circumventing the service desk altogether. As a result, the service desk is unable to gain the confidence of its customers and of the other groups in its customer service value chain. Without the support of these other groups, it is unlikely that the service desk's potential will be realized and its contribution recognized.

CASE STUDY: The Service Desk and DevOps

DevOps is a cultural and professional movement that emphasizes communication, collaboration, and integration between software developers (Dev) and IT operations professionals (Ops). DevOps responds to the demands of application and business unit stakeholders for an increased rate of production software releases. Driven by the adoption of agile development processes by IT development organizations, DevOps aims to help organizations rapidly produce quality software products and services.

Although the "Ops" in DevOps is often viewed as the technical and application management professionals who deploy and manage applications and their associated infrastructure (e.g., application servers, web servers, and database servers), the service desk supports the goals of DevOps in a number of ways. A goal of DevOps is to produce more frequent software releases. This means the service desk must be prepared to handle a faster rate of change. One way to ensure the service desk is prepared is to engage the service desk earlier in the service lifecycle. For example, some organizations are involving the service desk in testing activities. This enables the service desk to gain early exposure to releases and also capitalizes on the service desk's ability to log and track incidents. In some organizations, incidents logged during testing are referred to as preproduction incidents. The service desk can also begin logging problems and known errors. Although some problems and known errors may be resolved before a release is moved into production, some may be carried forward into the production environment. The service desk can ensure knowledge articles are in place that enable efficient handling of those errors when they are encountered. The service desk plays another invaluable role in that it captures data about incidents and problems affecting production systems. This data not only allows the handling of those incidents and problems, it is also an important part of the feedback loop that enables the development team to improve the quality of the next release and reduce the cost of handling errors associated with that release.

*DevOps aims to not only improve Ops's visibility into development activities, but also to improve Dev's visibility into the impact of changes on the production environment, particularly during early life support. ITIL defines **early life support (ELS)** as the stage in the service lifecycle that occurs at the end of a deployment and before the service is fully accepted into operation. During ELS the service desk works closely with development and deployment teams to ensure incident and problem management activities are occurring as efficiently and effectively as possible. This includes using and refining provided diagnostic tools and knowledge resources, ensuring clear escalation procedures are in place, and capturing and communicating user and customer complaints.*

Key goals of DevOps include better alignment of IT responsiveness and capabilities to business needs, and enabling companies to gain a competitive advantage by delivering better software, faster. To contribute to these goals, the service desk must build solid working relationships with development teams and other IT operations teams.

Building a Solid Team

To perform at maximum efficiency and effectiveness, each team member, including the leader, must embrace the characteristics of a successful team. That is, the team needs *a clear sense of purpose.* The team leader cannot simply choose a direction and instruct the team to follow blindly. Members of successful teams are committed to the goals of the team and to each other's ability to grow and be successful. To grow, team members must embrace *diversity.* Effective team members acknowledge their weaknesses, set individual goals, and take steps to improve, or rely upon, the strengths of their teammates to get the job done. As a team, members must acknowledge the unique skills that each player contributes and seek out and accept into the team people who can fill the team's voids. When people work together this way, the sum of their efforts is invariably greater than the efforts of any one person acting alone. This is because the combined experience of the team is greater than the experience of any one team member.

No one can be the best at everything. But when all of us combine our talents, we can be the best at virtually anything.

DON WARD

One of the greatest challenges that a team faces is establishing methods of communication that promote *openness and trust.* This is because the team must have in place ways of communicating within the team, between individual team members, and with groups outside the team. No team stands alone. Teams benefit when they have *positive relationships with other support groups* who can provide the funds, equipment, training, and information the team needs to succeed.

A group of people cannot become a team overnight. It takes time, an open, pleasant working environment, and a willingness to work through the stages of growth that all groups experience on their way to becoming a team. Figure 8-2 introduces the Tuckman Teamwork Model. Developed by Bruce W. Tuckman, Ph.D. (*Psychological Bulletin*, 1965, pp. 63, 384–399), this model is often used to describe the developmental stages that all teams experience.

- Forming
- Storming
- Norming
- Performing

Figure 8-2   Tuckman Teamwork Model

Stage 1: Forming

During this first stage, the team members are selected and the process of becoming a team begins. The team's mission and goals are defined along with the team members' roles and responsibilities. Team members often experience a range of emotions during this stage, including excitement, anxiety, and, perhaps, even fear. Little is achieved while a team is in this stage as team members get to know each other and as the team's purpose is defined. During the forming stage, team members are often on their best behavior and try to avoid conflict. The team leader is actively involved in this stage and provides the direction and resources the team needs to progress.

Stage 2: Storming

During the storming stage, the team begins to face the reality of turning its mission and goals into executable action plans. Team members often begin to feel the team's goals are unrealistic, and they may doubt the leader's ability to provide the team with what it needs. As the team members get to know each other, the polite facade begins to fade and they are more willing to disagree. Team members may experience frustration and self-doubt during this stage, and some defensiveness and competition may occur. The team leader coaches and counsels the team during this stage and repeatedly reminds the team to stay focused on its goals.

Stage 3: Norming

This stage represents the calm after the storm. Team members begin to take ownership for the team's performance, and they begin to have confidence in the team's abilities. They begin to feel a sense of camaraderie, and they begin to exhibit team spirit. Conflict is, for the most part, avoided as team members accept and welcome feedback rather than view it as criticism. The team leader steps away from the team during this stage and gets involved only when the team asks for support.

Stage 4: Performing

At this stage of the team's development, the team is achieving its goals and the team's members are participating fully in team activities. A spirit of cooperation and collaboration prevails, and team members trust each other and their leader. Team members feel a sense of pride and satisfaction, and the team has become a close-knit community. The team leader serves as head cheerleader and encourages the team to avoid complacency and continuously improve.

In the course of a team's development, it is inevitable that change will occur. New team members may be added, and old team members may leave. In the course of continuously improving, the team may rethink its mission or set new goals. The team may also be affected by changes to the company such as a reorganization, a merger, or an acquisition of some kind. When change occurs, it can affect the team's ability to maintain or advance its current stage of growth. The best teams accept and embrace change by taking a step back to the forming stage in an effort to clarify the team's purpose and team members' roles and responsibilities. They can then move quickly through the storming and norming stages back to peak performance. Figure 8-3 illustrates the way teams continually move through these developmental stages.

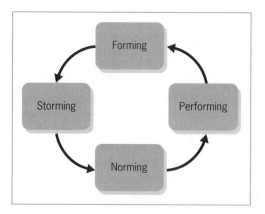

Figure 8-3 The ongoing nature of team development
Source: Bruce W. Tuckman, *Psychological Bulletin*, 1965, pp. 63, 384–399

Some teams never make it to the performing stage. For example, some teams avoid conflict during the storming stage and never develop the ability to deal with negative issues or achieve a consensus. A **consensus** is an opinion or position reached by all of a team's members or by a majority of its members. Conflict is inevitable in a team setting, and successful teams learn to work through it in a fair and constructive manner.

Reaching a consensus does not mean that team members agree with the majority just to avoid conflict. Typically, a consensus is reached when all team members can say that they agree with a decision or that they feel their point of view on a matter has been heard and understood, even if it has not been accepted. When a consensus is reached, some team members may still disagree with the decision but they are willing to work toward its success.

Managing Conflict in a Team Setting

Conflict is a normal part of human interaction that, when approached positively, can actually produce very creative and innovative results. In a team setting, conflict usually results from team members' varying perceptions and expectations. A team member who stays late every night may resent the fact that a team member who is dedicated to his family leaves "early"— that is, on time—one or two nights a week. In a technical setting, a team member may resent the fact that a coworker has been selected to work on a choice project and as a result will be acquiring state-of-the-art skills. Another team member may feel that her technical skills are not being fully utilized and as a result are becoming stagnant. Or, a team member may feel that his accomplishments are not being acknowledged and appreciated. Conflict can even arise simply as a result of the stress that is inherent in a service desk setting. A stressed team member may snap at coworkers, causing hurt feelings.

An issue is typically at the heart of a conflict. Because people often take the issue personally, they experience an emotional reaction, such as disappointment, hurt, and even anger. The best way to handle conflict is for team members to focus on the issue and not on the personalities of their teammates. Each team member must also be honest about his or her feelings, while striving to understand the feelings of his or her teammates. Engaging in a conflict is not a pleasant experience for most people. It is better, though, to resolve the issue rather than avoid it and allow it to turn into something even bigger.

Gossip is often a sign of unresolved conflict. It is best to avoid gossip by encouraging the parties who are gossiping—including yourself—to talk directly to the person or persons who are the subject of the gossip.

The following tips are helpful for resolving conflict in a team setting in a constructive manner. These tips also enable team members to maintain and perhaps even strengthen their relationship. When faced with a conflict, remember the following:

- The person on the other side of the conflict has a point of view that is just as legitimate and reasonable to him or her as yours is to you. Listen actively to the other person's point of view, and strive to understand his or her perspective.

- The other person may be as uncomfortable talking about the conflict or disagreement as you are. Suggest to your teammate that you want to have a positive working relationship and that you would like to find a mutually agreeable way to resolve the conflict.

- It is safer and wiser to keep to the issues of a discussion. Avoid making comments that attack your teammate's personal character or question his or her motives.

- Saying the same thing over and over will not resolve the conflict. If you feel strongly about your point of view and your teammate does not seem to be getting it, state your point of view in a different way or try presenting your point of view from the other person's perspective.

- Little can be gained by discussing or debating the past. Rather than dwelling on what or who caused the conflict, try to determine what can be done now and in the future to eliminate the source of conflict.

- The other person may be willing to accept a solution if you can make it sufficiently attractive. To achieve a compromise, both you and your teammate must be willing to make concessions. You must strive to identify a middle ground that you both find acceptable.

- It is okay to change your mind. Sometimes we form an opinion without having all of the facts. Should you discover through discussion that you were misinformed or that you were simply wrong, graciously acknowledge your teammate's point of view and, when appropriate, apologize for causing or prolonging the conflict.

- One-on-one collaboration may not always work or be appropriate. Know when it is time to engage a **mediator**, a negotiator who helps individuals resolve disputes. The mediator's role is to remain neutral, gather the facts, and discuss the conflict with all of the parties involved. The mediator then helps the parties work out a resolution in keeping with the company's policies, ethics, and goals.

Although it is typically best to resolve a conflict rather than avoid it, there are times when it is appropriate to delay discussing a difficult situation. It is appropriate to avoid an issue if the timing is wrong and more harm than good will come from engaging someone in a discussion. For example, the person may be very upset or angry and, as such, incapable of having a reasonable discussion. Or, you may be feeling highly emotional and unable to maintain an open mind. This does not mean you should avoid the issue altogether. Doing so may lead people to perceive you do not care about the outcome or that you are unwilling to be a team player. Instead, you should choose a time when both you and the person can calmly discuss the issue and seek a resolution. Being a team player requires that people work together in an effort to resolve not only their customers' problems, but problems within the team as well.

Being a Team Player

Being a team player requires personal commitment and a willingness to put the needs of the team ahead of personal goals. Team players contribute to the team's success by cooperating freely and communicating openly with their teammates. This does not mean they must abandon their personal goals to be team players. The most successful team players seek out a team setting that enables them to work toward their personal goals while contributing to the team's goals. People feel the greatest sense of job satisfaction when their skills are fully utilized and when their personal working style is acknowledged and accommodated. Some people like to continuously learn new skills and become bored when their work becomes routine. Other people enjoy routine and feel most comfortable when they have fully mastered the tasks they are expected to complete. A successful team is made up of a mix of people who contribute a variety of skills and personal working styles to the service desk and to the entire support organization.

Understanding Your Role in the Service Desk

A common misconception is that being a team player means going along with the crowd. Some people believe they will have to give up their individuality and become just like everyone else on the team. This is not true. For a team to succeed, all team members must understand that they have a unique role to play. The role a person plays is a sum of his or her skills, knowledge, experience, and personal style.

In his book, *Team Players and Teamwork*, Glenn M. Parker writes that research indicates that there are four types or styles of team players (*Team Players and Teamwork*, 2011). Figure 8-4 lists the four styles of team players.

- Challenger
- Collaborator
- Communicator
- Contributor

Figure 8-4   Team player styles

Each of these team player styles contributes to the team's goals in different ways. A *challenger* serves as the team's "devil's advocate" and often questions the team's goals, methods, and procedures. A *collaborator* is goal oriented and is willing to do what is needed to get the job done. A *communicator* is a good listener and encourages other team members to participate in team discussions and decisions. A *contributor* is task oriented and does everything possible to provide the team with the skills, knowledge, and information needed to achieve its goals.

Each team player style serves a purpose, and each shines brightest at different times during the stages of a team's growth. During the forming stage, a challenger will push the team to set high standards and may question the validity of the team's goals. During the storming stage, a communicator will facilitate discussion and encourage conflict resolution. During the norming stage, a contributor will help the team stay organized and will do the research needed for the team to succeed. During the performing stage, a collaborator will encourage the team to stay focused on its goals and, when needed, revisit its goals in an effort to continuously improve.

Each team player style can become ineffective if a team player overemphasizes his or her contribution or fails to acknowledge the contributions of others. Team players must be sensitive to the needs of the team and the needs of their teammates. A collaborator who jumps in and takes over a task from a coworker may believe that this is needed to get the job done. He or she may, however, be depriving that coworker of the opportunity to learn new skills. Furthermore, people can get "stuck in a rut," becoming a liability to the team. For example, there are times when it is no longer appropriate for a challenger to continuously question the team's goals and methods. Once a consensus has been achieved, the challenger must accept the goals and let the team move forward.

 It is the team leader's responsibility to deal with disruptive team members. Early intervention along with consistent feedback and follow-through are essential. The company's human resources (HR) policies and procedures should be consulted for guidance.

Although most people have one style that predominates, each person is capable of exhibiting all of these team player styles. In fact, people may exhibit different styles in different situations. Your challenge as a team player is to determine your personal style and use the strengths of that style to contribute to your team. Knowing your personal style will also help you to identify and overcome your weaknesses, or understand when your strength becomes a weakness. You can also strive to embrace the strengths of the other styles, thus increasing your ability to contribute to the team. People can change, and they can exhibit incredible flexibility. If you want to develop a new style in an effort to increase your effectiveness, learn more about team player styles and team dynamics. The more you know about these concepts, the more effective you can be in a team setting.

Personality tests, such as the Myers-Briggs Type Indicator (MBTI) and the Motivational Appraisal of Personal Potential (MAPP), can also be used by individuals to learn more about their work preferences and by companies to learn more about a job candidate. These tests measure qualities such as motivation, temperament, learning style, and people skills.

Appendix A lists books, magazines, and organizations you can use to obtain self-study training materials and additional information about teams and team player styles. To locate personality tests on the web, search for topics such as "personality test," "myers-briggs type indicator test," or "MAPP assessment."

Tests that provide the ability to assess and improve emotional intelligence are also useful in a team setting. Simply put, **emotional intelligence** is a form of intelligence relating to the emotional side of life. Emotional intelligence includes the ability to:

- Recognize and manage one's emotions and the emotions of others
- Motivate oneself and restrain impulses
- Effectively handle interpersonal relationships

Positive interpersonal relationships are an important element of teamwork, and they begin with self-awareness. The most effective—that is, emotionally intelligent—team players understand that negative behavior can affect the productivity of others and the overall success of the entire team. Emotionally intelligent team players are able to control their emotions, show empathy for the feelings of others, and promote cooperation and collaboration.

Team players who embrace the diversity that a team setting offers are invariably happier and more successful. They continuously learn new skills from their coworkers. They become more open-minded and learn to accept, and even invite, new and challenging opportunities. They learn to respect that people are entitled to their own viewpoints, and they strive to understand other people's perspectives. They enjoy the camaraderie that comes from working with others and the feeling of satisfaction that comes when a common goal is achieved.

The most successful team players value the opportunity to work with others who are equally unique. They learn to rely on other people for their knowledge, experience, and support. They appreciate and respect their teammates and want their teammates to appreciate and respect them in return. These feelings of mutual appreciation and respect also extend beyond the service desk to the entire support organization.

Understanding an Analyst's Role in the Company's Support Organization

Although each member of the service desk team plays a unique role, customers or other support groups tend to lump everyone together as "the service desk." This may not seem fair, but it is actually the essence of what makes a team a team. The service desk, as a team, has a role to play within the support organization. The service desk's mission and goals define what that role will be. The role of most service desks is to serve on the front line between a company or department and its customers. This is a most important role. Customers form opinions about the entire company or department based on their interactions with the service desk. The service desk's performance also influences how efficiently and effectively other support resources, such as level two, level three, and external suppliers, are used. Each and every member of the service desk team must embrace the service desk's mission and achieve his or her individual performance goals for the service desk team to achieve its goals.

Contributing to Team Goals

Each member of a team brings to the team a unique set of skills and a personal style. Those skills and that style are only of value if they enable the team to achieve its goals (the measurable objectives that support the service desk's mission). Service desk goals differ from one company to the next and may vary from one year to the next, based on a company's business goals and the needs and expectations of its customers. Sample service desk goals include:

- Achieve an average 4 out of 5 rating on the annual customer satisfaction survey.

- Provide each analyst 8 hours of training each month.

- Resolve 70 percent of reported incidents at level one.

- Reduce contacts to the service desk by 5 percent within 6 months.

- Increase contacts resolved using self-services by 15 percent within 6 months.

- Reduce support costs by 5 percent by year end.

- Maintain a cost per contact at or below the industry average.

 Goals typically assess characteristics such as cost, customer satisfaction, efficiency, effectiveness, employee satisfaction, and quality. The best companies strive to maintain a balanced set of goals because placing too great an emphasis on any one goal can negatively impact other goals.

Team performance is only as good as the performance of the analysts on the team. Every analyst influences the team's ability to achieve its goals and expected service levels. If every analyst in the service desk achieves his or her individual performance goals, then the team will achieve its goals. Data is needed to measure and manage both team and individual performance. Service desk analysts often create the needed data by using tools.

Some analysts mistakenly believe that management cannot measure their performance if the data is not available. This line of thinking is flawed: Management will still measure performance; it will simply do it without facts. In other words, management will measure performance based on what it *perceives* an analyst has accomplished. By capturing data and learning to use that data to create information, analysts can maximize their contribution to service desk goals and communicate that contribution to management.

Service desk tools that may be used to create metrics for individuals include an automatic call distributor (ACD), email response management system, and incident management system. The metrics captured with an ACD and email response management system can be combined with metrics produced using the service desk's incident management system. Table 8-1 shows individual performance metrics that can be captured.

Tool	Metric	Description
ACD	**Availability**	The length of time an analyst was signed on to the ACD compared to the length of time the analyst was scheduled to be signed on
	Average call duration	The average length of time required to handle a call
	Time idle	The average length of time an analyst was idle during a given period of time; an **idle state** means the analyst is logged on to the ACD but is not accepting calls
	Wrap-up time	The average length of time an analyst was in wrap-up mode during a given period of time; **wrap-up mode** is a feature that prevents the ACD from routing a new inbound call to an analyst's extension
Email response management system	**Average handle time**	The average length of time required to handle an email
	Average number of exchanges	The average number of email exchanges required to resolve an incident
Incident management system	**Reopen percent**	The percentage of closed incidents that had to be opened back up within a given time period
	Resolution percent	The percentage of incidents an analyst resolved compared to the total number of incidents that an analyst handled during a given time period
	Application of training investments	A comparison of an analyst's resolution percent and reopen percent before and after attending training

Table 8-1   Individual performance metrics

Customer satisfaction is another common individual performance metric. It is captured through the results of event-driven customer satisfaction surveys. Because event-driven surveys request customer feedback on a single service event, they are an excellent way to capture information about an individual analyst's performance.

Monitoring is yet another way that companies measure the performance of individual analysts. The most effective monitoring programs provide analysts with a checklist that describes the specific criteria that supervisors or team leaders are using to measure the quality of a contact.

A metric that directly influences customer satisfaction but that can be difficult to capture is first contact resolution rate. **First contact resolution rate** is the percentage of contacts (such as calls, emails, chats, faxes, and web requests) resolved during a customer's initial contact compared to the total number of contacts received at the service desk for a given period of time. With telephone calls and chats, this metric can be captured fairly easily because an analyst is able to verify a customer's satisfaction with a resolution before he or she closes the call. This metric is much more difficult to capture with emails because the service desk may not receive acknowledgment from the customer that a solution has worked. Many companies link customer satisfaction surveys to email-delivered solutions in an effort to solicit feedback from customers.

 The industry average first contact resolution rate has been decreasing in recent years. Much of this decrease can be attributed to improved self-services and problem management, both of which result in the service desk handling new and more complex incidents, rather than easier to solve recurring incidents.

Although not an indicator of individual performance, first contact resolution rate is also often used to measure the effectiveness of automated email response management systems and web-based knowledge management systems. Again, this metric is difficult to capture and so customer satisfaction surveys and exit polls are often used to determine the effectiveness of technology-delivered solutions.

Metrics are an excellent way for service desk management and staff to know whether they are achieving team and individual performance goals. It is important to note, however, that no single metric can be used to accurately measure team or individual performance. They all work together and can influence each other. The best service desks use metrics to monitor performance as well as to identify areas for improvement. Metrics can be used to identify the training needs of service desk analysts. They can be used to identify the need for new or improved tools or the need to refine the service desk's processes and procedures. Metrics can also be used to know when it is time to rethink the service desk's mission or revisit its goals.

Although management directs most of the performance metrics analysts must meet, you can suggest additional metrics and supply other information that further demonstrates your contribution to the team's goals. For example, you can prepare a brief report that shows how an FAQ you wrote has resulted in a reduction in the number of questions that customers ask about a new product. Remember to be specific. Indicate how many questions were asked for 1 or 2 months before you wrote the FAQ, and how many questions were asked during the month or two after the FAQ was published. Many managers try to involve their staff when establishing performance measures, and you may be encouraged to suggest ways to measure and improve team and individual performance. You can also suggest possible solutions to a problem rather than finding fault or complaining. For example, if poor communication is affecting team performance, you can suggest ways to improve communication. This positive, constructive approach will really raise your standing in management's eyes. By embracing performance metrics and, when appropriate, suggesting additional performance metrics, you can show management that you are a team player.

Communicating Effectively in a Team Setting

The way people communicate in a team setting influences their relationships with their teammates and the effectiveness of the entire team. In successful teams, team players communicate freely and in ways that encourage trust and respect. Communication is bi-directional and involves active listening. Team members not only freely share information, thoughts, and opinions, they encourage their coworkers to share as well. For example, team players:

- Originate and propose new ideas, and actively encourage others to contribute their ideas.

- Articulate the team's goals, and help to clarify the team's goals as needed.

- Regard conflict as a normal part of team growth, and strive to resolve conflict in a positive way.

- Actively encourage teammates to participate in team activities, and assert the right of each and every teammate to be heard.

- Express their feelings about issues affecting the team in a positive way, and seek to understand how teammates feel about issues.

- Assume responsibility for guiding the team when their expertise or team player style is needed.

- Encourage team growth by describing the benefits to be gained by making a change.

Communication is the key that unlocks the door to teamwork.

AUTHOR UNKNOWN

Another form of communication in a team setting is feedback. **Feedback** is communication from one team member to another about how the member's behavior is meeting the expectations of the team. Feedback is appropriate and necessary when a person does something well, a person's behavior does not appear to be aligned with the team's mission or goals, or a conflict needs to be resolved.

To be effective, feedback must be delivered in a considerate, humane, and helping fashion. It must also be specific and provide the recipient with a clear understanding of how his or her behavior affects the team. Sarcastically mumbling, "It's about time you showed up" as a chronically late coworker passes your desk does nothing to address the situation. A more appropriate form of feedback would be to let the coworker know how it affects the team when he or she is late: "When you are late, our work stacks up and we cannot respond to our customers in the time frame they expect. It also affects our ability to take breaks, and so things can get a little stressful. We really need for you to make it in on time."

He has the right to criticize who has the heart to help.

ABRAHAM LINCOLN

It is the responsibility of the person providing feedback to ensure the recipient received the correct message. It is the recipient's responsibility to receive the feedback in the spirit with which it was delivered. In other words, if a recipient becomes defensive or angry upon receiving feedback, it is the sender's responsibility to clarify the point he or she is trying to make and find a more positive way to communicate. In turn, the recipient must accept the fact that the person providing feedback is trying to be helpful and must try to glean from the feedback a positive message.

Interestingly enough, even positive feedback can be received negatively. Some people try to do their best day in and day out, and they may view a seemingly arbitrary compliment from a coworker such as "good job" as frivolous and patronizing. For other people, basic courtesies, such as saying "please" and "thank you," are all they ask in return for a job well done. If you praise a coworker and she replies, "I'm just doing my job," you can surmise that she tends to be self-motivated. Remember, though, a person's needs can vary from one day to the next. Even a person who tends to scorn praise likes to get a pat on the back now and then. By listening actively to your coworkers, you can get a feel for their feedback preference.

For a team to be successful, everyone must participate in the feedback process:

- Employees must provide feedback to other employees.

- Employees must provide feedback to supervisors and team leaders.

- Supervisors and team leaders must provide feedback to employees.

- Supervisors and team leaders must provide feedback to other supervisors and team leaders.

This feedback process is particularly important in a service desk setting. Although diversity is a hallmark of a successful service desk team, unfortunately, it can quickly lead to division unless team members communicate by providing each other with feedback. Successful teams insist that all team members share their feelings, ideas, and knowledge with the rest of the team. It is unacceptable for team members to withhold information or ideas that could be useful to the team. This includes feedback that acknowledges the efforts of a team member or that will provide a team member with information needed to improve.

The purpose of feedback is to help individuals understand their strengths and weaknesses and provide insights into aspects of their work that can be improved. Effective feedback is constructive and based on behaviors, not personality.

Communication in a team setting can occur formally or informally. Formal communication can occur during a team meeting or in the form of a publication, such as a newsletter or a procedures guide. Informal communication can occur when two or more team members interact. Teams that communicate effectively strive to use the most appropriate method of communication for each situation. For example, announcement of a new team goal or a team member's promotion is handled formally to ensure that everyone affected by the change is kept informed and involved. On the other hand, discussion of a conflict with a coworker is handled privately and informally with only the affected parties and perhaps a trusted mediator. This enables the affected parties to feel more comfortable and thus more willing to communicate freely.

Many teams use technology to aid communication and collaboration. Often referred to as **groupware**, these **collaboration technologies** enable multiple users to work together on related tasks. Technologies that aid communication include email, instant messaging systems, audio conferencing, video conferencing, and web conferencing systems. Social networking services such as LinkedIn and Twitter are also used to aid communication. Technologies that aid collaboration include document-sharing systems, project management systems, wikis, and knowledge management systems. Microsoft SharePoint is a collection of products commonly used to aid collaboration.

 A **social network** is a community of people who share similar interests or activities. **Social networking services** are web-based services that provide members a variety of ways to interact. Facebook is one of the most widely used social networking services in the world.

Effective communication enables teamwork. It ensures everyone on the team knows what the team must do to succeed and what he or she must do to contribute to the team's success. Ineffective communication can cripple a team and permanently damage the relationships that exist between team members. It is the responsibility of each and every member of the service desk team to do all he or she can to enhance communication. Remember that a team player, by definition, contributes to the success of a team by communicating openly with teammates. Remember, too, that in an effective team setting, even conflict is viewed as a normal part of a team's functioning. Team members are encouraged to deal with conflict in a positive way by getting issues out on the table and seeking a viable solution.

What to Do When You Are New to a Team

Whether you are starting work at a new company, or simply joining a new team at the company where you work, there are a few actions you can take to quickly get oriented. Remember that when joining a new team, you have to earn your place by working hard and showing a willingness to work with others, even if you have been hired to serve as the resident expert on a particular subject. Respect and trust must be earned. You cannot assume you know what the team needs, and you cannot decide what role you will play. The measures listed in Figure 8-5 can help you get settled into a new team as quickly as possible.

- Meet and get to know your teammates.
- Gain an understanding of the "big picture."
- Learn the lingo.
- Determine exactly what is expected of you.
- Volunteer.

Figure 8-5 Tips for settling into a new team

Meet and Get to Know Your Teammates

As you are introduced to each of your teammates upon joining the team, make an effort to go beyond simple introductions and get to know your teammates. During your first week or two, make it a point to have a one-to-one conversation with all of your teammates. Shake their hand. Ask them what their role is, what their area of expertise is, and what projects they are working on. Ask them to help you understand how the team operates. Let them know you are looking forward to working together. Even a brief conversation will build rapport and help each of you settle into a positive working relationship.

Gain an Understanding of the "Big Picture"

Ask your coworkers and team leader or supervisor questions, and ask for any documented policies and procedures. Make sure you receive a copy of the service desk's mission and its goals. Make sure you understand the factors that are critical to the team's success. In other words, make sure you understand why the team exists to begin with. You also want to gain an understanding of who your customers are and where the service desk fits into the overall support organization. Ask for copies of organization charts, or ask someone to draw a diagram that shows you how the service desk relates to other departments, such as level two support groups.

Learn the Lingo

Every company, and even each team within a company, has its own vocabulary. It may have unique naming standards for systems and network components or use a lot of acronyms. If available, get a glossary of terms and use it to learn the language of your new team. If a glossary of terms is not available, you may want to start one. Every time you hear a new term, write it down. Fill in the definitions as you go along. The next new team member will greatly appreciate your efforts.

 Learn what acronyms and jargon mean, and avoid using them or define them first when communicating with customers.

Determine Exactly What Is Expected of You

It does not matter how hard you are working if you are not working on the right things. Failing to do what is expected of you can also create a bad first impression that may be hard to overcome. Ask your supervisor or team leader for a detailed outline of what you should be doing during the first few months that you are with the team. It takes time to learn a team's culture, and it takes time to learn all of the processes, procedures, and tools you will be using to do your work. You cannot fully contribute until you understand how the team operates and the role you are expected to play. Let your supervisor or team leader know you want to be a team player and that you want to make a contribution.

Volunteer

Although you want to resist the temptation to take on more work than you can handle, volunteering is an excellent way to get involved with a team. If you see an area where your expertise can be put to work, offer it, or you can offer to help out with a social or charity event that the team may be planning. Volunteering is an excellent way to let your personal interests and unique talents shine through.

Joining a team can be intimidating, especially when you are joining one that has been working together for a while. You may be tempted initially to keep your head down, do what you are told, and stay out of people's way. You will never become a part of the team that way. A crucial element of teamwork is not only knowing what you are supposed to be doing, but also knowing what your teammates' roles and responsibilities are as well. When you first join a team, it may feel as if you have blinders over your eyes. By asking questions and learning how your contributions fit into the bigger picture, you can remove the blinders and see clearly what needs to be done.

Developing Positive Working Relationships with Teammates

A service desk can be a hectic place to work. On the other hand, working in a service desk can be extremely rewarding. You have the opportunity to help other people. You can work with technology. You get to solve problems and continuously learn new skills and acquire new knowledge. Life really is good and you have the opportunity—the choice—every day of making it great. During tough times, remember that you are not alone. You are a member of a team. The following tips are designed to help you put your best foot forward in a team setting. Like the tips aimed at helping you get settled into a new team, these tips help build the respect and trust that are needed in a team setting.

- Get to know your teammates.
- Extend common courtesies to your coworkers.
- Listen with interest to your teammates.
- Inquire about and acknowledge your teammates' feelings.
- Share your feelings openly and honestly.
- Be willing to learn and teach.
- Recognize your teammates' achievements.
- Ask for help when you really need it.

Figure 8-6 Tips for working with a team

Get to Know Your Teammates

You should know your teammates well enough to know their strengths and weaknesses relative to the goals of your team. You should also know what your teammates view as the priorities in their lives. If a teammate's children are very important to him, learn a little about his children and ask him how they are doing now and then. If a teammate is training for a marathon, ask her how the training is going and wish her well just before the big day. You do not have to be best friends. Simply acknowledge the fact that you work side by side with this fellow member of the human race day in and day out. Acknowledge and embrace each person's uniqueness. Only then can you expect them to embrace your uniqueness.

Extend Common Courtesies to Your Coworkers

Simply put, say, "Good morning, everyone" and "Have a good night, everybody" when you walk in and out of the door each day. Some workers slip in and out of work each day in hopes that no one will notice that they have come or gone. Unfortunately, this approach can quickly lead to animosity. Say, "Please" to your coworkers when you ask for their help and "Thank you" when you receive it. These simple phrases let your coworkers know that you respect and appreciate their time and effort. Offer to help a teammate who appears to be struggling with a difficult task. Some people are hesitant to ask for help, but most will appreciate and accept a sincere offer. Remember that simple courtesies go a long way in creating positive working relationships and positive personal relationships as well.

Listen with Interest to Your Teammates

Listen to your teammates as actively as you do your customers. The nice thing about communicating with teammates is that you often can communicate face to face. Be considerate. Resist the temptation to glance at your cell phone or tablet, work on your computer, or perform some other task when speaking with a coworker. Stop what you are doing. Make eye contact. Be attentive. If a conversation becomes too personal or lengthy, politely let your teammate know that you need to go back to work.

Inquire About and Acknowledge Your Teammates' Feelings

If a usually upbeat coworker seems to be having a bad day, ask if there is anything that you can do. This does not mean you should become a busybody. Just let your coworkers know that you care about their well-being and that if there is anything you can do to help, you are willing. You do not have to coddle people, but give them your support.

Share Your Feelings Openly and Honestly

No one feels comfortable around a person who has a scowl on his or her face and yet insists that nothing is wrong, or a person who is insecure and lacking direction and yet is unwilling to ask for help. Furthermore, no one likes to hear, after an extended time, that he or she has inadvertently offended a teammate but has not been given an opportunity to repair the relationship. By sharing your feelings openly and honestly with your teammates, you create a climate of trust. Your teammates will learn to view you as fair and reasonable and will respond by being open and honest with you in return.

Be Willing to Learn and Teach

Some people set out to learn something new every day, a philosophy that is easily quenched in a technical support setting. Some people, unfortunately, think they know it all. Others are content to get by knowing only the bare essentials, and defer to others when problems become complex. Still others are unwilling to ask questions—they fear they will look stupid or they will lose their standing as an expert. A service desk setting is an excellent place to be a perpetual student. Technology is constantly changing. Customer needs and the needs of your business are constantly changing. You will never be bored working in a service desk setting if you have an inherent sense of curiosity and are willing to say, "What is that?"

You must also be willing to share your knowledge and experience with your coworkers. It used to be considered "job security" if a person was the only one who possessed certain knowledge or experience. In this day and age, companies are looking for people who willingly share their knowledge and cross-train their coworkers. Techniques include contributing to blogs, wikis, and the knowledge management system; developing scripts and checklists; presenting what you learned in a recent training class at a team meeting; and so forth. Keep in mind also that if you are spending all of your time answering questions and handling difficult incidents in a given area of expertise, you may not have the time, or the energy, you need to pursue new skills. Spread your knowledge around.

Recognize Your Teammates' Achievements

Everyone wants to be appreciated for the work that he or she does and for the things he or she accomplishes. Sincerely congratulate your teammates when they successfully complete a project or solve an exceptionally complex problem. Encourage a coworker who is studying for a certification test or who is gearing up for final exams. Teammates who are just getting started especially need to be encouraged. The first steps in any endeavor are often the hardest, and teammates who are trying to acquire new skills need your encouragement and support. A positive side effect of recognizing and acknowledging your teammates' achievements is that they will give you positive feedback in return.

Ask for Help When You Really Need It

A team cannot perform well unless each of its members is performing well. In a team setting, you cannot, and you should not, try to do everything on your own. Asking for help when you need it is not a sign of weakness. It says that you want to do things in the most efficient, effective way possible so that you contribute to the team's success. Keep in mind, though, that your teammates are just as busy as you are and may be struggling with new challenges as well. Do not be lazy. It is not okay to ask for help simply because you have procrastinated or forgotten something or because you want to get out of doing your homework. Effort in a team setting is as much about attitude as it is about skills and ability. Let your *can do* attitude shine through. Remember, too, to help your teammates when they really need it.

Don't worry if you're feeling confused. Worry if you're not.

Tom Peters

If you want to work on a successful team that achieves its goals and reaps the associated rewards, you cannot be an inactive or ordinary team player. You also cannot leave it up to the team leader or to the other members of the team. Each and every member of a team has to contribute. This includes and begins with you. Know your role and know your strengths. Get clear on what is expected of you, and do your best to give the team what it needs. Remember, there is no *I* in team.

Chapter Summary

- Technical support lends itself to a team setting because no single person can know everything about all the products supported or provide all the support customers need. The demands are too great. A team is a group of people organized to work together toward the achievement of a goal. A team player is a person who contributes to the team's success by cooperating freely and communicating openly with his or her teammates.

- Assembling a group of team players does not make a successful team. To be successful, a team must share a clear sense of purpose, leadership, diversity, openness and trust, and positive relationships with other support groups. It must also have an open, pleasant working environment and a willingness to work through the stages of growth—forming, storming, norming, and performing—that all groups experience on their way to becoming a team. To reach the performing stage, teams must learn to work through conflict and achieve a consensus.

- Being a team player requires personal commitment and a willingness to put the needs of the team ahead of your own. This does not mean you have to give up your individuality. For a team to succeed, each team member must understand that he or she has a unique role to play. The role a person plays is a sum of his or her skills, knowledge, experience, and personal style. Team player styles include challenger, collaborator, communicator, and contributor. Each of these styles serves a purpose, and each shines brightest at different times during the stages of a team's growth. Your challenge as a team player is to determine your personal style and use the strengths of that style to contribute to your team. You can also strive to embrace the strengths of the other styles, thus increasing your ability to contribute to the team.

- The service desk's mission and goals determine the role the service desk plays within the support organization. Each and every member of the service desk team must embrace the service desk's mission and achieve his or her individual performance goals for the service desk team to achieve its goals. Data is needed to measure and manage both team and individual performance. Service desk analysts often create needed data by using tools such as an automatic call distributor (ACD), email response management system, and incident management system. Techniques such as customer satisfaction surveys and monitoring may also be used to capture information about an analyst's performance. In addition to measuring performance, service desk managers and staff can use the data these tools and techniques provide to identify ways they can improve.

- The ways people communicate in a team setting influence their relationships with their teammates and the effectiveness of the entire team. Team members must freely share information, thoughts, and opinions, and they must encourage their coworkers to share as well. Another form of communication in a team setting is feedback. To be effective, feedback must be delivered in a considerate, humane, and helping fashion. Ineffective communication can cripple a team and permanently damage the relationships that exist between team members. Effective communication ensures everyone on the team knows what the team must do to succeed and what he or she must do to contribute to the team's success.

- A service desk can be a hectic place to work. On the other hand, working in a service desk can be extremely rewarding. During tough times, remember that you are not alone. You are a member of a team. If you want to work on a successful team that achieves its goals and reaps the associated rewards, you cannot be an inactive or ordinary team player. You have to contribute. Remember, there is no *I* in team.

Key Terms

application of training investments—A comparison of an analyst's resolution percent and reopen percent before and after attending training.

availability—The length of time an analyst was signed on to the ACD compared to the length of time the analyst was scheduled to be signed on.

average call duration—The average length of time required to handle a call.

average handle time—The average length of time required to handle an email.

average number of exchanges—The average number of email exchanges required to resolve an incident.

collaboration technologies—Technologies that enable multiple users to work together on related tasks; also known as *groupware.*

consensus—An opinion or position reached by all of a team's members or by a majority of its members.

DevOps—A cultural and professional movement that emphasizes communication, collaboration, and integration between software developers (Dev) and IT Operations professionals (Ops).

early life support (ELS)—The stage in the service life cycle that occurs at the end of a deployment and before the service is fully accepted into operation (ITIL definition).

emotional intelligence—A form of intelligence relating to the emotional side of life.

feedback—Communication from one team member to another about how the member's behavior is meeting the expectations of the team.

first contact resolution rate—The percentage of contacts resolved during a customer's initial contact compared to the total number of contacts received at the service desk for a given period of time.

groupware—See *collaboration technologies.*

idle state—An ACD state that occurs when an analyst is logged on to the ACD but is not accepting calls.

318 **individual performance goals**—Measurable objectives for analysts that support the service desk mission.

326 **mediator**—A negotiator who helps individuals resolve disputes.

331 **reopen percent**—The percentage of closed incidents that had to be opened back up within a given time period.

331 **resolution percent**—The percentage of incidents an analyst resolved compared to the total number of incidents that the analyst handled during a given time period.

316 **service desk goals**—Measurable objectives that support the service desk mission.

318 **service desk mission**—A written statement describing the customers the service desk serves, the types of services the service desk provides, and how the service desk delivers those services.

335 **social network**—A community of people who share similar interests or activities.

335 **social networking service**—A web-based service that provides members a variety of ways to interact.

316 **team**—A group of people organized to work together toward the achievement of a goal.

316 **team player**—A person who contributes to the team's success by cooperating freely and communicating openly with his or her teammates.

331 **time idle**—The average length of time an analyst was idle during a given period of time.

319 **virtual team**—A group of people who work across time, space, and organizational boundaries.

331 **wrap-up mode**—A feature that prevents the ACD from routing a new inbound call to an analyst's extension.

331 **wrap-up time**—The average length of time an analyst was in wrap-up mode during a given period of time.

Review Questions

1. What is a team?

2. How does a team player contribute to a team's success?

3. What are the reasons technical support lends itself to a team setting?

4. What are the five characteristics of a successful team?

5. List the three components of a service desk mission.

6. Why is it important for a service desk to have a mission and goals that are clearly defined?

7. What is a key to success for multigenerational teams?

8. Why is it important for the service desk to have a positive working relationship with other support groups?

9. List and describe three ways the service desk supports the goals of DevOps.

10. List the four stages of development reflected in the Tuckman Teamwork Model.

11. How does the role of the team leader change as a team moves through these stages of growth?

12. Typically, when is a consensus reached?

13. Why does conflict usually occur in a team setting?

14. What should team members focus on when handling conflict in a team setting?

15. What must you remember about the other person's point of view when you are faced with a conflict?

16. When is it appropriate to avoid a conflict?

17. What qualities influence the role a person plays on a team?

18. List the four types of team player styles.

19. When can a team player style become ineffective?

20. Why is it important to determine your personal team player style?

21. List three characteristics of emotional intelligence.

22. What are the five most common tools and techniques that companies use to measure individual performance?

23. What are three ways that service desk management and staff can use metrics?

24. Why is communication important in a team setting?

25. What is feedback?

26. How must feedback be delivered to be effective?

27. What are two ways that teams use technology? Provide examples for your answers.

28. Whose responsibility is it to enhance communication in a team setting?

29. What are five things you can do to get settled into a new team?

30. What five basic courtesies, discussed in this chapter, will help you to have a positive working relationship with your teammates?

31. Why is it important to ask for help when you really need it?

Discussion Questions

1. Many people believe that because they have played on a sports team for years, they know how to be a team player at work. Is this a fair comparison? As a prelude to this discussion, consider taking an assessment. To locate assessments on the web, search for topics such as "team player assessment."

2. There is an old expression: "One bad apple spoils the bunch." Discuss traits that can get in the way of teamwork, such as negativity and insecurity. Develop a list of techniques you can use to deal with negative, insecure, and otherwise difficult people.

3. A common belief is that to achieve a consensus, someone must win and someone must lose. Another belief is that the majority rules, whether or not everyone on the team has been heard. Are these beliefs valid? Discuss the characteristics of a consensus decision, and then discuss ways to achieve a consensus in a team or life setting.

4. It is possible to encounter four generations of workers in the workforce: Seniors, Baby Boomers, Generation X, and Generation Y. Discuss how members of each generation view work and the workplace. Develop a list of ways these generations can benefit each other and avoid conflict.

Hands-On Projects

1. **Evaluate a team's success.** Interview a friend, family member, or classmate who works in a team setting. Describe for this person the characteristics discussed in this chapter of a successful team. Ask the following questions about the person's team:

    a. Does he or she work for a successful team? That is, is the team fulfilling its mission and achieving its goals?

    b. If yes, does the team exhibit all of the characteristics discussed in this chapter? How did the team develop these characteristics?

    c. If no, what characteristics could be improved to make the team more successful?

    Prepare a brief report that presents any conclusions you can draw from this interview.

2. **Determine a company's culture.** Visit the web site for the company where you work or where you would like to work. Alternatively, type "corporate culture" in your web browser and go to the site of a company that offers information about its culture. From the web site, determine the following:

    a. What is the company's mission or purpose?

    b. What are the company's core values?

    c. What is the company's philosophy toward its customers, and its employees and their work environment?

    Write a one-page report that summarizes your findings.

3. **Discuss the stages of team development.** Use your school's online message or discussion board to conduct a roundtable discussion within your class about the stages of team development. First, have each person in your class who is a member

of a team of any kind assess the stage of development that his or her team has achieved. They may belong to a team at work, or they may be a member of a sports team or a study group. Next, ask all of your classmates who are in, for example, the forming stage to relate their current experience to the description of the forming stage discussed in this chapter. For example:

a. What insight into the workings of their team have they gained while studying this chapter?

b. Given what they have learned in this chapter, how do they feel they can help their team move forward or improve?

c. What, if any, conclusions can you and your classmates draw from this discussion before moving on to the next stage of development?

Apply these questions to each of the four stages of team development. Briefly summarize the conclusions of your class. After you have finished this discussion, think of your class as a team. As a team, determine the stage of team development your class has achieved. Briefly outline the steps your team must take to achieve the next stage.

4. **Review your approach to managing conflict.** Conflict is an inevitable part of human interaction. Think about a conflict that you have faced or are facing at home, school, or work. Review the tips discussed in this chapter concerning how to resolve conflict in a constructive manner. Use these tips to assess your ability to manage conflict in a positive way. Using your own words, make note of one or two of the tips you can use to improve your conflict resolution skills.

5. **Discuss team player styles.** Assemble a team of three to five classmates or use your school's online message or discussion board. For each of the four team player styles described in this chapter, discuss the following:
    a. How does a team benefit by having a person who exhibits this team player style?

    b. How is a team affected if a team player who exhibits this team player style becomes ineffective?

Compare the results of your discussion to the findings of other teams in the class.

6. **Learn about personality testing.** On the web, search for topics such as "personality testing," "Myers-Briggs Type Indicator," or "Motivational Appraisal of Personal Potential." Determine how companies use personality testing and how you personally can use personality testing. Locate and take a free personality test. Write a short paper that describes how personality tests are used and what you learned about yourself by taking a personality test.

7. **Learn about emotional intelligence testing.** On the web, search for topics such as "emotional intelligence testing" or "emotional intelligence quotient (EIQ) testing." Determine how emotional intelligence contributes to success in both your professional and personal lives. Locate and take a free emotional intelligence test.

Write a short paper that describes how emotional intelligence tests are used and what you learned about yourself by taking an emotional intelligence test.

8. **Learn how team and individual performance are measured.** Interview a friend, family member, or classmate who works in a team setting. Ask this person the following questions:

   a. How is your team's performance measured?

   b. How is your individual performance measured?

   c. Do you feel that your manager has clearly communicated what you must do to contribute to the team's goals?

   d. Do you feel that your manager effectively uses metrics to identify improvement opportunities as well as to monitor performance?

   e. What techniques do you use to communicate your achievements to management?

   f. How do you feel about the tools you are required to use and the amount of data that you are required to provide management with regard to your performance? If you feel it is a burden, why?

   Prepare a brief report that presents any conclusions you can draw from this discussion.

9. **Assess your communication skills.** Prepare a list of the effective ways to communicate in a team setting discussed in this chapter. For each skill listed, rate yourself on a scale of 1 to 5, where 1 is very weak and 5 is very strong. Then, further assess your communication skills by answering the following questions:

   a. In what areas are your communication skills strong?

   b. In what areas can you improve your communication skills?

   Given what you have learned in this chapter, how can you improve your communication skills?

10. **Provide feedback.** The set of questions that follows is designed to enable constructive peer feedback (Thomas L. Quick, *Successful Team Building (The WorkSmart Series)*, AMACOM, 1992, p. 92). It could also be used to perform a self-assessment or by a team leader to evaluate each member of a team. Use this peer feedback form to:

    a. Assess your skills as a team member. You can apply these questions to your behavior at work, as a member of a sports team or study group, or as a member of your class.

    b. Provide feedback to a team member. Again, this may be a coworker at work, a member of a sports team or study group to which you belong, or a classmate.

Peer Feedback Evaluation

In each category, circle the number that you believe best represents the usual behavior of [*name of team member*]:

Initiates ideas

10	9	8	7	6	5	4	3	2	1
Frequently offers ideas and solutions			Initiates only moderately, but supports initiating by others				Tends to let others take most of the initiative and often reserves support		

Facilitates the introduction of new ideas

10	9	8	7	6	5	4	3	2	1
Actively encourages others to contribute without worrying about agreement			Provides support for ideas with which he or she agrees				Often resists the introduction of new ideas; looks for flaws		

Is directed toward group goals

10	9	8	7	6	5	4	3	2	1
Often helps to identify and clarify goals for the group			Sometimes helps the group define its goals; sometimes confuses it with side issues				Tends to place priority on own goals at the expense of the group's		

Manages conflict

10	9	8	7	6	5	4	3	2	1
Regards conflict as helpful in promoting different perspectives and in sharpening the differences in views			Generally disengages from conflict				Tries to smooth over points of disagreement; plays a pacifying role		

Demonstrates support for others

10	9	8	7	6	5	4	3	2	1
Actively encourages the participation of others and asserts their right to be heard			Encourages certain members part of the time, but does not encourage all members				Does not offer support or encouragement for other members		

Reveals feelings

10	9	8	7	6	5	4	3	2	1
Openly expresses feelings about issues; ensures that feelings parallel views			Sometimes disguises feelings or tries to keep them to self				Denies both the existence of own feelings and the importance of expressing them in the group		

Displays openness

10	9	8	7	6	5	4	3	2	1
Freely and clearly expresses self on issues so others know where he or she stands			Sometimes employs tact and speaks circumspectly to camouflage real views				Is vague about views on issues, even contradictory when pressed		

Confronts issues and behavior									
10	9	8	7	6	5	4	3	2	1
Freely expresses views on difficult issues and on team members nonproductive behavior			Is cautious about taking a visible position on issues and on others' actions without first ensuring widespread approval				Actively avoids issues and any conflict by talking about "safe" issues that are irrelevant to current group work		

Shares leadership									
10	9	8	7	6	5	4	3	2	1
Assumes responsibility for guiding the group when own resources are needed or when problems lend themselves to his or her solving			Competes with other members for visibility and influence				Dominates group discussions and exerts disproportionate influence that subverts group progress		

Exhibits proper demeanor in decision-making process									
10	9	8	7	6	5	4	3	2	1
Actively seeks a full exploration of all feasible options			Becomes impatient with a deliberate pace in generating and evaluating all options when he or she does not concur with them				Moves strongly toward early closure of discussion to vote on a preferred option		

Case Projects

1. **Service Desk Team Leader.** You were just promoted to team leader of your service desk. Research the subject of leadership and what it takes to be an effective team leader. Go to the library, search the web, or speak to people whom you respect and think of as leaders. Develop a list of three leadership qualities that you think are most important and that you want to develop. Present your list to the class. If you like, include a quotation about leadership that you consider meaningful.

2. **Recognizing Achievement.** You are the manager of a small service desk that is starting to perform well as a team. You have a very small budget, and it is difficult for you to give people monetary rewards when they accomplish good things. You would like the members of the team to acknowledge each other's accomplishments and not always look to you to dole out rewards. Using your school's online message or discussion board, conduct a brainstorming session with your classmates and identify creative ways the team can celebrate individual and team accomplishments.

3. **Back to Basics.** You recently began working as a service desk analyst. The service desk is very large, and you are trying to become more conscious about using common courtesies, such as saying, "Please," "Thank you," "Good morning," and "Good night," in an effort to build a positive working relationship with your new coworkers. You are also trying to make it a habit to use these basic courtesies whenever you interact with other people, whether they are friends, family members, coworkers, or even strangers you encounter during your day. For the next week, use these basic courtesies whenever you interact with others. Observe your feelings when people do not use these basic courtesies when interacting with you. Notice how you can influence others to use these basic courtesies by using them yourself. Discuss your observations with your classmates.

CHAPTER 9

Minimizing Stress and Avoiding Burnout

In this chapter you will learn:

◎ The causes of stress

◎ Effective coping skills to reduce the negative effects of stress in your life

◎ Proven techniques to manage your time wisely and achieve personal success

◎ The connection between time and stress management

Customer service is a stressful occupation. Because of this, service desk personnel need good self-management skills in addition to good business skills, soft skills, and technical skills. Self-management skills are the skills, such as stress and time management, that people need to complete their work effectively, feel job satisfaction, and avoid frustration or burnout. Self-management skills also include the ability to get and stay organized as well as to continuously and quickly learn new skills.

The support industry is particularly fast paced and things are never "normal." If you have good self-management skills, you will be able to enjoy the variety of responsibilities and challenging situations that a service desk offers. Self-management skills provide a solid foundation upon which you will always be able to draw regardless of how hectic the service desk becomes. Furthermore, skills such as stress management and time management are excellent life skills that will serve you well regardless of your chosen profession.

Reducing the Negative Effects of Stress

Stress is a normal and unavoidable side effect of living. **Stress** is the adaptation of our bodies and minds to the demands of life. In other words, stress is the wear and tear our bodies and minds experience as a result of life's ups and downs. When properly managed, stress is an excellent source of motivation and can be a positive part of life. Have you ever experienced the enormous sense of satisfaction that comes when you avert a crisis or meet a deadline? Have you ever felt the adrenaline rush that accompanies the attainment of a long sought-after goal? Eustress helped you to achieve that positive feeling. **Eustress** is a healthy form of stress that helps keep you motivated and enables you to feel a sense of accomplishment. Positive stress instills in you the need to stay focused and enables you to think creatively about how to accomplish your goals. It encourages you to work harder to accomplish your goals or to make positive changes in your life.

Conversely, high levels of stress can sap your motivation and become a negative feeling. Have you ever been so overwhelmed by a task that you simply gave up? Have you ever been so anxious about an upcoming event, such as a job interview, that you sabotaged yourself by staying out late the night before or leaving late for your appointment? Pessimism, being a perfectionist, taking on more than you can realistically accomplish, and failing to plan ahead are also characteristics of self-sabotage that lead to distress. **Distress** is a negative form of stress that causes strain, anxiety, or suffering.

For stress to be a positive part of life, it must be managed. Too little stress can lead to complacency, hopelessness, and boredom. Too little stress may be a result of choosing to go through life without goals or being unwilling to take risks. It can also be a result of avoiding situations that can cause stress such as trying new things or meeting new people. On the other hand, too much stress can lead to anxiety and panic. Too much stress may be a result of choosing to avoid proven techniques for managing your time and emotions. It can also be a result of failing to relieve the physical symptoms of stress. Either extreme can lead to health problems. According to one estimate, 75 to 90 percent of all visits to primary care physicians are for stress-related problems ("The Effects of Stress on Your Body" *www.webmd.com/mental-health/effects-of-stress-on-your-body*, accessed 1/9/14). Health problems that can be related to or aggravated by too much or too little stress include:

- Alcoholism
- Back and muscle aches
- Depression
- Drug abuse

- Eating disorders, such as anorexia and bulimia
- Serious illness, including heart disease, ulcers, chronic diarrhea, and cancer
- Fatigue
- Headaches, including migraine headaches
- Sleeplessness
- Low energy and concentration levels
- Premature aging

To manage stress and minimize its effects, you must first determine the causes of stress in your life.

Determining the Causes of Stress

A service desk is a particularly stressful place to work because analysts are exposed to multiple sources of stress. Figure 9-1 lists the sources of stress analysts may experience. People respond to each of these sources of stress in different ways.

- Institutional stressors
- Situational stressors
- Personal stressors

Figure 9-1   Sources of stress

Institutional Stressors

Institutional stressors are the stressors that accompany the type of business you are in or the state of the organization where you work. Nonprofit organizations often lack the financial resources of for-profit companies. Small companies often lack the redundancy in their workforce that is found in larger companies. Start-up companies often lack the infrastructure and discipline found in more mature companies. Institutional stressors exist anywhere you work. Your challenge is to figure out which institutional stressors you want to experience. For example, some people enjoy working for a start-up company. They relish being in on the ground floor and helping the company grow and flourish. They love the seat-of-the-pants approach that start-up companies tend to require. On the other hand, some people prefer a more stable environment and find the dynamic nature of a start-up company overwhelming. They may want to work for a company that has a proven track record or that offers a greater sense of job security. They may prefer the formality and discipline of a more mature company. You have very little ability to influence institutional stressors. They simply come with the territory. You can, however, choose where you work very carefully.

Situational Stressors

Situational stressors are the stressors that accompany the type of work you do. People who work in customer service must handle difficult customer situations. People who work in technical support are constantly exposed to new technologies and must continuously learn new skills. People who work in a service desk setting must be able to handle constant interruptions and must be able to juggle a number of outstanding issues at one time. Figure 9-2 lists some of the factors that cause situational stress in a service desk setting.

- Conflict with coworkers

- Difficult customer situations

- Heavy workload

- Inability to predict or control workload

- Insufficient training

- Insufficient time for training

- Insufficient tools such as incident management systems, knowledge management systems, and remote control systems

- Insufficient knowledge resources such as tools, procedures, and resident experts

- Interruptions

- Lack of career opportunity

- Lack of management commitment and direction

- Poor product quality in terms of the products supported by the service desk

- Response time restrictions

- Understaffing

Figure 9-2   Factors that cause situational stress in a service desk

Like institutional stressors, situational stressors exist anywhere you work. What you must determine is whether you have the attitude and the skills needed to handle these stressful situations. Some people enjoy handling difficult customer situations and view them as a personal challenge. They strive to turn a dissatisfied customer into one who raves about the service he or she received from the service desk. They also work hard to develop and continually refine the skills needed to handle these difficult situations. Other people would rather not interact directly with customers and lack the skills to do so. These people typically prefer to be in more of a supporting role.

You have a greater ability to influence situational stressors than institutional stressors by developing a positive attitude and skills. You can considerably reduce the amount of situational stress you experience by, for example, striking negative phrases from your vocabulary or using the techniques described in this book to become a better listener or to communicate more effectively. In other words, you can control the amount of stress you experience by choosing to deal positively with the sources of stress.

Stress is not what happens to us. It's our response to what happens. And response is something we can choose.

MAUREEN KILLORAN

Personal Stressors

Personal stressors are the stressors that accompany your individual life experiences. You may have lost your job or you may be starting a new job or planning a wedding. You may drive through heavy traffic each day to get to work or school. You may be having financial problems, or you may be dealing with an illness in your family. You may simply be fatigued from your physical fitness regimen and as a result have difficulty keeping up with your work.

CASE STUDY: Working for a Bad Boss

Working for a bad boss can be extremely stressful. A bad boss can squelch your motivation and undermine your efforts to advance your career. When working for a bad boss, use the opportunity to (1) focus on the goals of your company, (2) make yourself as marketable as possible, and (3) commit yourself to your personal goals and relaxation. If your boss fails to clearly communicate what you are expected to do, ask for clarification on the goals of your company and ensure your actions contribute to those goals. If your boss is taking credit for your work or seems unwilling to help you advance, get to know people in other departments or at other companies, and tell them about the good things that you and your team are doing. If your boss does not hesitate to point out your mistakes but rarely acknowledges your accomplishments, put your accomplishments in writing and ask that they be incorporated into your personnel file and considered at review time. If your boss will not authorize training, seek self-study opportunities. If your boss expects you to regularly work overtime, do your best to arrange your schedule in such a way that you can still participate in your exercise program or hobby. Simply put, figure out what you can do.

Table 9-1 lists some of the many factors that can cause personal stress. It is important to note that even positive life experiences, such as getting promoted or having a child, can cause stress. The good news is that you have the greatest ability to influence personal stressors (versus institutional or situational stressors). You can determine ways to either eliminate the stressor or minimize its effects on your life.

Stressor	Occurs
Change	When you alter anything important in your life, such as getting married, moving, changing jobs
Chemical	When you abuse chemicals such as drugs and alcohol; caffeine and nicotine are common chemical stressors
Commuting	As you travel to and from work
Decision	When you have too many choices to make and not enough time to make them
Disease	As a result of short- or long-term illnesses
Emotional	When you experience emotions such as sorrow, fear, or anxiety
Environmental	When your surroundings cause inefficiency or discomfort such as when your office is run down or poorly designed
Financial	As a result of your efforts to sustain your lifestyle
Pain	When you experience aches and pains from new and old injuries or diseases
Physical	When you overextend yourself such as if you exercise too strenuously or get inadequate sleep
Social	When you interact with other people
Work	When you experience tension and pressure on the job

Table 9-1   Factors that can cause personal stress

Having all these layers of stressors piled on top of each other can cause you to feel completely overwhelmed. To deal effectively with the stress in your life, take the time to identify the real source or sources of your stress. For example, when you are feeling exceptionally stressed, ask yourself the following questions:

Do you like the business you are in?

Do you like the work that you do?

Are you happy with your personal life?

There may be times when you answer "No" to one or more of these questions. That is normal. If you answer "No" to all of these questions all of the time, however, it is time to make a change. Otherwise, you may be risking your health. Identifying the sources of stress in your life will not make the stress go away, but it will enable you to develop a plan of action and a stress management program that works for you.

Developing Effective Coping Mechanisms

People's ability to influence the effect that a stressor has on their life depends on the source of the stress. Some stressors you can influence. For other stressors, you must either learn to live with them or find a way to minimize their effects. You can minimize the effects of stress by managing how you respond. Two key factors that affect how people respond to stress are (1) how much control a person has over a stressor, and (2) whether a person chooses to be exposed to a stressor.

How Much Control a Person Has over a Stressor

Some people want to control every aspect of their lives and become stressed when they feel they cannot control the events that occur throughout the day. The reality is that sometimes matters are beyond your control. For example, people working in a service desk cannot control the number of contacts they will receive on any given day. They can be proactive and try to manage the number of contacts they will receive, but they must also accept that a variable contact volume is a service desk characteristic. However, service desk analysts can be as prepared as possible for that variable contact volume by making it a habit to get focused. They can also strive to stay organized so they can work effectively when busy times hit. Remember, you may not be able to control what happens around you or what other people do, but there is always something you can do. You can choose whether or not to expose yourself to a stressor.

Whether a Person Chooses to Be Exposed to a Stressor

If you want to manage and minimize the stress in your life, you must understand this very important concept: *You choose the stress you experience each and every day.* When you cannot control a situation, you have two choices:

- Change the situation.
- Control the way you respond to the situation.

Say your drive to and from work each day has become unbearable. You have two choices. You can change the situation by changing the hours that you work so you arrive before the heaviest traffic begins, leaving for work after the heaviest traffic subsides, looking for a job that is closer to your home, or looking for housing that is closer to where you work. On the other hand, if you love where you work and live and you like the hours that you work, you can choose to accept the stressor and control the way you respond to the situation.

Once you choose to accept a stressor, stop complaining about it. Complaining simply makes you unhappy and may even magnify the stressor in your mind. Complaining may also annoy the people to whom you are complaining. Next, determine what you can do to minimize the effect the stressor is having on your life. You can buy soothing CDs and audiobooks that you can listen to while driving to work. Or, you can record study notes for a class you are taking and listen to them. You can also leave a little earlier than necessary each day so you do not become stressed if you encounter an accident on the way to work that causes a delay. Be positive. Continuously remind yourself that you are accepting this stressor for a reason.

There are two primary choices in life: to accept conditions as they exist, or accept the responsibility for changing them.

DENIS WAITLEY

Accepting responsibility for the stress you are experiencing is the most important step you can take in terms of coping with stress and avoiding burnout. **Burnout** is the physical and emotional exhaustion that is caused by long-term stress. People often experience burnout when they are not managing their stress day in and day out. To manage stress effectively, remember that you are not a victim. There is always something that you can do. You can determine the best course of action to take by staying calm and in control. If you feel yourself losing control and becoming incapable of making a good decision, use the following calming techniques, which were discussed in Chapter 5:

- Take a deep breath.
- Take a sip of water.
- Use positive imagery.
- Use positive self-talk.

These techniques help you to manage how you respond to stressors when they occur. Positive imagery and positive self-talk are particularly effective ways to handle ongoing stress and avoid burnout. For example, you may be going to school and holding down a full- or part-time job. Such a busy schedule may seem overwhelming at times. To minimize the stress, identify why you are choosing to expose yourself to such considerable stress. Do you want to get a better job? Do you want to change careers? Do you want to pay off your school loan by the end of the year? Whatever the reason, use positive imagery to stay focused on your goals. Imagine yourself working in the profession of your dreams. Imagine a gift that you will buy for yourself once your school loan is paid off. Periodically take a deep breath, and use positive self-talk to remind yourself that you can do it. You can and you will achieve your goals. These techniques will help you feel more in control and more able to handle the stress in your life.

How you respond to the people in both your personal and professional life can considerably influence your stress. To minimize stress, figure out how to get along with the people in your life. Recognize that although you cannot change another person, you can change how, or if, you interact with that person. If a person's habits or actions drive you crazy, practice deep breathing or consciously take sips of water when he or she is around. If a person makes you feel insecure or uncomfortable, use positive imagery and positive self-talk to boost your self-esteem and assert your rights. Work hard to become a better listener, and communicate what you want and need from others. You cannot change another person, but you can change the relationship you have with that person by figuring out what *you* can do to get along. You may find that by changing your behavior, you prompt a change in the other person's behavior as well.

Stress is a normal part of life and you cannot—and should not try to—eliminate it altogether. You can learn to identify the causes of stress in your life and develop effective coping mechanisms. You can also learn to use stress as a positive, motivating force.

Learning to Master Change

Advances in technology have dramatically changed when, where, and how people work and live. Computers are everywhere—at work, at home, at school, and in public places. We carry them with us in the form of smartphones and tablets. As a result, the business economy has shifted toward technology-related services and knowledge work. The good news is that tremendous opportunity exists for people who want to pursue a technology-related career. However, the pace of change means that today's technology will be replaced in a few years, if not sooner. In fact, some jobs, and even some professions, may not exist in the future. The rate of change keeps accelerating, and it is not likely to slow down any time soon. Job security is a thing of the past. That doesn't mean you cannot be highly employable.

Success in the business world belongs to the people who embrace change and who are ready and willing to reinvent themselves as needed to contribute to their company's goals. Companies want people who can quickly abandon outdated tools and methods and accept new and improved ways of working. The career opportunities go to people who can look to the future, anticipate coming changes, and quickly adapt.

It is not the strongest of the species that survive, nor the most intelligent, but the most responsive to change.

CHARLES DARWIN

The tips listed in Figure 9-3 will help you keep pace with the changing world of work. They will also enable you to take personal responsibility for your career. By accepting responsibility for your future, you can minimize much of the stress and fear that comes from putting your well-being in the hands of someone else, such as an employer.

- Recognize learning as the labor of the digital age.
- Develop flexibility.
- Speed up.
- Develop project management skills.

Figure 9-3 Tips for mastering change

Recognize Learning as the Labor of the Digital Age

Technology changes quickly, and it does not take long for technical skills to become obsolete. The skills and experience that served you well in the past may, at any time, outlive their usefulness or relevance. Take the time to continuously update and improve your technical skills as well as your business, soft, and self-management skills. For example:

- Stay in school or go back to school.

- Take advantage of training classes offered where you work or that are available online.

- Seek out self-study resources that you can use as time allows.

- Keep up with industry trends, and continuously evaluate how those trends affect your skills.

- Join organizations, and get to know the experts in your industry.

- Ask people who have the skills you need to serve as your mentor.

- Let your supervisor or team leader know what your interests are, and ask to be assigned to projects that will enable you to learn new skills.

- Share your knowledge and experience with others, freeing yourself to learn new skills.

Knowledge is power, and working in a service desk offers you a great opportunity to expand your knowledge and develop and enhance a broad base of skills. Do your homework and do not forget the extra credit—self-study—assignments. After all, it is your career.

Develop Flexibility

Many job descriptions contain the simple phrase, ". . . other duties as assigned." This means that you must expect on any given day to be asked to do something new, something you have never done before, perhaps even something you will never do again. People who need structure hate this phrase. However, everyone must learn to accept this phrase and the uncertainty that it implies. Do not push back and wait for your responsibilities to be described in perfect detail. Do not wait for the information you need to come to you. Develop the ability to quickly figure out what needs to be done and do it. Draw on past experience to get started. Use the Internet to gather additional ideas. If you need help, ask for it. Ask your team leader or supervisor for guidance in terms of the desired outcome. Ask your coworkers or a subject matter expert to collaborate with you or simply help you get started. If no help is available, do your best. Prove your worth by being willing to do what needs to be done for the company to achieve its goals.

Speed Up

In the business world, slow and steady no longer wins the race. Companies that fail to keep pace with their competition cannot survive. However, companies cannot go fast if their employees go slow. Approach all of your work with a sense of urgency. The goal is to get it done, get it done right, and get it done quickly. Avoiding a task or approaching it half-heartedly will not make it go away. You must also try not to get bogged down in endless discussion and planning in an effort to ensure that the outcome of a task is perfect. Some people give a task 120 percent of their effort and energy and get it done late. A better approach is to give a task 99 percent and get it done early. The reality is that you are probably the only person who will see value in that extra 21 percent. High quality is important, but you do not need to be perfect. Strive for excellence, and do it *fast*.

 Get in the habit of creating a to-do list each day and assigning each task a priority. Also, think about and write down the steps you need to perform before you begin a task. A little planning will help you to be more efficient.

Develop Project Management Skills

People often make the mistake of thinking that only people who work on large projects or develop new systems need project management skills. Furthermore, some service desks are too reactive to think about project management. In reality, anyone who has to juggle more than one task at a given time can use project management skills. Project management skills provide you with the ability to identify and attend to details, while at the same time staying focused on the big picture. They provide you with the discipline to think about and plan your efforts before you jump in and start to work. In a service desk setting, project management skills enable you to define the tasks that need to be completed in order to solve an incident or handle a service request. These skills also enable you to define the dependencies associated with those tasks (in other words, determine the tasks that must be completed before the next task can begin). Project management skills also provide you with the ability to proactively identify issues and communicate concerns that may affect the outcome of your efforts. As is the case with problem-solving skills, project management skills are skills that you can improve with practice.

To develop project management skills:

- Visit your local library or bookstore, and pick up a book on project management.
- Attend a seminar or buy a project management CD or DVD.
- Serve as a deputy, or assistant, on a project team.
- Ask someone who has a lot of experience to serve as your mentor.
- Trust, empower, and rely on your team. Do not try to do it all yourself.
- Learn from your mistakes, and thank everyone, even your critics, for their feedback.

Good project management skills take time to develop and can improve only through experience. Project management skills are highly transferable and will serve you well now and in the future.

 If you have never managed a project before, ask for the opportunity. Start with a small project, and then ask for and be willing to accept help and feedback.

You cannot stop the world from changing, and you cannot expect the company where you work to accommodate your desire to stay put. Rather than feel stressed, you must accept the fact that change is constant and learn to adapt—fast.

Learning to master change will open you up to greater opportunities and options. These skills will also give you the confidence to handle any challenges that come your way without wasting precious energy and enthusiasm.

INTERVIEW WITH...

Courtesy of Joe Leggiero

Joe Leggiero
Information Technology Consultant
Atlanta, Georgia
Joe Leggiero has more than 22 years of experience in managing professional services and systems integration. He began his career as a system developer for IBM mainframe systems. After working with a team of developers on a large project, he soon became a team leader. Building on team leader experiences led him to become a project manager and, in time, an independent consultant. As an independent consultant, he specializes in helping organizations make better use of technology and processes to improve enterprise operations. He has worked with large corporate clients, small businesses, and software publishers to design and implement technology and business process solutions. Joe Leggiero shares his thoughts on building a professional career.

A career is a journey of experiences. Each experience is a building block to the next position, the next opportunity, or the next level of responsibility. Every decision, good or bad, will influence the direction of your career and provide opportunities for personal growth and rewards.

In the business world, ethical behavior, strong effort, respect for others, dependability, and integrity are timeless characteristics of a professional. Business skills such as communicating with others, managing conflict, and handling criticism are also timeless skills. They help you deal with others and maintain an atmosphere of cooperation.

Companies measure employees based on their contributions to corporate goals. Being a professional requires working with others to achieve those goals. To do this, professionals must strive to understand and learn from the uniqueness of others. They must work hard to resolve conflicts quickly so those conflicts do not get in the way of working together. Professionals must also be able to accept feedback and criticism, and view both as tools for personal growth, not as a personal attack. Understanding others and graciously accepting feedback and criticism are essential, but difficult, business skills to learn.

On your career journey, as in life, learning never ends. Throughout your career, you will meet people who have years of experience using the very skills you seek. Ask questions. Use the knowledge these more experienced people have acquired through the years. Use the research skills you learned in school to keep your knowledge current and to continuously expand your skills. Apply the business skills you have learned and a good work ethic to every new situation you encounter. For example, in any technical position, problem-solving skills are important and universal. You don't have to relearn these skills for each new position or technology. You must simply adapt your skills to the new situation. Employers are always looking for individuals who can apply their knowledge and experience to new situations. Your ability to continuously draw from your portfolio of skills will help determine your value as an employee and will influence your ability to advance in a career.

Selecting and building a career is not easy. People who are unsure about their career path can still build a foundation of business skills as they are trying to decide on a college major or a career. For example, don't underestimate the value of courses heavy in communications, psychology, and writing when building the foundation for a professional career. Many of us start our careers working for a company in an entry-level position. A key to success is understanding that every position, even an entry-level position, offers the opportunity to acquire business skills. For example, you can learn about setting and achieving career goals, working in a team setting, and what it takes to be a leader.

At some point you will need to decide if you want to pursue a technical career path or a management career. Your business skills will apply within each career path. For example, on a technical path, communication skills may be used to describe the benefits of a technical solution. On a management path, communication skills may be used to explain goals and the importance of meeting those goals. Both paths require the ability to evaluate and communicate costs and benefits. The bottom line here is that, although technical skills can become obsolete, you can use most of the business skills you learn along the way regardless of the career path or profession you choose.

Whether pursuing a technical or managerial career path, at some point you may be presented the opportunity to assume a leadership position. That position may involve becoming a team leader, or it may involve serving as a project manager. People are typically chosen to be team leaders because they've demonstrated the ability to get things done and management believes they can provide guidance to others. First-time team leaders soon find that influencing others requires a new set of skills. For example, team leaders must learn to solve business problems, as opposed to technical problems, and they must learn to motivate and empower others. Some people excel as team leaders and go on to become successful managers and executives. For others, a team leader role convinces them to stay on a technical career path and solve problems with technology instead of with people and schedules.

Some people build leadership skills by becoming a project manager. Project managers use structured methods to plan and direct projects. Being a project manager involves assuming greater responsibilities, taking ownership of your actions and the actions of project team members, and recognizing and learning from failures or successes. It means helping others succeed at their tasks by helping them manage their time and resources. Experience as a team leader will help you in your role as project manager, but it is not required. A broad range of business skills are required. For example, project managers must understand and be able to justify the business goals of projects. They must also be able to communicate, manage conflict, and provide constructive feedback and criticism. Sound familiar?

The journey of your career will have many challenges, triumphs, and setbacks. While you cannot control the outcome of each situation, the decisions that you make will be based on what you learn along the way. The more you learn from each experience along the way, the more apt you will be to avoid making mistakes or missing opportunities in the future.

I have found that combining timeless professional characteristics with previous experience and a continuous quest for knowledge is the formula for building a successful professional career.

Getting and Staying Mentally and Physically Fit

Coping with stress and mastering change takes energy—physical and emotional energy. Stressful and challenging situations can sap your energy and cause your enthusiasm to waver. Stressful situations, even pleasurable ones such as a wedding or the birth of a child, cause a physical response that, left unchecked, can lead to illness.

Research shows that the immune system breaks down when we do not handle stress well. This breakdown of the immune system can lead to illnesses ranging from the common cold to cancer.

Our bodies and minds are tightly connected, particularly when it comes to stress. Upon perceiving a stressful event, our mind triggers an alarm that mobilizes our body for action. These physiological changes are known as the **fight-or-flight reaction**. Our ancestors, surrounded by predatory animals, needed this ability to instantly mobilize to survive. Today, most people are not even aware of their body's minute-to-minute responses to stressful— perceived or otherwise—situations. They may not notice that their heart has begun to beat faster or that their breathing has become shallow. We often learn to ignore or accept short-term stress responses, such as butterflies in our stomach, a lump in our throat, tension in our muscles, and the feelings of anxiety. In time, however, this tension can accumulate and lead to serious health problems.

The techniques listed in Figure 9-4 can help you relieve the physical tension that accompanies stress. These techniques will also help you to rejuvenate your spirit and acquire the emotional strength needed to handle everyday stress.

- Exercise.
- Drink plenty of water.
- Practice good nutrition.
- Avoid the use of stimulants.
- Get a good night's sleep.
- Align your workspace ergonomically.
- Take breaks.
- Let your sense of humor shine through.
- Commit yourself to relaxation.
- Set realistic goals.

Figure 9-4   Techniques for staying fit

Exercise

Exercise provides a way of releasing a great deal of the muscle tension that can accumulate from stress. Exercise can also be used to clear your mind. People who exercise report that spending time away from working diligently on a problem gives them a chance to sort things out in a more relaxed way. Try to fit in exercise during the workday. If your office has exercise facilities, use them at lunch or before or after work, or go for a brisk walk before or after you eat lunch. Try out one or more of the many fitness apps or gadgets that are designed to track and reward your efforts and to help you stay motivated.

Drink Plenty of Water

Our bodies are made up primarily of water and become dehydrated when the amount of water leaving the body is greater than the amount being taken in. Fatigue is one of the first signs of dehydration. Other early symptoms include headaches, dizziness, and a dry or sticky mouth. The easiest way to avoid dehydration is to drink plenty of water. Drinking plenty of water increases your energy level and mental capacities. A side benefit of drinking plenty of water is that your body lets you know when it is time to take a break.

Water has many sources. For example, fruits and vegetables are excellent sources of water when eaten whole or when added to plain water to improve its taste. Drinks such as fruit and vegetable juices, milk, and herbal teas can contribute to the amount of water you should get each day, although they may add extra calories to your diet. Drinking caffeinated beverages such as coffee, tea, and energy drinks can also contribute to your daily fluid intake, although they can have a mild diuretic effect when consumed in excess. Be aware, however, that caffeinated drinks often come with unwanted extras such as sodium, sugar, and fats. They can also act as stimulants.

Avoid the Use of Stimulants

Stimulants such as the caffeine found in coffee, tea, soda, and chocolate exaggerate all of the body's stress responses by causing a surge of adrenaline and other hormones. Excessive caffeine causes some people to feel nervous and jittery, and may even affect their ability to sleep at night. It is best to avoid stimulants altogether. But if you do choose to consume caffeine, limit your intake and time your consumption carefully. For example, having one cup of coffee or tea in the morning is far better than drinking two cups after dinner. Drinking plenty of water can also boost your energy level so you may also want to keep a water bottle at your desk for those times when you are tempted to reach for a soda.

Practice Good Nutrition

Skipping meals can cause you to feel irritable. Eating too much can cause you to feel sluggish and tired. Eating the right amount of food at the right time helps you sustain your energy level and maintain an even temperament. If allowed, have fruit or whole wheat crackers at your desk that you can eat when you feel hungry or when you need energy. Although some companies prohibit eating at one's desk, most have a break room and refrigerator where you can store food items. Bring your lunch from home so you can eat healthy food and have time to relax during your lunch break by taking a walk or stepping outside for a breath of fresh air. If you purchase lunch, substitute healthier options for ones that can sap your energy. If you know you are going to have a particularly stressful week, it is especially important to plan ahead and have healthy snacks and meals available.

Get a Good Night's Sleep

Failing to get a good night's sleep can have serious physical and mental effects on your health. Inadequate sleep impairs your ability to make decisions, concentrate, handle stress, maintain a healthy immune system, and moderate your emotions. You may also find that your memory and problem-solving capabilities are impaired.

Healthy habits such as exercise and avoiding stimulants such as alcohol, caffeine, the television, and video games contribute to your ability to get a good night's sleep. Trying to set a bedtime schedule and developing a bedtime routine are also effective techniques, along with resisting the temptation to oversleep.

An overly busy schedule, worry, and anxiety can make it difficult to fall asleep and can also cause you to wake up frequently during the night. Techniques such as updating your to-do list each evening or making simple preparations for the next day can help quiet your mind and help you to prepare for a good night's sleep. Some people keep a journal or pad of paper and pen near their beds to capture thoughts, ideas, or worries, allowing the mind to relax and fall asleep.

 Get additional tips and techniques by searching the Internet for "how to get a good night's sleep."

Align Your Workspace Ergonomically

A poorly designed workspace can cause physical symptoms such as headaches, wrist and shoulder pain, backaches, and swollen ankles. Ergonomics helps reduce these symptoms and prevent repetitive stress injuries. **Ergonomics** is the applied science of equipment design intended to maximize productivity by reducing operator fatigue and discomfort. **Repetitive stress injuries (RSIs)** are physical symptoms caused by excessive and repeated use of the hands, wrists, arms, and thumbs. These symptoms occur when people perform tasks using force, repeated strenuous actions, awkward postures, and poorly designed equipment. For example, too much typing on handheld devices such as smartphones could cause repetitive stress injuries to your thumbs. RSIs include carpal tunnel syndrome, tendonitis, bursitis, and rotator cuff injuries. **Carpal tunnel syndrome** is a common repetitive stress injury that affects the hands and wrists and is linked to repetitious hand movements, such as typing on a computer keyboard or working with a mouse.

Search the web for quick exercises you can use to prevent RSIs such as carpal tunnel syndrome. Examples include warming up before working and periodically releasing tension by bending your wrists, making fists, shaking out your hands, and performing shrugging exercises to relax your shoulders. Keep it loose!

Service desk analysts are susceptible to RSIs because they do a considerable amount of keyboarding. To help prevent RSIs, improve the ergonomics of your workspace by aligning your chair with your monitor and keyboard so when you sit up straight in the chair, the monitor is at or below eye level and your wrists are straight on the keyboard. Figure 9-5 illustrates the relationship between your chair, monitor, and keyboard.

Comstock Images/Stockbyte/Getty Images

Figure 9-5 Ergonomically aligned chair, monitor, and keyboard

Prolonged use of tablet computers can cause different forms of RSIs to the fingers and hands. To minimize these symptoms, use an external keyboard and consider purchasing an accessory that enables you to set the screen at eye level, just as you would a computer monitor or laptop.

Users of mobile devices are particularly susceptible to shoulder and neck pain. Good posture and frequent, short breaks can help minimize these symptoms.

Take Breaks

Working nonstop often leads to fatigue and burnout. Take time throughout the day to rejuvenate yourself. Stretch, spend a moment looking out the window, or simply close your eyes and take a few deep breaths to regain a sense of calm. Take a short walk, even if it is only to the restroom or to get a drink of water. Take a moment to chat with or encourage a coworker. Perform a less intensive task such as filing, organizing your desk, or catching up on what is happening in your industry via social media. We all, at times, need to step away from what we are doing in order to rejuvenate ourselves both physically and mentally.

Let Your Sense of Humor Shine Through

Laughter truly is the best medicine. It can cause you to relax when you are feeling tense, and it can restore your sense of optimism and self-confidence. Although work is not the place for harmful humor or off-color jokes, there are plenty of creative ways to have fun in the service desk. Some service desks have a funniest hat day or a mismatched clothes day. Some service desks have a box that contains stress-relieving toys such as stress balls and squeeze toys. Having a sense of humor is a great way to manage stress and maintain a positive and balanced perspective on life. In both your professional and personal life, surround yourself with positive people and seek them out when you need a good laugh. Seize opportunities to make others feel better by sharing a good laugh over the ups and downs of life.

Commit Yourself to Relaxation

A relaxing activity is one that leaves you free of tension and refreshed both physically and mentally. People relax in different ways. Some people enjoy hobbies such as gardening and astronomy. Some people like to read. Others enjoy activities such as yoga or Pilates, or activities that enable them to commune with nature such as hiking, walking, or biking. For optimum stress-relieving benefits, a relaxing activity should consume you to the extent that you temporarily forget about your stressors and focus on your personal well-being.

The time to relax is when you don't have the time.

AUTHOR UNKNOWN

Set Realistic Goals

Many people cause the very stress they are experiencing either by setting unrealistic goals or by failing to set goals at all. Setting realistic goals keeps you motivated and enables you to get what you want in life. Realistic goals are attainable. That does not mean they are easy to achieve. Do not set yourself up to fail by choosing goals that are so unrealistic they are impossible to achieve. Also, avoid goals where you will have to sacrifice so much to achieve them that they become worthless. Conversely, do not set goals that are so easy to achieve that they fail to provide you with a sense of accomplishment.

The most successful people have written short- and long-term goals as well as professional and personal goals. This balanced approach provides the ability to feel successful in all areas of your life and also provides you the impetus to continuously improve. At work, ask your supervisor or team leader to help you establish reasonable goals along with a timetable for reviewing your accomplishments. Make sure you also understand your team's goals and how your personal goals fit in with them.

If you want to live a happy life, tie it to a goal, not to people or things.

ALBERT EINSTEIN

Not having goals can also lead to stress. Goals give you a purpose in life. People with goals feel in control of their lives because they know the direction in which they are heading. Conversely, people without goals may feel dissatisfied with their lives and may feel they are just drifting aimlessly from one day to the next. If you are dissatisfied with some aspect of your life, it may be because you do not know what you want. Setting goals and, most importantly, writing down those goals and attaching a timeline allow you to choose a course of action for your life. Knowing where you want to go and what you want to do in life lets you focus your energies and avoid, or more easily tolerate, distractions along the way.

The bottom line is that in order to use stress as a positive, motivating force in your life, you must take care of yourself both physically and mentally. Take responsibility for how you experience each and every moment of your life. Take time every day to think about your physical and emotional needs, and devote time to fulfilling those needs. Remember, it is just as important to foster your mental health as it is to care for your physical well-being.

Live a balanced life. Learn some and think some and draw and paint and sing and dance and play and work every day some.

ROBERT FULGHUM

CASE STUDY: Ergonomically Aligning Your Workspace

A majority of ergonomic problems can be eliminated by making simple, no-cost adjustments to your personal workspace. You can easily adjust your chair, monitor, keyboard and mouse, telephone and headset, and lighting to create a workspace that fits your needs. Making these adjustments goes a long way toward helping you stay healthy on the job.

Chair. The placement and use of your chair, monitor, keyboard, and mouse are related and must be aligned properly with each other and with you. How you adjust and sit in your chair are equally important. You should adjust your chair until your back is erect, slightly back, and firm against the backrest. If necessary, further support your back with a lumbar pillow, back support, or a rolled up towel.

Thighs and legs should be relaxed and feet should be flat on the floor. You can also place a footrest, box, or stack of books under the desk, as shown in the picture, to keep your feet from dangling.

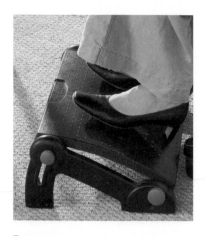

Footrest
© Image Point Fr/Shutterstock.com

Properly aligned monitor
Hill Creek Pictures/Photodisc/Getty Images

Monitor. The chair height can affect and be affected by the placement of your monitor. The best position for a monitor is directly in front of you at, or just below, eye level, as shown in the picture. When you are sitting straight with your head erect, the monitor should be no more than 24 inches away from your eyes. If necessary, place a book under the monitor to raise it up to the right level. If the monitor is too high, remove anything under it to make it lower, adjust your chair, or replace the desk or table with a lower one as a last resort.

Keyboard and Mouse. Correct placement and use of the keyboard and mouse can help you avoid repetitive stress injuries. The proper form for keyboarding and using the mouse is to keep your wrists straight and avoid resting them on hard surfaces. Keys should be pressed gently rather than pounded to prevent injury to both your hands and the keyboard. Also, the mouse should be gripped loosely. You can also consider using an ergonomic keyboard (as shown in the picture) and a sloping keyboard tray to reduce the symptoms of carpal tunnel syndrome. A **wrist**

Ergonomic keyboard
© Dmitry Melnikov/Shutterstock.com

rest, a firm cushion that lays parallel to the keyboard, can also help. Avoid overly soft wrist rests that wrists sink into because they put unnecessary pressure on your wrists.

Remember that all these components—chair, monitor, keyboard, and mouse—work together. Whenever you adjust your chair, you will most likely need to readjust your monitor, keyboard, and mouse.

Telephone headset

Stockbyte/Getty Images

Telephone and Headset. *A telephone is one of the most basic pieces of equipment at service desks. The type or style of telephone you use is less important than making sure the telephone is positioned correctly in relation to your computer. If you have to stretch or turn around to answer the telephone, you are at risk for a repetitive stress injury. A good rule of thumb is to place the telephone either directly in front of you, or at less than a 25-degree angle and no more than 10 inches away.*

A telephone headset rids you of a traditional handheld receiver. Headsets relieve stress and tension by freeing your hands for typing, and prevent neck pain by eliminating the need for you to balance a receiver between your tilted head and shoulder. In fact, a study conducted at Santa Clara Valley Medical Center in San Jose, California, found that headsets reduce neck, shoulder, and upper back tension by as much as 41 percent.

There are numerous styles of headsets, including over-the-ear headsets and headbands that fit over one ear or both ears. Wireless headsets provide you with the added ability to stand up and move about the service desk. If possible, you should try on several models before making a final selection. Although the style of headset you select is a matter of personal choice, there are a couple of factors to consider. You may prefer a headset that covers only one ear (as shown in the picture) so you can still remain aware of what is going on around you, or you may prefer a headset that covers both ears so you can block out noise. Some headsets offer a noise-canceling microphone to help filter out noise from the service desk that the customer may hear. Regardless of the style, a headset should keep your head and neck in a neutral position and free your hands for activities such as keyboarding. Consider also that your head is the heaviest part of your body. While headsets are fairly light, do not use a headset that encourages you to tilt or hang your head. Leaving your head tilted for even a short period of time causes tension in your neck, shoulders, and back.

Adjustable task lighting

Fuse/Getty Images

Lighting. *The brightness of your workspace can greatly affect your well-being. Too much lighting can produce a glare on the monitor, which can cause eyestrain, headaches, and fatigue. You can reduce this glare by spraying an antiglare coating on the glass surface or by installing an antiglare filter. Too little lighting can cause you to squint and strain in order to see paperwork or the monitor. Adjustable task lighting on the desk provides directed lighting to supplement the overhead lighting. Natural light, or the lack of it, can also influence your mood. To experience a positive psychological lift, make a conscious effort to look out a window or momentarily step outside periodically throughout the day.*

Any time you move into a new office or workstation, take the time to arrange the equipment to meet your requirements. If you need additional equipment, such as a task light or footrest, speak with your manager. After all, you are worth it!

Managing Your Time

Service desks are high-activity places to work, and some days can be very hectic. Analysts must handle incoming contacts with grace, stay on top of outstanding incidents and service requests, and assist their coworkers whenever possible. Along the way, they must make time to relieve stress and take care of their physical and emotional well-being. Analysts who manage time wisely are able to feel in control during exceptionally busy periods at the service desk and stay motivated during slow times. Good work habits, such as getting and staying organized, enable you to view work as a challenge to be enjoyed. Good work habits also enable you to maintain physical and mental fitness on the job and to achieve personal success.

Getting and Staying Organized

Strong organizational skills are the hallmark of an excellent service provider and enable analysts to stay on top of incoming and outstanding incidents and service requests. How you manage your workload will not only influence customer satisfaction and your relationships with other service providers, it will influence your personal stress level as well. The techniques listed in Figure 9-6 will help you get and stay organized. The following sections discuss these techniques in more detail.

- Create a beginning-of-day (BOD) checklist.
- Create a "What I Need to Know" list.
- Create a "What Coworkers Need to Know" list.
- Keep up with administrative tasks.
- Log all incidents and service requests in real time.
- Check the status of your open tickets regularly.

Figure 9-6   Techniques for getting and staying organized

Create a Beginning-of-Day Checklist

Successful analysts often develop routines that enable them to stay organized and remember things. A **beginning-of-day (BOD) checklist**, such as the one shown in Figure 9-7, is a list of tasks an analyst performs at the start of each workday.

✔ Greet coworkers.

✔ Check your personal and team calendars for meetings or deadlines.

✔ Check and respond to voice mail and email messages.

✔ Check the status of incidents or service requests you own via the incident management system.

✔ Follow up on any critical issues from the previous day.

✔ Create or update a to-do list for the day. Verify that you have completed any necessary preparations such as prereading in advance of a meeting or training class.

✔ Straighten your desk.

✔ Note any current major (systemwide) incidents.

✔ Check to see if any changes happened overnight that may be causing incidents.

✔ Check for any new system or user-generated incidents or service requests that need to be addressed.

✔ Take a deep breath.

✔ Get ready for anything.

Figure 9-7 Sample BOD checklist

Try to arrive at work a few minutes early so you can complete your BOD checklist before you begin handling contacts or greeting customers. Creating a BOD checklist is a habit that sets the tone for the rest of the day. Start the day off right.

In addition to encouraging each analyst to create a BOD checklist, some service desks create a BOD checklist for the entire service desk. An end-of-day (EOD) checklist is also a good idea. Service desks that work in shifts may also have a beginning- and an end-of-shift checklist. The policies of the service desk determine what tasks are included in these lists.

Create a "What I Need to Know" List

Lists of commonly used information are a great way for analysts to get and stay organized. Analysts should create a list of important telephone numbers, filenames, dates, and so on that they need on a fairly regular basis and place it in clear view such as on an erasable whiteboard. This information can also be maintained using a digital to-do list manager or digital sticky notes. These items are not necessarily ones they use daily, which analysts tend to memorize. Rather, they are pieces of information they use regularly but not often enough to memorize, or during a short time period, such as the roll-out date of a new system.

Create a "What Coworkers Need to Know" List

Similar to the "What I Need to Know" list, the "What Coworkers Need to Know" list contains important information coworkers may need to know if an analyst is out of the office for a period of days or weeks at a training class or on vacation, for example. This list should include the status of any current and ongoing projects, the names of folders or the location of documents the analyst is responsible for maintaining, the dates during which the analyst will be gone, and the names of people who provide backup in the analyst's absence. During work-related travel, such as attending a training class or an offsite meeting, analysts may include a way for coworkers to reach them in the event of an emergency.

 Some service desks have a quick meeting each morning where analysts share information that other analysts need to know, along with tips and tricks they recently learned.

Keep Up with Administrative Tasks

All jobs come with administrative tasks. You may be required to fill out a time sheet, prepare a status report, or maintain and close tickets in the incident management system. When you complete these tasks in a timely fashion, it takes less time because the information you need is fresh in your mind. Your coworkers and your supervisor or team leader also appreciate when you keep these items up to date because then they have the information they need to do their work if you are not available.

Managing administrative tasks is also a great way to reduce the stress associated with a large assignment. For example, if producing the month-end report is something you find stressful, take a break in the middle and fill out your expense report or time sheet, update your to-do list, or check for new email messages. This way, you can take a break, but still be productive. Do not do this too often, though, or you will lose your ability to focus on your main—and, most likely, higher-priority—task.

Log All Incidents and Service Requests in Real Time

Some analysts write customer and incident or service request data on a piece of paper during the contact and then log the information in the incident management system after they have hung up the telephone. They may even log the contact later in the day. This is an unproductive practice because they are handling the contact twice. They may also find later that they have not collected all of the information needed to log the incident or service request, making it necessary to contact the customer. This may prompt the customer to perceive that the service desk is disorganized or that no one has been working on his or her incident or service request. Logging contacts in real time ensures other analysts know an incident or service request exists and is also an excellent way for service desk managers to know and show when the service desk is short-handed. If you are logging contacts in real time and incidents and service requests are backing up, it is much easier to justify additional resources than if you work after hours or after your shift to do all of the logging.

Logging contacts in real time is a habit, and you may need practice to become proficient. Seek training to learn how to use your team's incident management system or any of the tools available to you more efficiently and effectively.

Check the Status of Your Open Tickets Regularly

Rather than keeping paper lists that can become out of date or disorganized, learn to use your company's incident management system to manage your tickets. Learn to create online reports or run queries that list all of the tickets you own so you can stay organized. If a high volume of tickets makes it difficult for you to check the status of each ticket as often as you would like, make a note in each ticket indicating when follow-up is absolutely needed.

You can never predict what will happen in a service desk on any given day. Regardless, your customers, coworkers, and supervisor or team leader are counting on you to manage your workload and take care of those tasks that are urgent. Getting and staying organized will enable you to assume your responsibilities and feel in control at all times.

Coping with Deadlines

Like stress, deadlines are a normal part of life and can be a positive, motivating force. If you have too much work or too little time, however, deadlines can become a considerable source of stress. The best way to cope with deadlines is to (1) clearly define the work to be done, and then (2) be realistic about what you can accomplish each day, week, and year. Overcommitting is a major cause of stress and can diminish your ability to do high-quality work. When facing deadlines, remember the guidelines listed in Figure 9-8.

- Avoid procrastination.
- Manage your priorities.
- Use your peak productivity times.
- Eliminate time robbers.

Figure 9-8   Guidelines for coping with deadlines

Avoid Procrastination

Putting off a task until the last minute can cause analysts to miss a critical deadline or produce a low-quality product. The best way to avoid this is to break large tasks into smaller ones and try to complete the task a little bit at a time. Also, you can set a time limit and work on a task for at least that period of time. Even if it is only 10 minutes, at least you will have started. Who knows, you may find the project captures your interest and you will want to keep going. Also, by breaking large tasks into smaller ones, you will know a lot sooner whether you can meet your deadline and can then inform your supervisor or team leader.

Manage Your Priorities

Many analysts create a to-do list that shows all of the tasks they are required to complete. Once you create your to-do list, you can assign a priority to each task that indicates the order in which you will work on tasks that day. A simple priority scale rates each task on a scale from A to D, as shown in Table 9-2.

Rating	Priority
A	Urgent: Must do today
B	Important: Should do this week
C	Do when time permits
D	Delegate.

Table 9-2   Simple priority scale

After each task has been assigned a priority rating, you should check for a balance of priorities. When faced with more *A* priority tasks than can be completed in one day, you can consider the following questions about each task:

1. Who asked me to complete this task?
   A task assigned by a customer or a manager may have a higher priority than a task assigned by a coworker.

2. What is the risk if I do not complete this task? What is the value if I do complete this task?
   Failing to complete a task may cause you (or someone waiting on your input) to miss a critical deadline. Completing a task may make you eligible for a promotion.

3. When am I expected to have this task done? That is, what is my deadline for this task?
   If the task is due that day, it is a high priority. If it is not due for several weeks, you can assign it a lower priority and strive to simply start the task.

 To avoid overcommitting yourself, ask the person assigning a task when it needs to be completed, rather than offering to complete it immediately. Also, ask how important the task is so you can assign an appropriate priority.

Based on your answers to these questions, you can refine the priorities of the tasks on your to-do list.

Some people find the task of assigning priorities to all of the tasks on their to-do lists overwhelming. Some people lack the time or inclination required to rewrite to-do lists at the end of each day or week and end up with multiple, out-of-date to-do lists, which tends to only make them feel more disorganized. A simple, effective solution can be to use an electronic organizer, such as Evernote (*www.evernote.com*), LeanKit Kanban (*www.leankitkanban.com*), OneNote (*www.office.microsoft.com/en-us/onenote*), or Todoist (*www.todoist.com*). These systems enable you to set up electronic folders or whiteboards that you can drag and drop to move around as priorities change. In these systems, you can also maintain pages or cards that describe each assigned project or task.

Regardless of what system you use, a key to success is collecting all of your to-do tasks, ideas, and project-related data in one place or system, and then developing the habit of regularly maintaining that system. Having an easy-to-use system not only will allow you to be more organized, it will also help to control the stress that is inevitable when you have an abundance of commitments.

Use Your Peak Productivity Times

Are you an early bird or a night owl? Most people have about 4 hours each day during which they are most productive and alert. Because this time varies from person to person, you should determine your personal peak productivity time. If possible, tackle your most difficult tasks during the time in which you function best. You can then handle easier tasks, such as paperwork or more routine tasks, during those times when your energy is waning.

Eliminate Time Robbers

Time robbers are activities that take up time and do not add value to the work you perform. In fact, time robbers usually decrease productivity and increase stress levels. Some time robbers, such as paperwork and email, are necessary. Others such as inadequate planning, failing to focus on a task, and procrastination can be avoided through good work habits. You can use the techniques discussed in the following sections to avoid time robbers.

LOG CONTACTS AS THEY COME IN This avoids the need to handle the contact twice, eliminates the possibility that you will forget critical information, and ensures that the time stamps, which indicate when the contact was recorded, correspond to the actual time when the customer reported the incident or service request. Also, when a major incident occurs that may affect many customers, such as a server being down, logging contacts as they come in ensures other analysts are aware of the incident.

AVOID DISTRACTIONS Overall, you should stay focused on your work and resist the temptation to let distractions get in your way. Resist the temptation to do someone else's job, even if you think you can do it better yourself. For example, you should not research airline prices to go to a conference if your company has a Travel department whose function is to schedule employee trips. Also, focus on tasks that match the policies of your department and your priorities, rather than tasks you feel like doing at the time. For example, you should not research an incident if the target escalation time has been exceeded and the incident is clearly in another group's area of responsibility. It is also important to resist the temptation to get involved in every conversation going on around you. Although it is appropriate for you to get involved when it appears there is a major incident and you need a status report, resist the temptation to get involved in resolving the incident unless it is your responsibility and your expertise is clearly needed.

AVOID GOSSIP AND EXCESSIVE SOCIALIZING Some socializing is appropriate and is, in fact, an important element of teamwork. Excessive socializing, however, is unproductive and may cause your coworkers to resent that you are not getting the job done. Sharing news about other people is a normal part of socializing when it is well-meaning and up front. For example, sharing the fact that a coworker just became engaged is okay unless the person is trying to keep this fact a secret. It is best to steer clear of gossip that is mean spirited or that reveals secrets.

ASK FOR HELP WHEN YOU REALLY NEED IT It is human nature to want to figure things out on your own, but sometimes we all need help. Try to distinguish between just "taking a little more time to figure things out" and really needing help and guidance to avoid aggravation and wasted time.

KEEP YOUR DESK AND FILES ORGANIZED Organization is a key to success. You should devise a system you can use to get and stay organized. Get in the habit of always putting away files after you use them and handling papers and folders only one time. A good guideline is: Do it, file it, or dump it (that is, throw away unneeded junk mail or other paperwork).

SUGGEST CONSTRUCTIVE WAYS TO MAKE IMPROVEMENTS Complaining wastes time. If you see opportunities to make improvements, tell your team leader or send an email message or memo that outlines the steps you think could help eliminate or minimize a problematic situation. Although your ideas may not always be accepted, they will be received far more positively than complaints.

AUTOMATE RECURRING TASKS Every job includes tasks that must be done on a regular or frequent basis. Identify these tasks, such as frequently accessing a web site or performing routine lookups in the incident management system, and then set up shortcuts and function keys that you can use.

Companies are increasingly asking employees to do more work with fewer resources. People who manage their time well can meet this challenge because they prioritize their work and stay focused on producing the desired results. An added benefit is that people who manage their time well experience lower levels of stress and burnout.

Your local library has numerous books on time and stress management. They contain many excellent tips about how to manage your time wisely and how to avoid and alleviate stress.

Understanding the Time/Stress Connection

Time management involves making an endless series of small and large decisions about what you will accomplish each day. Inappropriate decisions, such as those that result in wasted time, can lower self-esteem and increase stress levels. On the other hand, people who maintain a positive attitude, manage their priorities, and use time wisely feel good at the end of each day because they know they have done their best.

Time and stress management skills are tightly linked. People who are highly stressed may be contributing to that stress by making poor decisions about how they use their time. For example, some people believe that "If I want something done right, I have to do it myself." In reality, all that does is result in them having more work to do. A better approach is to teach and help others so they can in turn help you. Some people also have a hard time saying "No," particularly in the workplace. It is appropriate, however, to let your boss or coworkers know when you are feeling overwhelmed or do not know which of your tasks take priority. It is better to let people know that your plate is full than to miss a deadline or let them down because you run out of time. This does not mean you should whine. Calmly ask for clarification about what you should consider your priorities or state what you can do, as illustrated in the following examples.

I was planning to finish the month-end report this morning. Does this new task take priority over that one?

I'm working on a deadline today. Can I get that information to you tomorrow?

Failing to plan ahead is another common contributor to people's stress. People who are highly stressed may feel they do not have time to think about a future event, much less take time out to prepare in advance. In reality, minutes of planning prior to an event can often mean the difference between feeling stressed and confused when the event arrives and enjoying the event to its fullest (or at least feeling in control of the event). For example, if your boss asks you to work late in the coming week, take a moment to arrange child care or determine what, if any, appointments you may need to reschedule. Taking care of such tasks as soon as possible will eliminate panic, or the need for apologies, in the week ahead. Another simple example is to ask for directions before heading out for an appointment or a job interview. Rather than "winging it" and running the risk of being late, you may want to call ahead or go online for directions, and perhaps even drive to the location in advance.

Highly stressed people often feel they do not have time for time management or for training in stress management. It is important to remember, though, that you choose the stress you experience each and every day. Practicing good time and stress management will help you take control of your life and achieve your full potential.

If you choose a career in the service desk industry, an exciting and rewarding profession awaits. It is a rapidly growing and ever-changing field that offers tremendous opportunities to people who like working with technology and enjoy helping customers. To seize these opportunities, you must hone your soft and self-management skills, along with your business and technical skills. In developing these skills, you lay the foundation for a successful career, regardless of your chosen profession. You also develop the life skills needed to handle even the most challenging situations—whether in your professional life or in your personal life—with confidence and enthusiasm. Be optimistic. With your skills, the future is bright.

Chapter Summary

- Customer service is a stressful occupation, and service desk analysts need to develop good self-management skills, such as stress and time management. Stress is the adaptation of our bodies and minds to the demands of life. When properly managed, stress is an excellent source of motivation and can be a positive part of life. Too much stress or too little stress can lead to health problems. To deal effectively with the stress in your life, take the time to identify the real source or sources of your stress. Begin to develop a plan of action and a stress management program that will work for you.

- Two key factors that affect how people respond to stress are (1) how much control they have over the stressor, and (2) whether or not they choose to be exposed to the stressor. Remember that even when you feel a situation is out of your control, there is always something you can do. You can change the situation, or you can control the way you respond to the situation. Accepting responsibility for the stress you are experiencing is the most important step you can take in terms of coping with the stress and avoiding burnout.

- The rate of change in the business world keeps accelerating, and it is not likely to slow down any time soon. To be successful, learn to embrace change and be willing to reinvent yourself as needed to contribute to your company's goals. Take personal responsibility for your career. Keep learning, develop flexibility, speed up, and develop project management skills. By accepting responsibility for your future, you can minimize much of the stress and fear that come from putting your well-being in the hands of someone else, such as an employer.

- Coping with stress and mastering change take energy—physical and emotional energy. Stressful and challenging situations can sap your energy and cause your enthusiasm to waver. To relieve the tension that accompanies stress, and to use stress as a positive, motivating force in your life, take care of yourself both physically and mentally. Take time every day to think about your physical and emotional needs, and devote time to fulfilling those needs.

- Companies are increasingly asking employees to do more work, often with fewer resources. People who manage their time well are able to meet this challenge because they prioritize their work and stay focused on producing the desired results. Good work habits, such as getting and staying organized, will enable you to feel in control and make good time management decisions. An added benefit is that when you manage your time well, you will experience lower levels of stress and burnout. Time and stress management are tightly linked, and practicing both will help you take control of your life and achieve your full potential.

Key Terms

372 **beginning-of-day (BOD) checklist**—A list of tasks an analyst performs at the start of each workday.

358 **burnout**—The physical and emotional exhaustion that is caused by long-term stress.

367 **carpal tunnel syndrome**—A common repetitive stress injury that affects the hands and wrists and is linked to repetitive hand movements, such as typing on a computer keyboard or working with a mouse.

352 **distress**—A negative form of stress that causes strain, anxiety, or suffering.

367 **ergonomics**—The applied science of equipment design intended to maximize productivity by reducing operator fatigue and discomfort.

352 **eustress**—A healthy form of stress that helps keep you motivated and enables you to feel a sense of accomplishment.

364 **fight-or-flight reaction**—A set of physiological changes that occur when the mind, upon perceiving a stressful event, triggers an alarm that mobilizes the body for action.

353 **institutional stressors**—The stressors that accompany the type of business you are in or the state of the organization where you work.

355 **personal stressors**—The stressors that accompany your individual life experiences.

367 **repetitive stress injuries (RSIs)**—Physical symptoms caused by excessive and repeated use of the hands, wrists, arms, and thumbs; these symptoms occur when people perform tasks using force, repeated strenuous actions, awkward postures, and poorly designed equipment.

354 **situational stressors**—The stressors that accompany the type of work you do.

352 **stress**—The adaptation of our bodies and minds to the demands of life.

370 **wrist rest**—A firm cushion that lies parallel to the keyboard.

Review Questions

1. How do self-management skills benefit people in a service desk setting?

2. What is stress?

3. What are the symptoms of too little stress?

4. What are the symptoms of too much stress?

5. List five health problems that can be related to or aggravated by too much or too little stress.

6. How can you influence institutional stressors?

7. How can you influence situational stressors?

8. How can you influence personal stressors?

9. What two factors affect how people respond to stress?

10. What are your choices when you are faced with a situation that you cannot control?

11. What is burnout?

12. When do people experience burnout?

13. Why is it important to stay calm and in control when facing a stressful situation?

14. What calming techniques can you use if you feel yourself losing control?

15. Why is it important to take personal responsibility for your career?

16. What techniques can you use to keep pace in the changing world of work?

17. How can service desk analysts use project management skills?

18. Describe six symptoms our bodies and minds experience as a result of the flight-or-fight reaction.

19. How does exercise help relieve stress?

20. How does good nutrition help relieve stress?

21. List three symptoms you may experience if your workspace is not arranged ergonomically.

22. What service desk activity puts you at risk for repetitive stress injuries?

23. How can you improve the ergonomics of your workspace?

24. What are the benefits of laughter?

25. What are realistic goals?

26. What are the benefits of good work habits?

27. Why is it important to log all incidents in real time?

28. What are two ways to avoid procrastination?

29. What should you do after you have assigned a priority to each task on your to-do list?

30. What are time robbers?

31. What does time management involve?

32. Describe the relationship that exists between time and stress management.

33. Why is it important to let people know when you are feeling overwhelmed?

34. You _____ the stress you experience each and every day.

35. What are the benefits of practicing good time and stress management?

Discussion Questions

1. Occupational healthcare professionals have long debated whether job stress is a result of the work environment or the coping skills of the worker. What do you think?

2. People who procrastinate often defend putting off a task until the last minute by saying, "I do my best work under pressure." Is that possible?

3. Some people have a hard time saying "No." As a result, they may overcommit, lose sight of their priorities, and feel overwhelmed. Discuss appropriate ways to say "No" to your boss, coworkers, family members, and friends.

Hands-On Projects

1. **Interview a service desk employee.** Arrange to interview a manager or analyst who works in a service desk either at your school or in the community about how that person and his or her team minimize stress and avoid burnout. Before the interview, create a list of questions you would like answered and send it to the person so he or she can prepare. For example, you may ask the person to describe:

   a. What institutional stressors are inherent in your industry?

   b. What situational stressors do you encounter working in a service desk?

   c. What does your team do to minimize stress?

   d. What do you personally do to minimize stress?

   Write a report that summarizes what you learned from this person.

2. **Identify the causes of stress in your life.** Prepare a list of the causes of stress in your life, and consider the effect those stressors have on your life by answering the following questions:

   a. What, if any, institutional stressors are you experiencing? Do you like the business you are in?

   b. What, if any, situational stressors are you experiencing? Do you like the work that you do? (Consider your answers to Hands-On Project 1-9 when answering this question.)

   c. What, if any, personal stressors are you experiencing? Are you happy with your personal life?

   Given what you have learned in this chapter, what conclusions can you draw about the stress you are experiencing?

3. **Assess your stress management skills.** Using the list of stressors you identified in Hands-On Project 9-2, assess the effectiveness of your current efforts to manage stress in your life by answering the following questions:

   a. Am I doing all that I can do to control the effect this stressor has on my life?

   b. Am I choosing to be exposed to this stressor?

c. What changes, if any, can I make to (i) the situation and (ii) my response to the situation that will result in less stress?

d. What, if anything, can I do about an identified stressor (such as moving or starting a new job) to reduce its effect on me?

e. Can I reduce the stress I am experiencing by eliminating negative phrases and demonstrating a positive, *can do* attitude? (Consider your answers to Hands-On Project 1-8 when answering this question.)

Given what you have learned in this chapter, what conclusions can you draw about your stress management skills?

4. **Learn about mastering change.** Interview someone, such as an acquaintance, family member, or coworker, who has a career that you believe is interesting or challenging. Write a short paper that answers the following questions:

a. What changes have occurred in the business world since this person began working in his or her current profession?

b. What changes does this person anticipate in the future?

c. How does this person continuously improve his or her technical, business, soft, and self-management skills during and in anticipation of changing times?

d. Does this person have project management skills? If so, how did he or she develop those skills?

e. What advice, if any, can this person give you in terms of dealing with changing times?

5. **Learn to manage your fight-or-flight reactions.** For one week, keep a list of the physiological changes you experience when your mind perceives a stressful event. For example, when facing a stressful situation, does your heart begin to beat faster or does your breathing become shallow? For each physiological change you experience, identify a coping mechanism that you can use to relieve the symptom of stress and then try to apply it. As the month goes on, assess the effectiveness of your efforts to manage your fight-or-flight reactions. For example, have you found that by taking a deep breath you can relieve the butterflies in your stomach?

6. **Create a BOD checklist.** Create a BOD checklist for a typical day in your life. For example, if your typical day involves going to school and going to work, prepare a list of tasks you must complete before leaving the house to ensure you are ready for both. While creating your BOD checklist, think back over the last couple of weeks. Were there days when you felt disorganized or when you forgot items you needed? Include tasks on your BOD checklist that can prevent the frustration of this type of situation. Were there days when you really felt you had your act together? Include tasks on your BOD checklist that enable you to regularly feel that confident and organized. Post your BOD checklist in a place where you can view it each day in an effort to make these tasks a habit.

7. **Evaluate your workspace.** A properly arranged workspace increases productivity and reduces stress and fatigue. Look closely at the workspace where you complete most of your writing, computer work, and reading or studying. Then, briefly outline your answers to the following questions:

    a. Have you ever experienced any of the negative symptoms of a poorly designed workspace, such as headaches, wrist and shoulder pain, back pain, or swollen ankles?

    b. If so, given what you have learned in this chapter, were your symptoms the result of poor workspace design or poor work habits?

    c. In what ways can you improve the ergonomics of your workspace?

    d. In what ways can you improve your work habits?

    Unless you share your workspace with other people, arrange your workspace so it meets your ergonomic requirements.

8. **Manage your priorities.** Create a to-do list, or ensure your existing to-do list is complete. Consider investigating one or more of the electronic organizers mentioned in this chapter. Ensure each task has a priority rating. Review your to-do list. Do you have a balanced set of priorities? If not, use the questions contained in this chapter to refine your priorities. Given what you have learned in this chapter, what, if any, changes can you make in terms of how you manage your to-do list to better manage your priorities?

9. **Identify time robbers.** Using your school's online message or discussion board, discuss the list of time robbers presented in this chapter. Add to the list other time robbers that you and your classmates are exposed to in school or at work. Select three time robbers you and your classmates consider particularly unproductive. Brainstorm and prepare a list of ways to eliminate these time robbers.

Case Projects

1. **Lunch and Learn Training Session.** Your boss asks you to prepare for and facilitate an informal training session and discussion on stress management to be presented during a luncheon meeting. This meeting is optional, and people who want to attend can bring their lunch and participate in the meeting. Prepare a 10- to 15-minute presentation on stress—what it is, what causes it, and 10 ways it can be prevented or minimized. Submit an outline of your presentation to your boss (your instructor) for review.

2. **Vacation Checklist.** Your team is facing a vacation and holiday season during which many team members will be out of the office. In an effort to minimize the stress associated with having people out of the office, your team has decided to put together a vacation checklist. This checklist will ensure team members are consistent in their efforts to prepare for time out of the office and consistent in their

efforts to get up to speed quickly when they return to the office. Conduct a brainstorming session with your teammates via your school's online message or discussion board and develop the following:

a. A checklist to be completed before going on vacation

b. A checklist to be completed after returning from vacation

The checklist to be completed before going on vacation would include activities such as changing your voice mail message to one that indicates you are out of the office and when you will return, and transferring ownership of all your open incidents. The checklist to be completed when you return would include activities such as changing your voice mail greeting back to the standard greeting, and reading and responding to email messages.

3. **Carpal Tunnel Syndrome Prevention.** You have been hired as a consultant to help a large service desk prevent carpal tunnel syndrome. Several members of the service desk have recently developed carpal tunnel syndrome, and the manager wants you to help the staff understand what causes it, how it is treated, and how it can be prevented. Prepare an article for the service desk's monthly newsletter that answers the following questions:

a. What is carpal tunnel syndrome?

b. What are its symptoms?

c. What causes it?

d. How is it treated or how can its symptoms be controlled?

e. How long does it take to relieve the symptoms?

f. How can it be prevented?

Service Desk Site Visit

This Capstone Project is designed to be an active learning experience that brings together in a real-world setting all of the concepts and techniques described in this text. This project involves arranging to visit (as a class, if possible) the service desk at your school or at a company in your community. Communicate to the host ahead of time that the purpose of the visit is to understand how the service desk interacts with its customers and to obtain answers to questions such as:

- How does the service desk measure customer satisfaction?

- What training do employees receive to improve their soft and self-management skills, such as listening, communication, customer service, stress management, and time management?

- How is the service desk using technologies such as the telephone, email, incident management systems, knowledge management systems, and web-based technologies such as self-service, instant messaging, and chat?

- What steps does the company take to ensure these technologies are customer friendly?

- What types of documents and records do employees create, and what, if any, training do employees receive to improve their writing skills?

- What difficult customer situations do analysts experience, and how do they handle these situations?

- What techniques and training do analysts use to enhance and improve their problem-solving skills?

- What training or awareness techniques are used to increase analysts' business skills and understanding of business needs?

- What roles exist within the team, and what techniques are used to build a solid team?

- How does the team, and how do analysts within the team, manage stress and burnout?

Following the visit, use everything you have learned in this book to determine what conclusions can you draw from visiting the service desk. Write a report that summarizes your findings and conclusions, and share those findings and conclusions with your classmates.

Service Desk Resources

This appendix lists resources for additional information about the service desk industry that you can use to learn more about this dynamic field and advance your career. Many of these resources can be obtained through your local library or via the web. Many of the magazines can be obtained free of charge by subscribing through the magazine's web site. The magazines and the membership organizations are excellent sources of the most up-to-date information about the industry. The following resources are provided:

- Books
- Certification bodies
- Self-study programs
- Magazines
- Membership organizations

Books

American Accent Training: A Guide to Speaking and Pronouncing American English for Anyone Who Speaks English as a Second Language. A. Cook. Barrons Educational Series, 2012.

Calming Upset Customers, Fourth Edition. R. Morgan. Crisp Publications, 2009.

The Complete Idiot's Guide to MBA Basics. T. Gorman. Alpha Books, 2011.

Crucial Conversations: Tools for Talking When Stakes Are High, Second Edition. K. Patterson, J. Grenny, R. McMillan, and A. Switzler. McGraw-Hill, 2011.

Customer Service for Dummies, Third Edition. K. Leland and K. Bailey. Wiley Publishing, Inc., 2006.

Delivering Happiness: A Path to Profits, Passion, and Purpose. T. Hsieh. Business Plus, 2010.

Delivering Knock Your Socks Off Service, Fifth Edition. Performance Research Associates. AMACOM, 2011.

Dictionary of Business Terms and Economic Terms, Fifth Edition. J. Friedman. Barrons Educational Series, Inc., 2012.

The Elements of Style, Fourth Edition. W. Strunk Jr. E. B. White. Longman, 1999.

The Elements of Technical Writing, Third Edition. T. Pearsall. Longman, 2009.

The Essential Drucker. P. Drucker. HarperBusiness. 2001.

Getting Things Done: The Art of Stress-Free Productivity. D. Allen. Penguin Putnam, Inc., 2002.

A Guide to Computer User Support for Help Desk & Support Specialists, Fifth Edition. F. Beisse. Course Technology, 2009.

A Guide to Service Desk Concepts, Fourth Edition. D. Knapp. Course Technology Cengage Learning, 2014.

The Hamster Revolution: How to Manage Your Email Before It Manages You. M. Song, V. Halsey, and T. Burress. Berrett-Koehler Publishers, 2008.

The Handbook of Technical Writing, Tenth Edition. G. Alred. St. Martin's Press, 2011.

How to Prepare, Stage, and Deliver Winning Presentations. T. Leech. AMACOM, 2004.

Idiot's Guides: Project Management, Sixth Edition. G. Michael Campbell. Penguin Group, 2014.

Implementing Service and Support Management Processes: A Practical Guide. Authors (Various), C. Higday-Kalmanowitz (Editor), S. Simpson (Editor). Van Haren Publishing, 2005.

The Insider's Guide to Technical Writing, Tenth Edition. K. Van Laan. XML Press, 2013.

Instant Messaging Rules. N. Flynn. AMACOM, 2004.

ISO/IEC 20000-1: 2011 A Pocket Guide. M. Rovers. Van Haren Publishing, 2012.

ITIL® Continual Service Improvement. The Stationary Office, 2011.

ITIL for Dummies (ITIL® 2011 Edition). P. Farenden. John Wiley & Sons, Ltd., 2012.

ITIL® Service Design. The Stationary Office, 2011.

ITIL® Service Strategy. The Stationary Office, 2011.

ITIL® Service Operation. The Stationary Office, 2011.

ITIL® Service Transition. The Stationary Office, 2011.

IT Problem Management. G. Walker. Prentice Hall PTR, 2001.

Kanban and Scrum: Making the Most of Both. H. Kniberg and M. Skarin. C4Media, Inc. 2010.

Life Is a Series of Presentations: Eight Ways to Inspire, Inform, and Influence Anyone, Anywhere, Anytime. T. Jeary. Touchstone, 2005.

Metrics for IT Service Management. P. Brooks (Lead Author), Jan van Bon (Chief Editor). Van Haren Publishing, 2006.

Presentation Skills: Captivate and Educate Your Audience, Fourth Edition. S. Mandel. Axzo Press, 2010.

The Phoenix Project: A Novel About IT, DevOps, and Helping Your Business Win. G. Kim, K. Behr, and G. Spafford. IT Revolutionary Press, 2013.

The Portable MBA, Fourth Edition. R. Bruner (Contributor), M. Eaker, R. Freeman (Contributor), R. Spekman. John Wiley & Sons, 2002.

Process Mapping, Process Improvement, and Process Management. D. Madison. Paton Press LLC, 2005.

The Relaxation and Stress Reduction Workbook, Sixth Edition. M. Davis, E. Robbins Eshelman, P. Fanning, and M. McKay. New Harbinger Publications, 2008.

Six Sigma for IT Management. Authors (Various), Jan van Bon (Chief Editor). Van Haren Publishing, 2006.

The Social Media Handbook. N. Flynn. Pfeiffer, 2012.

Stress Management (A Comprehensive Guide to Wellness), Revised, Updated Edition. E. Charlesworth. Ballantine Books, 2004.

Team Players and Teamwork, Second Edition. G. Parker. Jossey-Bass Publishers, 2008.

Technical Writing 101: A Real-World Guide to Planning and Writing Technical Documentation, Third Edition. S. O'Keefe, A. Pringle. Scriptorium Publishing Services, Inc., 2011.

The Time Trap, Fourth Edition. A. MacKenzie, P. Nickerson. AMACOM, 2009.

When Words Collide: A Media Writer's Guide to Grammar and Style, Seventh Edition. L. Kessler and D. McDonald. Cengage Learning, 2013.

Writing Effective E-Mail, Revised Edition. N. Flynn, T. Flynn. Crisp Publications, 2003.

You Don't Need a Title to Be a Leader: How Anyone, Anywhere, Can Make a Positive Difference. M. Sanborn. Doubleday. 2006.

Certification Bodies

The Computing Technology Industry Association (CompTIA)
www.comptia.org

CompTIA works with experts and industry leaders from the public and private sectors, including training, academia, and government to develop broad-based, foundational exams that validate an individual's IT skill set.

HDI
www.thinkhdi.com

HDI certification is an open, standards-based, internationally recognized certification program for service desk professionals.

ITIL Exam Institutions
www.itil-officialsite.com/ExaminationInstitutes/ExamInstitutes.asp

ITIL-related examinations are offered by a number of accredited examination institutes (EIs). EIs work with a network of accredited training organizations (ATOs) and accredited trainers with accredited materials.

Project Management Institute (PMI)
www.pmi.org

PMI's family of credentials supports the project management profession and its practitioners and promotes ongoing professional development.

Technology Services Industry Association (TSIA)
www.tsia.com

TSIA offers a family of awards, recognition, and certification programs that are designed to recognize the accomplishments of and prepare support professionals at all levels.

Self-Study Programs (DVDs, CDs, and Seminars)

American Management Association (AMA)
www.amanet.org

The AMA offers seminars in topics such as communication, customer service, finance and accounting, leadership, management, project management, and time management.

Fred Pryor Seminars and CareerTrack
www.pryor.com

Fred Pryor Seminars and CareerTrack offers seminars in topics such as conflict and stress management, communication skills, computer skills, customer service, grammar and writing, team building, and time management.

HDI
www.thinkhdi.com

HDI publications include *SupportWorld* magazine and its Focus Book series. These publications provide timely articles on topics affecting the service desk.

ITSM Bookstore
www.itsmbookstore.com

ITSM Bookstore offers ITSM-related book titles including AXELOS' Official ITIL books, Key Element Guides, and Pocket Guides.

JWA Video
www.jwavideo.com

JWA Video offers seminars in topics such as customer service, communication skills, management and supervision, writing and presenting, and time management.

The Telephone Doctor
www.telephonedoctor.com

The Telephone Doctor offers soft skills training for customer service professionals. Other topics include leadership and management and meeting openers for staff meetings and training sessions.

Magazines

The following publications provide information resources for service and support professionals and are available by subscription or online:

Contact Professional
www.contactprofessional.com

SupportWorld
www.thinkhdi.com/resources/publications

Membership Organizations

Association of Support Professionals (ASP)
www.asponline.com

ASP is an international membership organization for customer support managers and professionals. ASP publishes research reports on a wide range of support topics and provides its members with career development services.

HDI
www.thinkhdi.com

HDI provides targeted information about the technologies, tools, and trends of the service desk and customer support industry. HDI offers a variety of services to meet the evolving needs of the customer support professional.

The IT Service Management Forum (*it*SMF)
www.itsmfi.org

*it*SMF is an independent and internationally recognized membership organization for IT Service Management professionals. *it*SMF has 53 officially approved chapters worldwide that offer membership, events, and publications to its members.

Technology Services Industry Association (TSIA)
www.tsia.com

TSIA is an industry trade group for service and support professionals. TSIA provides market research, programs, certifications, and information resources.

Glossary

24/7 support Service desk services that are provided 24 hours a day, 7 days a week.

A

abandon rate The percentage of abandoned calls compared to the total number of calls received.

abandoned call A call where the caller hangs up before an analyst answers.

acceptance criteria The conditions that must be met before the project deliverables are accepted.

acronym An abbreviation formed from the first letters of a series of words.

active listening Listening that involves participating in a conversation and giving the speaker a sense of confidence that he or she is being heard.

announcement system Technology that greets callers when all service desk analysts are busy and can provide valuable information as customers wait on hold.

anomaly A deviation or departure from the average or the norm.

application of training investments A comparison of an analyst's resolution percent and reopen percent before and after attending training.

automated attendant An ACD feature that routes calls based on input provided by the caller through a touch-tone telephone.

automatic call distributor (ACD) A telephone technology that answers a call and routes, or distributes, it to the next available analyst. If all analysts are busy, the ACD places the call in a queue and plays a recorded message.

automatic number identification (ANI) A service provided by a long-distance service provider that discloses the telephone number of the person calling.

availability The length of time an analyst was signed on to the ACD compared to the length of time the analyst was scheduled to be signed on.

available state An ACD state that occurs when an analyst is ready to take calls.

avatar A computer user's representation of himself or herself.

average call duration The average length of time required to handle a call.

average handle time The average length of time required to handle an email.

average number of exchanges The average number of email exchanges required to resolve an incident.

average queue time See *average wait time*.

average speed of answer (ASA) The average time it takes an analyst to pick up an incoming call.

average wait time The average number of seconds or minutes a caller waits for an analyst after being placed in the queue by an ACD; also known as *average queue time*.

B

baseline A metric used to show a starting point.

beginning-of-day (BOD) checklist A list of tasks an analyst performs at the start of each workday.

benchmarking The process of comparing the service desk's performance metrics and practices to those of another service desk in an effort to identify improvement opportunities.

best effort A policy that states analysts do their best to assist a customer within a predefined set of boundaries, such as a time limit.

best practice A proven way of completing a task to produce a near optimum result.

blog A journal kept on the Internet; short for *web log*.

brainstorming A technique performed by a group of people that is designed to generate a large number of ideas for solving a problem.

bring your own device (BYOD) The practice of using personally owned mobile devices to access business applications.

budget The total sum of money allocated for a particular purpose or period of time.

burnout The physical and emotional exhaustion that is caused by long-term stress.

business A commercial enterprise or establishment; also used to describe a person's occupation, work, or trade.

business analyst An individual who is skilled at working with end users to determine their needs.

business and IT alignment A process aimed at ensuring that information technologies support corporate goals and objectives.

business case A report that describes the business reasons that a change is being considered, along with its associated costs, benefits, and risks.

business productivity team (BPT) A team that has a singular focus on improving user productivity and business outcomes (Gartner definition).

business skills The skills people need to work successfully in the business world.

C

call center A place where telephone calls are made or received in high volume.

caller identification (caller ID) A service provided by a local telephone company that discloses the telephone number of the person calling and, where available, the name associated with the calling telephone number.

can do attitude Telling a customer what you *can do* rather than what you cannot do.

capture To collect.

caring attitude A service desk's ability to communicate that it wants to satisfy its customers' needs.

carpal tunnel syndrome A common repetitive stress injury that affects the hands and wrists and is linked to repetitious hand movements, such as typing on a computer keyboard or working with a mouse.

case-based reasoning (CBR) A searching technique that uses everyday language to ask users questions and interpret their answers.

cause and effect analysis A technique used to generate the possible causes of a problem or effect.

change control plan A description of how the project scope will be managed and how agreed upon changes will be incorporated into the project deliverables.

channel A route of communication to and from the service desk, such as the telephone, voice mail, email, and the web.

chat A simultaneous text communication between two or more people via a computer; also called *online chat*.

chat speak A term for the abbreviations and slang commonly used in email, IM, and chat messages for brevity or due to a limitation on the number of characters that can be used when sending messages.

client/server A computing model in which some computers, known as clients, request services, and other computers, known as servers, respond to those requests.

closed loop process A process that changes its output based on feedback.

closed-ended question A question that prompts short answers, such as "yes" and "no."

cloud computing Delivering hosted services over the Internet.

cold transfer A way of transferring a telephone call when you stay on the line only long enough to ensure that the call has been transferred successfully.

collaboration technologies Technologies that enable multiple users to work together on related tasks; also known as *groupware*.

communication The exchange of thoughts, messages, and information.

computer telephony integration (CTI) The linking of computing technology with telephone technology to exchange information and increase productivity.

configuration management system (CMS) A set of tools and databases for managing IT asset information and linking that information to related incidents, problems, known errors, changes, and releases.

consensus An opinion or position reached by all of a team's members or by a majority of its members.

considerations and concerns A description of all considerations and concerns identified during the development of the project scope.

contact A generic term used to describe different types of customer transactions such as questions, incidents, and service request.

contact center A call center that uses technologies such as email and the web in addition to the telephone.

contact volume The total number of contacts received during a given period of time.

content management system (CMS) Software used to manage the content of a web site.

cookie A very small text file created by a web server that is stored on a user's computer either temporarily for that session only or permanently on the hard disk.

cost An amount paid or the expenditure of something, such as time or labor.

cost effectiveness A metric that ensures a proper balance between the cost of service and the quality of service.

cost per contact The total cost of operating a service desk for a given period (including salaries, benefits, facilities, and equipment) divided by the total number of contacts received during that period; historically called *cost per call*.

cost per unit The total cost of operating a service desk for a given period (including salaries, benefits, facilities, and equipment) divided by the total number of units (such as devices and systems) supported during that period.

cost-benefit analysis A business calculation that compares the costs and benefits of two or more potential solutions to determine an optimum solution.

crowdsourcing Outsourcing a task traditionally performed by a single individual to a large group of people or community (in other words, a crowd).

customer A person who buys products or services.

customer data The identifying details about a customer.

customer record All of the data and text fields that describe a single customer.

customer satisfaction A measure of the difference between how a customer perceives he or she was treated and how the customer expects to be treated.

customer satisfaction survey A series of questions that ask customers to provide their perception of the support services being offered.

customer service value chain A linked set of activities during which value is added when serving customers.

customer support Services that help a customer understand and benefit from a product's capabilities by answering questions, solving problems, and providing training.

D

data A set of raw facts that is not organized in a meaningful way.

data analytics The science of examining raw data with the goal of finding meaningful patterns, unknown correlations, and useful information.

data field An element of a database record in which one piece of data is stored.

decision tree A branching structure of questions and possible answers designed to lead an analyst to a solution.

desktop virtualization The separation of a PC desktop environment from a physical machine using the client/server model of computing.

detailed incident description A comprehensive accounting of an incident and the circumstances surrounding the incident's occurrence.

DevOps A cultural and professional movement that emphasizes communication, collaboration, and integration between software developers (Dev) and IT Operations professionals (Ops).

digital agent A software routine that waits in the background and performs an action when a specified event occurs.

dispatch To send.

distress A negative form of stress that causes strain, anxiety, or suffering.

E

early life support (ELS) The stage in the service lifecycle that occurs at the end of a deployment and before the service is fully accepted into operation (ITIL definition).

effectiveness A measure of how completely and accurately services are delivered.

efficiency A measure of the time and effort required to deliver services in relation to their cost.

email response management system A system that enables service desks to manage high-volume chat, email, and web form messages.

emoticon A symbol used to convey feelings.

emotional intelligence A form of intelligence relating to the emotional side of life.

empathy The act of identifying with and understanding another person's situation, feelings, and motives.

employee satisfaction A measure of how satisfied an employee is with his or her job.

ergonomics The applied science of equipment design intended to maximize productivity by reducing operator fatigue and discomfort.

ethics The rules and standards that govern the conduct of a person or group of people.

eustress A healthy form of stress that helps keep you motivated and enables you to feel a sense of accomplishment.

event-driven survey A customer satisfaction survey that asks customers for feedback on a single, recent service event.

exchange An email transaction in which one email is received and another is sent.

exit poll A measurement technique that, on the Internet, combines questions such as "Was this information helpful to you?" with a set of choices that customers can use to provide feedback.

expectation A result that a customer considers reasonable or due to them.

external customer A person or company that buys another company's products or services.

external service desk A service desk that supports customers who buy its company's products or services.

extranet A web site that is accessed via the Internet—that is, it can be accessed by the general public—but requires a password to gain entry to all or parts of the site.

F

fax An image of a document that is electronically transmitted to a telephone number connected to a printer or other output device; short for *facsimile*.

fee-based support Support services that customers pay for on a per-use basis.

feedback Communication from one team member to another about how the member's behavior is meeting the expectations of the team.

fight-or-flight reaction A set of physiological changes that occur when the mind, upon perceiving a stressful event, triggers an alarm that mobilizes the body for action.

first contact resolution rate The percentage of contacts resolved during a customer's initial contact compared to the total number of contacts received at the service desk for a given period of time.

Five Whys A technique that involves repeatedly asking the question "Why?" until the root cause of a problem is determined.

flowchart A diagram that shows the sequence of tasks that occur in a process.

follow-through The act of keeping promises, including calling the customer back when you said you would—even if you do not have a resolution to the incident.

follow-up The act of having a service desk or company representative verify that the customer's incident has been resolved to the customer's satisfaction and that the incident has not recurred.

form A predefined document that contains text or graphics users cannot change and areas in which users enter data.

frequently asked questions (FAQs) Well-written answers to the most common customer queries.

front-line service provider A service desk staff member who interacts directly with customers.

fuzzy logic A searching technique that presents all possible solutions that are similar to the search criteria, even when conflicting information exists or no exact match is present.

G

Gantt chart A type of bar chart that is often used to illustrate a project schedule.

global support Support for customers anywhere in the world.

groupware See *collaboration technologies*.

H

help desk A single point of contact within a company for technology-related questions and incidents.

hot transfer A way of transferring a telephone call when you stay on the line with the customer and the service provider whom you are engaging in the call; also known as a *conference call*.

hyperlink Text or graphics in a hypertext or hypermedia document that allow readers to "jump" to a related idea; also called a *link*.

hypermedia A storage method that stores information in a graphical form so users can access the information in a nonlinear fashion using hyperlinks.

hypertext A storage method that stores information in a nongraphical form so users can access the information in a nonlinear fashion using hyperlinks.

I

idiom A group of words whose meaning is different than the meanings of the individual words.

idle state An ACD state that occurs when an analyst is logged on to the ACD but is not accepting calls.

impact A measure of the effect an incident, problem, or change is having on business processes (ITIL definition).

incident An unplanned interruption to an IT service or a reduction in the quality of an IT service (ITIL definition).

incident data The details of an incident or service request.

incident management The process responsible for managing the lifecycle of incidents (ITIL definition).

incident management system Technology that offers enhanced trouble ticketing and management reporting capability.

incident owner An employee of the support organization who acts as a customer advocate and ensures an incident is resolved to the customer's satisfaction.

incident record All of the fields that describe a single incident.

individual performance goals Measurable objectives for analysts that support the service desk's mission.

industry knowledge Business skills that are unique to the industry or profession the service desk supports.

information Data that is organized in a meaningful way.

Information Technology Infrastructure Library (ITIL) A set of best practices for IT service management.

inquiry A customer request for information.

instant messaging system Technology that enables two or more people to communicate in real time over the Internet.

institutional stressors The stressors that accompany the type of business you are in or the state of the organization where you work.

intangible A characteristic that is difficult to measure precisely, such as customer satisfaction, employee satisfaction, and quality.

integrated ITSM solution A suite of systems that companies use to manage their incident, problem, knowledge, change, service asset and configuration management, and request fulfillment processes; sometimes called *enterprise solutions*.

internal customer A person who works at a company and at times relies on other employees at that company to perform his or her job.

internal service desk A service desk that responds to questions, distributes information, and handles incidents and service requests for its company's employees.

Internet A global collection of computer networks that are linked to provide worldwide access to information.

intranet A secured, privately maintained web site that serves employees and that can be accessed only by authorized personnel.

ISO/IEC 20000 An international standard for IT service management.

IT planner The individual responsible for producing and maintaining the IT standards, policies, plans, and strategies that ensure the IT department's services meet the business' strategic needs.

IT service A service that is based on the use of information technology and supports business processes.

IT service management (ITSM) A discipline for managing IT services that focuses on the quality of those services and the relationship that the IT organization has with its customers.

J

jargon The specialized or technical language used by a trade or profession.

job shadowing Working side by side with another person in an effort to understand and potentially learn that person's job.

K

Kepner-Tregoe problem analysis A proprietary problem analysis technique developed by Charles Kepner and Ben Tregoe that involves defining and describing the problem, establishing possible causes, testing the most probable cause, and verifying the true cause.

keyword A descriptive word or phrase.

keyword searching The technique of finding indexed information by specifying a descriptive word or phrase, called a *keyword*.

knowledge The application of information along with people's experiences, ideas, and judgments.

knowledge base A logical database that contains data used by a knowledge management system.

knowledge base administrator (KBA) Another name for a *knowledge engineer*.

knowledge engineer A person who develops and oversees the knowledge management process and ensures that the information contained in the service desk's knowledge management system is accurate, complete, and current; also called a *knowledge base administrator (KBA)*.

knowledge management system (KMS) A set of tools and databases that are used to store, manage, and present information sources such as customer information, documents, policies and procedures, incident resolutions, and known errors.

Knowledge-Centered Support (KCS) A knowledge management strategy for service and support organizations developed by the Consortium for Service Innovation (*www.serviceinnovation.org*).

known error A problem that has a documented root cause and a workaround (ITIL definition).

known error database (KEDB) A database that contains known error records.

L

level zero Customers resolving incidents on their own; also referred to as *tier zero* or *self-help*.

link See *hyperlink*.

listening To make an effort to hear something; to pay attention.

M

major incident An incident that is causing significant business impact.

mediator A negotiator who helps individuals resolve disputes.

metrics Performance measures.

milestone A key or important event in the life of a project.

monitoring When a supervisor or team leader observes an analyst's interactions with customers in order to measure the quality of that analyst's performance.

multi-level support model A common structure of service desks, where the service desk refers incidents it cannot resolve to the appropriate internal group, external vendor, or subject matter expert.

N

network and system administration Activities that include day-to-day tasks such as setting up and maintaining user accounts, ensuring the data that the company collects is secure, and performing email and database management.

network monitoring Activities that use tools to observe network performance in an effort to minimize the impact of incidents.

network monitoring system A tool used to observe network performance.

nonprofit A company established for charitable, educational, or humanitarian purposes rather than for making money; also known as *not-for-profit*.

nonverbal communication The exchange of information in a form other than words, including facial expressions, body language, and clothing.

notification The activities that inform all of the stakeholders in the incident management process (including management, the customer, and service desk analysts) about the status of outstanding incidents.

O

off-the-shelf A personal computer software product that is developed and distributed commercially.

one-to-many relationship One resolution that resolves many incidents or service requests.

open-ended question A question that cannot be answered with a "yes" or "no" response.

Operational Level Agreement (OLA) An agreement between internal support groups that underpins a Service Level Agreement by ensuring that all parties involved in meeting SLA targets understand their respective responsibilities.

outsource To provide services through an outside supplier instead of providing them in-house.

overall satisfaction survey A customer satisfaction survey that asks customers for feedback about all contacts with the service desk during a certain time period.

ownership The tracking of an incident to ensure that the customer is kept informed about the status of the incident, that the incident is resolved within the expected time frame, and that the customer is satisfied with the final resolution.

P

page hit A web page visit.

paraphrase To restate the information given by a customer using slightly different words in an effort to verify that you understand.

Pareto analysis A technique for determining the most significant causes from a list of many possible causes of a problem.

passive listening Listening that involves simply taking in information and shows little regard for the speaker.

payback period The period of time over which the benefits of an investment are received.

peer-to-peer support A practice in which users bypass the formal support structure and seek assistance from coworkers or someone in another department.

people The service desk component that consists of the staff and structure put in place within a company or department to support its customers by performing processes.

personal stressors The stressors that accompany your individual life experiences.

pitch The highness or lowness of vocal tone.

positive imagery The act of using mental pictures or images to influence your thinking in a positive way.

positive self-talk The act of using words to influence your thinking in a positive way.

priority A category that defines the relative importance of an incident, problem, or change and that is based on impact and urgency (ITIL definition).

probable source The system, network, application, or product that is most likely causing an incident.

problem The cause of one or more incidents (ITIL definition).

problem management The process responsible for managing the lifecycle of problems (ITIL definition).

problem manager An employee of the support organization who coordinates all problem management activities and ensures problems are resolved within SLA targets.

problem-solving skills The thinking skills used to answer a question or resolve a difficult situation; also known as *troubleshooting skills*.

procedure A step-by-step, detailed set of instructions that describes how to perform the tasks in a process.

process A collection of interrelated work activities that take a set of specific inputs and produce a set of specific outputs that are of value to a customer.

profile A collection of personal data associated with a specific user; also called a *user profile*.

project A temporary endeavor undertaken to create a unique product, service, or result (Project Management Institute definition).

project charter A short document that formally authorizes the project and gives authority to the project manager.

project deliverable An item to be delivered as a result of a project, such as a product, system, service, report, or plan.

project management The process of planning and managing a project.

project manager The person who leads the project team and is assigned the authority and responsibility for overseeing the project and meeting the project's objectives.

project objective A measurable goal in terms of time, money, and quality that the project must achieve to be considered successful.

project overview A summary of the project and of the business need driving the project.

project plan A summary document that describes a project, its objectives, and how the objectives are to be achieved.

project scope A description of the work to be done in a project.

project sponsor The person who has ultimate authority over a project.

project stakeholder A person or group that is involved in or may be affected by project activities.

Q

quality A characteristic that measures how well products or services meet customer expectations.

query by example (QBE) A searching technique that uses queries, or questions, to find records that match the specified search criteria; can include search operators.

question A customer request for instructions.

queue A line; can be used to refer to a list of calls, tickets, email messages, or chat requests waiting to be processed.

R

record A collection of related fields.

recording system Technology that records and plays back telephone calls.

remote control and diagnostic systems Systems that allow the service desk to take remote control of the keyboard, screen, or mouse of connected devices and then troubleshoot problems, transfer files, and even provide informal training by viewing or operating the customer's screen.

remote control system A technology that enables an analyst to view and take control of a connected device to troubleshoot incidents, transfer files, provide informal training, or collaborate on documents.

reopen percent The percentage of closed incidents that had to be opened back up within a given time period.

repetitive stress injuries (RSIs) Physical symptoms caused by excessive and repeated use of the hands, wrists, arms, and thumbs; these symptoms occur when people perform tasks using force, repeated strenuous actions, awkward postures, and poorly designed equipment.

request for change (RFC) A request to change the production environment.

requirement Something that is necessary or essential.

resolution A definitive solution to an incident or service request, or a proven workaround.

resolution data The details that describe how an incident was resolved.

resolution percent The percentage of incidents an analyst resolved compared to the total number of incidents that the analyst handled during a given time period.

responsiveness The service desk's ability to be available when customers need help and to make it easy for customers to obtain help.

return on investment (ROI) A business calculation that measures the total financial benefit derived from an investment and then compares it with the total cost of the project.

root cause The most basic reason for an undesirable condition or problem, which, if eliminated or corrected, would prevent the problem from existing or occurring.

root cause analysis A methodical way of determining why problems occur and identifying ways to prevent them.

S

scope creep A term used to describe unplanned changes to a project's scope.

screen pop A CTI function that enables information about the caller to appear, or pop up, on an analyst's monitor based on caller information captured by the telephone system and passed to a computer system.

script A standard set of text and behaviors.

search criteria The questions or symptoms entered by a user.

search operator A connecting word such as AND, OR, and NOT.

self-management skills The skills, such as stress and time management, that people need to complete their work effectively, feel job satisfaction, and avoid frustration or burnout; also includes the ability to get and stay organized and to continuously and quickly learn new skills.

self-help Customers resolving incidents on their own; also referred to as *level zero* or *tier zero*.

self-service A service that enables customers to help themselves.

service desk A single point of contact within a company for managing customer incidents and service requests.

service desk goals Measurable objectives that support the service desk mission.

service desk mission A written statement describing the customers the service desk serves, the types of services the service desk provides, and how the service desk delivers those services.

service industry knowledge Knowledge of the customer service and support industry.

Service Level Agreement (SLA) A written document that spells out the services the service desk will provide the customer, the customer's responsibilities, and how service performance is measured.

service request A formal request from a user for something to be provided (ITIL definition).

short incident description A succinct description of the actual results a customer is experiencing.

situational stressors The stressors that accompany the type of work you do.

skill The service desk's ability to quickly and correctly resolve customer incidents and service requests.

skills-based routing (SBR) An ACD feature that matches the requirements of an incoming call to the skill sets of available analysts or analyst groups; the ACD then distributes the call to the next available, appropriately qualified analyst.

social listening The process of identifying and evaluating what is being said about a company, individual, product, or brand on the Internet; also known as *social media listening*.

social network A community of people who share similar interests or activities.

social networking service A web-based service that provides members a variety of ways to interact.

soft skills The qualities that people need to deliver great service, such as active listening skills, verbal communication skills, customer service skills, problem-solving skills, temperament, teamwork skills, and writing skills.

spam Unsolicited email.

speakerphone A telephone that contains both a loudspeaker and a microphone.

standard change A preapproved change that is low risk and follows a procedure.

status data The details about an incident that are used to track the incident throughout its lifecycle.

stress The adaptation of our bodies and minds to the demands of life.

style guide A set of standards for designing and writing documents.

subject matter expert (SME) A person who has a high level of experience or knowledge about a particular subject.

swarming A work style characterized by a flurry of collective activity by anyone and everyone conceivably available and able to add value (Gartner, Inc. definition).

symptom A sign or indication that an incident has occurred.

T

tangible A characteristic that is capable of being measured precisely, such as exactly how much something costs or how long it takes to complete a task.

target escalation time A time constraint placed on each level that ensures incident resolution activities are proceeding at an appropriate pace.

target resolution time The time frame within which the support organization is expected to resolve an incident.

team A group of people organized to work together toward the achievement of a goal.

team player A person who contributes to the team's success by cooperating freely and communicating openly with his or her teammates.

technical skills The skills people need to use and support the specific products and technologies the service desk supports; also includes basic computer and software literacy.

technical support A wide range of services that enable people and companies to effectively use the information technology they acquired or developed.

technical writing A technique that involves writing documentation that explains technical issues in ways that nontechnical people can understand.

technology An invention, process, or method that enables the creation and enhancement of tools.

template A predefined item that can be used to quickly create a standard document or email message.

text field A field that accepts free-form information.

ticket A term commonly used to describe a record stored in a database that contains the details of a customer contact; also known as *case, incident, log, record*, and *service request*.

time idle The average length of time an analyst was idle during a given period of time.

tool A product or device that automates or facilitates a person's work.

trend analysis A methodical way of determining and, when possible, forecasting service trends.

troubleshooting skills See *problem-solving skills*.

turnover rate The ratio of the number of workers who had to be replaced in a given period of time to the average number of workers.

U

urgency A measure of how long it will be until an incident, problem, or change has a significant impact on the business (ITIL definition).

user A person who consumes products or services.

V

value The perceived worth, usefulness, or importance of a product or service to a customer.

verbal communication The exchange of information using words.

virtual team A group of people who work across time, space, and organizational boundaries.

voice mail An automated form of taking messages from callers.

Voice over Internet Protocol (VoIP) A technology that translates voice communications into data and then transmits that data across an Internet connection or network.

voice response unit (VRU) A technology that integrates with another technology, such as a database or a network management system, to obtain information or to perform a function; also called an interactive voice response unit (IVRU).

W

warm transfer A way of transferring a telephone call that occurs when you introduce the customer and the service provider to whom you are transferring the call but you do not stay on the line.

Web 2.0 A concept that emphasizes enabling web users to interact, collaborate, and generate content via, for example, blogs, wikis, and social networking sites, rather than passively view content created by others.

weight A rating scale of importance.

wisdom The judicious application of knowledge.

work breakdown structure (WBS) A task-oriented breakdown of the work to be done.

workaround A temporary way to circumvent or minimize the impact of an incident.

world class Refers to a company that has achieved and sustains high levels of customer satisfaction.

wrap-up mode A feature that prevents the ACD from routing a new inbound call to an analyst's extension.

wrap-up time The average length of time an analyst was in wrap-up mode during a given period of time.

wrist rest A firm cushion that lies parallel to the keyboard.

Index

Note: Page numbers in boldface indicate key terms.